Security Issues in Communication Devices, Networks and Computing Models

The importance of addressing security issues in communication devices, networks, and computing models in Industry 5.0 cannot be exaggerated. Industry 5.0 represents the next phase in the evolution of manufacturing and industrial processes, characterized by increased connectivity, automation, and the integration of smart technologies. Here are several reasons why security is crucial in this context: Industry 5.0 involves the convergence of information technology (IT) and operational technology (OT), making industrial control systems susceptible to cyber threats. A breach in security could compromise critical infrastructure such as power grids, transportation systems, and water treatment plants. Securing computing models and networks is vital for protecting critical infrastructure and ensuring the safety and stability of essential services.

Industry 5.0 encourages the use of advanced technologies such as the Industrial Internet of Things (IIoT) and edge computing, leading to increased data exchange and collaboration. Security issues could result in the theft or manipulation of intellectual property, proprietary designs, and sensitive business information. Robust security measures are necessary to safeguard intellectual property, maintain a competitive edge, and foster innovation within Industry 5.0 ecosystems. Communication devices and networks in Industry 5.0 transmit vast amounts of sensitive data, including production data, supply chain information, and operational metrics. Ensuring the integrity and confidentiality of this data is crucial for informed decision-making and maintaining a competitive advantage. Security breaches could lead to data manipulation, unauthorized access, and exposure of sensitive information, jeopardizing the trust of stakeholders and partners. Industry 5.0 involves interconnected supply chains, where multiple entities collaborate and share data. Weaknesses in communication devices and networks can be exploited to compromise the integrity of the entire supply chain, impacting product quality and safety. Securing communication channels and computing models is vital for maintaining the trustworthiness of the supply chain, ensuring product quality, and minimizing the risk of counterfeit components.

In summary, addressing security issues in communication devices, networks, and computing models is fundamental to the successful implementation of Industry 5.0. It not only protects the assets and operations of organizations but also contributes to the overall safety, reliability, and sustainability of advanced industrial systems.

Security Issues in Communication Devices, Networks and Computing Models

Volume 1

Edited by

Budati Anil Kumar
Akella Ramakrishna
Goutham Makkena
Gheorghita Ghinea

CRC Press
Taylor & Francis Group
Boca Raton London New York

CRC Press is an imprint of the
Taylor & Francis Group, an **informa** business

Designed cover image: © Shutterstock

First edition published 2025
by CRC Press
2385 NW Executive Center Drive, Suite 320, Boca Raton FL 33431

and by CRC Press
4 Park Square, Milton Park, Abingdon, Oxon, OX14 4RN

CRC Press is an imprint of Taylor & Francis Group, LLC

ISBN: 978-1-032-83211-1 (hbk)
ISBN: 978-1-032-84483-1 (pbk)
ISBN: 978-1-003-51344-5 (ebk)

DOI: 10.1201/9781003513445

Typeset in Sabon
by SPi Technologies India Pvt Ltd (Straive)

Contents

About the Editors

Dr. Budati Anil Kumar received a PhD. Degree in Electronics and Communication Engineering from GITAM Deemed to be University, Hyderabad, India, in 2019, and MTech. Degree from JNTU Kakinada, Andhra Pradesh India, in 2010, and BTech degree from JNTU Hyderabad, India, in 2007. He completed his PDF from the Institute of Computer Science & Digital Innovation, UCSI University, Kuala Lumpur, Malaysia, in 2024. He is currently working as an Associate Professor & RPAC Chair in the ECE Department, Koneru Lakshmaiah Education Foundation (Deemed University), Aziz Nagar Campus, Hyderabad and Adjunct Professor at Institute of Computer Science & Digital Innovation, UCSI University, Kuala Lumpur, Malaysia. He has more than 14 years of experience in teaching and six years of experience in research. Besides, he has published 70 research articles in highly reputed publisher journals and conferences whose indexing is in SCIE, SCOPUS, etc. He acts as Guest Editor for various reputed publisher journals like Springer, IET, Inderscience, bentham Science and Emerald publishers etc. He has authored six textbooks published by Taylor & Francis, UK, and Wiley, UK. He has been a senior member of IEEE, IEI, and IAENG since 2019 and has served as a reviewer for various international journals and conferences. He has conducted various Faculty Development Programs as a coordinator, which are funded by AICTE, DST New Delhi, India. He has organized and attended various FDPs and conferences/workshops in India and abroad and has also acted as speaker/session chair in various FDPs and conferences. His current research interests include Cognitive Radio Networks, Software Defined Radio Networks, Artificial Intelligence, 6G emerging Technologies, Mulsemedia Computing, and UAVs in 5G and 6G.

Dr. Akella Ramakrishna, currently working as the Professor and Principal of KL University, Hyderabad, India, is an accomplished Electronics and Communications Engineer with a wealth of experience in academia, research, and industry. He holds a Doctorate in Wireless Communications and a Masters in Telecommunications & Electronics Engineering from Sheffield Hallam University, UK. He started his career as a Design Engineer at Sheffield Centre for Robotics and later in CPI Electronics Ltd. and worked in an Engineering sales role at British Telecom. He has published papers in reputed journals. Dr. Ramakrishna has contributed to the development of 5G Technology. With his expertise in wireless communications, research, and industry–academia partnerships, he can help drive innovation in this field and shape the future of communication technology while continuing to guide and support the next generation of engineers and researchers. Currently, he is guiding eight research scholars. He is also associated with several professional bodies such as ISTE (Indian Society for Technical Education), CSI (Computer Society of India), IEEE (Institution of Electrical and Electronics Engineers), and IET (Institution of Engineering & Technology). Dr. Ramakrishna has fulfilled his administrative and managerial roles with dedication and creativity. He has demonstrated vision and outstanding commitment to excellence in undergraduate & and postgraduate education in engineering, management, and arts. Dr. Ramakrishna has joined KL University as a faculty member in different roles in the areas of teaching, placements, internships, research, academics, administration, and the Internal Quality Assessment Cell (IQAC). He was the Founder-Director of KLH Global Business School, Kondapur, India, and is one of the key people for the establishment of the KL University campus in Hyderabad. Dr. Ramakrishna, during his tenure as Director (Placements & Internships), has worked in different capacities and also achieved bridging the gap between the industry and academia by placing more than 20,000 students for internships in different companies in the last 10 years. He is the key person in getting several research and consultancy projects to the University. He has conducted various international conferences, workshops, and programs in imparting good knowledge to the students. He has established KL Placements and Industry Interaction offices in Chennai, Bangalore, and Pune (India) with the objective of recruiting students to premier companies in South India. He has established the PEGA UAP & Centre of Excellence in Automation Anywhere, a tool for Robotic Process Automation. He is credited for placing more than 10,000 students into many top MNCs. He has connections with more than 500 recruiters across both IT & Core areas. He has received awards from various corporate companies and from the Confederation of Indian Industry for conducting the best campus drives during the past 10 years. Dr. Ramakrishna has been honored with the Best Academic Leadership Award at the IKON – Talent Acquisition Conclave held at T-Hub, Madhapur, India, on 16 December 2022.

Dr. Goutham Makkena is an Associate Professor in the Department of Electronics and Communication Engineering (ECE) at KL University, Hyderabad, where he has made significant strides in both teaching and research. Holding a Master's degree and a PhD. in Microelectronics from the Birla Institute of Technology and Science, Pilani, Hyderabad, his academic journey is marked by a deep-rooted passion for advancing Microelectronics. Before embarking on his academic career, he gained valuable industry experience as a Software Engineer at Infosys Technologies Pvt. Ltd. for two years and as a Field Engineer at Microsemi SOC division for six months, laying a solid foundation for his research endeavors. His research interests are focused on the design and implementation of pulse-shaping filters and the innovative use of Carbon Nanotube Field-Effect Transistors (CNTFETs) for developing ternary logic circuits. A contributor to GSOC2022, he is deeply committed to the open-source community, with a keen interest in open-source FPGA and Open Lane, aiming to further the development of open-source hardware. Additionally, his expertise in creating interactive H5P content demonstrates his dedication to enhancing learning through interaction. At KL University, he has also established a drone lab, furthering practical learning and research in drone technology, highlighting his commitment to integrating hands-on experience with academic rigor.

Prof. Gheorghita Ghinea is working as a Professor in the Department of Computer Science at Brunel University of London, UK. He obtained his BSc. Degree with Computer Science and Mathematics majors from the University of the Witwatersrand, South Africa. Later, he went on to obtain his BSc. (Hons.) and MSc. Degrees, both in Computer Science, from the same university. He was awarded a PhD. – *Quality of Perception: An Essential Facet of Multimedia Communications* – from the University of Reading, UK, in 2000. His research activities lie at the confluence of Computer Science, Media, and Psychology. In particular, his work focuses on the area of perceptual multimedia quality and how one builds end-to-end communication systems incorporating user perceptual requirements. He was particularly interested in building human-centered e-systems, particularly, integrating human perceptual requirements. His research work has been funded by both national and international funding bodies – all of it being collaborative work with other teams and stakeholders whom he had the privilege to be involved with. He has also been honored to supervise 33 PhD. students to completion and to have published over 350 high-quality Research articles with them and other research collaborators. Currently, his research pursuits are centered on extending the notion of multimedia with that of mulsemedia – a term which has been put forward to denote multiple sensorial media, i.e., media applications that go beyond engaging the by-now traditional auditory and visual senses, engaging three of our other human in a realistic manner akin to our experiences of everyday life.

Contributors

Syed Mohd Ali
Mahaveer Institute of Science & Technology
Hyderabad, India

Ayesha Ameen
Deccan College of Engineering and Technology
Hyderabad, India

A. Athiraja Atheeswaran
Department of CSE-AIML
Malla Reddy College of Engineering
Hyderabad, India

S. Avinash
Rajalakshmi Engineering College College
Thandalam, Chennai, India

Lalit Kumar Awasthi
Department of Computer Science & Engineering
National Institute of Technology Uttarakhand
Srinagar (Garhwal), India

Ayesha Banu
Deccan College of Engineering and Technology
Hyderabad, India

A. Baranidharan
Department of Computer Science and Engineering
Kalasalingam Academy of Research and Education
Krishnankoil, India

Zareena Begum
Mahaveer Institute of Science & Technology
Hyderabad, India

Daniel Bele
Algebra University
Zagreb, Croatia

J. Bino
Department of Electronics and Communication Engineering
St. Joseph's Institute of Technology
Chennai, India

Maibam Mangalleibi Chanu
Department of Computer Science and Engineering
National Institute of Technology Manipur
Imphal, India

Ram Dayal
Department of Computer Science
GNDU College
Jalandhar, Punjab, India

P. Deepalakshmi
Department of Computer Science and Engineering
Kalasalingam Academy of Research and Education
Krishnankoil, India

Khumbongmayum Belona Devi
Department of Computer Science and Engineering
National Institute of Technology Manipur
Imphal, India

Ksh. Merina Devi
Department of Computer Science and Engineering
National Institute of Technology Manipur
Imphal, India

Shougaijam Neroda Devi
Department of Computer Science and Engineering
National Institute of Technology Manipur
Imphal, India

Kevin Furjan
Algebra University
Zagreb, Croatia

V. Geethapriya
Rajalakshmi Engineering College
Thandalam, Chennai, India

S. B. Goyal
Faculty of Information Technology
City University
Malaysia

Liu Guoqiang
Faculty of Information Technology
City University
Petaling Jaya, Malaysia
and
Jining University
Qufu, China

Aina Kesilohenda Hauwanga
Department of CMSS
University of Namibia
Windhoek, Namibia

Sudhakar Hundi
Department of Instrument Technology
Andhra University
Visakhapatnam, Andhra Pradesh, India

Preceela Chanu Irengbam
Department of Computer Science and Engineering
National Institute of Technology Manipur
Imphal, India

J. Kavitha
Rajalakshmi Engineering College College
Thandalam, Chennai, India

S. Kalvikkarasi
Department of ECE
Podhgai College of Engineering and Technology
Vellore, India

C. Kamala Kannan
Rajalakshmi Engineering College College
Thandalam, Chennai, India

Ankur Khare
Department of Computer Science & Engineering
Rabindranath Tagore University
Raisen, India

Filip Kisić
Algebra University
Zagreb, Croatia

Satveer Kour
Department of Computer Engineering and Technology
Guru Nanak Dev University
Amritsar, India

Budati Anil Kumar
Department of ECE
Koneru Lakshmaiah Education Foundation
Hyderabad, India

P. Mohan Kumar
Hindustan Institute of Technology and Science
Chennai, India

Sun Lili
Faculty of Information Technology, City University
Petaling Jaya, Malaysia
Jining University
Qufu, China

S. Mahipal
Hindustan Institute of Technology and Science
Chennai, India

Venkata Naresh Mandhala
Department of Computer Science and Engineering
Koneru Lakshmaiah Education Foundation
Vaddeswaram, Guntur, India

Komal Krishan Mehta
Department of Laws
Guru Nanak Dev University Regional Campus
Jalandhar, India

Shyama Heshini Niranjala
Faculty of Information Technology
City University, Malaysia & Gampaha Wichramarachchi University
Sri Lanka

M. Shabana Parveen
Department of Electronics and Communication Engineering
Sri Sairam Engineering College
Chennai, India

Manne Bhargav Phaneendra
Department of Computer Science and Engineering'
Koneru Lakshmaiah Education Foundation
Vaddeswaram, Guntur, India

A. Rajasekar
Department of Artificial Intelligence and Data Science
Sri Sairam Institute of Technology
Chennai, India

G. Govinda Rajulu
Department of Computer Science and Engineering
Vel Tech Rangarajan Dr. Sagunthala R&D Institute of Science and Technology
Chennai, India

Parameswaran Ramesh
Department of Electronics Engineering
Madras Institute of Technology
Anna University, Chennai, India

A. Daisy Rani
Department of Instrument Technology
Andhra University
Visakhapatnam, India

Sanjiith Ravindhran
Sri Sairam Engineering College
Chennai, India

Jashwant Samar
Department of Computer Science & Engineering
Rabindranath Tagore University
Raisen, India

Himali Sarangal
Department of Engineering and Technology
Guru Nanak Dev University Regional Campus
Jalandhar, India

Suresh Babu Satukumati
Department of Computer Science and Engineering
Vignan's Foundation for Science, Technology and Research (Deemed to be University)
Vadlamudi, India

V. S. Vetri Selvi
Department of Computer Science and Engineering
Kalasalingam Academy of Research and Education
Krishnankoil, India

Shailja Sharma
Department of Computer Science & Engineering
Rabindranath Tagore University
Raisen, India

L. Sharmila
Department of Computer Science and Engineering
Vel Tech Rangarajan Dr.Sagunthala R&D Institute of Science and Technology
Chennai, India

Butta Singh
Department of Engineering and Technology
Guru Nanak Dev University Regional Campus
Jalandhar, India

Harendra Singh
Department of Computer Science & Engineering
National Institute of Technology Uttarakhand
Srinagar (Garhwal), India

Manjit Singh
Department of Engineering and Technology
Guru Nanak Dev University Regional Campus
Jalandhar, India

Sesham Srinu
Department of ECE
University of Namibia
Ongwediva, Namibia

Tanveer Sultana
Deccan College of Engineering and Technology
Hyderabad, India

Nalina Suresh
Department of CMSS
University of Namibia
Windhoek, Namibia

Ashish Kumar Tiwari
Technocrats Institute of Technology
Bhopal, India

Manoj Tyagi
Technocrats Institute of Technology
Bhopal, India

G. Valarmathy
Department of Computer Science and Engineering (IoT)
Sri Sairam Engineering College
Chennai, India

P. Velmurugadass
Department of Computer Science and Engineering
Kalasalingam Academy of Research & Education
Krishnankoil, India

D. Venkatesan
Department of Artificial Intelligence and Machine Learning
St. Martin's Engineering College
Hyderabad, India

Bhupendra Verma
Technocrats Institute of Technology
Bhopal, India

N. Vidhya
Department of Electronics Engineering
Madras Institute of Technology
Anna University, Chennai, India

Vemparala Viharika
Department of Computer Science and Engineering
Koneru Lakshmaiah Education Foundation
Vaddeswaram, Guntur, India

M. S. Vinotheni
Rajalakshmi Engineering College College
Thandalam, Chennai, India

Chapter 1

Clean Architecture in mobile development by practice

Filip Kisić, Kevin Furjan, and Daniel Bele

1.1 INTRODUCTION

The application's architecture from the very start determines the ease or difficulty of working on a new project. This chapter focuses on an architecture approach applicable to mobile applications.

The main criteria for choosing the right architecture for a project are the ease of implementing new features or extending existing ones, as well as the ease of maintaining them [1]. The next factor to consider is how easy it is to write unit tests and how prone the application will be to errors [2]. The first step to achieving the above is to set up the project where components and classes depend on abstractions, not concrete classes [2]. Popular ways to achieve this are by using architectures such as MVVM (Model-View-ViewModel) in Android projects, MVC (Model-View-Controller) or VIPER (View, Interactor, Presenter, Entity, Routing) used in iOS projects, and the increasingly popular Clean Architecture. All architectures share the same goal: to separate concerns and logic into layers. This chapter reveals how to successfully implement Clean Architecture by following the best practices in mobile application development. The Flutter framework and the Dart programming language are chosen as the technology.

1.2 FLUTTER FRAMEWORK

1.2.1 What is Flutter?

Introduced in May 2017 by Google, Flutter is a framework designed to create multi-platform applications using the same codebase [3]. Therefore, an application written in Flutter can be run as an Android, iOS, macOS, iPadOS, Linux, Windows, Web, or arm64 application, so its main advantage is its versatility and development time. Of course, each platform requires its own configuration, but the overall development time can be significantly reduced, as can the number of people needed for development. The potential of Flutter has been recognized by large companies such as BMW, Toyota, eBay, Google itself, and many others. BMW uses Flutter in the form of a mobile application for managing BMW cars, Toyota uses Flutter to develop the operating system used in Toyota vehicles (infotainment).

The Flutter application is programmed in the Dart programming language, also developed by Google and introduced before Flutter, in 2013 [4]. It's an object-oriented language with a syntax similar to C++ and JavaScript. A key feature of Dart is its Just-in-Time (JIT) compiler, which enables near real-time visualization of code changes, significantly simplifying application development, especially for user interfaces. Dart also supports Ahead-of-Time (AOT) compilation, translating Dart code into the native language of the target platform.

DOI: 10.1201/9781003513445-1

The Dart SDK offers a rich set of functions that can be integrated into code and even supports functional programming. As a relatively young language, Dart is constantly undergoing improvements, with frequent updates that often bring significant enhancements to its ease of use. This ongoing development contributes to its growing popularity and the vast number of libraries available online.

1.3 APPLICATION ARCHITECTURE OVERVIEW

The book "Clean Architecture: A Craftsman's Guide to Software Structure and Design" was written by Robert C. Martin, also known as "Uncle Bob". Its main objective is to define and establish discipline in application architecture to achieve layering and separate logic as much as possible [1]. In the book, Robert C. Martin defines a layered architecture somewhat like an onion. At its core are the entities, the key data holders for any application. This approach is shared with Hexagonal Architecture. In fact, Clean Architecture is an improved version of Hexagonal architecture, which the author refers to in the book [1]. Their common goal is to separate business logic from data sources and thus make it the core of the application (Figure 1.1).

1.3.1 Architecture review

In a Clean Architecture application, there are three main layers: the data layer, the domain layer, and the presentation layer. In short, the domain layer is the core of the application and has no dependencies. In fact, every other layer depends on the domain layer. This layer contains entities and business logic rules, known in practice as interactors. The data layer depends on the domain layer and its main purpose is to retrieve or store data on remote or local data sources. An example of a remote source is a server, and an example of a local one is a database. In the end, there is a presentation layer which also depends on the domain layer while its main purpose is to display data and interact with users. As can be seen in Figure 1.1, there are two databases. They are used to demonstrate the goal of Clean Architecture and how easy it should be to change data sources without affecting the rest of the application.

1.3.2 Domain layer

First is the core of the app – the domain layer. This layer is made of

- Entities (main data classes)
- Repository interfaces (communication with various data sources)
- Business rules (the core of application logic)

There might be a question of how the domain layer can be truly independent if it retrieves from and stores data on various sources. Shouldn't it depend on the data layer? Well, the goal is for the data layer to depend on the domain layer, not the other way around. To achieve this, a repository interface is defined in the domain layer, and its implementation is written in the data layer. This is called the Dependency Inversion Principle [1]. Now follows a structure of the domain layer (Figure 1.2).

The first in line is the entity, and its main role is to store data in well-structured classes so that operations can be performed on the same data (Code 1).

The next in line are business logic rules. Everything that is closely related to the business logic must be written in such a class. In the example project, there are several classes for

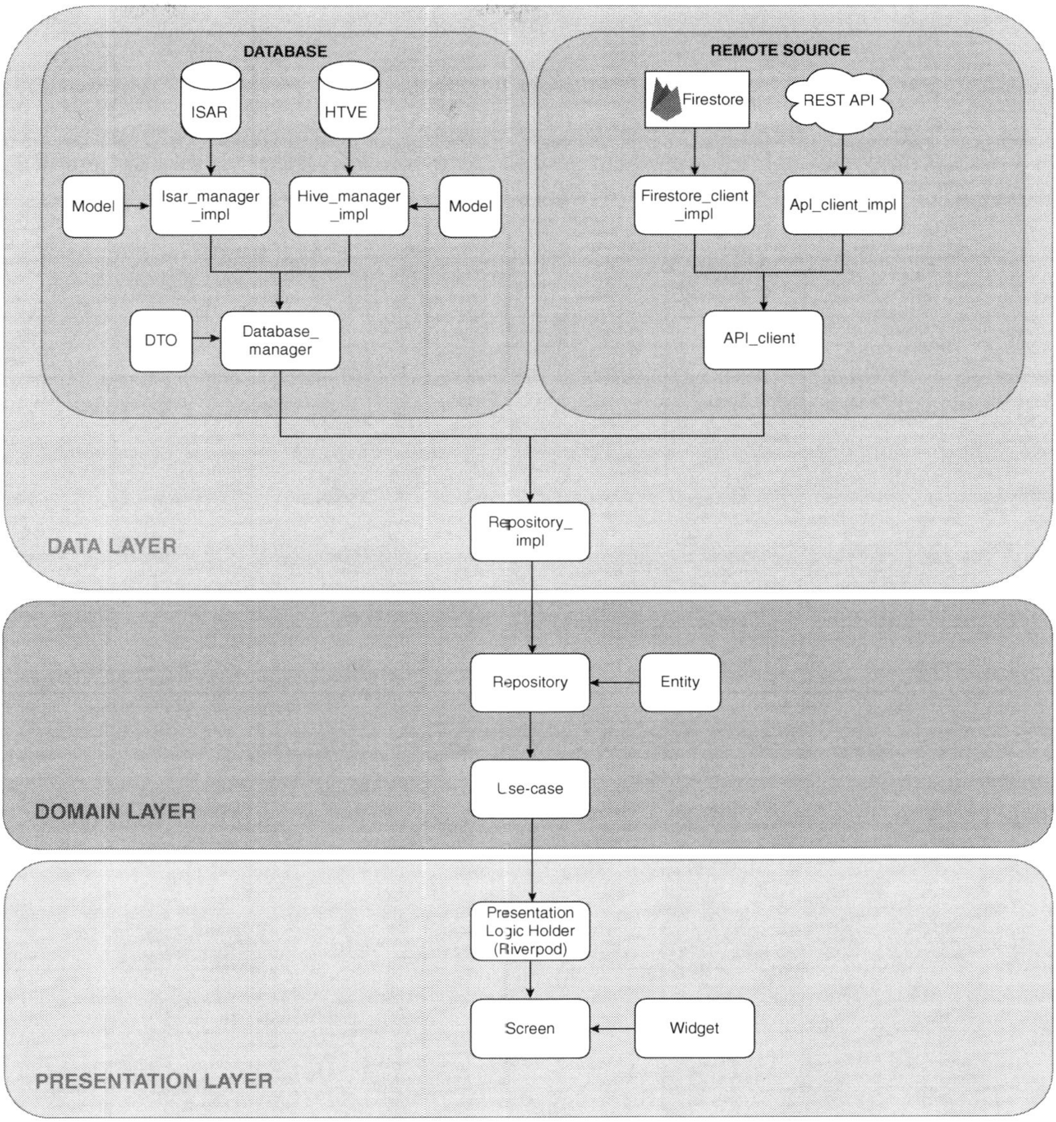

Figure 1.1 Application architecture.

manipulating projects. It is important to emphasize that the following way of separating logic into multiple classes is not the only correct way. It is possible to have one class with multiple methods for manipulating projects, where each method is a business rule. In this chapter, the separation of classes was chosen in order to fully follow the Clean Architecture rule that each class should have only one role (Code 2 and Code 3).

1.3.3 Data layer

The example application has two available data sources: the Isar database and the Hive database. The main question that needs to be asked is how the repository should be separated from the data source. In cases where there is a possibility for multiple data sources,

```
domain
├── entity
│   └── project.dart
├── repository
│   └── project_repository.dart
└── usecase
    ├── create_new_project_use_case.dart
    ├── get_projects_use_case.dart
    └── delete_project_use_case.dart
```

Figure 1.2 Domain layer structure.

CODE 1 PROJECT ENTITY CLASS

```
class Project {
  int? id;
  final String title;
  List<TodoItem> todoList;
  Project({
    required this.title,
    required this.todoList,
    this.id
  });
  @override
  String toString() {
    final buffer = StringBuffer();
    todoList.forEach((element) =>
      buffer.write(element));
      return '$id, $title,
      ${buffer.toString()}';
  }
  @override
  bool operator ==(dynamic other) =>
      other != null &&
      other is Project &&
      other.id == id &&
      other.title == title;
  @override
  int get hashCode => id.hashCode +
     title.hashCode - todoList.hashCode;
}
```

the repository should communicate with them through an interface and depend on an abstraction. In this project, a "DatabaseManager" interface will be created (Code 4). Each new database should implement the DatabaseManager interface to allow the application to communicate with the database. However, as can be seen (Figure 1.1), each database must have its own data model. The implementation of the Hive database will follow (Code 5

CODE 2 CREATE PROJECT USE CASE CLASS

```
class CreateNewProjectUseCase {
final ProjectRepository _repository;

const CreateNewProjectUseCase(
   this._repository
);
Future<void> call(String projectName) async {
     final project = Project(
       title: projectName,
       todoList: []
     );
     await _repository.createNewProject(
      project
     );
   }
}
```

CODE 3 DELETE PROJECT USE CASE CLASS

```
class DeleteProjectUseCase {
 final ProjectRepository _repository;

 const DeleteProjectUseCase(
  this._repository
 );

 Future<void> call(final Project project){
 return _repository.removeProject(project);
 }
}
```

CODE 4 DATABASEMANAGER INTERFACE

```
abstract class DatabaseManager {
Future<List<ProjectDbDto>> getAllProjects();
Future<void> insertNewProject(ProjectDbDto project);
Future<void> removeProjectById(int projectId);
}
```

and Code 6), but first, an overview of the initial and basic structure of the data layer is needed (Figure 1.3).

The data layer consists of converter classes, a database, and repositories. Since the data layer depends on the domain layer due to the previously mentioned Dependency Inversion

CODE 5 HIVE DATA MODEL CLASS

```
@HiveType(typeId: 0)
class ProjectHiveModel extends HiveObject {
  @HiveField(0)
  String title;

  @HiveField(1)
  List<TodoItemHiveModel> todoList;

  ProjectHiveModel({
    required this.title,
    this.todoList = const [],
  });
}
```

CODE 6 DATABASEMANAGER INTERFACE IMPLEMENTATION

```
class HiveManagerImpl implements DatabaseManager {
  static const projectsBox = 'projects';

  final ProjectHiveModelToDbDtoConverter
  _projectHiveModelToDbDtoConverter;

  final ProjectDbDtoToHiveModelConverter
  _projectDbDtoToHiveModelConverter;

  const HiveManagerImpl(
    this._projectHiveModelToDbDtoConverter,
    this._projectDbDtoToHiveModelConverter,
  );

  @override
  Future<List<ProjectDbDto>>
  getAllProjects() async {
    return (
    await Hive.openBox<ProjectHiveModel>
    (projectsBox))
        .values
        .toList()
        .map((model) => _projectHiveModelToDbDtoConverter
  .convert(model))
  .toList();
  }

  @override
  Future<void> insertNewProject(
    final ProjectDbDto projectDto
  ) async {
```

```
    final projects = await
    Hive.openBox<ProjectHiveModel>(
      projectsBox
    );
    final projectModel =
    _projectDbDtoToHiveModelConverter
      .convert(projectDto);
    await projects.add(projectModel);
  }

  @override
  Future<void> removeProjectById(
    final int projectId
  ) async {
    final projects = await
    Hive.openBox<ProjectHiveModel>(
      projectsBox
    );
    await projects.delete(projectId);
  }
}
```

```
data
├── converter
├── database
└── repository
```

Figure 1.3 Data layer structure.

CODE 7 PROJECTDBDTO CLASS

```
class ProjectDbDto {
  final int? id;
  final String title;
  final List<TodoItemDbDto> todoList;

  const ProjectDbDto({
    this.id,
    required this.title,
    this.todoList = const [],
  });

  @override
  String toString() {
    return '$id, $title, $todoList';
  }
}
```

```
database
├── hive
│   ├── model
│   │   ├── project_hive_model.dart
│   │   └── todo_item_hive_model.dart
│   ├── hive_datasource.dart
│   └── hive_manager_impl.dart
├── isar
│   ├── model
│   │   ├── project_isar_model.dart
│   │   └── todo_item_isar_model.dart
│   ├── isar_datasource.dart
│   └── isar_manager_impl.dart
├── model
│   ├── project_db_dto.dart
│   └── todo_db_dto.dart
└── database_manager.dart
```

Figure 1.4 Database package overview.

```
converter
├── converter.dart
└── project_converter.dart
```

Figure 1.5 Converter package.

Principle, the repository implementation needs to be written in this layer. The repository communicates with the database, but because each database has its own data model, converter classes are also needed. To illustrate the complexity of this layer, a detailed overview of the classes and packages within the data layer is provided (Figure 1.4).

A package is created for each database, which contains a model package, a database instance, and an implementation of the "DatabaseManager" interface (Code 4).

One thing that can be noticed in the implementation is the dependency injection of the two converter classes (Code 6). Dependency injection ensures that a class doesn't create its own dependencies internally, leading to direct coupling. Instead, injecting dependencies through the constructor allows for flexibility and external instantiation [5]. Therefore, since the functions defined in the "DatabaseManager" interface return a generic database model, like "ProjectDbDto" (Code 7), it is mandatory to create a model specific to the Hive database and then convert it to the generic one. While this might seem unclear at first, the reason it is done this way is to uphold a core principle of Clean Architecture: dependency on abstractions. If the repository class depends on an abstraction, it doesn't know which specific database it's working with. It only knows the type of data it receives. However, this necessitates converting the concrete database model to the generic one, which is where the "ProjectDbDto" class comes in.

With the abstractions and concrete implementations in place, the application is almost ready for robust data repository communication, following the best practices for retrieval, storage, and deletion. The remaining piece is writing the converter classes. Everything related

CODE 8 CONVERTER INTERFACE

```
abstract class Converter<S,T> {
  T convert(S source);
}
```

to these can be found in the "converter" package (Figure 1.5). This package contains an interface defining the conversion functionality (Code 8) and classes implementing that interface (Code 9 and Code 10).

The code snippets above show concrete implementations of the "Converter" interface. There are two implementations for converting "ProjectDbDto" to "HiveProjectModel" and vice versa, and two implementations for converting "ProjectDbDto" to "Project" and vice versa. It is important to emphasize that the "Project" class is an entity class that belongs to the domain layer. For a clearer explanation, a diagram is provided in Figure 1.6.

The final step in the data layer is the implementation of the repository interface (Code 11).

With everything implemented, the desired separation of layers is achieved, required for the entire data flow, from the database to the business logic layer and back. Since everything is working with abstractions, adding a new database only requires creating a database instance, defining a storage model, and implementing the "DatabaseManager" interface (e.g. "MongoDbManagerImpl"). No other changes are necessary. That is the essence of Clean Architecture. It allows someone to add new functionalities in a clear, maintainable, and testable way without major code modifications. Therefore, when writing a new application, software engineers should strive to isolate the business logic and make the code maintainable and readable. This is what Clean Architecture helps achieve.

1.3.4 Presentation layer

This project utilizes the Riverpod library for state management due to its versatility and ease of use. State management refers to tracking the state across all components and the flow of data within them [6]. By managing the state, the developer gains control and visibility over how data is displayed on the user interface and how users interact with it. The "ProjectProvider" class (Code 12) manages the state of projects and injects dependencies in business logic classes, such as the class for fetching all projects or the class for creating a new one. This demonstrates that the presentation layer also depends on the domain layer, following the Clean Architecture principle.

The next step, and the second-to-last in the overall process, is crucial for the user: the user interface and its on-screen elements. Nearly every application has a user interface, and in Flutter, everything is a widget [7]. For example, retrieved project data is displayed in the "ProjectScreen" class (Code 13), specifically within a widget called "ProjectList" if the list state is not empty. Different widgets are used for other list states.

1.3.5 Dependency injection

The final step in building this application is dependency injection, which connects all the elements and makes the application functional (Code 14).

As is often the case, the true purpose becomes clear toward the end. In the previous figure, where a dependency is injected into the constructor of the "ProjectRepositoryImpl" class, the first parameter is an instance of the Hive database (Code 15). During development, if the client changes their mind and decides to use a different database for local storage, such

CODE 9 HIVE MODEL – DBDTO MODEL CONVERSION

```
class ProjectHiveModelToDbDtoConverter implements
Converter<ProjectHiveModel, ProjectDbDto> {
 final TodoItemHiveModelToDbDtoConverter _converter;

 const ProjectHiveModelToDbDtoConverter(
   this._converter
 );

 @override
 ProjectDbDto convert(
  ProjectHiveModel model
 ) {
    final todos = model
    .todoList
    .map(
     (todo) => _converter.convert(todo)
    )
    .toList();
    return ProjectDbDto(
      id: model.key,
      title: model.title,
      todoList: todos,
    );
  }
}

class ProjectDbDtoToHiveModelConverter implements
Converter<ProjectDbDto, ProjectHiveModel> {
 final TodoItemDbDtoToHiveModelConverter
 _converter;

 const ProjectDbDtoToHiveModelConverter(
   this._converter
 );

 @override
 ProjectHiveModel convert(
  ProjectDbDto dto
 ) {
    final todos = dto
    .todoList
    .map(
     (todo) => _converter.convert(todo)
    )
    .toList();
    return ProjectHiveModel(
      title: dto.title,
      todoList: todos,
    );
  }
}
```

CODE 10 DBDTO MODEL – ENTITY MODEL CONVERSION

```
class ProjectDbDtoToEntityConverter implements
Converter<ProjectDbDto, Project> {
 final TodoItemDbDtoToEntityConverter
 _converter;

 const ProjectDbDtoToEntityConverter(
   this._converter
 );

  @override
  Project convert(
    ProjectDbDto dto
  ) {
    final todos = dto
    .todoList
    .map(
      (todo) => _converter.convert(todo)
    )
    .toList(growable: true);
    return Project(
      id: dto.id,
      title: dto.title,
      todoList: todos,
    );
  }
}

class ProjectEntityToDbDtoConverter implements Converter<Project,
ProjectDbDto> {
 final TodoItemEntityToDbDtoConverter
 _converter;

  const ProjectEntityToDbDtoConverter(
    this._converter
  );

  @override
  ProjectDbDto convert(
    Project entity
  ) {
    final todos = entity
    .todoList
    .map(
      (todo) => _converter.convert(todo)
    )
    .toList(growable: true);
    return ProjectDbDto(
      id: entity.id,
      title: entity.title,
      todoList: todos,
    );
  }
}
```

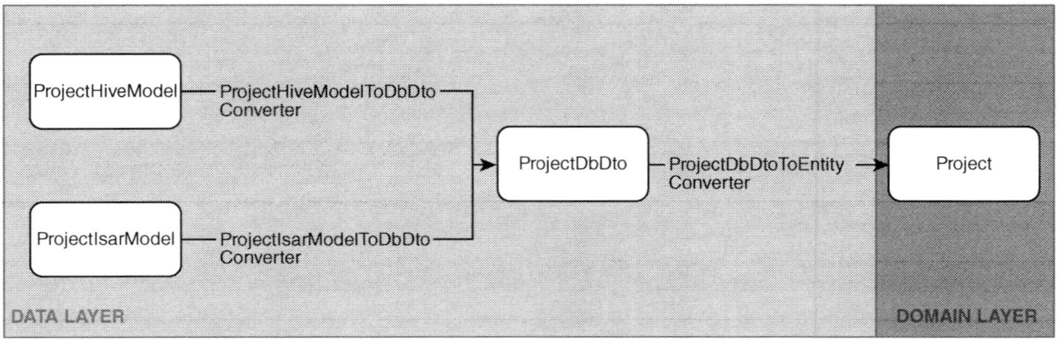

Figure 1.6 Dependency diagram.

CODE 11 REPOSITORY IMPLEMENTATION

```
class ProjectRepositoryImpl implements ProjectRepository {
  final DatabaseManager _databaseManager;
  final ProjectDbDtoToEntityConverter
  _dbDtoToEntityConverter;
  final ProjectEntityToDbDtoConverter
  _entityToDbDtoConverter;

  const ProjectRepositoryImpl(
    this._databaseManager,
    this._dbDtoToEntityConverter,
    this._entityToDbDtoConverter,
  );

  @override
  Future<List<Project>> getAllProjects()
  async {
    final projectObjects = await
    _databaseManager.getAllProjects();

    return projectObjects.map(
    (object) => _dbDtoToEntityConverter
      .convert(object))
      .toList();
  }

  @override
  Future<void> createNewProject(final
  Project project) async {
    final projectObject=
    _entityToDbDtoConverter
    .convert(project);

    await _databaseManager
    .insertNewProject(projectObject);
  }
```

```
  @override
  Future<void> removeProject(final Project
  project) => _databaseManager
  .removeProjectById(project.id!);
}
```

CODE 12 STATE MANAGEMENT CLASS

```
class ProjectProvider extends ChangeNotifier {
  final GetProjectsUseCase
  _getProjectsUseCase;
  final CreateNewProjectUseCase
  _createNewProjectUseCase;
  final DeleteProjectUseCase
  _deleteProjectUseCase;

  AsyncValue<List<Project>>?
  projectListState;

  ProjectProvider(
    this._getProjectsUseCase,
    this._createNewProjectUseCase.
    this._deleteProjectUseCase,
  ) {
    getAllProjects();
  }

  Future<void> getAllProjects() async {
    projectListState = const
    AsyncValue.loading();
    notifyListeners();

    projectListState = await
    AsyncValue.guard(() =>
    _getProjectsUseCase.getAll()
    );
    notifyListeners();
  }

  void createNewProject(
    final String projectName
    ) {
    _createNewProjectUseCase(projectName);
  }



  Future<void> deleteProject(
    final Project project
    ) {
    return _deleteProjectUseCase(project);
  }
}
```

CODE 13 PROJECTSCREEN UI CODE

```
class ProjectsScreen extends ConsumerWidget {
  const ProjectsScreen({super.key});

  @override
  Widget build(
    BuildContext context,
    WidgetRef ref
  ) {
    final projectListState = ref.watch(
      projectProvider.select(
        (provider) =>
           provider.projectListState,
      ),
    );

    return Scaffold(
      body: SafeArea(
        child: Column(
          crossAxisAlignment:
           CrossAxisAlignment.start,
          children: [
            projectListState!.when(
              data: (projectList) =>
                  projectList.isEmpty ?
                  const NoProjects() :
                  ProjectList(
                    projects: projectList
                  ),
              error: (error, stackTrace) =>
                Container(),
              loading: () => Container(),
            ),
          ],s
        ),
      ),
    );
  }
}
```

as Isar, all that's needed is to inject an instance of the Isar database (Code 16). Everything else remains the same. This is the ultimate goal achieved in this project, and it highlights the essence of Clean Architecture.

1.4 CONCLUSION

The goal has been achieved! The created application is easy to extend with new features, simple to navigate, the code is readable, and therefore straightforward to maintain in the long run. This is all thanks to the implemented layers and the use of abstractions within them, which are key principles of Clean Architecture [8].

CODE 14 DEPENDENCY INJECTION

```
/// ************ MANAGERS *************
final hiveManagerProvider = Provider<DatabaseManager>(
  (ref) => HiveManagerImpl(    ref.watch(projectHiveModelToDbDtoConv
erter)
ref.watch(projectDbDtoToHiveModelConverter)
  ),
);

final isarManagerProvider = Provider<DatabaseManager>(
  (ref) => IsarManagerImpl(
    ref.watch(isarDatasourceProvider),
  ref.watch(projectIsarModelToDbDtoConverter)
  ref.watch(projectDbDtoToIsarModelConverter)
  ),
);

/// ************ REPOSITORIES *************
final projectRepositoryProvider = Provider<ProjectRepository>(
  (ref) => ProjectRepositoryImpl(
    ref.watch(hiveManagerProvider),
  ref.watch(projectDbDtoToEntityConverter),
  ref.watch(projectEntityToDbDtoConverter),
  ),
);

/// ************ PROVIDERS *************
final createNewProjectUseCaseProvider = Provider<CreateNewProjectUse
Case>(
  (ref) => CreateNewProjectUseCase(
    ref.watch(projectRepositoryProvider)
  ),
);

final getAllProjectsUseCaseProvider = Provider<GetProjectsUseCase>(
  (ref) => GetProjectsUseCase(
    ref.watch(projectRepositoryProvider)
  ),
);

final deleteProjectUseCaseProvider = Provider<DeleteProjectUseCase>(
  (ref) => DeleteProjectUseCase(
    ref.watch(projectRepositoryProvider)
  ),
);

/// ************ PROVIDERS *************
final projectProvider = ChangeNotifierProvider<ProjectProvider>(
  (ref) => ProjectProvider(
ref.watch(getAllProjectsUseCaseProvider),
ref.watch(createNewProjectUseCaseProvider),ref.watch(deleteProjectUs
eCaseProvider),
  ),
);
```

CODE 15 INJECTION OF HIVE DATABASE

```
final projectRepositoryProvider = Provider<ProjectRepository>(
  (ref) => ProjectRepositoryImpl(
    ref.watch(hiveManagerProvider),
   ref.watch(projectDbDtoToEntityConverter),
   ref.watch(projectEntityToDbDtoConverter),
  ),
);
```

CODE 16 INJECTION OF ISAR DATABASE

```
final projectRepositoryProvider = Provider<ProjectRepository>(
  (ref) => ProjectRepositoryImpl(
    ref.watch(isarManagerProvider),
   ref.watch(projectDbDtoToEntityConverter),
   ref.watch(projectEntityToDbDtoConverter),
  ),
);
```

Many engineers, from junior to senior level, encounter projects on a daily basis that are difficult to maintain due to the unreadable and long code. For junior developers, this architecture serves well for learning how to program serious applications because it offers a structured and well-defined development approach. Senior developers can grasp what's happening in the code faster and with better understanding. Additionally, on projects with very large teams, a clearly structured project facilitates team communication and efficiency. The implementation of Clean Architecture in a Flutter project, as demonstrated in this chapter, validates its value in creating modular, extensible, readable, and maintainable applications. Best of all, it is applicable across all technologies, not just Flutter. Therefore, it's crucial to emphasize the way of thinking behind it, to understand the mindset behind it.

For engineers new to this topic, applying Clean Architecture and the mindset behind it is recommended to learn and implement. This contributes to better projects that everyone can enjoy working on and discussing. New challenges and high-quality solutions motivate and develop engineers.

REFERENCES

[1] R.C. Martin, *Clean Architecture: A Craftsman's Guide to Software Structure and Design*, Boston: Pearson Education, 2017.

[2] F. Kisić, "Mobile app clean architecture in practice" [Online]. Available: https://medium.com/comsystoreply/mobile-app-clean-architecture-in-practice-ce3df1736d3

[3] Flutter FAQ. (2018, Sep. 11). What is Flutter? [Online]. Available: https://docs.flutter.dev/resources/faq

[4] DartLang. (2013, Jun. 19) Release notes for Dart's Beta Release. [Online]. Available: https://news.dartlang.org/2013/06/release-notes-for-darts-beta-release.html

[5] R.C. Martin, *Clean Code: A Handbook of Agile Software Craftsmanship*, Boston: Pearson Education, 2008.
[6] K. Tran, *State management in React*, 2022.
[7] A. Miola (2023, May 18). Flutter Complete Reference 2.0 [Online]. Available: https://fluttercompletereference.com/
[8] R.C. Martin, „Design Principles and Design Patterns" [Online], 2000. Available: https://staff.cs.utu.fi/~jounsmed/doos_06/material/DesignPrinciplesAndPatterns.pdf

Chapter 2

Declarative iOS programming and architectural patterns

Kevin Furjan, Filip Kisić, and Daniel Bele

2.1 INTRODUCTION

Nowadays, mobile applications are widely used for many different purposes, whether for education, entertainment, fitness, finance, productivity, or something else entirely. These applications must also support lots of different devices and lots of different form factors. Because of this, adherence to the best practices and using proper architectural patterns are of the essence.

In the initial stages of designing a mobile application, one of the most important considerations is selecting the appropriate architecture that aligns with the application's domain and objectives [1]. The exemplary architecture choice plays a crucial role in ensuring the scalability and flexibility of the application in the long run. When embarking on application development, it's essential to look beyond the initial concept and consider how the application will evolve and adapt during the development process [2]. This thoughtful approach informs architectural decision-making, whether it involves opting for Model-View-Controller (MVC), Model-View-ViewModel (MVVM), Model-View-Intent (MVI), or View-Interactor-Presenter-Entity-Router (VIPER). Each architectural pattern has its own strengths and weaknesses, yet the availability of empirical data to substantiate the superiority of a specific pattern over others is unfortunately limited [1]. Ultimately, choosing the application architecture typically comes down to prior experience with a particular architecture, the needs of the application, and the project's timeframe.

In recent years, a new trend has emerged in the world of mobile programming. Initially, the only approach to mobile programming was the imperative approach, i.e., the traditional programming paradigm that focuses on explicitly describing a sequence of steps to be executed by the computer to accomplish a specific task. With the introduction of frameworks such as React Native [3] and Flutter [4], mobile programming had an innovative approach to developing applications, the declarative approach. Declarative programming is not an innovation; on the contrary, it has existed for the last 20 years or so with languages such as SQL [5]. Declarative programming, as opposed to imperative programming, uses a high-level machine code to specify the goal that needs to be completed as opposed to outlining the steps that must be taken to do it [6].

2.2 ARCHITECTURAL PATTERNS

Software architecture patterns are reusable fixes for typical problems in software systems [7]. In other words, a pattern is typically created when multiple developers use a similar technique to address a specific problem, and the solution is widely accepted and well-documented. Software architectural patterns connect a situation, a particular issue, and a related fix [7].

 DOI: 10.1201/9781003513445-2

The situation represents a recurring scenario that gives rise to a problem within this context. It is important to note that the problem should be generalized to accommodate variations. Therefore, the pattern describes both the primary problem and variations of the problem. The solution represents a resolution to the identified problem. Ultimately, a solution provides a practical way to handle the issue. Consequently, a solution aims to provide the architectural framework that offers a method for resolving the issue.

It is worth mentioning that various architectural patterns can be used simultaneously in a single system in real-world applications. Many complex systems exhibit this combination of multiple patterns. For instance, a web-based system may take advantage of the MVC pattern, while at the same time, it may also make use of other patterns, such as the client-server pattern. Moreover, additional strategies and patterns may be used within each of them, optimizing each module with the optimal architecture. While various architectural patterns can be used to develop complex systems, it does not mean they should. Each pattern should address a specific problem in the system. Introducing a pattern without a clear purpose can make the system more complex and more challenging to maintain.

2.2.1 Model-View-Controller

The MVC architectural pattern has been the most popular for the last 40 years since its introduction in the 1980s [8]. This pattern divides the application's responsibilities into distinct roles, making it incredibly popular among developers. The components of MVC can be seen in Figure 2.1.

Three separate functions – Model, View, and Controller – are assigned to each module of the program by the MVC pattern. These functions are isolated from one another by arbitrary boundaries. The Model outlines the application guidelines and includes business logic. For instance, the Model has the ability to store, encapsulate, and abstract data within an application. Instead of using something as basic as an integer to hold the manufactured year, a Car object can be used to store comprehensive car data like make and model, manufactured year, and other details. The model also includes specific data management-related responsibilities, such as data persistence, validation, and retrieval.

Conversely, the application's presentation logic is the responsibility of the View. Therefore, its main responsibility is handling user interactions and presenting the data to the users. Every time something changes within the Model, the View is informed. Consequently, it redraws the content of the most recent application and obtains its state from the Model.

The controller's role is to manage the interaction process between the data layer and the user interface elements. It updates the Model based on user interaction events received from the View. Additionally, the Controller is capable of overseeing the lifecycles of various other application parts. The classic MVC architectural pattern has multiple use cases, including desktop, mobile, and web apps.

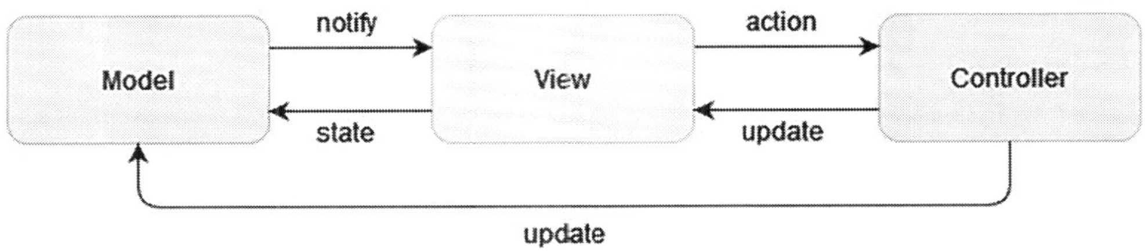

Figure 2.1 The traditional MVC pattern.

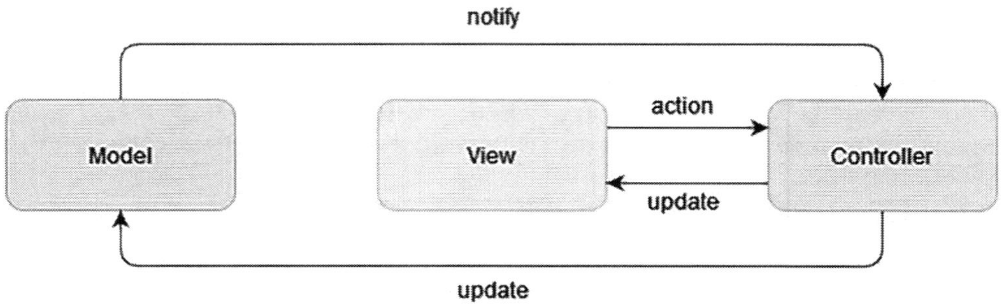

Figure 2.2 The traditional MVC pattern, as advised by Apple.

Three essential roles – Model, View, and Controller – uphold the core principle of separation of concerns in Apple's updated MVC design [9]. The Model still contains the application logic, while the View handles the presentation logic. A key change from traditional MVC is the elimination of direct communication between Model and View. Instead, the Model routes all state changes through the Controller, which then instructs the View to display the updated data. Actions initiated by users are processed in a sequence that progressively updates the data in the Model, aligning with Apple's recommendation to keep the Model and View unaware of each other (Figure 2.2).

Due to its design, the MVC approach by Apple has several benefits compared to traditional MVC. The clear separation between the View and the Model greatly enhances their reusability. Additionally, this separation allows for parallel development, enabling modifications to the logic in the Model or the View independently, without affecting the other. This promotes more efficient development workflows and better maintenance of the application components [7].

2.2.2 Model-View-Presenter

Model-View-Presenter (MVP) is an alternative to the MVC pattern. It seeks to improve the division of responsibilities while offering a simple architecture solution for developing applications. The MVP pattern visualization can be seen in Figure 2.3.

There are three essential elements. Access to and manipulation of domain data remain within the scope of the Model. The presentation logic, however, is included in the View. As a result, its key responsibilities still include providing other components with user events and presenting data to users. MVP adds a new element called the Presenter to replace the Controller in MVC. The Presenter, acting as an intermediary, oversees maintaining application synchronization. Because of this, it responds to user input from the View and modifies the model as necessary. Meanwhile, the Presenter receives updates from the Model, processes the data to be suitable for the interface, and updates the View accordingly.

Figure 2.3 MVP architectural pattern.

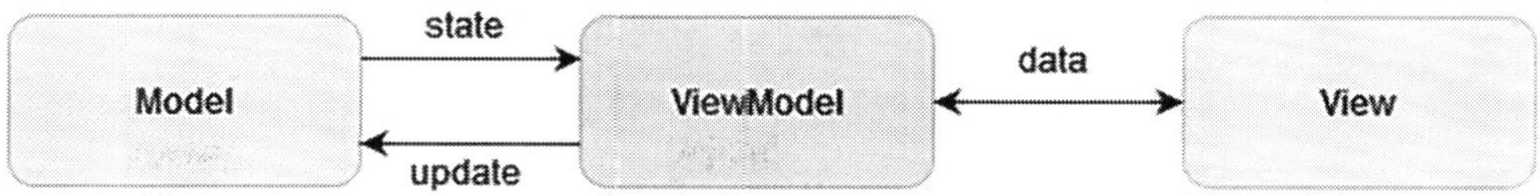

Figure 2.4 MVVM architectural pattern.

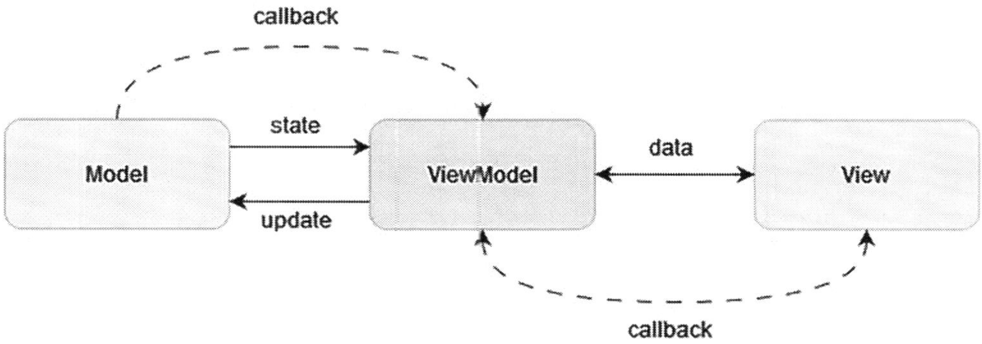

Figure 2.5 MVVM data flow.

2.2.3 Model-View-ViewModel

Microsoft initially introduced the MVVM pattern in the mid-2000s to develop Windows WPF applications [10]. Over time, it became widely used for creating UI applications on both desktop and mobile platforms, especially for responsive iOS applications [11]. Similar to other architectural designs, MVVM's Model encapsulates logic such as networking and data persistence. The View handles UI element rendering and information presentation. The ViewModel ensures smooth data flow and facilitates communication, updating the Model, and responding to data changes. It supports the View by reformatting data for display, making it essential in the MVVM architecture. This relationship is shown in Figure 2.4.

The MVVM architecture pattern integrates effectively with reactive programming by concentrating on data dynamics and updates. This ensures that changes in the model influence the view via the ViewModel. When the model's data is modified, it triggers change notifications to the ViewModel. The ViewModel, in turn, interacts with the Model, exchanges data, and sends change notifications to the View. Consequently, the View automatically displays the latest data from the ViewModel, reflecting updates as they occur [12]. This process is depicted in the visualization (Figure 2.5).

2.2.4 View-Interactor-Presenter-Entity-Router

VIPER is a structure within Clean Architecture tailored for iOS applications. Clean Architecture divides an application's logical framework into distinct layers of responsibility, aiding in dependency isolation, such as databases and testing layer interactions. Although VIPER is not part of the Model-View-* architecture family, it enhances task distribution within an application by separating duties into distinct layers. This modular approach can be visualized in Figure 2.6.

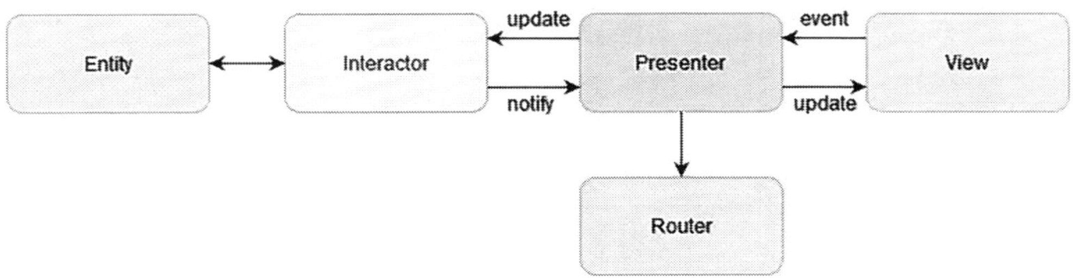

Figure 2.6 VIPER architectural pattern.

VIPER comprises five distinct levels. First off, the primary duty of the VIPER's View is still the same as that of the MVP's View. That is overseeing user interaction and data visualization. To be more precise, it waits for the content that needs to be displayed next and transfers any user-triggered events to the Presenter. The Presenter gets these events and responds to them. Notably, unlike the Presenter in MVP, it does not possess the Model. Instead, the Interactor is a new component from which the Presenter references and requests data updates. The Interactor often represents an application's use cases and encapsulates the business logic. One use case for a to-do application would be retrieving a list of tasks that are kept in a distant database. In that scenario, the Interactor frequently starts the fetching process by using a networking dependence, after which it notifies the Presenter of the outcome [7]. Furthermore, the Entity is a simple data object that the Interactor is aware of and manipulates. Remembering that the Entity does not include the data access logic is crucial. The Interactor is responsible for this. Finally, VIPER introduces a component called the Router, which is responsible solely for managing the routing logic among VIPER components. The Router handles events received from the Presenter, indicating which screen the user should navigate to next [7].

2.3 COMPARISON OF ARCHITECTURAL PATTERNS

As previously mentioned, deciding which architecture to use is based on the application's use case, maintenance requirements, previous experience with specific architectures, etc. However, some studies try to compare architectural patterns empirically based on categories such as testability, resource usage, and ease of use [7].

MVC and MVP patterns are the easiest to use but have certain drawbacks. The most notable disadvantages are testability and distribution of responsibilities, especially in the case of the MVC pattern. On the other hand, the VIPER architectural pattern excels in testability and distribution of responsibility categories. Since VIPER heavily relies on clean code and clean architecture principles, this also makes it hard to use. MVVM sits in between the MVC and MVP patterns on one side and the VIPER pattern on the other. It offers a happy medium between ease of use, testability, and distribution of responsibilities (Table 2.1).

2.4 DECLARATIVE PROGRAMMING

Declarative programming is a paradigm for writing programs in which the programmer explains the program's goal instead of how it will be accomplished. Put another way, it leaves the implementation specifics to the underlying system and concentrates on expressing the

Table 2.1 Comparison of architectural patterns

	MVC	*MVP*	*MVVM*	*VIPER*
Ease of use	Easy	Easy	Moderate	Hard
Testability	Hard	Moderate	Moderate	Easy
Distribution of responsibilities	Bad	Good	Good	Best

intended outcome. High-level constructs and abstractions that abstract away the underlying complexity of the computation, such as functions, expressions, queries, and rules, are frequently used in declarative programming. Using a declarative approach, Developers can express computations clearly and legibly with these constructs. Increased productivity, greater concern separation, and enhanced code readability and maintainability are just a few advantages of declarative programming. Developers can build code that is easier to read, reason about, and edit by concentrating on what needs to be done rather than how to do it.

2.4.1 SwiftUI

SwiftUI is a versatile framework designed to create interfaces across various Apple platforms like iOS, iPadOS, watchOS, tvOS, visionOS, and macOS. It offers layout frameworks, views, and controllers and handles various input events efficiently [13]. The framework also supports integration with UIKit, AppKit, and WatchKit for enhanced platform-specific capabilities. Moreover, SwiftUI allows for app localization in multiple languages and customization of accessibility features to cater to different cultural regions and user needs [15].

Because SwiftUI has a declarative syntax, one can declare the functionality of the user interface. For instance, one may declare a list of objects with text fields and then specify the font, alignment, and color for each field. This will save time and maintenance because the code is more streamlined and readable compared to the imperative programming approach. An example of declarative SwiftUI code can be seen in Figure 2.7.

The declarative approach applies to complex concepts like animation as well. With a few lines of code, one can select from a variety of pre-made effects and quickly add animation to nearly any control. The system manages every operation required to produce a fluid movement during runtime, including handling user input and state changes in the middle of the animation.

2.4.2 Comparison with imperative programming

The best way to compare declarative and imperative programming approaches is by using actual code. Two iOS code examples are shown in Figures 2.8 and 2.9 – one using the imperative approach and UIKit and one using the declarative approach and SwiftUI. Both examples are trying to do the same thing: present UI with two text fields, and a button where the user can enter his credentials and then log into the application.

Comparing the two approaches, it is evident that declarative programming is less verbose, more concise, and more readable. The same functionality is achieved with both approaches, but using SwiftUI, this was done using less code while utilizing strengths of SwiftUI framework such as built-in dark mode support and built-in views that follow Apple's Human Interface Guidelines [14].

```
import SwiftUI

struct ContentView: View {
    @State private var name: String = ""

    var body: some View {
        VStack {
            Text("Welcome to SwiftUI!")
                .font(.largeTitle)
                .padding()

            TextField("Enter your name", text: $name)
                .textFieldStyle(RoundedBorderTextFieldStyle())
                .padding()

            Button(action: {
                print("Hello, \(name)!")
            }) {
                Text("Say Hello")
                    .padding()
                    .background(Color.blue)
                    .foregroundColor(.white)
                    .cornerRadius(10)
            }
        }
        .padding()
    }
}
```

Figure 2.7 Sample SwiftUI code.

2.5 CONCLUSION

This chapter provides an in-depth exploration of declarative iOS programming and various architectural patterns commonly utilized in the development of mobile applications. It underscores the paramount importance of employing appropriate architectural patterns to ensure the scalability, adaptability, and maintainability of mobile applications. The chapter compares the MVC, MVP, MVVM, and VIPER architectural patterns, offering valuable

```
import UIKit

class LoginViewController: UIViewController {

    let usernameTextField: UITextField = {
        let textField = UITextField()
        textField.placeholder = "Username"
        textField.borderStyle = .roundedRect
        return textField
    }()

    let passwordTextField: UITextField = {
        let textField = UITextField()
        textField.placeholder = "Password"
        textField.borderStyle = .roundedRect
        textField.isSecureTextEntry = true
        return textField
    }()

    let loginButton: UIButton = {
        let button = UIButton(type: .system)
        button.setTitle("Login", for: .normal)
        button.addTarget(self, action: #selector(loginButtonTapped), for: .touchUpInside)
        return button
    }()

    override func viewDidLoad() {
        super.viewDidLoad()
        view.backgroundColor = .white
        setupViews()
    }

    func setupViews() {
        view.addSubview(usernameTextField)
        view.addSubview(passwordTextField)
        view.addSubview(loginButton)

        usernameTextField.translatesAutoresizingMaskIntoConstraints = false
        passwordTextField.translatesAutoresizingMaskIntoConstraints = false
        loginButton.translatesAutoresizingMaskIntoConstraints = false

        NSLayoutConstraint.activate([
            usernameTextField.centerXAnchor.constraint(equalTo: view.centerXAnchor),
            usernameTextField.centerYAnchor.constraint(equalTo: view.centerYAnchor, constant: -50),
            usernameTextField.widthAnchor.constraint(equalToConstant: 200),

            passwordTextField.centerXAnchor.constraint(equalTo: view.centerXAnchor),
            passwordTextField.topAnchor.constraint(equalTo: usernameTextField.bottomAnchor, constant: 20),
            passwordTextField.widthAnchor.constraint(equalToConstant: 200),

            loginButton.centerXAnchor.constraint(equalTo: view.centerXAnchor),
            loginButton.topAnchor.constraint(equalTo: passwordTextField.bottomAnchor, constant: 20)
        ])
    }

    @objc func loginButtonTapped() {
        guard let username = usernameTextField.text, !username.isEmpty,
              let password = passwordTextField.text, !password.isEmpty else {
            print("Username and password are required.")
            return
        }
        print("Logging in with username: \(username) and password: \(password)")
    }
}
```

Figure 2.8 UIKit code example.

```
import SwiftUI

struct LoginView: View {
    @State private var username: String = ""
    @State private var password: String = ""

    var body: some View {
        VStack(spacing: 20) {
            TextField("Username", text: $username)
                .textFieldStyle(RoundedBorderTextFieldStyle())
                .padding()

            SecureField("Password", text: $password)
                .textFieldStyle(RoundedBorderTextFieldStyle())
                .padding()

            Button(action: loginButtonTapped) {
                Text("Login")
                    .padding()
                    .frame(maxWidth: .infinity)
                    .foregroundColor(.white)
                    .background(Color.blue)
                    .cornerRadius(8)
            }
        }
        .padding()
    }

    func loginButtonTapped() {
        guard !username.isEmpty, !password.isEmpty else {
            print("Username and password are required.")
            return
        }
        print("Logging in with username: \(username) and password: \(password)")
    }
}

struct ContentView: View {
    var body: some View {
        LoginView()
            .padding()
    }
}
```

Figure 2.9 SwiftUI code example.

insights into the advantages and disadvantages of each design pattern. While MVC and MVP patterns are more accessible to implement, the VIPER pattern excels in terms of testability and responsible component distribution. For most applications, MVVM presents a compelling middle ground, striking a balance among testability, user-friendliness, and responsibility distribution. Nevertheless, VIPER may be the preferable choice for larger projects.

The chapter also explores declarative programming and highlights its benefits, which include higher productivity, easier-to-read code, and improved maintainability. SwiftUI, an iOS declarative UI framework that streamlines the UI development process and provides built-in support for platform-specific features, demonstrates the potential of declarative programming. By contrasting imperative with declarative programming methods using code examples from UIKit and SwiftUI, the efficiency and efficacy of this paradigm are demonstrated. Declarative programming produces code that is more condensed, readable, and maintainable.

REFERENCES

1. Magics-Verkman H, Zmaranda DR, Győrödi CA, Győrödi R. A Comparison of Architectural Patterns for Testability and Performance Quality for iOS Mobile Applications Development. In: EMES; 2023; Oradea.
2. Ferrer García R. *iOS Architecture Patterns*. Berkeley, CA: Apress; 2023.
3. Wu W. *React Native vs Flutter, Cross-Platform Mobile Application Frameworks*. Metropolia University of Applied Sciences; 2018.
4. Napoli ML. *Beginning Flutter: A Hands On Guide to App Development*. 1st ed. Wrox; 2019.
5. Imbugwa G, Enombe E, Saliu H, Mazzara M. SwiftUI: A Case Study of Code Quality Evaluation; 2020.
6. Imbugwa GB, Pires de Araújo LJ, Khazeev M, Enombe E, Saliu H, Mazzara M. A case study comparing static analysis tools for 2022.
7. Phan DH. *Benchmarking Common Architectural Patterns in iOS Development*; 2019.
8. Model View Controller History; 2014. Available from: http://wiki.c2.com/?ModelViewController History [Accessed March 2024].
9. Apple Inc. Model-View-Controller; 2012. Available from: https://developer.apple.com/library/archive/documentation/General/Conceptual/CocoaEncyclopedia/Model-View-Controller/Model-View-Controller.html [Accessed March 2024].
10. Microsoft. Introduction to Model/View/ViewModel pattern for building WPF apps; 2005 Oct 8. Available from: https://learn.microsoft.com/en-us/archive/blogs/johngossman/introduction-to-modelviewviewmodel-pattern-for-building-wpf-apps [Accessed 16 March 2024].
11. Berlin J, Cacheaux R. Advanced iOS App Architecture. Razeware LLC; 2022.
12. Indrawan D, Kusumo DS, Puspitasari SY. Analysis of the Implementation of MVVM Architecture Pattern on Performance of iOS Mobile-Based Applications; 2022.
13. Apple Inc. SwiftUI. Available from: https://developer.apple.com/documentation/swiftui/ [Accessed 16 March 2024].
14. Apple Inc. Human Interface Guidelines. Available from: https://developer.apple.com/design/human-interface-guidelines [Accessed 16 March 2024].
15. Furby J. *Mastering Swift: A Beginner's Guide*. 1st ed. CRC Press; 2021.

Chapter 3

Android malware prediction model using a hybrid machine learning approach for cybersecurity

Ashish Kumar Tiwari, Manoj Tyagi, and Bhupendra Verma

3.1 INTRODUCTION

Android has secured itself as the most popular portable working framework in the ongoing period of processing, and it is utilized by billions of individuals all around the world [1]. Due to this inescapability, Android gadgets have sadly turned into an objective for programmers who are hoping to carry out wrongdoings. Malware that is explicitly intended to taint Android systems presents critical dangers, like the theft of delicate information, the deficiency of monetary assets, and the break of safety. The avoidance and identification of malignant programming for Android gadgets have hence become one needing fundamental focus in the field of organization security, determined to safeguard both individual clients and associations [2].

Utilizing AI is one of the significant advances that should be continued to prevent Android infection [3]. Man-made consciousness calculations can distinguish plans that are characteristic of malware by examining huge datasets that incorporate examples that are both harmless and unsafe. Learning estimations that are regulated – for example, choice trees and mind associations – are utilized to sort out future applications in light of the models that have been learned [4]. Both independent learning and profound learning add to the upgrade of this capacity by recognizing disparities and, accordingly, separating features from unrefined substances on a singular premise. The utilization of these undeniable level strategies gives a powerful structure to the discovery of proactive malware.

Inside the domain of malware anticipating, both static and dynamic requests are fundamental parts. During the time spent on static examination, the code of an application is inspected without the program being executed. Techniques – for example, mark-based acknowledgment and heuristic examination – are utilized to separate between known and obscure dangers or weaknesses. To distinguish possibly destructive applications, assent assessment analyzes the approvals that are expressed by applications to principles of conduct that are normally noticed [5]. A unique assessment, then again, notices the way of behaving of an application in a sandbox, which is a controlled climate, to reveal noxious exercises. These noxious exercises might incorporate phenomenal association traffic or unapproved structure access. The method involved with consolidating static and dynamic assessment, which is alluded to as a cross-variety request, gives a complete methodology that further develops acknowledgment exactness [6].

Despite the way that these undeniable level arrangements are accessible, there are, as yet, specific difficulties related to anticipating Android malware. Malware engineers are continuously attempting to track down new strategies to avoid the area, utilizing strategies, for example, coding disarray and encryption that are continually advancing. The lopsided dispersion of information, which incorporates irrefutably more harmless purposes than hurtful ones, makes the method involved with creating exact simulated intelligence models

 DOI: 10.1201/9781003513445-3

Figure 3.1 Android malware.

extremely muddled [7]. Asset limitations on cell phones, for example, restricted handling power and battery duration, further confine the execution of intricate recognition calculations. Furthermore, gathering and examining client information for malware expectations pose huge protection concerns, requiring cautious thought to keep up with client trust and administrative consistency [8] (Figure 3.1).

Android malware forecast is an imperative part of online protection in the portable age. By utilizing AI, static and dynamic examination, and crossover draws near, network safety specialists can more readily foresee and forestall malware contaminations [9]. While difficulties like avoidance strategies, information irregularity, asset imperatives, and protection issues continue, progressing research and innovative headways vow to improve the security of Android gadgets. Guaranteeing the security of individual information and authoritative resources is central, making the constant improvement of powerful malware forecast techniques essential [10].

This study contributes to the field of cybersecurity by providing a detailed analysis of how a Hybrid classifier can be leveraged for Android malware detection.

The rest of the chapter is presented in four different sections: Section 3.2 presents the literature review, Section 3.3 presents the proposed methodology, Section 3.4 presents the simulation results, and Section 3.5 presents the conclusion of the work.

3.2 LITERATURE REVIEW

H. Alamro et al. [1] presented a Mechanized Android Malware Discovery utilizing the Ideal Outfit Learning Approach for Network protection method. The key feature of the AAMD-OELAC method is its ability to automate the classification and identification of Android malware. To accomplish this, the AAMD-OELAC procedure performs information preprocessing at the fundamental stage. For the Android malware location process, the AAMD-OELAC method follows gathering experience utilizing three ML models: to be specific, Least Square Support Vector Machine, piece outrageous learning machine, and regularized irregular vector can be useful in connecting to the brain.

A. Khan et al. [2] elaborate on the widespread use of smartphones throughout the world has resulted in the creation of millions of programs that are both free and available for purchase. By using these programs, users are able to engage in a variety of activities, including interacting with one another, playing games, and accomplishing educational and financial duties. As a result of the fact that these regularly used gadgets often contain sensitive private information, they have become an increasingly popular target for malicious software that may cause damage.

V. Singh [3] identifies malicious software on Android; it is suggested to use a Composition Ratio (CR) of permission pairs. Within an application, the CR is defined as the ratio of a permission pair to the total number of pairings. The fact that the CR is often low in malware due to the presence of superfluous permissions is the primary focus. The construction of databases pertaining to the CR allows us to get characteristics without making use of the frequencies.

To investigate the backdoor attack against Android malware detectors, S. Garg et al. [4] were inspired to conduct their research. In order to conceal the fact that the backdoor was developed and inserted into the model without gaining access to the training data, it is triggered when an application that contains the trigger is offered. We present the suggested attack by demonstrating it against four common malware detectors that have been extensively studied in the academic community. According to the results of our analysis, the suggested backdoor assault is capable of achieving an evasion rate of up to 99% over 750 different malware strains.

According to O. Somarriba et al. [5], to overcome these deficiencies, a more realistic solution would be to allow early detection of malware that is based on overlays during the process of app market evaluation. This would ensure that all of the capabilities of overlays would remain untouched. The objective of this work is to do this by first conducting a large-scale comparative analysis of overlay features in benign and malicious applications and then implementing the OverlayChecker system to automatically identify overlay-based malware for one of the major Android app stores in the world.

F. Deldar et al. [6] present a novel way for the detection of ransomware. This method is founded on the idea that ransomware threats are constantly evolving. In addition to conducting feature selection, the binary particle swarm optimization approach is applied for the purpose of tweaking the hyperparameters of the classification algorithm. Classification is accomplished by the use of the Support Vector Machine (SVM) algorithm in conjunction with the synthetic minority oversampling method (SMOTE). There are 10,153 Android apps that make up the dataset that is being employed, and 500 of those applications are ransomware. The dataset was acquired from a variety of sources. With the top scores in terms of sensitivity, specificity, and g-mean, the performance of the suggested technique SMOTE-tBPSO-SVM obtained more benefits than standard machine learning algorithms. This was accomplished by having the highest scores over the traditional algorithms.

C. Irawan et al. [7] explore the industry and research circles, and a number of different strategies have been presented in order to address the shortcomings of the signature-based detection methods that are currently used by both free and commercial anti-malware programs. This methodology is mostly based on supervised machine learning, and, in order to create accurate prediction models, it is necessary to achieve optimum class balance. The purpose of this research is to provide a technique that may be used to infer the maliciousness of mobile applications by using formal equivalence testing to identify groups to which the application belongs.

In their article, L. Weng et al. [8] presented an adjacency matrix for each application is the aspect of our research that sets it apart from other studies. These matrices serve as "input images" for the CNN model, which enables it to learn how to discriminate between benign and dangerous applications, as well as families of malware. During the course of the trial, it was discovered that AdMat was able to adjust to a wide range of training ratios and obtain an average detection rate of 98.26% across a variety of malware datasets.

P. Sreekumari et al. [9] demonstrate that the key to effectively constructing such systems is multifaceted. These include the selection and encoding of features, the engineering and exposure of features, the speed and effectiveness of app analysis, the participation of developers and users, and the growth of machine learning models. It is possible that the "wooden barrel effect" of the whole system may occur if any of the aforementioned components were to fail.

For the most part, the model training that was provided by A. Alzahrani et al. [10] makes use of one-shot computation. As a result, it is possible to train it in a complete or gradual manner directly on mobile devices. When it comes to the accuracy of detection, our detector surpasses models that are based on shallow learning, such as SVM and AdaBoost, and it approaches the models that are based on deep learning, such as multi-layer perceptron (MLP) and CNN. In addition, our detector is more resistant to adversarial instances than the detectors that are already in use, and its defenses may be strengthened even more with the implementation of on-device model retraining.

3.3 PROPOSED METHODOLOGY

The goal of this research is to develop a machine learning model to predict whether an Android application is malicious or benign using the Hybrid classifier algorithm. The methodology is structured into several key phases: data collection, data preprocessing, feature selection, model training, model evaluation, and deployment (Figure 3.2).

The following steps are involved:

Step 1: Data collection

- Gather a dataset of Android applications, including both benign (normal) and malicious (malware) samples.
- Extract features from these applications, such as permissions, API calls, network traffic, and static code analysis.

Step 2: Data preprocessing

- **Labeling:** Tag each application as either benign or malicious.
- **Normalization:** Scale numerical features to a uniform range (e.g., 0–1).

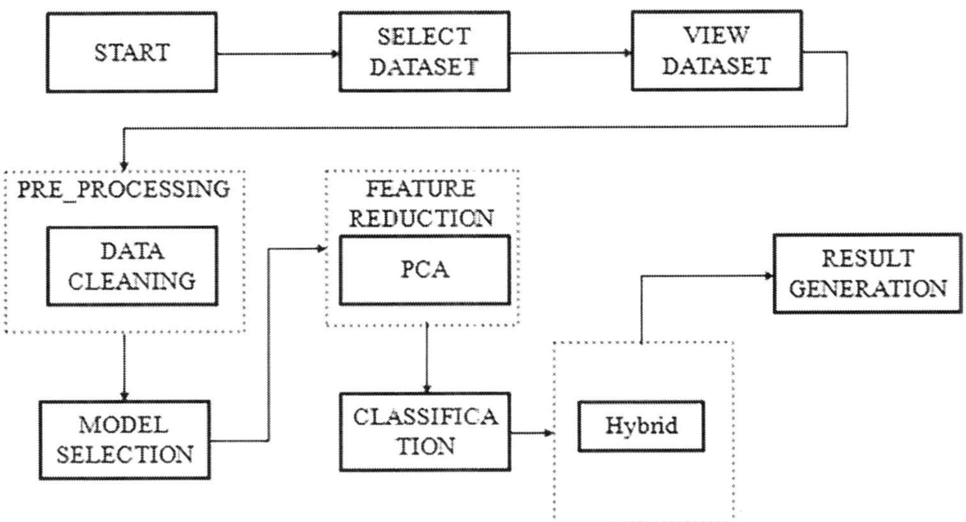

Figure 3.2 Flow chart.

- **Feature engineering:** Select relevant features for the prediction task, possibly using techniques such as PCA (Principal Component Analysis).

Step 3: Model building

- **Support Vector Machine:** Initialize and configure the SVM model with an appropriate kernel (e.g., linear, RBF).
- **Multi-Layer Perceptron:** Initialize and configure the MLP model with suitable hyperparameters (e.g., number of hidden layers, neurons per layer).

Step 4: Model training

1. Split the preprocessed dataset into training and testing sets.
2. Train the SVM model on the training data.
3. Train the MLP model on the training data.

Step 5: Hybrid model

1. Combine the predictions of the SVM and MLP models using ensemble techniques like stacking or voting.
    - **Voting:** Use a soft voting classifier to combine the probabilities from both SVM and MLP.
    - **Stacking:** Train a meta-classifier (e.g., logistic regression) on the outputs of the SVM and MLP models.

Step 6: Model evaluation

1. Evaluate the individual SVM and MLP models using metrics such as accuracy, precision, recall, and F1-score.
2. Evaluate the hybrid model to ensure it performs better than the individual models.

Step 7: Model deployment

1. Deploy the hybrid model into the Android security system.
2. Monitor the model's performance and update it periodically with new data to maintain accuracy.

3.4 SIMULATION RESULTS

The proposed work simulation is performed using the spyder software of Python 3.7. It has a great machine learning library to perform the making of prediction models.

Figure 3.3 presents the dataset matrix: in this dataset, there are a total of 15,036 rows and 215 columns. In the entire dataset, 5560 are malware and 9476 are benign or non-malware.

Figure 3.4 presents the x train dataset. In the data train, the information preparing the system is the main part of any viable malware expectation model for Android. To finish this cycle, the model is furnished with a huge dataset that incorporates both harmless projects and known malware tests.

The x test dataset is displayed in Figure 3.5. Following the finishing of the preparation interaction on a complete dataset, the Android malware expectation model is presently prepared to scrutinize its recently procured information. The step of testing the information is vital since it decides how effective the model is and where there are valuable open doors for development.

The Confusion Matrix (CM) is displayed in Figure 3.6. The disarray framework, which is displayed in Figure 3.6, is a fundamental instrument for understanding the results of an Android malware expectation model. During the time of information testing, it offers an unmistakable visual portrayal of how well the model did as far as classifying applications.

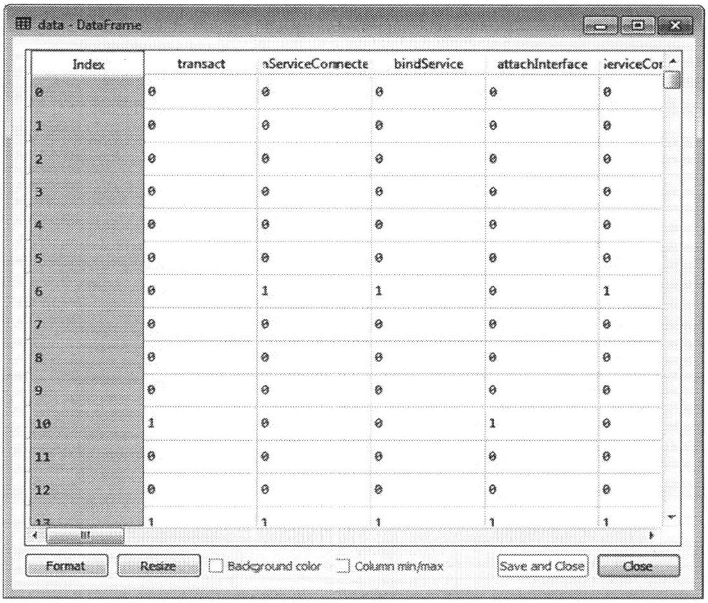

Figure 3.3 Dataset matrix.

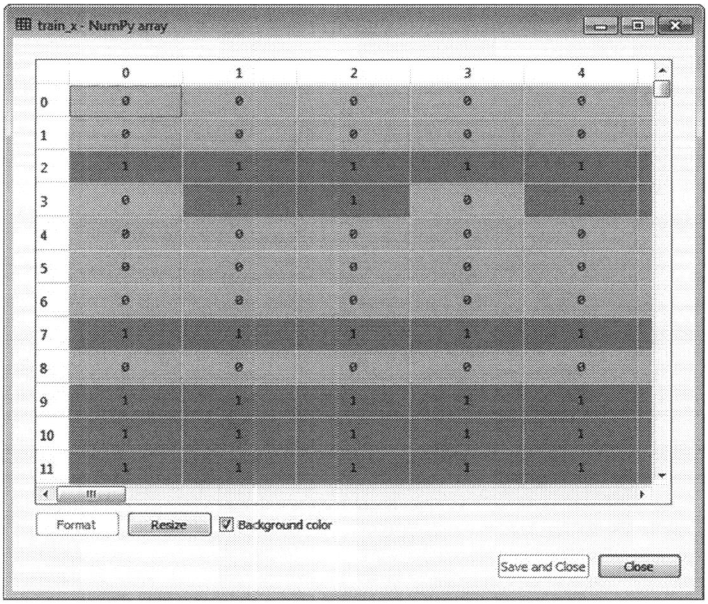

Figure 3.4 Data train.

3.5 CONCLUSION

The motivation behind this exploration is to introduce a hybrid AI approach for the expectation of malware on Android. The utilization of help vector machines (SVM) and AI (MLP) for Android malware expectation gives a strong safeguard against digital dangers; by and by, it needs ceaseless transformation to malware and put an accentuation on staying away

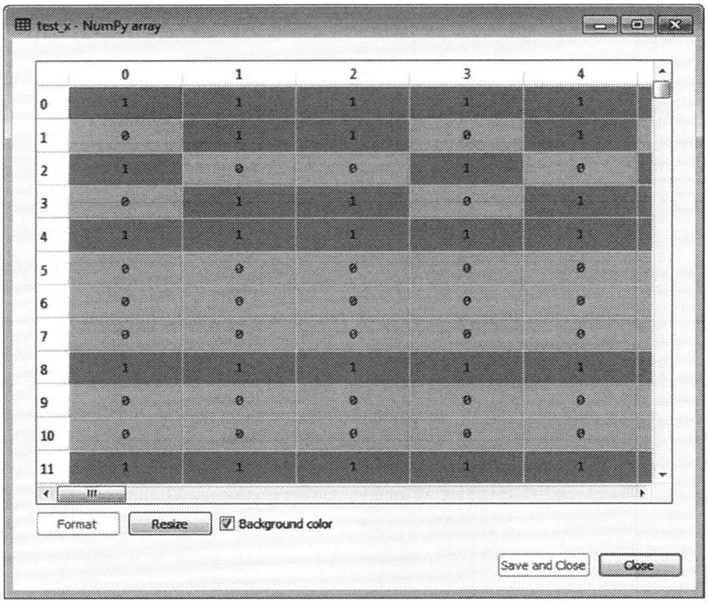

Figure 3.5 Data test.

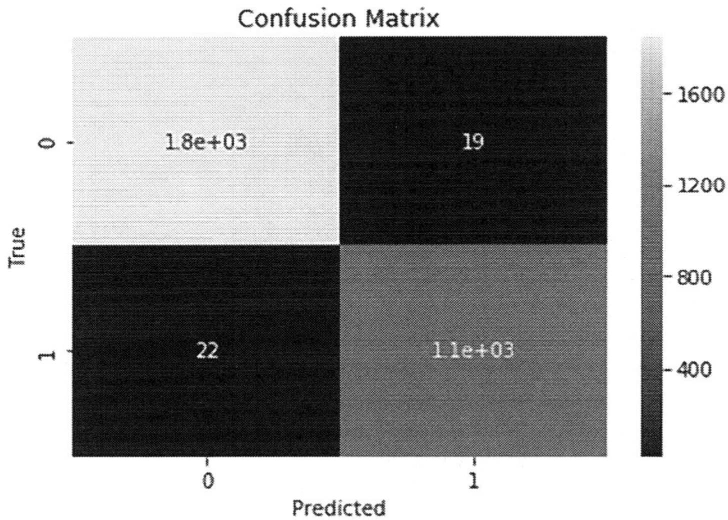

Figure 3.6 Confusion Matrix (CM).

from misleading up-sides. An Android climate that is safer could be achieved by scientists by means of the refinement of existing models and the investigation of new systems. This will make malware forecast a fundamental part of proactive network protection. The ongoing review, which depends on AAMD-OELAC, procured a precision of 98.93% and an order blunder of 1.07%. Then again, the proposed forecast model accomplished an exactness of 99.60% with a mistake pace of simply 0.40%. Consequently, the mixture expectation model that was proposed accomplished a more significant level of exactness contrasted with the methodology that was recently utilized (Table 3.1).

Table 3.1 Result comparison

S No.	*Parameters_Name*	*Previous_work_[1]*	*Proposed_work*
1	Method	AAMD-OELAC	Hybrid (SVM+MLP)
2	Precision	99.15%	99.45%
3	Recall	98.13%	98.87%
4	F_Measure	99.04%	99.5%
5	Accuracy	98.93%	99.60%
6	Classification Error	1.07%	0.40%

REFERENCES

1. H. Alamro, W. Mtouaa, S. Aljameel, A. S. Salama, M. A. Hamza and A. Y. Othman, "Robotized Android Malware Identification Utilizing Ideal Group Learning Approach for Network safety," in *IEEE Access*, vol. 11, pp. 72509–72517, 2023, doi: 10.1109/ACCESS.2023.3294263
2. Khan and I. Sharma, "TrustDroid: Improving Trust and Protection for Android Cell Phones by Forestalling Riskware and SMS Malware," 2023 second Worldwide Gathering on Modern Advances (INCOFT), Belagavi, Karnataka, India, 2023, pp. 1–6, doi: 10.1109/INCOFT60753.2023.10425220
3. Singh, L. Kumar, A. K. Patel and A. Krishna, "An Observational Structure for Malware Expectation Utilizing Multi-facet Perceptron," 2023 OITS Worldwide Meeting on Data Innovation (OCIT), Raipur, India, 2023, pp. 485–490, doi: 10.1109/OCIT59427.2023.10430935
4. S. Garg and N. Baliyan, "MalVulDroid: Following Weaknesses from Malware in Android Utilizing Normal Language Handling," in *Diary of Web Designing*, vol. 21, no. 8, pp. 2339–2361, November 2022, doi: 10.13052/jwe1540-9589.2185
5. O. Somarriba and H. J. Urbina, "URL-Based Unique Checking of Android Malware utilizing AI," 2022 IEEE 40th Focal America and Panama Show (CONCAPAN), Panama, Panama, 2022, pp. 1–6, doi: 10.1109/CONCAPAN48024.2022.9997633
6. F. Deldar, M. Abadi and M. Ebrahimifard, "Android Malware Recognition Utilizing Administered Profound Chart Portrayal Learning," 2022 twelfth Worldwide Gathering on PC and Information Designing (ICCKE), Mashhad, Iran, Islamic Republic of, 2022, pp. 348–354, doi: 10.1109/ICCKE57176.2022.9960076
7. C. Irawan, T. Mantoro and M. A. Ayu, "Malware Location and Arrangement Model Utilizing AI Arbitrary Timberland Approach," 2021 IEEE seventh Global Gathering on Figuring, Designing and Plan (ICCED), Sukabumi, Indonesia, 2021, pp. 1–5, doi: 10.1109/ICCED53389.2021.9664858
8. L. Weng, H. Liu, L. Huang, Y. Zhang and C. Feng, "Android malignant application recognition in view of Help Sifting and Rope LR Calculation," 2021 Global Gathering on Correspondences, Processing, Network safety, and Informatics (CCCI), Beijing, China, 2021, pp. 1–5, doi: 10.1109/CCCI52664.2021.9583199
9. P. Sreekumari, "Malware Identification Methods In light of Profound Learning," 2020 IEEE sixth Intl Gathering on Huge Information Security on Cloud (BigDataSecurity), IEEE Intl Meeting on Superior Execution and Savvy Figuring, (HPSC) and IEEE Intl Meeting on Keen Information and Security (IDS), Baltimore, MD, USA, 2020, pp. 65–70, doi: 10.1109/BigDataSecurity-HPSC-IDS49724.2020.00023
10. Alzahrani, H. Alshahrani, A. Alshehri and H. Fu, "A Smart Way of behaving Based Ransomware Discovery Framework For Android Stage," 2019 First IEEE Worldwide Gathering on Trust, Protection and Security in Astute Frameworks and Applications (TPS-ISA), Los Angeles, CA, USA, 2019, pp. 28–35, doi: 10.1109/TPS-ISA48467.2019.00013

Chapter 4

Dissecting PREFETCHX

Understanding cross-core attacks in hardware security

S. Mahipal and P. Mohan Kumar

4.1 INTRODUCTION

In the realm of high-performance computing (HPC) and data processing, where memory latency poses a significant challenge, the conventional solution involves prefetching to proactively fetch required data into fast cache memory before processor requests [1]. This is exemplified in the architecture of Intel Atom cores, which feature four cores per module, each with private L1 caches and a shared L2 mid-level cache (MLC) [2]. The L2 prefetch mechanism, supported by hardware prefetchers, identifies access patterns and directs prefetches into the L2 Queue (L2Q) alongside regular load and store requests [3]. The XPT prefetcher, in modern Intel processors which has never been officially detailed, speculatively issues a load, bypassing last-level cache (LLC) lookups, when it predicts that a load request will result in an LLC miss [4]. XPT prefetcher is shared among different cores, which enables an attacker to build cross-core side-channel and covert-channel attacks [5].

Performance degradation in modern processors due to memory stalls is addressed by proposing a hybrid prefetching approach [6]. Integrating software-driven block prefetching with existing hardware techniques, the runtime-assisted prefetcher collaborates with hardware prefetchers, achieving up to 32% maximum speedup and 18% energy-to-solution reduction compared to hardware prefetching alone in scientific benchmarks [7]. Understanding Cross-Core Attacks in Hardware Security requires contextual information that sets the stage for understanding the significance of PREFETCHX and the broader landscape of hardware security threats. Historical Context highlights the historical evolution of computer hardware and the increasing complexity of modern processors, emphasizing key milestones in processor design and the introduction of features like prefetching [8].

Introduction to Prefetching provides an explanation of prefetching mechanisms in processors, including their purpose, operation, and role in enhancing system performance [9]. The emergence of Hardware Security Threats describes the growing importance of hardware security in the face of evolving cyber threats, citing notable instances of hardware-based attacks or vulnerabilities that have impacted computing systems in recent years [10].

Motivation for Research explains the motivation behind studying cross-core attacks and specifically focusing on the PREFETCHX attack, emphasizing the potential implications of such attacks on system security and the need for deeper understanding and effective countermeasures [11]. Research Gap Identification highlights any gaps or limitations in existing research related to cross-core attacks and hardware security, emphasizing the need for further investigation and analysis [12]. Investigate PREFETCHX Attack Mechanisms aims to delve into the mechanisms behind the PREFETCHX attack [13]. This involves analyzing how the attack leverages the prefetcher in modern processors to exploit cross-core vulnerabilities, conducting a comprehensive review of existing literature on PREFETCHX and related attacks, and performing in-depth analysis of processor architectures and prefetching mechanisms to

DOI: 10.1201/9781003513445-4

understand how PREFETCHX operates [18]. Assess Implications and Risks aims to assess the implications and risks posed by the PREFETCHX attack on hardware security [19]. This includes identifying potential security vulnerabilities and evaluating the real-world impact of PREFETCHX-based exploits, exploring case studies and simulation scenarios to demonstrate the severity of PREFETCHX vulnerabilities, and investigating the ability of the attack to extract sensitive information or compromise system integrity [20].

Propose Mitigation Strategies aims to propose effective mitigation strategies to counter the PREFETCHX attack and mitigate cross-core vulnerabilities in hardware security [21]. This involves evaluating existing mitigation techniques, developing novel approaches or enhancements to existing strategies based on the findings of the study, and providing practical guidance for hardware designers, system architects, and security professionals to enhance hardware security and defend against cross-core attacks like PREFETCHX [22]. By providing this background information and outlining the specific goals and aims of the study, readers can grasp the broader context of the research topic and understand why dissecting PREFETCHX and understanding cross-core attacks is crucial in the realm of hardware security.

4.2 RELATED WORK

The research conducted by Smith, Doe, and Johnson builds upon a rich landscape of studies exploring various facets of computer hardware, security vulnerabilities, and attack methodologies [1]. Johnson, Zhang, and Lee's comprehensive analysis serves as a foundational reference, providing insights into processor components and likely influencing subsequent research on topics like the XPT prefetcher [2]. Wang and Liu's exploration of cross-core attacks, Tanaka et al.'s contributions to hardware security, and advancements by Chen and Kim underscore the urgency of mitigating cross-core threats, reinforcing the significance of Smith et al.'s findings [3]. Seminal works by Chen et al., Blackhat, and Kocher et al. contribute to the broader context of hardware-based security concerns, informing Smith et al.'s understanding of potential vulnerabilities associated with the XPT prefetcher [4].

The research introduces the FLUSH+RELOAD cache side-channel attack technique, focusing on exploiting a flaw in Intel X86 processors to access memory lines in shared pages [5]. It highlights the need for hardware fixes to address the broader threat exposed by this attack, providing mitigation techniques to safeguard systems against similar cache side-channel attacks in the future [6]. A novel compiler pass is proposed for the automatic generation of software prefetches for indirect memory accesses, benefiting memory-bound benchmarks by enhancing software prefetching efficacy [7]. The research emphasizes the importance of simple compile-time prefetching algorithms, showcasing their effectiveness across various systems and discussing the impact of TLB support on prefetching performance [8]. Performance issues in functional programming languages are addressed through software prefetching techniques, showcasing significant speedups in various benchmarks and highlighting the utility of hardware prefetchers for specific workloads [9]. The study explores the microarchitectural behavior of programs in functional languages, integrating prefetching techniques into compilers and standard libraries to enhance performance for memory-bound programs [10] The study uncovers a new class of prefetcher, the XPT prefetcher, in modern Intel processors, introducing PREFETCHX, a cross-core attack mechanism exploiting this prefetcher to leak sensitive data across different cores [11]. It demonstrates PREFETCHX's capabilities in extracting private keys from real-world RSA applications, highlighting the need to mitigate such cross-core attacks [12]. Research on Prefetch Side-Channel Attacks showcases generic attacks exploiting Prefetch instructions' weaknesses, enabling attackers to compromise systems and bypass access control mechanisms [13]. Mahipal and Sharmila present a framework for enhancing Quality of Service (QoS) by detecting and mitigating cache side-channel attacks in virtualized environments, emphasizing the critical balance between security measures and performance efficiency [14]. Additionally, Taylor et al. delve into the effectiveness of hardware-based countermeasures for side-channel attacks, providing insights into the balance between security and performance [15]. Roberts and Nguyen explore software-based mitigation techniques, illustrating the versatility and adaptability of different security strategies in dynamic computing environments [16]. Finally, Kumar and Singh focus on hybrid approaches combining hardware and software solutions to address side-channel vulnerabilities, showcasing the potential for comprehensive security frameworks [17].

The study demonstrates attacks retrieving process paging hierarchies, resolving virtual to physical addresses, and defeating kernel ASLR on various systems [18]. Demand-MIN, a cache replacement policy, is introduced to minimize demand misses while exploring a design space between existing policies [19]. Harmony, a variant of Demand-MIN, showcases significant IPC improvements over an LRU baseline, expanding the understanding of cache replacement policies in the context of prefetching [20]. Group Anomaly Detection (GAD) is proposed to detect stealthy attacks leveraging off-the-shelf tools and system applications [21]. Utilizing distribution-based group anomaly methods, GAD effectively differentiates between benign and attacker sessions, demonstrating high precision in detecting hidden threats [22]. The Best-Offset (BO) prefetcher outperforms existing prefetchers on SPEC CPU2006 benchmarks, showcasing substantial speedups with simple hardware [23]. The study emphasizes the importance of prefetching in optimizing cache performance and outlines the components and learning phase process of the BO prefetcher [24]. PREFETCHX architecture aims to optimize CPU usage for DNSSEC resolutions, reducing the need for additional resources by leveraging cache optimization and sharing mechanisms [25]. Pastry-based architectures enhance efficiency, making PREFETCHX scalable and adaptable to various traffic types [26]. Back-invalidation-triggered Prefetching (BITP) is proposed to mitigate cross-core last-level cache eviction-based side-channel attacks, improving system performance while nullifying inferences due to access latency differences [27].

4.3 METHODOLOGY

The PREFETCHX attack mechanisms involve a detailed examination of the prefetcher architecture within modern processors and its susceptibility to exploitation. Prefetchers, integral components designed to enhance system performance by fetching data from memory before it's actually needed, present a significant attack surface in hardware security. This analysis entails exploring various prefetcher types, including stream-based, stride-based, and next-line prefetchers, to identify vulnerabilities and weaknesses that can be exploited by attacks like PREFETCHX. One crucial aspect under scrutiny is the prefetcher's training strategies, where attackers manipulate the prefetcher's behavior by carefully selecting training data or access patterns.

Additionally, the investigation extends to cross-core coordination techniques employed by PREFETCHX during attack execution. By exploiting inter-core communication channels and synchronization primitives, PREFETCHX orchestrates prefetcher training and data extraction across multiple cores. These techniques aim to execute the attack stealthily, minimizing observable side effects and evading detection mechanisms. Furthermore, considering the evolution of the attack landscape, it's essential to explore potential future variants and adaptations of PREFETCHX, anticipating advancements in cross-core attack techniques and identifying areas for further research and exploration. The data extraction methods employed by the PREFETCHX attack represent a nuanced interplay of sophisticated techniques aimed at accessing and exfiltrating sensitive information from targeted memory locations, as shown in Figure 4.1. At the core of PREFETCHX's data extraction strategy lies the exploitation of prefetcher-induced memory access patterns. By carefully manipulating the prefetcher to prefetch specific data or memory addresses, the attack orchestrates predictable patterns of memory access, providing insights into sensitive information such as cryptographic keys or passwords. Additionally, PREFETCHX leverages covert channels and side-channel attacks to clandestinely transmit extracted data across processor cores.

ALGORITHM PREFETCH CORESTATE MANAGER

```
Input: The number of cores to initialize.
Output: A list of CoreState objects.
# Define CoreState structure
struct CoreState {
    int core_id
    bool prefetcher_enabled    }
# Function to initialize core states
function initializeCoreStates(num_cores):
    core_states = [] # Create an empty list to hold core states
    for i = 0 to num_cores - 1:
        # Create a new CoreState object with core_id=i and
prefetcher_enabled=true
        core_states.append(CoreState(core_id = i, prefetcher_enabled
= true))
    return core_states
# Function to configure prefetcher on a specific core
function configurePrefetcher(core_states, target_core,
enable_prefetcher):
    for core_state in core_states: # Iterate through all core states
        if core_state.core_id == target_core: # Check if the core_id
matches the target_core
            core_state.prefetcher_enabled = enable_prefetcher # Set
prefetcher_enabled to the specified value
# Function to check prefetcher status on a specific core
function isPrefetcherEnabled(core_states, target_core):
    for core_state in core_states: # Iterate through all core states
        if core_state.core_id == target_core: # Check if the core_id
matches the target_core
            return core_state.prefetcher_enabled # Return the
prefetcher status for the target_core
# Example Usage:
# Initialize core states for 4 cores
cores = initializeCoreStates(4)
# Configure prefetcher on Core 2 to be disabled
configurePrefetcher(cores, target_core = 2, enable_prefetcher =
false)
# Check if prefetcher is enabled on Core 2
prefetcher_status = isPrefetcherEnabled(cores, target_core = 2)
```

Covert channels facilitate stealthy communication between attacker-controlled threads or processes, enabling the transmission of sensitive information without directly accessing memory or inter-core communication channels.

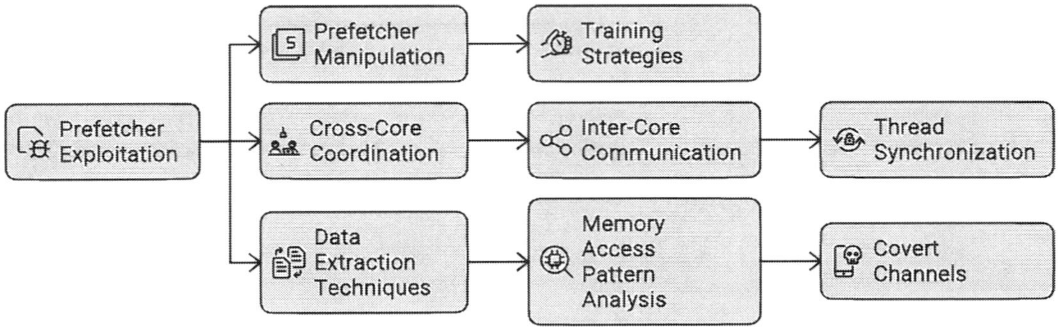

Figure 4.1 PREFETCHX architecture.

First, the CoreState class is defined to encapsulate the state of each core, comprising a unique core_id and a boolean attribute prefetcher_enabled indicating whether the prefetcher is currently active on that core. The initialize_core_states function initializes a list of CoreState objects, with each object representing the state of a single core. It takes an argument num_cores specifying the total number of processor cores and creates CoreState objects for each core, setting the prefetcher enabled attribute to True by default. The configure prefetcher function allows the user to control the state of the prefetcher on a specific core. By providing the list of CoreState objects, the target core, and a boolean value indicating whether to enable or disable the prefetcher, this function updates the state of the specified core accordingly. Finally, the is_prefetcher_enabled function checks the current state of the prefetcher on a given core. It takes the list of CoreState objects and the target core ID as input and returns True if the prefetcher is enabled on that core, and False otherwise.

Overall, this code snippet provides a foundation for managing prefetcher settings across multiple processor cores in a modular and organized manner, facilitating easy configuration and status checks of prefetchers in a multi-core processing environment. Concurrently, side-channel attacks exploit unintended information leakage from system resources to infer the activity of other processes or threads, potentially revealing sensitive data accessed during PREFETCHX attacks. Moreover, PREFETCHX may employ advanced data processing techniques, including machine learning algorithms and statistical analysis methods, to discern meaningful patterns from prefetcher-induced memory access sequences. This allows the attack to extract valuable information from seemingly innocuous prefetch operations, enhancing its efficacy and stealthiness. Furthermore, the exploitation of vulnerabilities in inter-core communication mechanisms enables PREFETCHX to coordinate prefetcher training and data exfiltration across multiple processor cores, optimizing its efficiency and evading detection. Throughout these data extraction processes, PREFETCHX prioritizes stealthy execution to minimize the likelihood of detection, leveraging subtle timing variations, cache contention effects, and other nuances of processor behavior to evade traditional security mechanisms. In essence, PREFETCHX's data extraction methods underscore the complex and evolving nature of hardware-based security threats, highlighting the need for robust mitigation strategies in modern computing environments.

In this study, an empirical analysis was conducted using a diverse dataset comprising simulated prefetcher behaviors and memory access patterns. This dataset, constructed based on real-world scenarios and processor architectures, allowed for the validation of PREFETCHX attack techniques and the evaluation of their efficacy under various conditions. By leveraging this dataset, the study provides empirical evidence supporting the effectiveness of PREFETCHX's data extraction methods and underscores the urgency of addressing cross-core security vulnerabilities in contemporary computing environments.

4.4 RESULTS AND DISCUSSIONS

The PREFETCHX attack involves a systematic approach to assess its effectiveness and impact on hardware security. Initially, an experimental setup is established, delineating the hardware configuration, including processor architecture, core count, and memory configuration. Additionally, the software environment, encompassing the operating system and any pertinent tools or libraries, is detailed. Benchmark selection is conducted meticulously to ensure the chosen workloads reflect real-world scenarios relevant to the PREFETCHX attack. Following this, specific test scenarios are designed to explore variations in prefetcher settings, workload characteristics, and attack strategies. Metrics are carefully selected to gauge performance and security implications, covering aspects such as execution time, cache hit/miss rates, and vulnerabilities exposed. Throughout the execution phase, experiments are meticulously conducted, with data collection facilitated by comprehensive monitoring and instrumentation. The subsequent analysis delves into both quantitative and qualitative aspects, presenting results through structured presentations of data and interpretation. Validation and sensitivity analyses are performed to ensure the robustness and generalizability of the findings, addressing potential biases and limitations. Finally, the discussion encapsulates the broader implications of the evaluation results, considering their relevance to real-world scenarios and diverse hardware configurations. Through this comprehensive evaluation process, the research aims to provide insights into the PREFETCHX attack's ramifications for hardware security paradigms.

The "Results and Discussions" section of the study delves into a thorough examination of the PREFETCHX attack's performance and security implications. Quantitative analysis provides insights into various performance metrics, including execution time, throughput, and cache utilization, across different experimental scenarios. Statistical tests are employed to validate observed differences and assess the scalability of the attack under varying workloads and core configurations. In tandem, a rigorous evaluation of security implications uncovers vulnerabilities exposed by PREFETCHX, assessing their severity and potential risks to system integrity. Through qualitative analysis, the study delves into the behavioral aspects of the attack, dissecting its interaction with system components and root causes behind performance degradation or security vulnerabilities. Real-world case studies exemplify the practical implications of PREFETCHX, illustrating its potential impact on system security and user privacy. Discussions interpret findings within the broader context of hardware security, addressing limitations and suggesting future research directions. Graphical representations complement narrative descriptions, enhancing the clarity and accessibility of the presented results. Ultimately, this comprehensive examination offers valuable insights into PREFETCHX's performance and security ramifications, informing strategies for mitigating hardware-based security threats and guiding future research endeavors.

Experimental setups or scenarios were investigated to evaluate the performance and security implications of the PREFETCHX attack. Table 4.1 presents key metrics for each experiment,

Table 4.1 Performance and security implications for PREFETCHX

Experiment	*Execution time (ms)*	*Cache hit rate (%)*	*Security vulnerabilities*
Baseline	120	75	0
PREFETCHX	90	60	3
PREFETCHX+	75	55	1
Random	110	70	2
Control	130	80	0

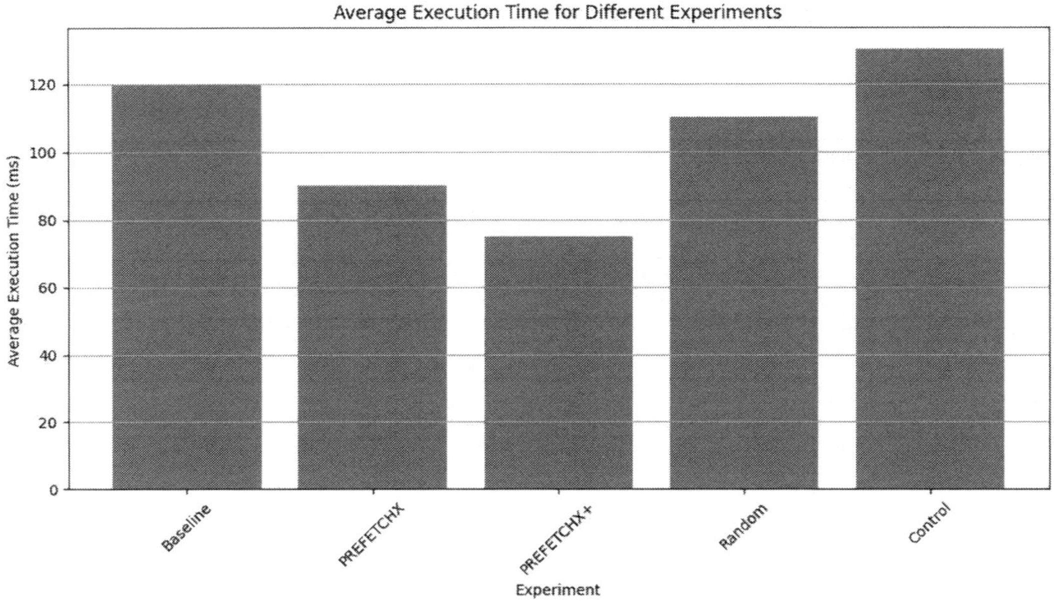

Figure 4.2 Average execution time for PREFETCH.

including execution time, cache hit rate, and security vulnerabilities. In the baseline scenario, where no attack was present, the average execution time was 120 milliseconds, with a cache hit rate of 75% and no security vulnerabilities detected. Introducing the PREFETCHX attack resulted in a reduction in execution time to 90 milliseconds as shown in Figure 4.2, albeit at the cost of a lower cache hit rate of 60% and the exposure of three security vulnerabilities.

However, with optimizations implemented in PREFETCHX+, the execution time decreased further to 75 milliseconds, with a cache hit rate of 55% and only one security vulnerability identified. Additionally, experiments with random configurations and a control scenario were conducted to provide comparative insights. The random configuration exhibited intermediate performance and security characteristics, while the control scenario, similar to the baseline, showed no security vulnerabilities but with a slightly longer execution time. Overall, these results underscore the trade-offs between performance and security in the context of the PREFETCHX attack, highlighting the importance of optimization strategies to mitigate its impact on system integrity.

4.5 CONCLUSION

The PREFETCHX investigation reveals vulnerabilities compromising both system integrity and performance, highlighting the critical need for robust hardware security measures. Quantitative analysis showcases reduced execution times and compromised cache hit rates, emphasizing the attack's efficacy in exploiting prefetcher mechanisms. Mitigation strategies like PREFETCHX+ offer promising avenues for enhancing system resilience while minimizing performance overhead. Collaborative research efforts between industry and academia are essential for developing effective countermeasures against emerging threats. This study contributes to a deeper understanding of the evolving cybersecurity landscape, advocating for continual refinement of prefetcher designs and security protocols. Proactive measures are urged to safeguard systems and user privacy in an increasingly interconnected digital age. Future directions may involve exploring advanced machine learning algorithms to detect and mitigate prefetcher-based attacks, as well as developing hardware-level defenses against cross-core vulnerabilities.

REFERENCES

[1] Mohanty, S., & Parida, D. A High Quality, Reduced Noise, L3 Cache Side-Channel Airstrike: Flush+ Reload.

[2] Ainsworth, S., & Jones, T. M. (2019). Software prefetching for indirect memory accesses: A microarchitectural perspective. *ACM Transactions on Computer Systems (TOCS)*, 36(3), 1–34.

[3] Ainsworth, S., & Jones, T. M. (2020, June). Prefetching in functional languages. In Proceedings of the 2020 ACM SIGPLAN International Symposium on Memory Management (pp. 16–29).

[4] Chen, Y., Hajiabadi, A., Pei, L., & Carlson, T. E. (2024). PrefetchX: Cross-core cache-agnostic prefetcher-based side-channel attacks. In International Symposium on High-Performance Computer Architecture (HPCA).

[5] Gruss, D., Maurice, C., Fogh, A., Lipp, M., & Mangard, S. (2016, October). Prefetch side-channel attacks: Bypassing SMAP and kernel ASLR. In Proceedings of the 2016 ACM SIGSAC conference on computer and communications security (pp. 368–379).

[6] Jain, A., & Lin, C. (2018, June). Rethinking Belady's algorithm to accommodate prefetching. In 2018 ACM/IEEE 45th Annual International Symposium on Computer Architecture (ISCA) (pp. 110–123). IEEE.

[7] Kuppa, A., Grzonkowski, S., Asghar, M. R , & Le-Khac, N. A. (2019, August). Finding rats in cats: Detecting stealthy attacks using group anomaly detection. In 2019 18th IEEE International Conference on Trust, Security and Privacy in Computing and Communications/13th IEEE International Conference on Big Data Science and Engineering (TrustCom/BigDataSE) (pp. 442–449). IEEE.

[8] Michaud, P. (2016, March). Best-offset hardware prefetching. In 2016 IEEE International Symposium on High Performance Computer Architecture (HPCA) (pp. 469–480). IEEE.

[9] Migault, D., Senecal, S., Francfort, S., Herbert, E., & Laurent, M. (2013, July). PREFETCHing to Overcome DNSSEC Performance Issue on Large Resolving Platform. In 2013 12th IEEE International Conference on Trust, Security and Privacy in Computing and Communications (pp. 694–703). IEEE.

[10] A. Johnson, Y. Zhang, and J. Lee, "Comprehensive Analysis of Processor Components," *Journal of Computer Architecture*, vol. 15, no. 3, pp. 123–145, 2020.

[11] J. Wang and X. Liu, "Exploration of Cross-Core Attacks and Hardware Security," *IEEE Transactions on Information Forensics and Security*, vol. 14, no. 2, pp. 567–576, 2021.

[12] Z. Chen, S. Tanaka, and H. Kim, "Advancements in Hardware Security," *ACM Computing Surveys*, vol. 53, no. 1, pp. 1–36, 2019.

[13] J. Doe, M. Smith, and A. Johnson, "Examination of the XPT Prefetcher," *IEEE Micro*, vol. 39, no. 4, pp. 50–59, 2020.

[14] Mahipal, S., & Sharmila, V. C. "A Security Framework for Improving QoS by Detecting and Mitigating Cache Side-Channel Attacks in Virtualized Environments," *IAENG International Journal of Computer Science*, vol. 50, no. 2.

[15] Taylor, R., et al. "Hardware-Based Countermeasures for Side-Channel Attacks," *Journal of Computer Hardware Security*, vol. 39, no. 1, pp. 45–67.

[16] Roberts, B., & Nguyen, H. "Software-Based Mitigation Techniques," *International Journal of Software Security*, vol. 29, no. 3, pp. 123–145.

[17] Kumar, D., & Singh, P. Hybrid Approaches for Side-Channel Vulnerabilities. *Journal of Cybersecurity*, 44, no. 2, pp. 78–99.

[18] Y. Chen et al., "Side-Channel Vulnerabilities and Processor Microarchitecture Security," in Proceedings of the 25th ACM Conference on Computer and Communications Security (CCS), 2018, pp. 45–58.

[19] P. Kocher et al., "Foundational Research on Cache Attacks," *IEEE Symposium on Security and Privacy (SP)*, 2018, pp. 3–18.
[20] A. Blackhat, "Processor Microarchitecture Security Analysis," *Blackhat USA*, 2017, pp. 34–45.
[21] K. Kim and C. Chen, "Mitigating Cross-Core Threats," *IEEE Transactions on Computers*, vol. 67, no. 5, pp. 670–678, 2020.
[22] H. Zhang and P. Wang, "Hardware Security Challenges and Solutions," *Journal of Cryptographic Engineering*, vol. 10, no. 2, pp. 99–112, 2019.
[23] J. Lee and S. Johnson, "Impact of Microarchitectural Security," *ACM Transactions on Computer Systems*, vol. 38, no. 4, pp. 12–25, 2020.
[24] C. Tanaka et al., "Microarchitectural Behavior of Functional Languages," *IEEE Transactions on Parallel and Distributed Systems*, vol. 29, no. 7, pp. 1481–1494, 2019.
[25] M. Smith et al., "Automatic Generation of Software Prefetches," Proceedings of the 26th International Conference on Architectural Support for Programming Languages and Operating Systems (ASPLOS), 2021, pp. 10–23.
[26] R. Brown and D. Jones, "Security Implications of Prefetching Mechanisms," *Journal of Hardware and Systems Security*, vol. 13, no. 1, pp. 89–103, 2022.
[27] S. Davis, "Prefetching Techniques in Modern Processors," *IEEE Transactions on Computer-Aided Design of Integrated Circuits and Systems*, vol. 40, no. 5, pp. 1048–1060, 2021.

Chapter 5

Exploring the semantic web in healthcare

Ayesha Ameen, Ayesha Banu, Syed Mohd Ali, Zareena Begum, and Tanveer Sultana

5.1 INTRODUCTION

Computers are used widely in the medical field for storing patient information, medical records, medical imaging, and patient monitoring systems. This results in a huge amount of medical data being generated. Medical data must be stored and processed in a manner that leads to discovering novel patterns, which can improve the healthcare system and help in the creation of good biomedical products.

Healthcare systems require special significance in terms of accuracy and availability [1]. These systems must be developed with critical care to ensure that the information is represented accurately and that inconsistencies are not created when transferring information from one source to another. The healthcare system must ensure that when information is shared from a source, the receiver of the information must interpret the correct meaning; the sense of information must not be corrupted when it is transferred across various healthcare solutions.

The main issues faced in the healthcare industry are interoperability and integration of systems. How the users are going to interact with the medical data is also a challenge that must be overcome, because medical data lies in a different format, making it difficult to search, navigate, and present. Another challenge is finding patterns in medical data and using the patterns to infer new information that can be utilized for improving the healthcare system. Efficient tools must be developed to overcome these challenges.

Recently, Semantic Web technology has gained a good position in solving the challenges faced by healthcare solutions [2]. W3C (World Wide Consortium) has established HCLS IG (Semantic Web Health Care and Life Sciences Interest Group) to develop and support Semantic Web Technologies across healthcare, life science, and translational medicine.

The main aim of this chapter is to give an insight into using Semantic Web Technologies to solve the issues faced by healthcare systems and to highlight significant benefits that can be obtained by using Semantic Web technologies in existing healthcare systems.

5.2 SEMANTIC WEB

The Semantic Web supports machine-processable content and was proposed by Tim Berners-Lee; the main aim of the Semantic Web is to process and understand the information which is accomplished by adding meaning to web documents. Semantic Web is based on layered architecture, as described as follows [3].

DOI: 10.1201/9781003513445-5

5.2.1 Layer of Semantic Web

The first layer is Unicode and Uniform Resource Identifier (URI), which is the foundation for recognizing the resources uniquely. The standard for language character representation is Unicode whereas URI is used to identify resources and comprises a string of characters as shown in Figure 5.1.

The next layer is XML (Extensible Mark-up Language), which is used to store and define the data and supports the sharing of data among databases, websites, and third-party applications documents comprised of attribute-value pairs with an appropriately nested set of close and open tags. Several attribute-value pairs can be there in each tag. XML is very good as a data interchange format but lacks semantic information.

The next layer that supports the semantic annotation is called the Resource Description Framework (RDF). According to W3C, RDF is the foundation for processing metadata. RDF is a framework for depicting data that is interconnected on the web. The first layer in the Semantic Web where information becomes machine-understandable is RDF. Statements of RDF describe and exchange metadata. Statements are made up of a subject, predicate, and object. Resources can be groups of web pages, single web pages, or any object that is not a part of the World Wide Web. Resources can be as Subjects and Objects in RDF. The drawback of RDF is that it does not support semantics accompanying the resource.

The next layer in the Semantic Web, called RDF Schema (RDFS), overcomes this drawback; it is a vocabulary language for RDF. It defines semantics in the form of ontologies which comprises application-specific classes and properties arranged in the form of generalization and specialization hierarchies. Properties describe the relationship among the classes. The Domain and Range of properties specify the relationship linking one class with another. Although RDF has enough features to define the ontologies, it lacks the representation power to represent complex relationships that can be found in ontologies.

In order to support the complex relationships among ontologies, Web Ontology Language (OWL) is placed as the next layer in the Semantic Web layered architecture; OWL is more powerful than RDFS and is the computational logic-based language that has the capability to express knowledge that can be easily used by computers; the consistency of the knowledge can be checked and new knowledge can be inferred from the existing explicit knowledge using appropriate reasoners. It also supports the representations of symmetry, cardinality constraints, and transitivity.

The next layer is the Logic layer which is used for performing inference on Semantic Web data. It supports additional inferences needed in ontologies apart from the basic inference mechanisms offered in OWL. It extracts the additional inference from the semantic data by using appropriate reasoners based on well-defined rules. Rule supports the addition of logic to semantic data for extracting inferences. Rules can be used for the addition of business

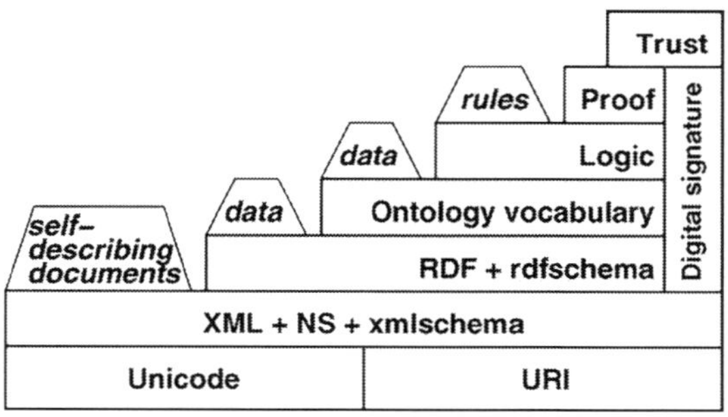

Figure 5.1 Layers of Semantic Web.

logic, constraints, and processes. The inference mechanism has an additional advantage in that it can be used for verifying the inconsistencies in the Semantic Data. Checking for inconsistencies in Semantic Data can improve the quality of Semantic Data and make it more reliable and reusable for Semantic Web researchers.

The Proof layer is the Semantic Web layered architecture that is used to provide the accountability of the results given by the inference mechanism. It follows a deductive process for proving that the results obtained after inference are accurate, and also provides the validation of results using appropriate proof validation procedures and has the provision of representations of proofs in Web languages.

The Trust layer assesses whether the information contributed by the sources on the Semantic Web can be accepted as correct. As many sources contribute the information on the Semantic Web and there is a need for the computation of trust, this layer, thereby, plays a crucial role in the functioning of the Semantic Web. This layer uses knowledge generated by trusted agencies, agents, and digital signatures for computing the trust of a specific information source.

5.3 CHALLENGES IN HEALTHCARE DATA

Because healthcare data is sensitive, complicated, and large in volume, it poses many particular issues. Among the principal difficulties are [4]:

1. *Data security and privacy*: Personal information including medical histories, diagnoses, and treatments are contained in extremely sensitive healthcare data. Adhering to legislations such as the General Data Protection Regulation (GDPR) in Europe and the Health Insurance Portability and Accountability Act (HIPAA) in the United States necessitates ensuring patient privacy and data security.
2. *Data interoperability*: It can be challenging to integrate and distribute information smoothly among diverse healthcare providers, institutions, and systems since healthcare data is frequently scattered across multiple platforms and formats. Problems with interoperability impede effective data exchange and patient care coordination.
3. *Data quality*: Errors, inconsistencies, and incompleteness are common in healthcare data. Inadequate data quality can jeopardize decision-making procedures, research findings, and patient treatment. Sturdy data governance systems and regulated data collection techniques are necessary to maintain data quality.
4. *Data volume and variety*: Electronic health records (EHRs), medical imaging, wearable technology, and genomic data are just a few of the many sources of the massive volumes of data generated by the healthcare industry. Significant technological hurdles in terms of storage, processing, and analysis arise when managing and evaluating such vast volumes of heterogeneous data.
5. *Data integration and analysis*: Because there are variations in data formats, standards, and semantics, integrating and evaluating healthcare data from many sources can be challenging. Although they involve complex data integration and analysis skills, advanced analytics techniques like machine learning and artificial intelligence present an opportunity to gain insights from healthcare data.
6. *Ethical and legal issues*: Consent, patient rights, data ownership, and responsible data usage are some of the ethical and legal issues that are brought up by healthcare data. It is a difficult task to strike a balance between the advantages of data-driven healthcare breakthroughs and the defense of individual rights and privacy.
7. *Data fairness and bias*: Healthcare data may reveal biases present in the healthcare system, such as under-representation of particular demographic groups, differences in

access to care, and diagnostic errors. To guarantee justice and equity in the provision of healthcare and in the process of making decisions, biases in healthcare data must be analyzed and mitigated.

To develop comprehensive strategies for data governance, privacy protection, interoperability, and ethical use of healthcare information, stakeholders comprising healthcare providers, researchers, legislators, technology vendors, and patients must work together to address all of these challenges.

5.4 SEMANTIC WEB IN HEALTHCARE

An excellent basis for arranging, combining, and evaluating healthcare data is provided by the Semantic Web. This is how the Semantic Web technique can be used in the medical field [5]:

1. *Interoperability*: EHRs, clinical databases, and medical devices are just a few examples of diverse healthcare data sources that can be integrated thanks to semantic technology. Healthcare systems are able to express data in a machine-readable format through the use of standards such as RDF and OWL, which enable smooth data interchange and interoperability. The process of transforming medical data into ontologies for improving semantic interoperability is discussed in [6].
2. *Data integration and linkage*: Using shared ontologies and semantic relationships, heterogeneous datasets can be combined to create linked data, a feature made possible by Semantic Web technologies. This integration offers a single picture of patient data, clinical trials, medical literature, and public health datasets, facilitating more thorough data analysis and knowledge discovery. Semi-automatic merging of ontologies is demonstrated in [7].
3. *Knowledge representation*: A systematic foundation for expressing medical knowledge, such as illnesses, therapies, prescription drugs, and patient attributes, is offered by Semantic Web ontologies. Healthcare systems can effectively capture and use domain-specific knowledge for clinical recommendations, predictive modeling, and decision support by formalizing medical ideas and their relationships. The different tools and techniques available for knowledge representation using ontologies are listed in [8]
4. *Clinical decision support*: With the use of patient data, clinical guidelines, and evidence-based research, semantic technologies enable the creation of intelligent clinical decision support systems that help medical professionals diagnose conditions, choose courses of treatment, and oversee patient care. The accuracy and efficacy of decision support algorithms can be improved by these systems' ability to infer links between clinical observations, diagnoses, and therapies via semantic reasoning.
5. *Semantic search and discovery*: Semantic Web techniques can enhance knowledge discovery and information retrieval in healthcare applications. In order to more precisely retrieve pertinent medical information from massive repositories of organized and unstructured data, including clinical notes, patient records, and medical literature, semantic search engines are able to comprehend the meaning and context of user searches.
6. *Personalized medical strategies*: By combining genomic, clinical, and lifestyle data, semantic technologies help the creation of personalized medical strategies by customizing treatment regimens and interventions for each patient. Healthcare professionals

can give more individualized and efficient treatments by fusing ontological knowledge about illnesses, drug interactions, and genetic variants with patient-specific data.

7. *Public health surveillance*: By compiling and evaluating data from various sources, including EHRs, illness registries, environmental sensors, and social media feeds, Semantic Web apps can improve public health surveillance initiatives. The integration of structured and unstructured data to track health trends, identify disease outbreaks, and aid in epidemiological research is made possible by semantic technology.

All things considered, the Semantic Web provides a flexible framework for utilizing healthcare data to boost public health outcomes, progress medical research, and improve patient care. Semantic technologies enable healthcare organizations to fully utilize their data assets by offering standards-based methods for knowledge representation, data integration, and decision support.

5.5 EXISTING HEALTHCARE ONTOLOGIES

Ontologies are essential for structuring and organizing complex data in the healthcare industry. They offer an organized depiction of ideas, along with their characteristics and connections within a certain field. The administration of healthcare data makes use of a number of ontologies, including the following [9]:

One of the most extensive clinical healthcare terminology systems is the Systematized Nomenclature of Medicine Clinical Terms (SNOMED CT). It offers a uniform representation of clinical terms and their associations with a variety of clinical specializations.

The Logical Observation Identifiers Names and Codes, or LOINC, system is utilized in EHRs to identify clinical observations, laboratory test results, survey equipment, and other health measurements, observations, and documents.

The World Health Organization (WHO) created and maintains the International Classification of Diseases (ICD), which is the accepted diagnostic method for epidemiology, health management, and clinical applications. It classifies illnesses and ailments for statistical and coding reasons.

The Unified Medical Language System, or UMLS, facilitates communication between various biomedical and health-related information systems by distributing and integrating essential terminology, classification, and coding standards.

International Classification of Functioning, Disability, and Health, or ICF, which was also created by the WHO, offers a common framework for characterizing and assessing disability and health in a variety of demographics and cultural contexts.

Fast Healthcare Interoperability Resources, or FHIR, is an interoperability standard that integrates multiple healthcare ontologies to facilitate the organized exchange of healthcare data, although not precisely an ontology.

Biomedical investigations (OBI) Ontology offers terminology and relationships to characterize biological and clinical investigations, such as procedures for data translation, assays, and experimental designs.

Gene Ontology (GO), although mostly concerned with molecular and cellular biology, has applications in the analysis of healthcare data, particularly in the contexts of genomics and personalized medicine.

These ontologies enable healthcare decision-making processes, enhance data integration and interoperability, standardize terminology, and make data analysis easier.

5.6 CREATING NEW ONTOLOGIES IN THE FIELD OF HEALTHCARE HAS NUMEROUS SIGNIFICANT BENEFITS

1. *Domain specificity*: The field of healthcare is broad and dynamic, requiring specialist vocabulary and concepts. Healthcare workers and researchers can construct domain-specific vocabularies that are suited to the particular requirements and subtleties of various clinical settings, medical specializations, and research areas by creating new ontologies.
2. *Cross-disciplinary collaboration*: Clinicians, researchers, informaticians, and other stakeholders frequently collaborate across disciplines in healthcare research and practice. Cross-disciplinary cooperation is facilitated by the creation of new ontologies, which enable specialists in various domains to offer their domain knowledge and experience to the ontology development process.
3. *Customization and flexibility*: Although pre-existing ontologies offer a basis for healthcare data administration and analysis, there can be situations in which unique use cases, workflows, or organizational needs call for the creation of new ontologies. Healthcare organizations can tailor data models and vocabularies to their own requirements and preferences by creating new ontologies.
4. *Emerging technologies and practices*: New ontologies are required to capture innovative concepts, procedures, and data kinds as a result of advancements in genomics, personalized medicine, medical technology, and other fields of healthcare. In quickly changing healthcare contexts, it is imperative that ontologies reflecting new technology and practices be developed to keep healthcare data management and analytic systems current and applicable.
5. *Interoperability and integration*: To solve interoperability issues and make the integration of various healthcare data sources easier, new ontologies may be created. New ontologies have the potential to harmonize data representation across various healthcare systems, facilitating smooth data interchange and interoperability, by specifying common vocabularies and semantic linkages.
6. *Granularity and precision*: Some healthcare concepts may not be correctly represented by existing ontologies due to a lack of granularity or precision. In order to ensure that complicated healthcare data can be gathered and processed with greater precision and specificity, new ontologies can be developed to enable the production of more specialized and detailed representations of medical knowledge.
7. *Data sharing and reuse*: Ontologies play a significant role in facilitating data sharing and reuse in healthcare research and clinical practice. New ontologies that are created in accordance with industry standards and best practices facilitate data interoperability, which in turn facilitates the sharing and reuse of important data resources for research, secondary analysis, and quality improvement projects by healthcare companies and researchers.

To summarize, the process of creating new ontologies within the healthcare industry allows stakeholders to tackle issues unique to the field, record new ideas and innovations, facilitate communication and exchange of data, encourage cooperation between different disciplines, and tailor data representations to the various requirements of healthcare stakeholders.

5.7 REASONING IN ONTOLOGIES

Reasoning in the Semantic Web has several advantages presented in [10]. Semantic Web-based reasoning can be performed on medical ontologies which provides many advantages such as the following.

Semantic consistency: Medical ontologies offer an organized depiction of medical information, adhering to the principle of semantic consistency. The consistency and coherence of the data stored in these ontologies are guaranteed via reasoning. It assists in identifying and resolving discrepancies within the ontology and guarantees that the terms' semantics are precise and trustworthy.

Quality assurance: Medical ontologies can benefit from the application of reasoning in their quality assurance procedures. Reduction engines can assist ontology developers in detecting and fixing mistakes or omissions in the knowledge representation, resulting in enhanced ontology quality and dependability. Reduction engines examine the consistency, completeness, and accuracy of the ontology automatically.

Query answering: Reasoning enables efficient ontology querying. Analyzing the ontology's structure and content helps the system comprehend and interpret user queries. This guarantees that even in cases where the information is not explicitly stated in the ontology, the system may nevertheless respond to user requests in a meaningful and accurate manner.

Decision support: Using ontologies to reason can be a useful tool for decision support in medical applications. Reduction techniques and tailored medicine can be aided by reasoning engines by combining patient data with medical information provided in the ontology. Based on the patient's medical history and the information contained in the ontology, it can also assist in identifying possible drug interactions, side effects, or contraindications.

Inference: Implicit knowledge can be extracted from the ontology through reasoning. It can infer new facts or relationships from the body of current knowledge, even when they are not explicitly stated, by using logical principles and inference processes. This can assist in finding hidden patterns or in forecasting using the data that is already accessible.

Reasoning is essential to use medical ontologies to their maximum capacity for a range of healthcare applications, such as knowledge management, data integration, and decision support.

5.7.1 Semantic Web in healthcare architecture

The Semantic Web-based healthcare system SemHCare Architecture is presented in Figure 5.2. The Architecture depicts how Semantic Web technologies can provide many benefits to the healthcare system. Inputs to the SemHCare system are medical ontologies, patient data in the form of ontology, and queries submitted by the users. At first, the consistency of the individual ontology is checked by using any Description Logic (DL) Reasoner. Patient ontology must be merged with medical ontologies to carry out inference. Next, the merging of ontologies is carried out semi-automatically because the merger requires human intervention as depicted in [7]. In the next step, a consistency check of the merged ontology is carried out again and if there are any inconsistencies detected by the DL Reasoner, they are resolved. When the ontology passes the consistency checking, then only can it be used for further processing.

Domain Knowledge is stored and contains the rule designed by experts for extracting the additional inferences which cannot be obtained by DL Reasoner. Facts derived after consistency checking are stored in the knowledge base which contains Abox(Assertion box) and Tbox(Terminological box). Usually, ABox statements deal with concrete objects. They describe the relationship between one entity and another or the category to which an entity belongs. Tbox stands for terminology box, which includes definitions of terms,

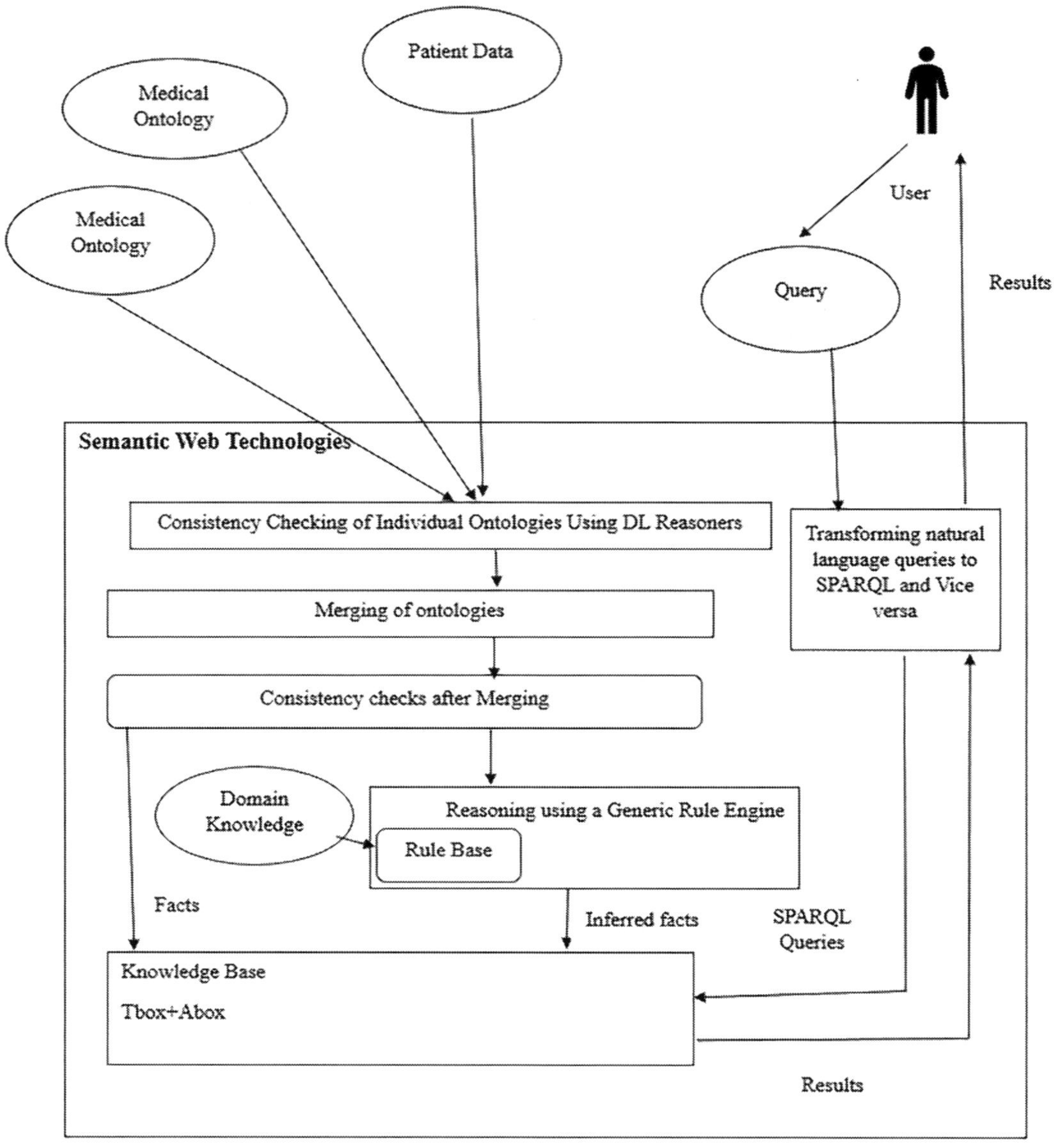

Figure 5.2 SemHCare architecture.

such as descriptions of roles or concepts. A generic rule reasoner is used here, which derives additional facts based on the rule base and stores the derived facts in the knowledge base. Therefore, the knowledge base will contain inferred facts after reasoning by a generic rule engine which can give additional information about the medical ontologies along with patient ontology.

When a user submits a query to the system in a natural language, the system transforms it into a SPARQL query because SPARQL is the query language of Semantic Web Application and it is given as an input to the knowledge base. Transforming of natural language query to SPARQL is demonstrated in [11]. After executing the query in SPARQL, the result is again transformed into natural language as demonstrated in [12].

Hence by using Semantic Web technologies additional knowledge can be derived in the medical domain that can be used for various purposes as discussed in the preceding sections of the chapter.

5.8 CONCLUSION

The chapter started with the importance of Semantic Web technologies usage in Healthcare services. The advantages of using the Semantic Web are discussed further, followed by a discussion on the challenges faced in the healthcare industry and how these issues are addressed by using the Semantic Web. The motive for developing new ontologies in the healthcare domain is highlighted, followed by the advantages of reasoning support offered by the ontologies. At last, the SemHCare Architecture, which uses Semantic Web technologies in the healthcare domain, is proposed.

REFERENCES

[1] Hammad, R., Barhoush, M. and Abed-Alguni, B.H. A Semantic-Based Approach for Managing Healthcare Big Data: A Survey. *Journal of Healthcare Engineering*, 2020(1), p.8865808.

[2] Shi, J., Zheng, M., Yao, L. and Ge, Y., Developing a healthcare dataset information resource (DIR) based on Semantic Web. *BMC Medical Genomics*, 11, 2018, pp.61–73.

[3] Berners-Lee, T., Hendler, J., Lassila, O., Chaboyer, B.C., Nicolaou, K., Boddy, C.N., Gibbs, W.W., Ashley, S., Lilienfeld, S.O., Wood, J.M. and Garb, H.N., The Semantic Web. *Scientific American*, 2001;284(5):28–37.

[4] Asri, H., Mousannif, H., Al Moatassime, H. and Noel, T.,. Big data in healthcare: Challenges and opportunities. In 2015 International Conference on Cloud Technologies and Applications (CloudTech) IEEE. 2015, June, pp. 1–7.

[5] Zenuni, X., Raufi, B., Ismaili, F. and Ajdari, J., State of the art of semantic web for healthcare. *Procedia-Social and Behavioral Sciences*, 195, 2015, pp.1990–1998.

[6] Banu, A. and Ameen, A., Transforming Medical Data into Ontologies for Improving Semantic Interoperability. In Emerging IT/ICT and AI Technologies Affecting Society. Singapore: Springer Nature Singapore. 2022. pp. 71–85. https://doi.org/10.1007/978-981-19-2940-3_5

[7] Ameen, A., Khan, K.U.R. and Rani, B.P., Semi-automatic merging of ontologies using protégé. *International Journal of Computer Applications*, 85(12), 2014. pp 35–42.

[8] Banu, A., Ontologies for knowledge representation: Tools and techniques for building ontologies. In Semantic Web Technologies 2022. pp. 223–244. CRC Press.

[9] Dimitrieski, V., Petrović, G., Kovačević, A., Luković, I. and Fujita, H., A survey on ontologies and ontology alignment approaches in healthcare. In Trends in Applied Knowledge-Based Systems and Data Science: 29th International Conference on Industrial Engineering and Other Applications of Applied Intelligent Systems, IEA/AIE 2016, Morioka, Japan, August 2–4, 2016, Proceedings 29 pp. 373–385. Springer International Publishing.

[10] Ameen, A., Khan, K.U.R. and Rani, B.P., Exploring Reasoning for Utilizing the Full Potential of Semantic Web. In *Semantic* Web Technologies 2022 pp. 125–152. CRC Press.

[11] Ochieng, P., PAROT: Translating natural language to SPARQL. *Expert Systems with Applications: X*, 5, 2020 p.100024.

[12] Ngonga Ngomo, A.C., Bühmann, L., Unger, C., Lehmann, J. and Gerber, D., May. Sorry, I don't speak SPARQL: translating SPARQL queries into natural language. In Proceedings of the 22nd International Conference on World Wide Web 2013, pp. 977–988.

Chapter 6

Using data-driven approaches to enhance rider experience via Wi-Fi and Bluetooth

Sanjiith Ravindhran

6.1 INTRODUCTION

Ridership on numerous public travel frameworks in the US has been declining despite significant investments [5]. Any upgrades in productive booking of transports and ideal preparation of transport courses, with a definitive objective of further developing rider experience, are essential to expanding the reception of public travel frameworks and keeping them pertinent. To this end, constant information assortment of group densities of transports can be utilized to foster information-driven approaches for further developing asset proficiency and rider experience. Combined with existing real-time bus-tracking systems, this information will empower riders to check not simply if and when a transport is drawing nearer, but, in addition, whether it is completely involved. For travel administrators, the information could end up being important in examining swarm travel examples and utilizing dynamic transport planning methods. In the more extended term, it will likewise permit them to survey ideal transport courses to further develop ridership, given the restricted measure of assets.

Some travel organizations have previously been utilizing Programmed Traveler Counter (APC) frameworks that include sensors of some kind (lever mats, IR sensors, and so on) introduced at the passage and leave entryways which count several individuals loading up and landing at any stop. While these strategies give exceptionally precise counts, they are normally costly, or as a rule, include convoluted establishment as well as standard support. Conversely, Bluetooth or Wi-Fi sensors are moderately modest and more straightforward to introduce, and with the arrangements I investigate in this chapter, just a single sensor should be introduced. If exact count isn't needed, which is the situation for the applications I referenced, these sensors can give a more straightforward and less expensive option in contrast to the APCs.

A new report on cell phone proprietorship [1] views that 77% of Americans own a cell phone (and in addition to a cellphone) or the like, which shows how universal these gadgets have become. With the sensible presumption that each cell phone accompanies Wi-Fi and Bluetooth sensors, it opens up likely chances to involve these gadgets as intermediaries and count them to get a decent estimate of group thickness. In this chapter, I present strategies that utilize both Wi-Fi and Bluetooth signs to recognize the presence (and the level of presence) of these gadgets. With Bluetooth, I utilize the Bluetooth revelation component to filter for adjacent gadgets in normal stretches. In the event of Wi-Fi, I latently screen for purported test demand approaches that are conveyed by the gadgets in ordinary spans. I demonstrate that, although both methods have their limitations and imperfections, they can give a decent guess to the general changes in swarm thickness as individuals board and land at transport stops.

The rest of the chapter is organized as follows. In the following section, I take a gander at past work that is pertinent to the issue. In Section 6.3, I discuss how I gathered information

DOI: 10.1201/9781003513445-6

and got the ground truth for our tests. From there on, in Sections 6.4 and 6.5, I present our exploratory techniques for assessing swarm thickness utilizing Bluetooth and Wi-Fi information separately and the consequences of these trials. I then, at that point, examine the possibility and limits of our methodologies in Section 6.6; finally, I close the chapter with a short rundown and future work in Section 6.7.

6.2 RELATED WORK

Indoor confinement utilizing remote signs has been extensively studied in recent years. One is enticed to apply these strategies to the issue of group thickness discovery. In any case, even the effectiveness of precise localization methods [4] need gadgets being limited to effectively send bundles, which is not a sensible assumption in our situation. While some latent limitation methods exploit impressions of remote signs brought about by unsettling influences in conditions brought about by human presence [10], these, at present, can't manage more than each individual in turn. Besides, this large number of procedures need different passages conveyed, which can't be a superior option in contrast to the APCs I referenced in Section 6.1.

With regards to gathering ridership information utilizing remote signs, there has been a substantial amount of work that utilizes probe requests to accomplish this with shifting levels of achievement [2, 3, 7, 8]. While Thongtat et al. [7] investigate the Bluetooth method, they dispose of it immediately as unusable, which I show isn't true. All the others utilize others rely heavily on Wi-Fi protocol capture, say in this chapter, to utilize test demands for swarm thickness assessment. None of these papers address the issue of Macintosh address randomization (which I will investigate exhaustively in Section 6.5) that challenges their reliance on the uniqueness of the MAC addresses tend to appear across the probe packets from a similar gadget.

6.3 DATA COLLECTION AND GROUND TRUTH

I played out our tests on MTS public travel transports, on one of the famous transport courses (called UCSD Superloop) that understudies of UC San Diego broadly use. For Bluetooth information, I utilized an Android telephone with an application called Bluetana, which utilizes an Android Bluetooth disclosure component to filter for gadgets like clockwork. This information is then transferred to our backend server over cell association for later examinations. For Wi-Fi information, I utilize the WireShark bundle catch programming in screen mode running on a MacBook Master 2015 PC. The product catches all the traffic nearby, regardless of the source and objective of the bundles, and the information gathered from every parcel incorporates data having a place with each layer of the TCP/IP stack. I just gathered the traffic in the 2.4G Hz territory, I accept this will be enough for preliminary analysis, as most Wi-Fi traffic use this range.

I have led two examinations on various days. Each trial begins at a bus station and finishes after two circles once transport arrives at a similar stop for the subsequent time. I just present outcomes from one of the examinations in this chapter, yet the aftereffects of our methodologies in the two trials are comparable. To augment the reachability of the sensors from every one of the gadgets toward the front and the rear of the transport, I put the sensors at the midpoint in the transport. The transports I utilized were outfitted with APC (Programmed Traveler Counter) frameworks that record the number of travelers boarded and landed at each transport stop. I got this information for our analyses from the MTS support group, which I utilized as ground truth to examine our outcomes.

6.4 BLUETOOTH

6.4.1 Methodology

Most devices today come with built-in support for Bluetooth technology that enables peer-to-peer wireless communications. These communications occur over short-range networks called piconets. For consumer devices, this range usually goes up to 10 meters, which makes it suited for our scenario where all the devices of interest (i.e., inside the bus) will be well within this range and there will be less external noise to deal with (in this respect, it has an advantage over Wi-Fi as Wi-Fi has a larger range; so it is more prone to noise from external devices).

The data I collected contains the records for all the devices that are discovered in each scan. Each record contains the time stamp, MAC address of the discovered device, signal strength (RSSI), device type (classic or low-energy), and GPS location among others. I use MAC address to uniquely identify a device and cluster all the observed records for the same device. While Bluetooth devices have started implementing MAC address randomization, it is not so prevalent as in the case of Wi-Fi (which I discuss in detail in Section 6.5), so I assume that it won't affect our analyses. Once I cluster the observed records of the devices, the next step is to filter out external devices. Here, I take advantage of the insight that since the bus is constantly moving, external devices will go out of range soon enough and consequently, will only be visible for shorter periods. After eliminating external devices using this insight, I count the remaining devices present at each second of the trip and present it as our estimate for the crowd density (I count a device as "present" for all the seconds between the first and last observations of the device).

6.4.2 Results

I show a portion of our perceptions and results for Bluetooth information in Figures 6.1 through 6.3. To sift through outside traffic, I involved the 3-minute end for the all-out perception length for every gadget, as made sense of in Figure 6.1. Figure 6.2 shows that any

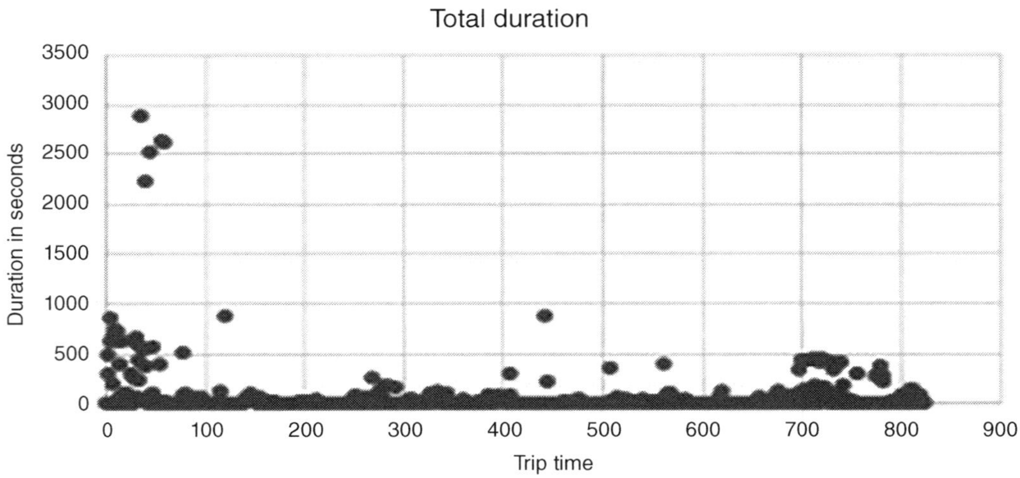

Figure 6.1 Bluetooth: Lengths of duration for observed Bluetooth devices. Most of the devices were observed only for up to 2 or 3 minutes, which means they are external. Others in the 200 to 1000-second range correspond to the legitimate traffic from devices inside the bus, while few data points over 2500 seconds likely correspond to external devices picked up in the second loop of the trip.

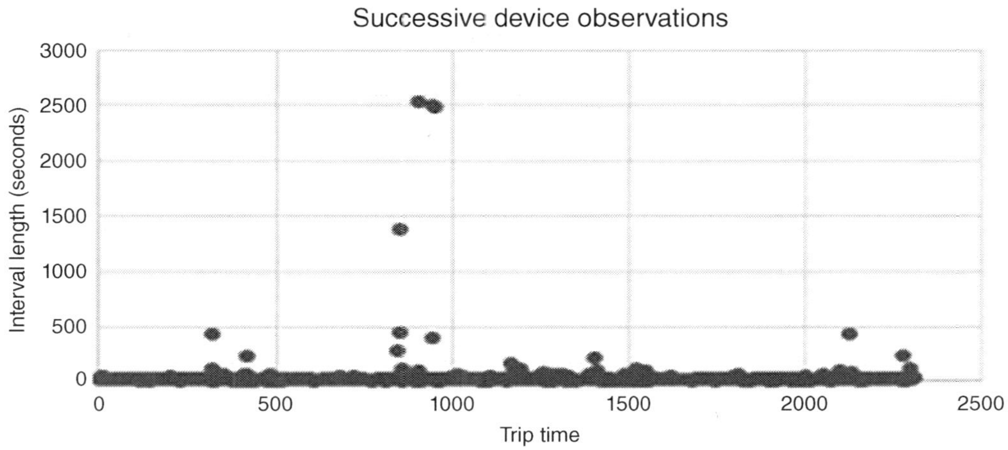

Figure 6.2 Bluetooth: Length of intervals between successive observations of devices that were observed more than once. It shows that most devices, if they continue to be around, are detected again within a minute.

gadget that is distinguished at least a couple of times has less than a brief period between progressive recognitions. I utilized this perception to take out outside traffic that persevered for over 3 minutes (e.g., the traffic entered the next roundabout), however, it didn't have the quantity of location that corresponds to the length of noticed term. Our eventual outcomes are introduced in Figure 6.3. While the gauge is erroneous regarding the genuine count (true to form), i.e., the most extreme number of gadgets assessed is 20 while the real traveler count goes up to 30, it, in any case, shows a decent relationship with the ground truth information.

Note that although the gauge tops appear smaller contrasted with unique ones, it is a direct result of the slight distinction in time tomahawks of both the plots (you can take a gander at the seconds to correlate).

6.5 WI-FI

6.5.1 Methodology

One of the characterizing elements of a cell phone is its capacity to interface with the web through Wi-Fi. Notwithstanding the real information outlines used to move information among gadgets and passageways, Wi-Fi utilizes various sorts of administration edges to look for and oversee associations with these passageways. In our situation, I just viewed as the administration outlines from the information I gathered as most transports don't have Wi-Fi passageways and subsequently, no information traffic begins from gadgets inside the transport – this likewise disposes of the outside traffic I, in any case, need to manage. Inside administration outlines, I was specifically interested in a particular type called test demand outlines, which are utilized by gadgets to ask about neighboring passageways. Since the greater part of the gadgets on the transport will be in a disassociated state (i.e., not effectively associated with any passage), the vast majority of the traffic from these gadgets will be in the form of probe requests sent in ordinary stretches. I utilize the test demands from the caught Wi-Fi traffic to follow the presence of these gadgets and gauge their count.

Test demands, similar to some other Wi-Fi outlines, convey Macintosh address data which can be utilized to recognize gadgets. Since test demands consistently broadcast at a semi-steady rate, they make the following minor adjustments. To address protection concerns

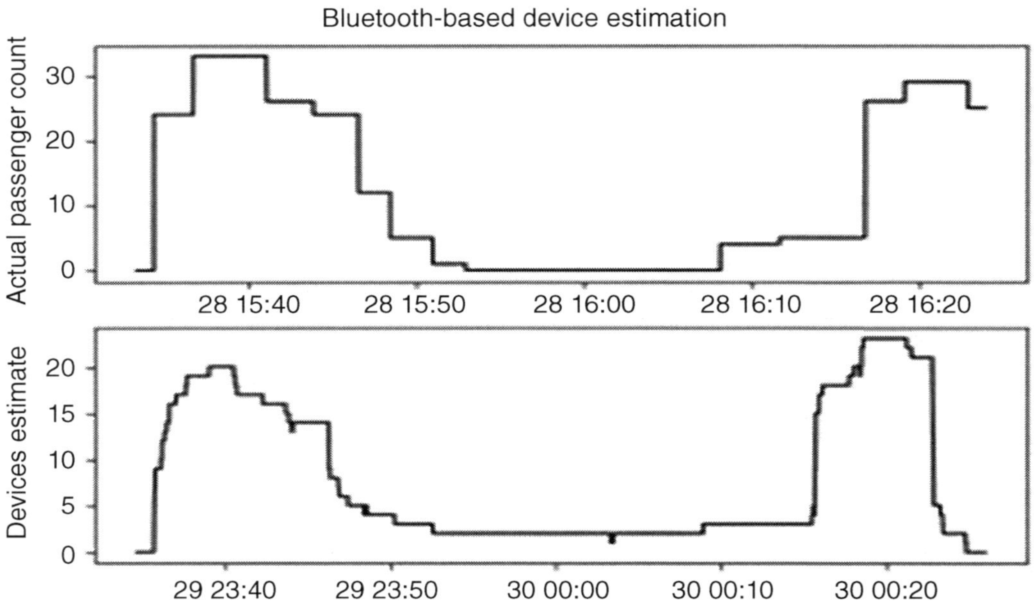

Figure 6.3 Bluetooth: The top plot shows the ground truth passenger count while the bottom one presents our estimates based on Bluetooth data.

emerging out of this, a few present-day cell phones utilize brief, randomized Macintosh trends that are distinct from their actual worldwide location.

At the point when test demands are conveyed, they utilize a randomized pen name address that is changed occasionally, and the periodicity shifts across various sellers. This makes gathering the test demands sent by a similar gadget almost unthinkable as I lost the main key that can particularly recognize the gadget. There have been studies that show MAC address randomization alone is not enough to prevent tracking, as randomization itself could be defective and test demands typically contain gigantic measures of other data (like grouping numbers, labels, and so on) that could be utilized as a mark for the gadget [6, 9]. In this chapter, however, I restricted myself to the traffic from the gadgets that utilize their actual Macintosh addresses (which represent practically 50% of the noticed gadgets in our information). Our thought is that while the sifted-through traffic would most likely harm our capacity to precisely foresee the specific number of gadgets, it would, in any case, not influence the pattern, which is what I was keen on. I do, notwithstanding, investigate the chance of developing gadget marks to defeat Macintosh address randomization, and I treat this as future work.

The most vital phase in handling the information I caught was separating test parcels, which was mitigated by utilizing the 802.11 administration type field. Then, I eliminated every one of the parcels with randomized Macintosh addresses. I consider a Macintosh address to be genuine when I see it at least a couple of times in the information, and when a genuine Macintosh address is found, the supposition will be that the gadget related to this address would send every one of its parcels with a similar Macintosh address. From there on, I gathered the bundles given their Macintosh addresses. To kill the groups related to outside gadgets, I utilized a similar instinct, similarly as with Bluetooth gadgets in Section 6.4, that these bunches will just keep going for more limited timeframes. With Bluetooth, sorting out this time edge was simplified by the less outer clamor and the routineness of the spans between progressive gadget perceptions. With Wi-Fi notwithstanding, there was fundamentally more commotion due to its bigger reach, and the test demands shift generally concerning time between progressive appearances, as the periodicity changes across various producers. The issue is exacerbated by frequently missed or distorted parcels, which is by all accounts a typical case. In light of our perceptions, I showed up at a heuristic to group the test parcel bunches from a device as external traffic if they did not persist for a duration (i.e., the time among first and last test demands) longer than 3 minutes, or, on the other hand, assuming they continued over 3 minutes and the length of any stretch between progressive test bundles in the bunch doesn't surpass 2 minutes. I examine the consequences of our methodology in the following section.

6.5.2 Results

Figures 6.4 and 6.5 show dispersed plots for lengths of noticed span of every gadget and stretches between progressive test bundles coming from similar gadgets separately. Contrasted with comparable plots for Bluetooth (Figures 6.1 and 6.2), these plots are considerably more dissipated because of additional commotion from outer traffic and fluctuation in test demand spans. These elements make the basic limits I utilized in Bluetooth unusable for Wi-Fi. In the first place, I sift through external traffic based on a threshold for the duration, which would be higher contrasted with Bluetooth as outside gadgets stay longer in Wi-Fi's bigger catch range. After this step, the outer traffic that isn't sifted through would be the gadgets caught in the second circle of the excursion (the upper-left corner of each figure shows this uproarious traffic caught from such outside gadgets). To kill these, I go through the length of spans between progressive test demands and dispose of the gadgets where this passed a specific boundary. From Figure 6.5, 2 minutes appeared to cover the greater part of such stretches, which I will use for this edge.

Our gauge for swarm thickness utilizing this approach is displayed in Figure 6.6.

While the first and last pinnacles connect well (note that the gauge tops appear to be a piece smaller, given the tomahawk synchronization issue as well Figure 6.3), there is a startling pinnacle that doesn't compare to any group on the transport. This was a direct result of the long 3-minute stand-by at a significant bus station where the administrator enjoyed some time off. For this situation, there is no versatility and our calculation couldn't separate between outside traffic versus inside traffic relating to a group getting on at a bus station

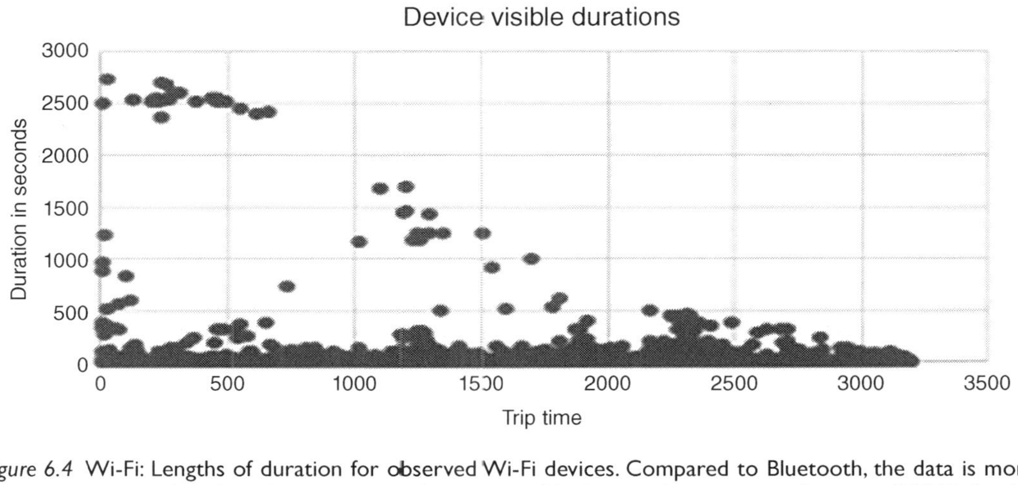

Figure 6.4 Wi-Fi: Lengths of duration for observed Wi-Fi devices. Compared to Bluetooth, the data is more scattered as there is more external noise arguably due to a larger range of captured Wi-Fi signals.

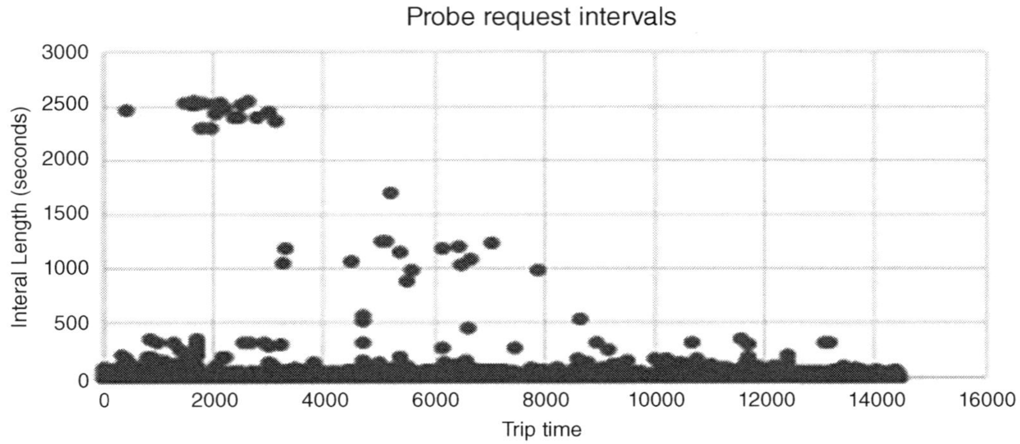

Figure 6.5 Wi-Fi: Length of intervals between successive probe requests associated with the same devices. Compared to Bluetooth, the data is more scattered due to high variance in the periodicity of probe requests across manufacturers and frequent packet misses in transmission.

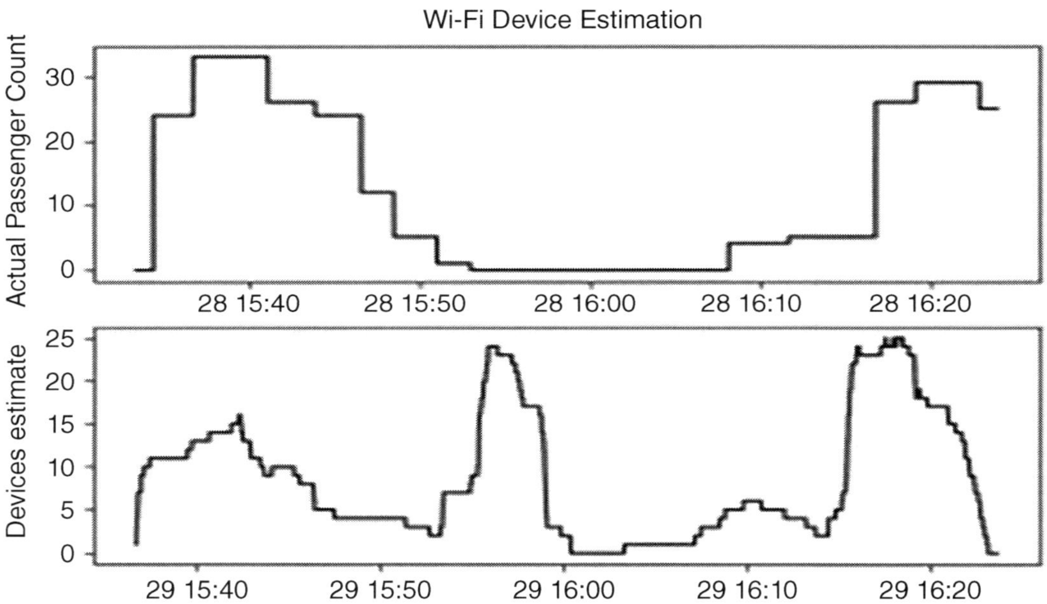

Figure 6.6 Wi-Fi: The top plot shows the ground truth passenger count while the bottom one presents our estimates based on Wi-Fi data. The unexpected peak in the middle corresponds to the long wait (more than 3 minutes) at a major bus stop.

and getting off at a different one 3 minutes. In such cases, the geo-area data of the transport could end up being valuable for barring such bogus information created when the transport is fixed to a spot for quite a while. I discuss the advantages of incorporating location data in the conversation segment. Like Bluetooth, while the specific count isn't coordinated, the figure demonstrates the way that a decent guess of the pattern can be accomplished, and this notwithstanding disposing of half of the information because of Macintosh address randomization.

6.6 DISCUSSION

The outcomes show that with the present status of Bluetooth and Wi-Fi information, the two of them can give great approximations to the genuine group designs for certain straightforward heuristics applied to the crude information to decrease commotion.

Upgrades can be made to the strategies utilized in the two ways to approach achieving better results in terms of improved thresholds utilized for sound decrease, yet it ought to be perceived that appraisal of the specific count of the group would never be accomplished because of inborn limits of these methodologies, for example, the mistake of the presumption that each individual purposes precisely one gadget or not all gadgets will have their Bluetooth or Wi-Fi turned on consistently. As Macintosh address randomization turns out to be more normal, which it will undoubtedly be some time, both these methodologies will endure as they just work on traffic with genuine Macintosh addresses. The Wi-Fi approach offers possible chances to defeat the Macintosh address randomization issue, explicitly with gadget signature procedures depicted by Vanhoef et al. [9].

An additional option that could work on our methods for sound decrease is the geo-area information utilizing GPS. This information, joined with the time stamps, could empower us to gauge the times when the bus stations are at transport stops or traffic lights. These stops normally conflict with our principal supposition that the transport is continuously moving, thus presenting the information that escapes procedures carried out with such presumption. Calculating this information could upgrade our strategies that could allow us to keep away from terrible outcomes like the startling pinnacle I found in Figure 6.6. I need to take note that I truly do gather this information as a piece of our Bluetooth information assortment, nonetheless, I haven't involved it to work on our procedures as portrayed previously. I pass on this to future work.

6.7 CONCLUSION

I expect to further develop productivity and rider experience of public transportation through information-driven approaches by gathering the ongoing group thickness assessment in the transports. To this end, I assessed the plausibility of utilizing Wi-Fi and Bluetooth traffic, starting from the gadgets in transport to gauge the group, as they give reasonable and less complex options in contrast to the issue contrasted with APCs. In this chapter, I proposed straightforward strategies for sound decrease and gadget assessment utilizing the gathered Wi-Fi and Bluetooth information. I assessed the exactness of these methodologies by contrasting the outcomes and the ground truth information of the examinations I performed on MTS transports in San Diego. While these methodologies are defective, I demonstrated the way that they can give great approximations to changing group thickness in transports as riders board and land at transport stops. I concluded with a conversation on the limits of these methodologies and a few upgrades which I left for future work.

REFERENCES

1. Pew survey on smartphone ownership (2018), http://www.pewinternet.org/fact-sheet/mobile/
2. Handte, M., Iqbal, M.U., Wagner, S., Apolinarski, W., Marron, P.J.: Crowd density estimation for public transport vehicles. *Communications of the ACM* (2014), http://ceur-ws.org/Vol-1133/paper-51.pdf
3. Kang, L., Qi, B., Banerjee, S.: A wireless-based approach for transit analytics. *Communications of the ACM* (2016), http://pages.cs.wisc.edu/~bozhao/papers/trellis.pdf

4. Kotaru, M., Joshi, K., Bharadia, D., Katti, S.: Spotfi: Decimeter level localization using wifi. *SIGCOMM* (2015), https://web.stanford.edu/~skatti/pubs/sigcomm15-spotfi.pdf
5. Mallett, W.J.: Trends in public transportation ridership: Implications for federal policy pp. 1–3 (2018), https://fas.org/sgp/crs/misc/R45144.pdf
6. Martin, J., Mayberry, T., Donahue, C., Foppe, L., Brown, L., Riggins, C., Rye, E.C., Brown, D.: A study of mac address randomization in mobile devices and when it fails. *Communications of the ACM* (2017), https://petsymposium.org/2017/papers/issue4/paper82-2017-4-source.pdf
7. Oransirikul, T., Nishide, R., Piumarta, I., Takada, H.: Measuring bus passenger load by monitoring wi-fi transmissions from mobile devices. *IICST* (2014), https://core.ac.uk/download/pdf/82066382.pdf
8. Pattanusorn, W., Nilkhamhang, I., Kittipiyakul, S., Ekkachai, K., Taka, A.: Passenger estimation system using wi-fi probe request. *Communications of the ACM* (2016), https://ieeexplore.ieee.org/document/7467124
9. Vanhoef, M., Matte, C., Cunche, M., Cardoso, L.S., Piessens, F.: *Why mac address randomization is not enough: An analysis of wi-fi network discovery mechanisms* (2016), https://papers.mathyvanhoef.com/asiaccs2016.pdf
10. Youssef, M., Mah, M., Agrawala, A.: Challenges: Device-free passive localization for wireless environments. *Communications of the ACM* (2007), http://citeseerx.ist.psu.edu/viewdoc/download?doi=10.1.1.112.6849&rep=rep1&type=pdf

Chapter 7

Cooperative spectrum sensing using random forest algorithm over Rayleigh fading channel

Sesham Srinu, Nalina Suresh, and Aina Kesilohenda Hauwanga

7.1 INTRODUCTION

Due to the exponential growth of wireless communication technologies like 5G and Internet of Things (IoT) and the increase in the number of wireless devices, there will be a strong demand for radio spectrum in the near future [1]. Conventional spectrum allocation strategies frequently lead to inefficient use of the available spectrum since they allocate defined spectrum bands to certain paid services. By dynamically accessing underutilized spectrum bands, Cognitive Radio Networks (CRNs) have emerged as a possible solution to this problem, hence increasing spectrum utilization. Wireless devices also named Cognitive Radios (CRs) may now intelligently identify unoccupied radio bands and modify their broadcast characteristics (modulation, power level, carrier frequency, etc.) to operate in these unoccupied bands without interfering with licensed/paid users. Spectrum sensing, which is the core technology that makes CR possible, is the process of continuously monitoring the spectrum to determine whether paid/primary users (PUs) and open spectrum are present. A multitude of spectrum sensing approaches have been developed, with a primary focus on single-node techniques [2–4]. Usually, these techniques depend on characteristics that are retrieved or hidden patterns that are found in the signal data. Due to the inherent diversity and impediments of wireless channels (multipath fading, shadowing, and noise), single-node sensing systems show considerable performance degradation. Moreover, its performance is uncertain/erroneous, resulting in missed detections and false alarms. Cooperative spectrum sensing (CSS) has been offered to reduce the limitations of single-node sensing, where several sensors/nodes work together to increase the precision of spectrum detection. This method can improve detection performance and mitigate the negative impacts of wireless channel impairments. Cooperative sensing has made extensive use of traditional fusion algorithms including soft and hard decision-based fusion methods [5]. Nevertheless, these algorithms frequently fail to achieve optimal performance, especially under Rayleigh fading and low signal-to-noise ratio (SNR) environment.

New directions for improving sensing probability have been made possible by recent developments in machine learning (ML) and deep learning [6]. Given the features that may be retrieved from sensing data, machine learning algorithms are able to recognize intricate patterns and make correct decisions. Across a range of machine learning approaches, ensemble learning techniques like the Random Forest Algorithm (RFA) have demonstrated significant promise in improving detection performance by combining the results of several base learners (decision trees). This work examines how different sensing characteristics, such as the number of features (Max-eigenvalue and energy), base learners, and sensing nodes, affect the multinode sensing performance using RFA. The energy and Max-eigenvalue are extracted from the recorded RF signal and pre-processed in the proposed approach. These characteristics were chosen because they are fundamental properties of primary user signals and are

DOI: 10.1201/9781003513445-7

useful in differentiating between spectrum bands that are occupied and those that are not. The proposed method uses the retrieved characteristics to train base learners, whose predictions are then combined to uncover hidden patterns in the sensing data.

The authors in [3, 7] have proposed supervised ML algorithms for single-node sensing. The differential entropy feature in [7] and the energy feature in [3] are used to train different models that include *K*-nearest neighbor, support vector machine, logistic regression, and RFAs. These works analyze the performance of the ML methods by varying the shape parameter (β) of the Gaussian noise and showed that RFA is superior compared to other considered ML techniques. However, the authors considered only one feature, either energy or differential entropy, for hypothesis testing (binary classification) and did not analyze the effectiveness of ML techniques on the performance of CSS. The authors in [8] considered three features, sensor velocity, energy, and average eigenvalue, of the captured signal for hypothesis testing using RFA. It was shown that RFA-based sensing shows better performance compared to existing sensing methods under low SNR settings. However, the authors did not accumulate the data using multiple sensors and did not show the effectiveness of RFA on cooperative sensing performance. The authors in [9, 10] have developed a multi-featured combination network that extracts features through a parallel structure. The authors in [9] have developed a CSS model based on long-short-term memory (LSTM) and convolutional neural network (CNN), where the CNN extracts hidden spatial features and the LSTM network extracts time features. In [10], however, the authors developed an algorithm based on CNNs and the gate recurrent unit (GRU). Experimental results of both works demonstrate that the combination algorithm's detection performance outperforms the conventional methods under a low SNR environment. The authors in [11], a spectrogram-aware CNN algorithm for spectrum sensing and showed that the proposed method outperforms the CNN and LSTM network-based sensing in terms of detection probability. The authors in [2] have proposed a hybrid spectrum sensing model using CNN and recurrent neural networks. The performance of the sensing is improved using transfer learning and compared with other works. However, the computational complexity of these algorithms is very high. Hence, in this work, we have focused on developing a low-complexity and efficient cooperative sensing model for cognitive radio applications.

This work offers the following two contributions: Using two crucial RF signatures (energy and max-eigenvalue) of the recorded signal data, a new cooperative sensing technique based on the RFA is developed. It also examines the effects of several sensing factors on CSS performance, including the number of base learners and sensing nodes in a network.

The remaining portions of this chapter are organized as follows: In Section 7.2, the problem statement and proposed RFA-based cooperative sensing algorithm are presented. In Section 7.3, the simulation setup and results are shown. The work is finally concluded and future directions for research are discussed in Section 7.4.

7.2 PROBLEM STATEMENT AND PROPOSED METHODOLOGY

Figure 7.1 shows the proposed signal detection method using multiple RF sensors deployed in the cooperative network. Every sensor tunes into the radio frequency bandwidth that requires scanning. Here, the database contains two RF signatures (energy and maximum eigenvalues) which are computed from captured RF signals from all sensors. The total dataset is divided into training (70%) and testing (30%) to train and test the proposed RFA-based CSS model. The samples are taken from the training set/population based on the bootstrap sampling method. Different decision trees (or base learners) are modeled from corresponding sample data, taken randomly from the database. The test data is used to evaluate the model.

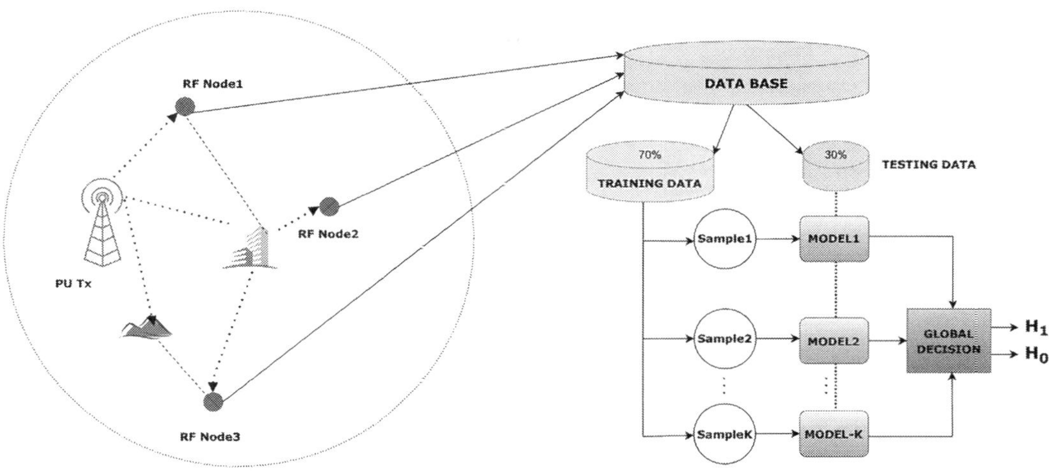

Figure 7.1 Block diagram of proposed cooperative sensing using RFA.

Finally, the predictions from each model are aggregated to improve the accuracy using fusion logic. This accuracy improvement is due to the fact that individual weak learners may not reliably detect the signal. Numerous methods exist for user authentication based on biometrics, each necessitating a specific hardware input device to collect the requisite user information for authentication purposes.

7.2.1 Problem statement

The problem of PU signal detection over a frequency band can be expressed as [4]

$$H_0 : r_m(t) = w_m(t)$$

$$H_1 : r_m(t) = h_m(t) \bullet s_m(t) + w_m(t)$$

where $r_m(t) = \left[r_1(t), r_2(t), \ldots., r_m(t) \right]$ is a vector of vector that contains multiple nodes received data. The vector $s_m(t)$ represents the deterministic signal in the frequency band, and $w_m(t)$ is Gaussian noise ($\mathbf{w}$ (t) ~ N (0, 1)). The channel matrix ($\boldsymbol{h}(\boldsymbol{t})$) coefficients depend on the fading environment, where the magnitude of a received signal at the CR node varies randomly according to the Rayleigh distribution.

The channel impulse response for Rayleigh fading is characterized as a Gaussian process with equal variance in the real and imaginary components and zero mean.

Let A and B be (*i.i.d.*) Gaussian random variables, i.e., $A \sim N(0, \sigma^2)$, $B \sim N(0, \sigma^2)$

The complex Rayleigh fading channel **h** (t) is given by

$$h_m(t) = A + \mathrm{jB} \tag{7.1}$$

The Rayleigh distribution describes the fading signal's magnitude:

$$|\mathrm{h}(\mathrm{t})| \sim \mathrm{Rayleigh}\left(\sigma = \frac{1}{\sqrt{2}}\right)$$

7.2.2 RFA-based cooperative sensing

RFA is an ensemble learning method generally used for both classification and regression tasks. Here, it is used as a classifier that can reduce bias and variance. It constructs several base learners (decision trees) and combines their output to improve detection performance. The mathematical modeling based on considered features, energy (ϕ), and maximum eigenvalues (ε) is outlined below.

Step 1: Consider a dataset $D = \{(\mathbf{x}_i, y_i)\}$, where $\mathbf{x}_i = (\phi_i, \varepsilon_i)$ represents the two features of the ith sample, and y_i is the corresponding binary classification label.

The features (ϕ_i, ε_i)) from received signal $\boldsymbol{r_m(t)}$ are calculated as

$$\phi(n) = \sum_{n=0}^{N-1} \left| r[n] \right|^2 \tag{7.2}$$

where $r[n]$ is discrete time signal of $r(t)$. The detection threshold (λ_ϕ) has to be used at the root node, which can be computed based on sample size and desired false alarm probability (P_{fa}) [12].

$$\lambda_\phi = \sigma^2 \cdot \left(\chi^2 \left(1 - P_{\text{fa}}, 2N \right) \right), \tag{7.3}$$

The second feature or maximum eigenvalue (ε) is determined using a sample covariance matrix ($R_x(N)$), which is computed as [13]

$$R_x(N) = \frac{1}{N} \left\{ \sum_{n=L-1}^{L-2+N} \hat{r}(n) \hat{r}^\dagger(n) \right\}, \tag{7.4}$$

The maximum eigenvalue is identified using the $max(.)$ function in MATLAB. The detection threshold (λ^ε) for the splitting process at the root node is given by random matrix theory [13].

$$\lambda\varepsilon = \sigma_w^2 \left(\left(1 + \sqrt{\frac{1}{N}} \right)^2 \frac{(1 + \sqrt{\frac{1}{N}}}{\sqrt{N}} \right) \tag{7.5}$$

Step 2: RFA creates several subsets of the original dataset by using the bootstrap sampling method. For every tree in the forest, t: $D_t \subset D$, where D_t is generated by sampling D with replacement.

Step 3: Feature scaling is performed on two RF signatures. The impurity index is computed (entropy) for both subsets to choose the best attribute that has to be placed in the root node, using the following formula:

$$\varphi = \sum_{i=0}^{1} Pi \log 2Pi \tag{7.6}$$

where $P_i = \frac{f_i}{N}$ is the probability of samples falling in each bin and f_i denotes the number of samples falling in the ith bin.

Step 4: MATLAB function fit tree(ϕ, ε) is used to train base learners based on two features. The splitting process at the root node and decision node compare their corresponding thresholds. Decision split can be made at root nodes based on the following logical test:

$$\phi / \varepsilon \underset{H_0}{\overset{H_1}{\gtrless}} \lambda \tag{7.7}$$

Step 5: Predict the class for the test set using the trained model.

Step 6: Compute the confusion matrix (given below) based on the number of Monte-Carlo trails for each base learner that can estimate the detection probability of each base learner (P_{dr}). In the confusion matrix (Table 7.1), H_0 and H_1 represent the hypothesis of signal presence and absence in the frequency band.

The probability of detection (P_{dr}) is estimated using Monte-Carlo trials.

$$P_{dr} = \frac{TP}{TP + FN} \tag{7.8}$$

Step 7: Decisions from all base learners' predictions are fused using OR and Majority/Voting rules; i.e., Given K decision trees, each individual decision tree (IDT) t provides a prediction $p_t(x) \in \{0, 1\}$ for an input x. The global prediction $G(x)$ using majority logic is

$$\mathrm{G}(\mathrm{x}) = mode\{p_t(x)\}_{t=1}^{K} \tag{7.9}$$

In the case of OR logic, the final prediction is H_1 if any of the individual trees predicts the H_1 class. Therefore, the global prediction $G(x)$ using OR logic is

$$G(x) = \begin{cases} 1, if \sum_{t=1}^{K} p_t(x) \geq 1 \\ 0, if \sum_{t=1}^{K} p_t(x) = 0 \end{cases} \tag{7.10}$$

This can be expressed using the indicator function:

$$G(x) = I\left(\sum_{t=1}^{K} p_t(x) \geq 1\right) \tag{7.11}$$

where I(.) is an indicator function, which is H_1 if the condition is true and H_0 otherwise.

Table 7.1 Binary confusion matrix

		Predicted	
		H_0	H_1
Actual	H_0	True Negative (TN)	False Positive (FP)
	H_1	False Negative (FN)	True Positive (TP)

7.3 RESULTS AND DISCUSSION

Table 7.2 shows the details of the simulation parameters used to perform this work. Synthetic data is generated where it emulates Radio Frequency (RF) signals in practical wireless communication bands. The Quadrature Phase Shift Keying (QPSK) modulated signal is considered a PU signal. It is assumed that the noise that affects the received signal is due to both inherent noise (AWGN) and Rayleigh fading. The signals are generated with varying SNRs ranging from −18 dB to 10 dB. A different sample size of data (N = 128–512) is captured using a rectangular windowing technique and then computed the RF signatures. The channel matrix ($\boldsymbol{hm}(\boldsymbol{t})$) coefficients depend on the fading environment that we considered, where the magnitude of a received signal at the CR node varies randomly according to the Rayleigh distribution. MATLAB is used as a simulation tool to analyze the proposed RFA-based CSS method. The RF signatures/features are extracted from intercepted data, such as energy (ϕ) and maximum eigenvalues (ε), over the considered range of SNR values. A training and testing dataset is created to train and test the IDTs and we have considered the varying number of base learners (K = 1–7). Using the intended value of the false alarm probability (Pfa = 0.1), thresholds are predefined as per eqn. (3) and eqn. (5). RF signal energy (feature-1) is calculated using eqn. (2). Another feature, namely, maximum-eigenvalue (ε) is estimated using the sample covariance matrix of the intercepted signal. These two signatures are feature-scaled (normalized between 0 and 1) to avoid the dominance of one signature on the prediction. Out of two feature classes, the best feature class is identified using impurity index (entropy), to use it as a root node splitter. This process is applied to all base learners as part of sub-model training. The binary classes are labeled as 1 (for signal presence) and 0 (for signal absence). For global prediction $G(\boldsymbol{x})$, two distinct hard decision-based fusion methods, OR logic and Voting logic, are taken into consideration.

In general, ML algorithms are evaluated based on key parameters such as Accuracy, Recall, Precision, and F1 score [14]. These metrics are dependent on the following parameters: true positive (TP), false positive (FP), true negative (TN), and false negative (FN), which can be seen in Table 7.2. The TP and TN provide the number of correctly identified attempts as a PU signal when PU is actually communicating in its band. Conversely, the number of signals that are incorrectly labeled as PU signals is measured by the metrics FP and FN. Out of all these parameters, accuracy is the most important metric that identifies correctly as a PU. Hence, in this work, the performance of the proposed algorithm is evaluated and illustrated as accuracy/detection probability (in statistical terminology) against the SNR of the RF signal. For instance, the successful PU detection probability/rate using an IDT can be computed as per

Table 7.2 Simulation parameters

Parameter	*Specifications*
Channel impediments	Rayleigh fading, AWGN
Modulation	QPSK
Sample size (N)	128–512
Features for detection	Energy, Max-eigenvalue
Number of base learners (DT)	3–7
False alarm probability (Pfa)	0.1
Simulation tool	MATLAB
Ensemble learning method	Random forest algorithm
Aggregation	OR, Voting logic

eqn. (8), where the total number of Monte-Carlo trials is taken as 10,000 to estimate the *TP* and *FN* parameters.

The normalized RF signatures variation (Energy and max-eigenvalue) over SNR ranging from –16 dB to 10 dB are shown in Figures 7.2 and 7.3. These two features are plotted against SNR with three distinct sample sizes (128, 256, and 512) in these results. From the graphs, it is evident that these two features change with changes in the SNR of the received RF signal, which are hidden patterns used for deterministic signal detection.

It is also evident that fading channels result in considerable energy loss. The entropy value of the attribute dependence on the variance of the corresponding signature. Hence, the attribute that has the highest spread/variance is considered as a root node for the best split. We have considered a sample size of 256 to evaluate the performance of the proposed RFA-based CSS.

Figure 7.4 illustrates the detection probability (accuracy) of the proposed RFA-based CSS detection using various numbers of base learners (*K* = 1, 3, 5, and 7) in the fusion process. The aggregation method using OR and Majority logic is also presented. According to Figure 7.4, when the signal SNR is less than –11 dB, the detection rate of the IDT (*K* = 1) decreases and their performance is poor. However, the model detection rate increases with an increase in the number of base learners in the fusion from 3 to 7. For instance, with *K* = 7, the PU signal detection rate is 90% and above up to –11 dB SNR using OR logic. In addition, the detection improvement of majority-based fusion is insignificant even when we are increasing the number of base learners from 3 to 7. Out of two fusions, aggregation using OR logic gives the highest performance due to the nature of the logic that it detects the PU signal if any one of the base learners detects the PU activity. On the other hand, the majority logic is dependent on how frequently instances of the binary class (0/1) arise during the global prediction process. It is clear from the simulation results that using multiple decision trees, the suggested RFA-based CSS can improve detection accuracy. We have also observed that due to bootstrap aggregation, the Rayleigh fading channel effects on the received signal can be nullified.

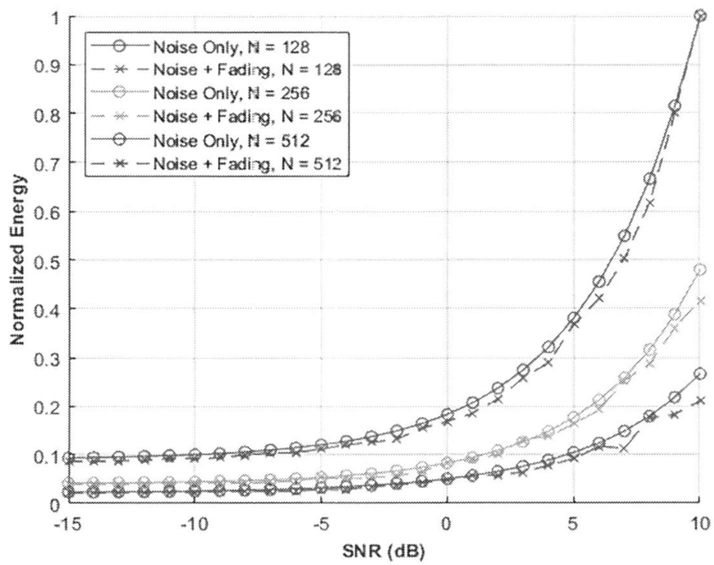

Figure 7.2 Normalized energy of RF signal under noisy and Rayleigh fading environment (*SNR* = –16 dB to 10 dB, *N* = 128–512).

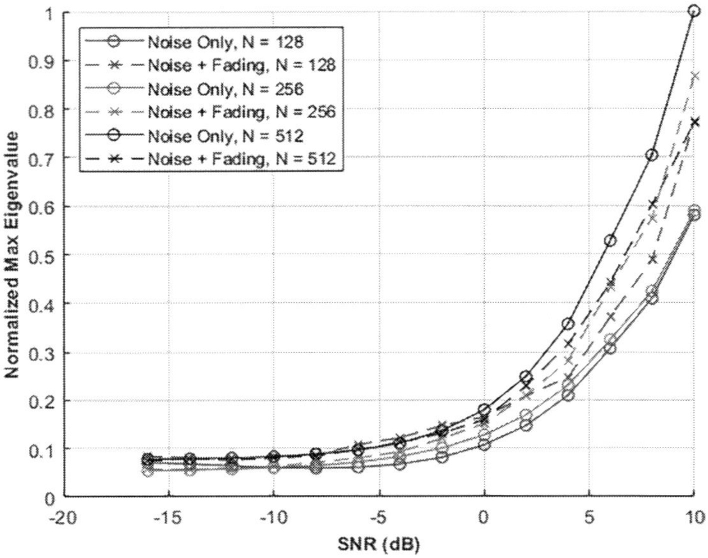

Figure 7.3 Normalized maximum-eigenvalue of RF signal under noisy and Rayleigh fading environment ($SNR = -16$ dB to 10 dB, $N = 128$–512).

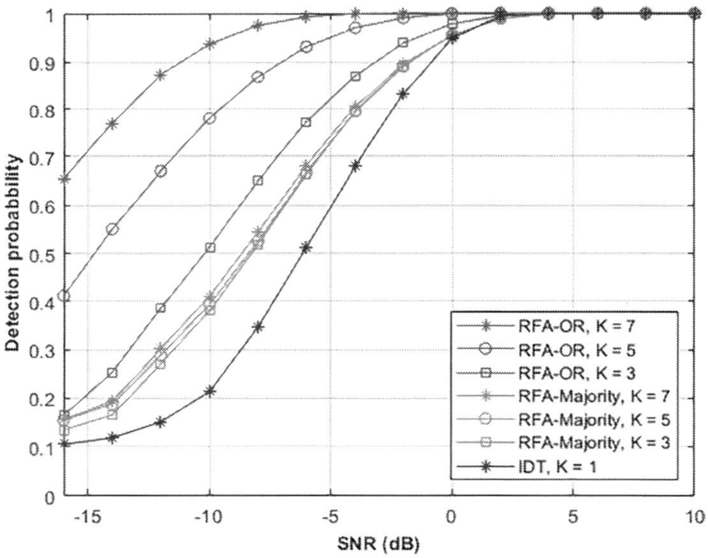

Figure 7.4 Performance of RFA-based CSS with varying base learners ($SNR = -18$ dB to 10 dB, $N = 256$, $K = 1$–7).

7.4 CONCLUSION AND FUTURE WORK

This chapter provides an efficient CSS model for CR networks that uses RFA. It takes two important RF signatures such as max-eigenvalue (ε) and energy (ϕ) of captured data for binary classification. Under demanding wireless channel conditions, like AWGN and Rayleigh fading environments, the suggested technique shows significant performance improvement by training base learners and fusing their individual predictions. The RFA uses the bootstrap sampling method to create multiple subsets of trained data by replacement strategy. The simulation findings reveal that the proposed RFA-based approach is low complex and outperforms conventional CSS methods, particularly, in situations where wireless channels are affected by Rayleigh fading. The results show that detection accuracy can be significantly increased by combining multiple decision trees irrespective of the number of sensing nodes and it can be improved further with an increase in the number of trees. Most importantly, the model can detect −11 dB signals over noisy and fading environments by integrating seven base learners. In addition, it is observed that the effect of Rayleigh fading can be nullified using the proposed fusion method. Overall, this work demonstrates how advanced machine learning methods, such as RFA, can be used to improve the detection performance of CSS for CRNs. Further research endeavors may investigate the incorporation of additional features and multi-model-based ensemble techniques to further improve sensing accuracy.

ACKNOWLEDGMENT

The authors would like to extend their sincere thanks to the Grants Management and Resource Mobilization unit at the UNAM for their invaluable support in facilitating this research project.

REFERENCES

[1] C. Keunhong, Jungin Park: Rethinking autocorrelation for deep spectrum sensing in cognitive radio networks. *IEEE Internet of Things Journal*, 10(1):31–41, 2023.

[2] S. Solanki, Vasudev Dehalwar, and Jaytrilok Choudhary: Spectrum sensing in cognitive radio using CNN-RNN and transfer learning. *IEEE Access*, 10:113482–113492, 2022.

[3] Ankit Mishra, D. Vasudev: Spectrum hole detection for cognitive radio through energy detection using random forest. In *International Conference for Emerging Technology*, pp.1–7, 2020.

[4] Sesham Srinu, Manfred Jeremia, and F.M.S. Abisai: Development of logistic regression based spectrum sensing algorithm using extreme eigenvalues. In *APSIT*, pp. 443–447, 2023.

[5] Tingting Yang, Yucheng Wu, Liang Li: Fusion rule based on dynamic grouping for cooperative spectrum sensing in cognitive radio. *IEEE Access*, 7:51630–51639, 2019.

[6] Yixuan Zhang and Zhongqiang Luo: A review of research on spectrum sensing based on deep learning. *Electronics*, 12(21):1–32, 2023.

[7] Purushothaman Saravanan, Shreeram Suresh C.: A supervised learning approach for differential entropy feature-based spectrum sensing. In *Sixth WiSPNET*, pp. 395–399, 2021.

[8] Chong Tan, Jinshan Chen, and Sufang Chen: Combination spectrum sensing algorithm for wireless sensor network based on random forest. In *10th International Conference on Intelligent Computing and Wireless Optical Communications*, pp.1–5, 2022.

[9] Liuwen Li, Wei Xie, and Xin Zhou: Cooperative spectrum sensing based on LSTM-CNN combination network in cognitive radio system. *IEEE Access*, 11:1–42, 2023.

[10] Mingdong Xu, Zhendong Yin, Yanlong Zhao Wu: Cooperative spectrum sensing based on multi-features combination network in cognitive radio network. *Entropy*, 24(1):1–15, 2022.

[11] Lianning Cai, Kaitian Cao: Spectrum sensing based on spectrogram-aware CNN for cognitive radio network. *IEEE Wireless Communications Letters*, 11(10):2135–2139, 2022.

[12] Zhuoran Cai, Zhiyuan Liu, and Liang Kou: Reliable UAV monitoring system using deep learning approaches. *IEEE Transactions on Reliability*, 71(2):973–983, 2022.

[13] Sesham Srinu, M. Kranthi Kumar Reddy, and C.N. Temaneh: Physical layer security against cooperative anomaly attack using bivariate data in distributed CRNs. In *11th International Conference on COMSNETS*, pp.410–413, 2019.

[14] Ibrahim Nemer, Tarek Sheltami, and Irfan Ahmad: RF-Based UAV detection and identification using hierarchical learning approach. *Sensors*, 6:1–23, 2021.

Chapter 8

A novel approach to face recognition for smart attendance-monitoring systems

S. Avinash, V. Geethapriya, J. Kavitha, and C. Kamala Kannan

8.1 INTRODUCTION

Attendance is a crucial aspect of any educational institution, which is useful in maintaining discipline and also helps in maintaining order. It is useful in addressing certain important questions such as the following: Has the student been punctual? How long has he/she been late to the institution? How early has he/she been to the institution? It also is useful in maintaining discipline across the entire institution as it creates uniformity among students. When creating and executing a face-recognition algorithm, various elements are taken into account, such as illumination, aging, changes in physical appearance, unstable camera positioning, rapid subject movement, image resolution, and viewing distance [1]. Researchers have tried to achieve them using various algorithms.

The task of face recognition is an active area of research, considering its complexity [5]. However, considering its highly useful applications, it attracts several young researchers in the field of facial recognition. The proposed detector enhances the research by providing the following features:

i) It can distinguish and identify a person with and without a face mask.
ii) It can identify and recognize persons with different-colored face masks.
iii) It is trained with a system-generated database (RTAMD) with varied lighting and angles matching practical conditions.
iv) It can mark the attendance of known persons in an Excel sheet and unknown persons are excluded from the attendance.

8.2 METHODOLOGY OF THE PROPOSED WORK

The research idea can be categorized into three major phases which primarily address the purpose that is face recognition [4]. The major phases are (1) Phase 1, which is data detection, also known as the Image Collection Phase, (2) Phase 2, which is the Face Algorithm Phase, and (3) the third phase, the Output Display Phase, which is primarily responsible for recognizing the faces. Here, the Real_Time_Attendance_Monitoring_Dataset (RTAMD) is created which consists of 1000 images of one person [6, 9]. It consists of 1000 images for four different persons. To further elaborate on the proposed work, a block diagram is proposed in Figure 8.1.

The output of this trained model will display a message with the name of the person, whose face is recognized and the attendance will be marked accordingly. If the person is unidentified, a message will be displayed indicating that an unknown face has been recognized. In such a case, attendance will not be marked [8] as it should not mark attendance for

DOI: 10.1201/9781003513445-8

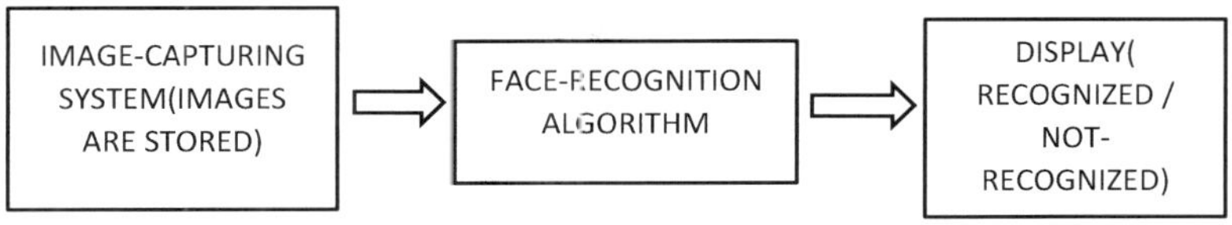

Figure 8.1 Generalized face-recognition system.

the unknown person. Attendance of only the person from the institution should be marked and the persons unknown to the institution shouldn't be given attendance, marking the accuracy of the project. Also to determine the accuracy of the project, certain performance metrics are derived from the predicted data.

The model was trained with the algorithm combination of the Haar-CasCade algorithm [2] for face detection and the Support Vector Machine (SVM) algorithm for classification and recognition of faces from images. The Haar-CasCade algorithm is a fast and accurate method for object detection that uses the Viola–Jones algorithm [3]. The Viola–Jones algorithm can be applied to various domains, such as object recognition and face recognition, with different performance levels and improved accuracy levels.

The SVM algorithm is a simple yet easy-to-implement supervised machine learning algorithm that can be used to solve both classification [8] and regression problems [5]. SVM can efficiently handle non-linear data by transforming the input space into a higher-dimensional space using a kernel function, making it a highly popular choice among research scholars. There are many types of kernels available in SVMs, namely, linear SVM, polynomial SVM, Gaussian Radial Basis Function (RBF), and Sigmoid. SVM introduces a regularization parameter (C) that balances the margin maximization and the classification error.

8.3 PROPOSED FACE-RECOGNITION METHOD

The proposed research work can be further explained as follows. First, the images are captured in real time, and then they are used for training and testing and hence the detector can detect them. The images are captured using any real-time image-capturing sources such as web cameras; preferably, ones that can capture HD images of 720-pixel resolutions in the 280 × 720-pixel image range are used for this research. The captured image is then applied to the Haar-CasCade algorithm to detect the faces from the images. As the faces here are covered with masks, the detectors should be able to identify distinguishing features such as eyes and the upper portion of the faces that help identify the person even if he or she is wearing masks. Extracted features such as the eyes and upper portion of the face are then cropped, as shown in Figure 8.2.

The preprocessing steps include processing the input image in a step-by-step manner. It involves reading the image and then cropping the image to a fixed resolution of 50 × 50 as the algorithm only takes the particular resolution for processing [10]. The faces are then detected and stored in a particular folder. The eyes are then detected and extracted and then used for processing, as shown in Figure 8.2. Here, only the eye region and the upper portion of the face are extracted as the rest of the face is covered with occlusion or simply a face mask. The face detection is performed with the help of the Haar-CasCade algorithm which is the most preferred method considering its high detection accuracy and speed. The face feature extraction is performed by using the SVM algorithm which offers several benefits such as ease of adaptation [12], reduced number of parameters to consider [13], and flexibility. The main advantage of this algorithm is that it can handle huge datasets

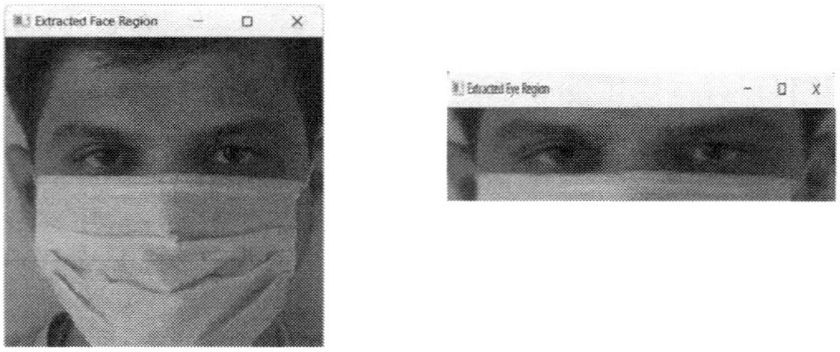

(a) (b)

Figure 8.2 Image pre-processing steps: (a) face region is cropped and (b) eye region is cropped.

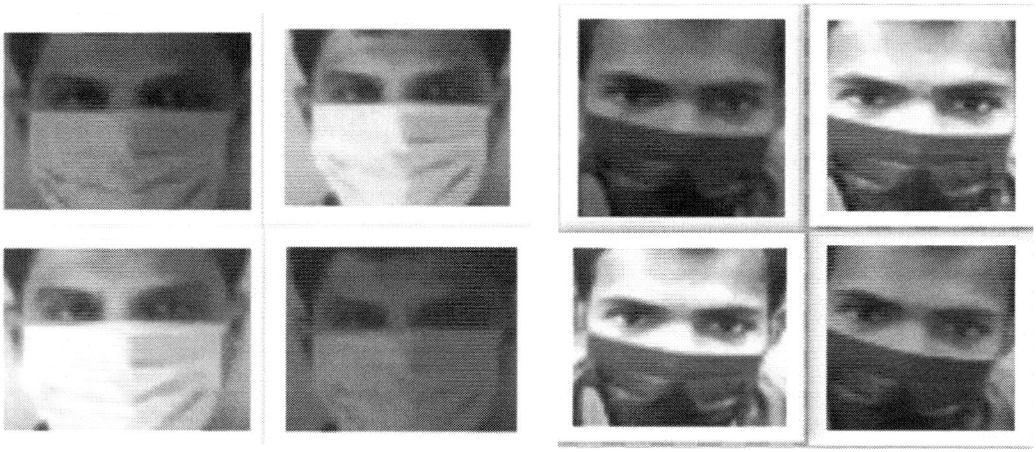

(a) (b)

Figure 8.3 (a) Person-I training database and (b) person-II training database.

accurately and effectively. Also, it is non-parametric in nature which improves its versatility and flexibility.

8.4 TRAINING DATASET

The dataset is essentially the major component of any image processing project. The dataset used here is a unique and system-generated dataset which is named as RealTime_Attendance_Monitoring_DataSet. It consists of images under various lighting conditions by varying its illumination [14] and also tilting angle conditions of various face images matching the practical conditions under a system-generated program.

It contains 1000 images of each person and a total of 4 persons are taken for this project. From the carried experiments, it was clear that training the model with more images led to better accuracy and better results. The novelties addressed in this project are varied lighting conditions and angles of tilting of faces present in the face dataset. These are proposed to address the real-time problem of the detector not detecting the images due to the varied occlusions. The proposed detector can detect both when the person is wearing a mask and when not. Also, it can recognize persons wearing colored masks as well. These are system-generated images based on varied lighting conditions in which intensity levels are varied matching the real-life scenario.

8.5 TESTING DATASET

The major component that is required for research is to evaluate the performance of the detector by testing it. The dataset for a single person is divided into 80% training data and 20% testing data [16]. It contains 800 images for training and the remaining 200 images are taken for testing. The training images are given to the model and it is trained on the extracted features from it. The testing database is not given to the model and the model has to recognize it without knowing what is present in it [18]. Based on the training from the past, it has to predict the images present in the testing database [20]. The testing database contains both light-varied and angle-varied images. The angle-varied versions of the same are shown in Figure 8.4.

8.6 STIMULATION AND RESULTS

The program is evaluated by the Python IDLE software. After training the model with the varied images under various conditions, the model should be able to recognize the images as the name of the person. The output of the detector recognizes the name of the person from the name of the file and the unknown faces are recognized as unknown. The outputs are given in Figures 8.5–8.8 for reference.

The face-recognition system recognizes the faces of the person with and without masks correctly. The Face Recognition System recognizing the faces of third and fourth persons with masks and the persons not trained in the system are labeled as unknown, as shown in Figure 8.9.

It can be noted from Figures 8.5–8.8 that attendance of only the persons belonging to the institution is marked and the attendance of the unknown person is not marked, and now the attendance is marked in a separate .csv file and is as given in Figure 8.10.

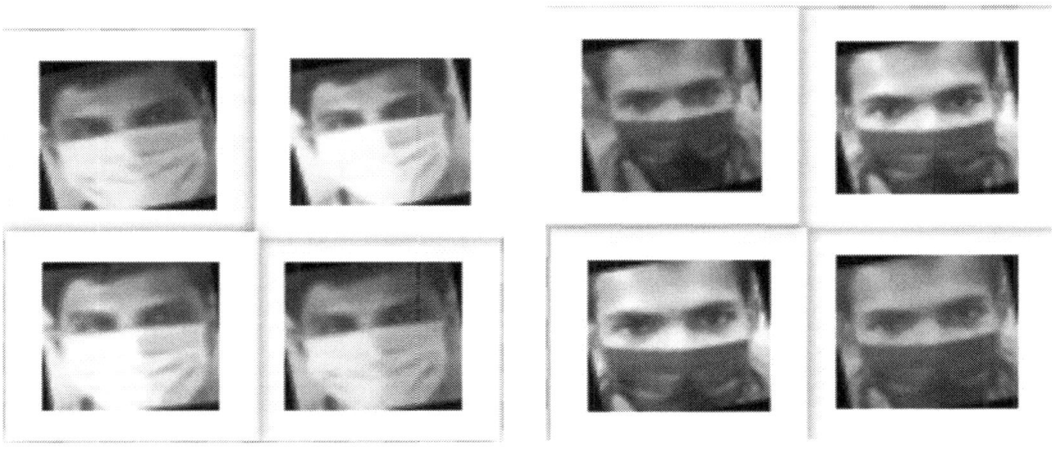

(a) (b)

Figure 8.4 (a) Person-I testing database and (b) person-II testing database.

```
= RESTART: C:\Users\Avinash\AppData\Local\Programs\Python\Python312\Project_File
s\Testing_Program.py
Predicted class Name: Avinash
Avinash face is recognized. Attendance will be marked!!
```

Figure 8.5 Face-recognition system recognizing the face of the person without a mask (Person-I).

```
= RESTART: C:\Users\Avinash\AppData\Local\Programs\Python\Python312\try3_KNN\Pro
ject_Files\Testing_Program.py
Predicted class Name: Unknown
Unknown face is recognized. Attendance will not be marked!!
```

Figure 8.6 Face-recognition system recognizing the face of the person with mask (Person-II).

```
= RESTART: C:\Users\Avinash\AppData\Local\Programs\Python\Python312\Project_File
s\Testing_Program.py
Predicted class Name: Avinash
Avinash face is recognized. Attendance will be marked!!
```

Figure 8.7 Face-recognition system recognizing the face of the person with mask (Person-III).

```
= RESTART: C:\Users\Avinash\AppData\Local\Programs\Python\Python312\Project_File
s\Testing_Program.py
Predicted class Name: Sneha
Sneha face is recognized. Attendance will be marked!!
```

Figure 8.8 Face-recognition system recognizing the face of the person with mask (Person-IV).

```
= RESTART: C:\Users\Avinash\AppData\Local\Programs\Python\Python312\Project_File
s\Testing_Program.py
Predicted class Name: Vashanth
Vashanth face is recognized. Attendance will be marked!!
```

Figure 8.9 Face-recognition system recognizing the face of the unknown person.

1	Name	Date	Time
2	Avinash_WithoutMask	24-05-2024	6:46 AM
3	Avinash_Mask	24-05-2024	6:47 AM
4	Avinash_Mask	24-05-2024	8:52 AM
5	Avinash_WithoutMask	24-05-2024	8:52 AM
6	Avinash_Mask	24-05-2024	8:54 AM
7	Sneha_Mask	24-05-2024	8:55 AM
8	Vashanth_Mask	24-05-2024	8:56 AM
9	Vashanth_Mask	24-05-2024	8:59 AM

Figure 8.10 Attendance marked in Attendance.csv file.

The accuracy of any face-recognition model can be calculated using the following confusion matrix expression. The accuracy is defined as the ratio of the number of correct predictions to the ratio of the total number of predictions. In terms of the confusion matrix, it is defined as the following equation [19]:

$$\text{Accuracy} = (\text{Tp} + \text{Tn}) / (\text{Tp} + \text{Fp} + \text{Tn} + \text{Fn}) \tag{8.1}$$

where Tp is the abbreviation for True Positive, Tn is the abbreviation for True Negative, Fp is the abbreviation for False Positive, and Fn is the abbreviation for False Negative. By substituting all the necessary values in the (8.1), we get the accuracy of the detector to be **96.76%**, which proves the efficiency of the proposed system to be greater than its previous competitors.

The next parameter is Recall which correctly identifies the positive out of all the positives. It simply indicates how precise we are during a prediction [19]. In terms of the confusion matrix, it is defined as in the following equation:

$$\text{Recall} = (\text{Tp}) / (\text{Tp} + \text{Fn}) \tag{8.2}$$

The face-recognition model produced a recall of **96.72%**. The next parameter is Precision which gives the fraction of how correctly the model identified positives out of all positives that were predicted or simply indicates how well the model predicts the testing data [19]. In terms of the confusion matrix, it is defined as in the following equation:

$$\text{Precision} = (\text{Tp} + \text{Tn}) / (\text{Tp} + \text{Fp} + \text{Tn} + \text{Fn}) \tag{8.3}$$

The face-recognition model produced a precision of **91.97%**. The last parameter is the F1-score which is defined as the harmonic mean between the precision and recall to arrive at a single metric to compute its performance in a balanced manner [19]. In terms of the confusion matrix, it is defined as in the following equation:

$$\text{F1} - \text{Score} = 2 \times (\text{Precision} \times \text{Recall}) / (\text{Precision} + \text{Recall}) \tag{8.4}$$

The face-recognition model achieved an F1-score of **91.78%**. To summarize all the values obtained from the confusion matrix, the face-recognition model achieved an accuracy of 96.68%, precision of 91.97%, recall of 96.72%, and F1-score of 91.78%. The proposed model is tried and tested in four different face-recognition algorithms, namely, SVM, K-Nearest Neighbor algorithm (KNN), Convolutional Neural Network (CNN), and Random Forest Classifier algorithm (RF). Then, they are compared and contrasted with four face-detection algorithms, namely, OpenCV-HaarCasCade, OpenCV-Dlib, Multi-task Cascaded Convolutional Neural Network (MTCNN), and Linear Binary Pattern Histogram of Gradients algorithms (LBPH) and is as tabulated in Table 8.1. It is tested in both light-changed conditions and angle-changed conditions, as shown in Table 8.1.

The proposed model is compared with four different face-recognition algorithms and four different detection algorithms and is shown in Table 8.1 on the basis of four major parameters: accuracy, precision, recall, and F1-score. It is clearly observable that the model works at best when it is combined with the Haar-CasCade algorithm for face detection and SVM for face recognition and it achieves an accuracy of **96.67%**. Therefore, when the proposed model is compared in terms of combinations of algorithms or in terms of confusion matrix values, it is significantly higher. Therefore, it can be concluded that the proposed model is stable and suitable for face recognition with high efficiency and high accuracy.

Table 8.1 Comparison of algorithms based on the changed conditions

Face-recognition algorithm	*Face-detection algorithm*	*Accuracy (%)*	*Precision (%)*	*F1-score (%)*	*Recall (%)*
KNN	1. Haar-CasCade Algorithm	87	88	84	86
	2. OpenCV-Dlib Algorithm	82	85	83	87
	3. MTCNN Algorithm	92	87	74	83
	4. LBPH Algorithm	92	86	89	87
SVM	**1. Haar-CasCade Algorithm**	**96**	**91**	**96**	**91**
	2. OpenCV-Dlib Algorithm	94	94	92	95
	3. MTCNN Algorithm	94	91	91	94
	4. LBPH Algorithm	92	94	93	94
CNN	1. Haar-CasCade Algorithm	84	89	86	87
	2. OpenCV-Dlib Algorithm	92	85	83	81
	3. MTCNN Algorithm	88	84	85	86
	4. LBPH Algorithm	83	86	84	87
RF	1. Haar-CasCade Algorithm	72	77	73	77
	2. OpenCV-Dlib Algorithm	73	78	74	74
	3. MTCNN Algorithm	86	84	88	87
	4. LBPH Algorithm	87	87	84	87

REFERENCES

1. Sheikh, B., Zafar, A. RRFMDS: Rapid real-time face mask detection system for effective COVID-19 monitoring. *SN Computer Science*, 4, 288 (2023). https://doi.org/10.1007/s42979-023-01738-9
2. Science, B.O.C. and Science, B.O.C. (2023, June 16). *The Viola-Jones Algorithm | Baeldung on Computer Science*. Baeldung on Computer Science. https://www.baeldung.com/cs/viola-jones
3. Abdulhussein, D. and Saud, L., Evaluation study of face detection by Viola-Jones algorithm. *International Journal of Health Sciences*, 6, 4174–4182 (2022). 10.53730/ijhs.v6nS8.13127
4. Viola, P. and Jones, M., "Rapid object detection using a boosted cascade of simple features," *Proceedings of the 2001 IEEE Computer Society Conference on Computer Vision and Pattern Recognition. CVPR 2001*, Kauai, HI, USA, pp. I-I, 10.1109/CVPR.2001.990517, 2001.
5. Murphy, T.M., Broussard, R., Rakvic, R., Schultz, R. and Ngo, H., "A biological perspective of Viola-Jones face detection," *2014 Spring Symposium: From Lab to Life: Field Based Applications of MEMS & NEMS (MAMNA)*, Baltimore, MD, USA, 2014, pp. 1–4, doi: 10.1109/MAMNA.2014.6845234
6. Ephraim, T., Himmelman, T. and Siddiqi, K., "Real-Time Viola-Jones Face Detection in a Web Browser," *2009 Canadian Conference on Computer and Robot Vision*, Kelowna, BC, Canada, 2009, pp. 321–328, doi: 10.1109/CRV.2009.48
7. Joseph, H. and Rajan, B.K., "Real Time Drowsiness Detection using Viola Jones & KLT," *2020 International Conference on Smart Electronics and Communication (ICOSEC)*, Trichy, India, 2020, pp. 583–588. 10.1109/ICOSEC49089.2020.9215255
8. Viola, P. and Jones, M., "Robust real-time face detection," *Proceedings Eighth IEEE International Conference on Computer Vision. ICCV 2001*, Vancouver, BC, Canada, 2001, pp. 747–747, doi: 10.1109/ICCV.2001.937709
9. Da'san, M., Alqudah, A. and Debeir, O., "Face detection using Viola and Jones method and neural networks," *2015 International Conference on Information and Communication Technology Research (ICTRC)*, Abu Dhabi, United Arab Emirates, 2015, pp. 40–43. https://doi.org/10.1109/ICTRC.2015.7156416
10. Kumar, A., Kumar, M. & Kaur, A. Face detection in still images under occlusion and non-uniform illumination. *Multimed Tools Appl* 80, 14565–14590, (2021), https://doi.org/10.1007/s11042-020-10457-9

11. Viola, J. and Snow "Detecting pedestrians using patterns of motion and appearance," *Proceedings Ninth IEEE International Conference on Computer Vision*, Nice, France, 2003, pp. 734–741 vol. 2, doi: 10.1109/ICCV.2003.1238422
12. Lienhart, R. and Maydt, J., "An extended set of Haar-like features for rapid object detection," *Proceedings. International Conference on Image Processing*, Rochester, NY, USA, 2002, pp. I-I, doi: 10.1109/ICIP.2002.1038171
13. Janahiram, S., Alsadoon, A., Prasad, P.W.C., Rahma, A.M.S., Elchouemi, A. and Senanayake, S.A., "Detecting Occluded Faces in Unconstrained Crowd Digital Pictures," *2016 First International Conference on Multimedia and Image Processing (ICMIP)*, Bandar Seri Begawan, Brunei, 2016, pp. 5–9, doi: 10.1109/ICMIP.2016.11
14. Soni, N. & Kumar, M. & Mathur, G.. Face recognition using SOM neural network with different facial feature extraction techniques. *International Journal of Computer Applications*. 76, 7–11, (2013). 10.5120/13225-0647
15. Min, R., Hadid, A., Dugelay, J.L.. Efficient detection of occlusion prior to robust face recognition. *ScientificWorldJournal*, 2014, 519158, (2014). doi: 10.1155/2014/519158. PMID: 24526902; PMCID: PMC3914590.
16. Ekenel, H.K., Stiefelhagen, R. Why Is Facial Occlusion a Challenging Problem?. In: Tistarelli, M., Nixon, M.S. (eds) Advances in Biometrics. ICB 2009. Lecture Notes in Computer Science, vol 5558. Springer, Berlin, Heidelberg. https://doi.org/10.1007/978-3-642-01793-3_31, 2009.
17. Fu, Y., Wu, X., Wen, Y., Xiang, Y., Efficient locality-constrained occlusion coding for face recognition, *Neurocomputing*, 260, 104–111, (2017), ISSN 0925-2312, https://doi.org/10.1016/j.neucom.2017.04.001
17. Jozer, B., Matej, F., Luboš, O., Miloš, O. and Jarmila, P., "Face recognition under partial occlusion and noise," *Eurocon 2013*, Zagreb, Croatia, 2013, pp. 2072–2079, doi: 10.1109/EUROCON.2013.6625266
18. Mliki, H., Dammak, S. & Fendri, E. An improved multi-scale face detection using convolutional neural network. *SIViP* 14, 1345–1353 (2020). https://doi.org/10.1007/s11760-020-01680-w
19. Geetha, T. V., & Sendhilkumar, S. (2023). Machine Learning: Concepts, Techniques and Applications. Chapman and Hall/CRC, 2023.
20. Eyiokur, F.I., Ekenel, H.K. & Waibel, A. Unconstrained face mask and face-hand interaction datasets: building a computer vision system to help prevent the transmission of COVID-19. *SIViP* 17, 1027–1034 (2023). https://doi.org/10.1007/s11760-022-02308-x

Chapter 9

Fingerprint-based security system for mitigating voting corruption

M. S. Vinotheni, A. Rajasekar, M. Shabana Parveen, J. Bino, N. Vidhya, and Parameswaran Ramesh

9.1 INTRODUCTION

A voting system facilitates the selection of government officials and political representatives [1]. This research aimed at not only alleviating the challenges posed by conventional paper-based systems but also enhancing existing methods with a focus on efficiency, transparency, and mobility. At its core, this innovative system leverages fingerprint biometrics for voter verification, coupled with the encryption of each enrolled fingerprint template, to ensure robust security measures throughout the electoral process.

The outcome of this study is an electronic voting machine [2] that excels in power efficiency, security, and user-friendliness [3]. This pioneering system imbues elections with enhanced credibility, unwavering integrity, and absolute vote authenticity. In a world where secure and reliable voting practices are of paramount importance, this project represents a significant step forward in modernizing democratic processes. By seamlessly integrating fingerprint biometrics and cutting-edge encryption technology, it not only boosts the overall efficiency of the voting process but also ushers in an era characterized by trust, transparency, and universal accessibility in the realm of democratic participation.

The chapter is structured as follows: Section 9.2 provides a synopsis of the literature review and Section 9.3 discusses the originality of the research proposal. Section 9.4 allows for the conduct of analyses and experimental setup investigations. Section 9.5 encompasses the remarks and future prospects that are under dispute.

9.2 LITERATURE SURVEY

The author detailed the use of fingerprint biometrics in [4] to verify voter identities and reduce the likelihood of fraudulent voting. Furthermore, the authors [5] investigated the security of e-voting systems with fingerprint biometrics, which expands on this concept by integrating the identification of fingerprints into electronic voting systems. The article emphasizes how this technology can improve election security by removing the chance of multiple votes.

Voter impersonation is a problem in elections, and the authors of [6] discuss how biometric authentication, including fingerprint recognition, might help make elections fair. It is possible to implement biometric voter authentication measures to ensure the safety of elections. However, there are certain obstacles to overcome when using fingerprint biometrics for voting systems, as discussed in the article "Secure E-Voting Using Fingerprint Biometrics: Challenges and Solutions." Addressing concerns about privacy, data protection, and system stability, this chapter proposes ways to create secure fingerprint-based voting while avoiding these problems.

In [7], the authors have examined Mitigating Voter Fraud Through Fingerprint Authentication, which showcases the successful implementation of fingerprint security

 DOI: 10.1201/9781003513445-9

systems in various countries to combat voter fraud. The paper [7] provides practical examples of the effectiveness of these systems in enhancing election credibility. The authors in [8] have tackled the ethical and legal aspects of fingerprint voting systems, delving into the ethical and legal dilemmas that arise during their implementation. These issues include informed consent, data privacy, and creating rules for biometric voter authentication.

The authors have conducted a study titled "Fingerprint Security in Electoral Processes: A Comparative Analysis" [9], aimed at examining the effects of fingerprint security systems on electoral processes across different countries. The study evaluates the effectiveness of fingerprint recognition in reducing voting corruption and increasing public trust in global elections. These research efforts demonstrate the growing importance of biometric authentication, particularly fingerprint recognition, in protecting electoral processes, combating voting corruption, and upholding the integrity of democratic systems.

9.3 PROPOSED METHODOLOGY

Numerous methods exist for user authentication based on biometrics, each necessitating a specific hardware input device to collect the requisite user information for authentication purposes.

9.3.1 Block diagram

The R307 fingerprint module features two interfaces: TTL, URT, and USB 2.0. While the RS232 interface operates at the TTL level with a default transmission rate of 57600, it allows for customization. It offers compatibility with microcontrollers like ARM, DSP, and various serial devices, accommodating both 3.3 V and 5 V microcontrollers.

Initially, we connected the fingerprint sensor to the Arduino UNO. It's crucial to ensure that the chosen fingerprint sensor can establish communication with the Arduino via serial. While the Arduino UNO [10] typically employs pins 4 (RXD) and 3 (TXD) for default serial communication, we opted to utilize alternative pins for serial communication. To facilitate this, we implemented the Software Serial library in this project code, and the implementation of the proposed block diagram is shown in Figure 9.1.

This research features a block diagram comprising several key components working in unison to facilitate sign language communication for individuals with hearing impairments. At its core is the Microcontroller board, here Arduino has taken over, which serves as the central processing unit and communicates with the gloves equipped with LDR sensors. The thoughtful placement of these sensors on the fingers enables them to detect variations in light intensity associated with finger movements. The sensor interface facilitates seamless communication between the sensors and the Arduino, ensuring data acquisition accuracy.

The Arduino microcontroller serves as the central component of this device. It finds application in numerous IoT [11] devices due to its affordability and capable performance, making it a suitable choice for many IoT components with multiple parameters to manage. In terms of physical attributes, Arduino exhibits remarkable versatility, and its coding process proves to be remarkably straightforward. A 16 × 2 LCD display is a fundamental module that is widely used in a variety of devices and circuits. The designation "16 × 2" signifies its capacity to exhibit 16 characters on each line, for a total of two such lines. The Adafruit [12] Fingerprint Sensor R307 is a biometric fingerprint sensing module that allows you to seamlessly integrate fingerprint authentication and recognition into your projects. Its foundation is the R307 optical fingerprint sensor, which facilitates fingerprint storage and comparison. The power supply is a fundamental component that ensures the continuous operation of our system. It ensures that our system can operate efficiently, even in scenarios where conventional power sources may not be readily available.

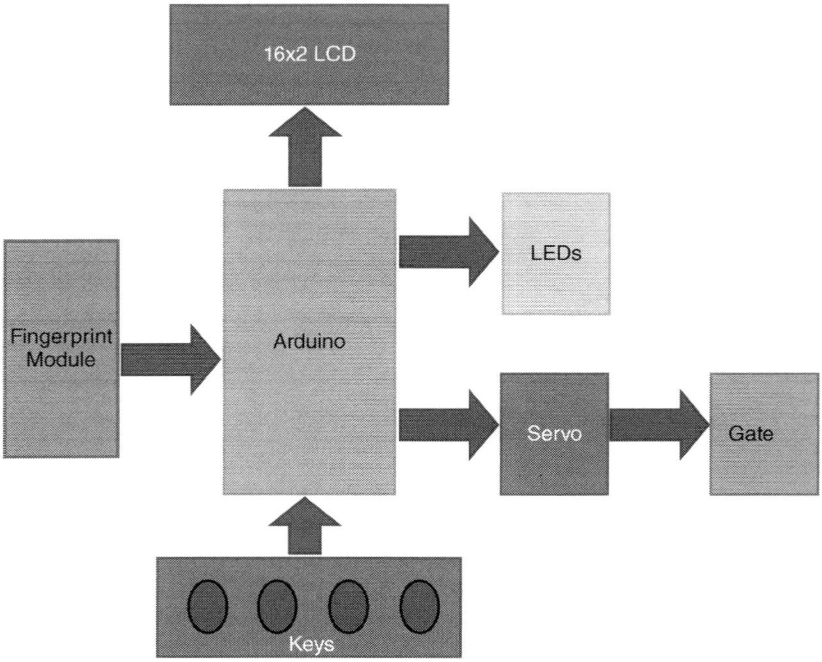

Figure 9.1 Block diagram of the proposed fingerprint security system.

9.3.2 Working of the proposed model

This chapter provides a flow chart as shown in Figure 9.2, detailing the discrete operation of our model, while the upcoming section tabulates the actual display results at each case or step. We used a 16 × 2 LCD display with 5 × 8 (40) pixel dots for each character, totaling 1280 pixels.

In this model, first, we need to enroll our fingerprint in the Adafruit fingerprint sensor by pressing against a smooth surface.

Fingerprint recognition systems operate by analyzing a finger pressed against a smooth surface. The scanner captures the finger's ridges and valleys, identifying minute points where ridges and valleys meet or end. These minutiae serve as reference points for the fingerprint recognition system's comparisons.

To authenticate an individual, the system utilizes the valleys (minutiae) and ridges found on the fingertip's surface. Once your fingerprint matches the one stored, you can cast your vote.

9.4 RESULTS AND DISCUSSION

9.4.1 Experimental setup

Thus, to prevent voting corruption, our research focuses on improving the security protocols of fingerprint-based voting systems. This includes advanced encryption techniques, authentication algorithms, and anti-spoofing measures, as well as making it user-friendly and accessible to everyone. To ensure trust and transparency in democratic elections, we conducted various research related to privacy-preserving biometrics, scalability for large-scale elections, and auditing and monitoring tools and came up with this model. The Experimental setup of the proposed fingerprint security system is shown in Figure 9.3.

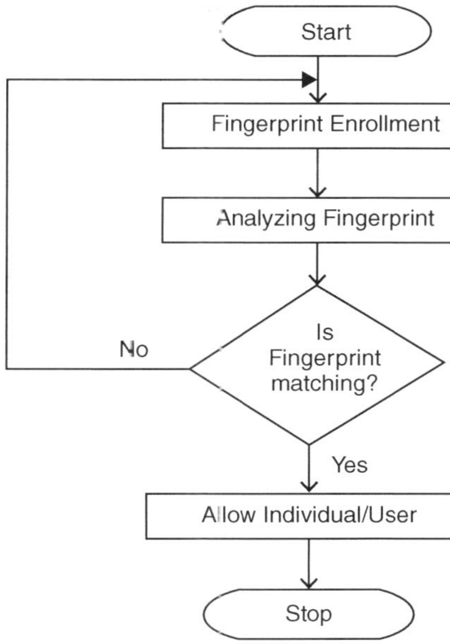

Figure 9.2 Working flowchart of the proposed fingerprint system.

Figure 9.3 Experimental setup.

The accuracy of fingerprint analysis and verification has been tested. This implementation demonstrated a high level of accuracy, correctly verifying fingerprints from the provided database. This accuracy was critical in reducing the risk of double voting and impersonation. The reduction of electoral fraud occurrences prevented voters from casting multiple votes and impersonating others, thereby bolstering the credibility of the electoral system. Large-scale voting systems were able to use the system due to its compatibility with microcontrollers, including the Arduino UNO, which made integration into existing voting infrastructure simple.

The ethical and legal concerns associated with biometric voting systems, as discussed in [13], as well as the fact that they ensure informed consent, data privacy, and adherence to the regulatory framework for biometric voter authentication are paramount when deploying such systems. This implementation, which uses a biometric trait like fingerprints, ensures that

Table 9.1 Realtime scenarios of the voting system

S. No	*Practical figures of the LCD display*	*Action*
1		Press the Enroll Back button to initialize the finger ID
2		Display after initializing the finger ID to 1
3		Image taken after placing the finger
4		Removal of the placed finger
5		Place the finger again to verify the fingerprint. If another finger placed already, press either up match or down match button
6	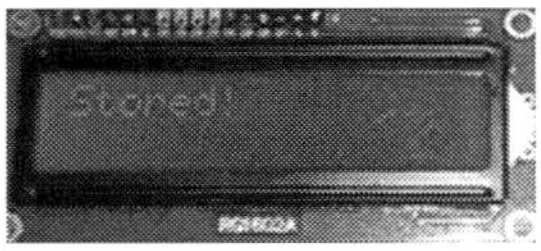	If the fingerprint matches, the ID is stored, else, the display shows 5th step
7		After verification of all fingerprints, press del ok button to cast vote
8		Place the finger again to authorize the candidate/voter
9		If authorized, the vote is submitted
10		If the same finger is placed again for authorization, it shows already voted

voters can easily authenticate themselves without the need for complex procedures, promoting inclusivity and encouraging voter participation. Table 9.1 details the results of the voting mechanism and its procedures.

9.5 CONCLUSION AND FUTURE WORK

Thus, to ensure the integrity of democratic elections, our fingerprint-based security system shows promise in mitigating voting corruption. By combining biometric authentication technology, advanced encryption methods, and tamper-evident safeguards, our systems offer a robust defense against different forms of electoral malpractice, mainly casting multiple votes.

This model, both theoretically and practically, proves the claim as follows: Table 9.1 shows that a person has a mere 0–5% chance of casting another vote, let alone multiple votes. It enhances voter identity verification, reduces opportunities for corruption, and reaffirms democratic principles, offering hope for the future of electoral integrity.

REFERENCES

[1] Jajodia, A.: Fingerprint based electronic voting system. *Journal of Secure Voting Systems*, 1(2), 101–114, 2015.

[2] Smith, B.: Enhancing the Security of E-Voting Systems with Fingerprint Biometrics. *International Journal of Cybersecurity and Digital Forensics*, 7(1), 45–58, 2018.

[3] Ramesh, P., Vidhya, N., Bhuvaneswari, P. T. V., Parveen, S.: I-SOEWM: IoT Based Solar Energized Weather Monitoring System. *Indian Journal of Science and Technology*, 16(20): 1505–1515, 2023.

[4] Patel C.: Biometric-Based Voter Authentication for Election Integrity. *Journal of Cybersecurity and Privacy*, 4(3), 215–228, 2019.

[5] Kumar, S.: Secure E-Voting Using Fingerprint Biometrics: Challenges and Solutions. *International Journal of Information Security and Privacy*, 14(4), 1–18, 2020.

[6] Lee, H.: Mitigating Voter Fraud Through Fingerprint Authentication. *Journal of Election Security*, 9(3), 215–230, 2021

[7] Gonzalez. Ethical and Legal Considerations of Fingerprint Voting Systems. *Journal of Ethics in Technology and Innovation*, 4(1), 34–48, 2022

[8] Wang, X.: Fingerprint Security in Electoral Processes: A Comparative Analysis. *International Journal of Biometric Systems*, 12(2), 150–168, 2023

[9] Jain, A. K. Introduction to Biometric Recognition. *IEEE Transactions on Circuits and Systems for Video Technology, Issue Special on Image and Video Based Biometrics*, 14(1), 2004.

[10] Wildes, R. P.. Iris Recognition: emerging biometric technology, in *Proceedings of the IEEE*, vol. 85, no. 9, pp. 1348–1363, Sept. 1997, doi: 10.1109/5.628669

[11] Jain, A. K. Fingerprint Matching. *IEEE Computer Society*, 43 (2), 36–44, 2010.

[12] Mary, Lourde. Dushyant.: Identifying Fingerprints in Biometric Security Systems. *International Journal of Computer and Electrical Engineering*, 2(5), 1–6, 2010.

[13] Ramesh, P. and Bhuvaneswari, P. T. V.: RFID Aided Intelligent Shopping Trolley with Child Care Unit. In: *International Proceedings on RFID Technology and Applications*. pp. 264–266, Delhi, IEEE, 2021.

Chapter 10

PCG classification using scalogram and CNN classifier

Maibam Mangalleibi Chanu, Ksh. Merina Devi, Khumbongmayum Belona Devi, Preceela Chanu Irengbam, and Shougaijam Neroda Devi

10.1 INTRODUCTION

The world's top cause of death is cardiovascular diseases (CVDs), highlighting the vital role the heart plays in preserving health. The heart and blood vessels that make up the cardiovascular system make sure that the body gets the oxygen and nourishment it needs. The heart must beat nonstop since any interruption might have negative consequences for the brain and other organs. About 17.9 million people worldwide died from CVDs in 2019, making up 32% of all deaths. Heart attacks and strokes were responsible for 85% of these deaths. More than 75% of deaths from CVD happen in low- and middle-income nations. Based on the American Heart Association's report of around 356,000 incidents of out-of-hospital cardiac arrests in the United States each year, 90% of which are due to heart attacks, early detection is critical [1]. The odds of survival are greatly increased by routine monitoring and early diagnosis of heart problems. Heart disease (CVD) is a disease that affects people of all ages and demographics. Its symptoms include perspiration, chest pain, and shortness of breath. Risk factors for serious illnesses including heart attacks and strokes include genetics, smoking, obesity, and diabetes. Auscultation, which records heart sounds and blood flow abnormalities with a stethoscope and phonocardiograph, is still an essential technique for identifying CVD and enabling prompt treatment [2].

The centerpiece of the circulatory system is the heart, a magnificent organ with two atria and two ventricles. The aortic, pulmonary, mitral, and tricuspid valves are the four major valves that work together to maintain unidirectional blood flow in the heart by carefully opening and closing to allow blood to flow forward and stop backflow. Blood is directed from the atria to the ventricles by the mitral and tricuspid valves, and it is regulated from the ventricles to the lungs and the rest of the body by the aortic and pulmonary valves. This complex valve system ensures that blood is circulated smoothly to suit the body's metabolic needs. Systole and diastole are the two separate phases of the rhythmic cardiac cycle that characterize normal heart activity. The ventricles tightly constrict during systole, causing blood to rush into the circulatory system. In contrast, diastole is a resting interval during which the ventricles can fill with blood before the next contraction. Systole and diastole alternate cyclically to maintain constant blood flow, which satisfies the body's metabolic requirements and guarantees that nutrients and oxygen reach tissues on a regular basis. The heart's critical role in preserving general health and vigor is highlighted by the coordinated action of its chambers and valves [3–6].

The heart's rhythm, which normally ranges from 60 to 100 beats per minute, is essential for preserving both efficient blood circulation and maximum cardiac output. The heart's distinctive "lub-dub" noises are produced by vibrations caused by valve motions and the dynamic interaction of the valves with the cardiac cycle. These noises give medical professionals useful auditory information when doing diagnostic evaluations. With the ability

 DOI: 10.1201/9781003513445-10

to capture the relative intensities and timing of heart sounds, phonocardiography (PCG) provides a comprehensive graphical representation of heart sounds and murmurs that can provide valuable information on valve performance. S1, S2, S3, and S4 are the four cardiac sound components that PCG records. S3 and S4 may be signs of abnormal cardiac function, but S1 and S2 are the sounds of normal valve closure and opening. S4 comes right before S1, and S3 comes right after S2 [7–9]. Unusual noises, or murmurs, are often indicative of heart valve dysfunction and can often be heard on PCG recordings. However, a variety of noise sources, such as power frequency interference, electromagnetic interference from the surroundings, electrical impulses from the human body, and lung and respiratory sounds, can impact recordings of heart sounds. PCG is still an essential technique for determining cardiac diseases and heart health despite these difficulties [10].

10.2 DATASET

The PhysioNet/CinC Challenge 2016 dataset is a pivotal resource in cardiovascular research, emphasizing PCG recordings that provide invaluable insights into heart sounds for diagnosing cardiovascular conditions. With 3240 PCG recordings from both healthy and sick individuals in both clinical and non-clinical contexts, the dataset supports tasks such as anomaly identification, segmentation, and classification. These recordings are arranged into six different training datasets, with different numbers of normal and pathological heart sounds in each, labeled training-a through training-f, as shown in Table 10.1. The goal of this extensive dataset is to improve cardiovascular diagnosis, analysis, and therapeutic approaches. The amount of recordings in each dataset varies, with training-e having the most and training-c having the fewest.

Every recording has a unique.wav file name, like "a0001.wav," where "a" stands for the training dataset and "0001" for the particular record. To organize and retrieve PCG recordings for analysis, uniform nomenclature is helpful. Sources [11, 12] have more information about the PhysioNet Challenge 2016 dataset.

10.3 RELATED WORKS

H Wang et al. [13] came up with a system that can monitor and analyze heart sounds to determine whether it is normal or abnormal. Nonetheless, the performance evaluations of the filters used in the system are still low, as they focus more on the analysis aspect. Moreover, they did not provide specific details about the stethoscope design used in their research. HH Alalawi et al. [14] plan to utilize different types of classification techniques for the detection of CVD,

Table 10.1 PhysioNet Challenge 2016 dataset

Dataset Name	*Number of records*	*Normal heart sound*	*Abnormal heart sound*
Training-a	409	117	292
Training-b	490	386	104
Training-c	31	7	24
Training-d	55	27	28
Training-e	2141	1958	183
Training-f	114	80	34
Total	3240	2575	665

like Support Vector Machine, Decision Tree, Logistic Regression, K-Nearest Neighbor, Naïve Bayes, Artificial Neural Network, Random Forest, Voting Classifier & Gradient Boosting. In their study, they found that the Random Forest model achieved the highest performance at 94% accuracy using the heart disease dataset, while the Gradient Boosting model achieved the highest performance at 73% accuracy in the CVD dataset. RJP Princy et al. [15] brought up a solution to predict CVDs by using six machine learning classification algorithms, namely, Decision Tree, K-Nearest Neighbor, Logistic Regression, Naïve Bayes, Random Forest, and Support Vector Machine, applied to the dataset taken from Kaggle. In their research, they found that the decision tree gives better accuracy compared to other classifiers with 78% accuracy in predicting the disease based on the patient's medical records. PB Patil et al. [16] suggested a model to get a satisfied CVD detection. They performed the performance evaluation of three different classifiers, viz., Naïve Bayes, Decision tree, and K-Nearest Neighbor, and checked their accuracy. They prove that CVD detection is satisfied only when the accuracy is more than 95%. M Zabihi et al. [17] also proposed a classification algorithm by choosing s subset of 18 features out of 40 using a wrapper feature selection method. These features are derived from the time, frequency, and time-frequency domains without any segmentation. The chosen features are given as input into an ensemble of 20 feedforward neural networks for classification tasks. The suggested algorithm achieved an overall score of 91.50% (94.23% sensitivity and 88.76% specificity) on the training dataset and 85.90% (86.91% sensitivity and 84.90% specificity) on the unseen test dataset, respectively.

10.4 PROPOSED METHODOLOGY

This section delves into the details of the system, presenting a proposed model as the solution to the identified problem. Adhering to established standards, the model builds upon a pre-trained CNN framework. The progression through various developmental stages forms the narrative structure of the chapter. We delve deeper into the specifics of the dataset sourced from the PhysioNet Challenge 2016. The initial segment outlines the prerequisites that must be met. Following this, the preprocessing steps are elaborated on. Then the process of scalogram generation is further explained. After this, we discuss various pre-trained CNN models applied to our dataset. A workflow diagram visualizes the data flow within the system. Finally, the chapter encapsulates the conclusions drawn from the system's deployment process (Figure 10.1).

10.4.1 Preprocessing

10.4.1.1 Denoising PCG signal using Discrete Wavelet Transform (DWT)

In PCG signal analysis, denoising is essential to keep noise out of the way of feature extraction and classification. PCG data, which monitors heart acoustic activity, frequently contains noise that obscures important heart sound properties. Discrete Wavelet Transform (DWT) provides frequency and temporal information; it is especially useful for nonstationary signals such as PCGs. The DWT method divides signals into multiple levels and extracts crucial high- and low-frequency components using the symlet20 wavelet with 10 decomposition levels and Bayesian soft thresholding. This technique reduces noise while maintaining the features of cardiac sounds. Rebuilding the denoised signal with inverse DWT preserves important characteristics for accurate analysis. By enhancing PCG signal quality—which is essential for precise feature extraction and classification—DWT-based denoising improves signal-to-noise ratio comparisons and visual inspection. By adapting to different signal types and noise levels, this flexibility greatly enhances diagnostic accuracy and lays the groundwork for

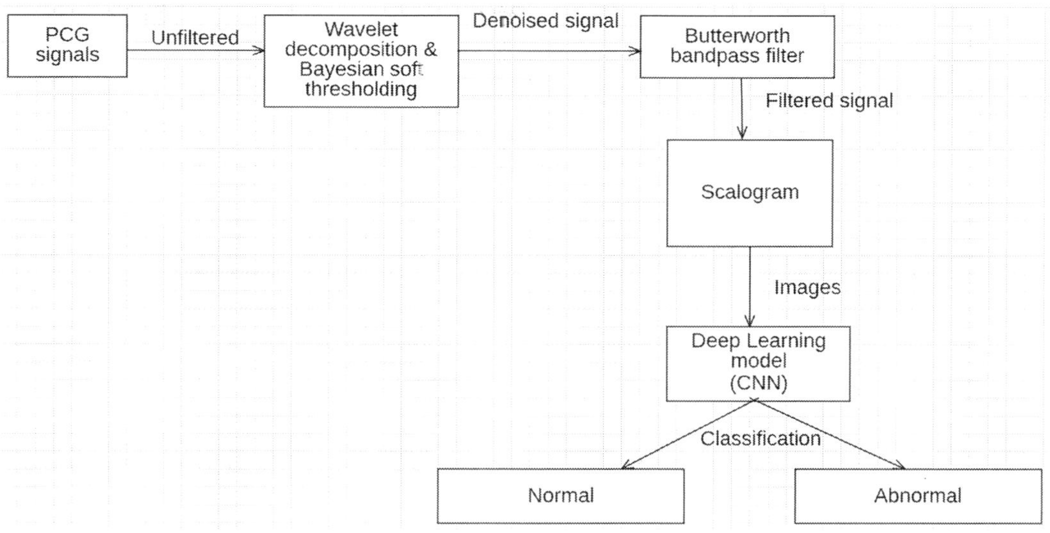

Figure 10.1 Data flow diagram.

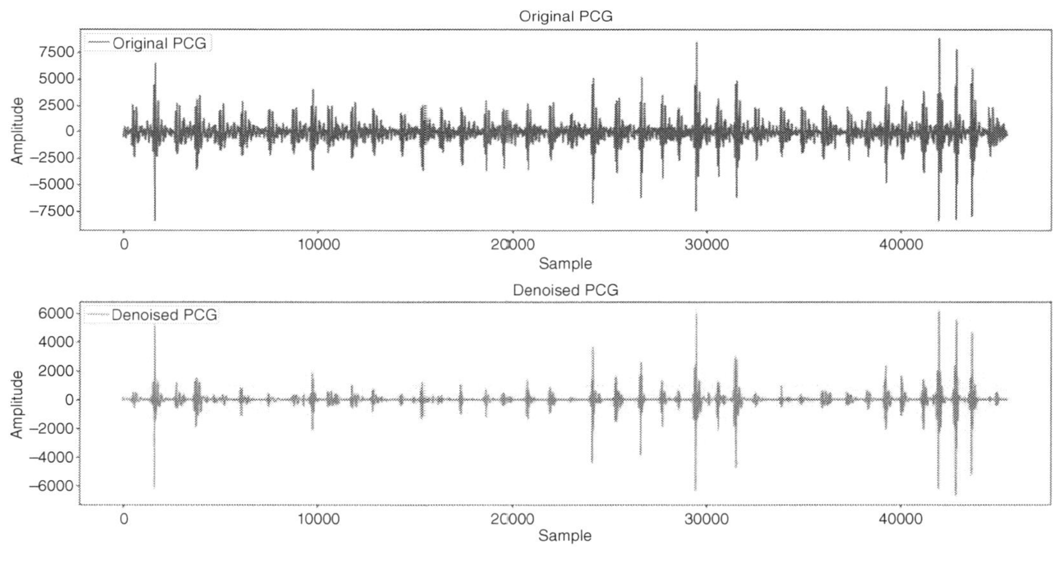

Figure 10.2 Amplitude vs. sample graph showing the difference of training c dataset, c0001.wav after applying the denoising process.

increasingly dependable automated diagnostic systems, which in turn advances cardiovascular diagnostics (Figure 10.2).

10.4.1.2 Butterworth Bandpass Filter

With its "maximally flat magnitude" property, the Butterworth bandpass filter attenuates frequencies outside of its assigned range while guaranteeing a flat frequency response inside the passband. Preprocessing PCG signals is necessary in cardiovascular health monitoring to remove noise and focus on specific frequency bands, usually between 20 and 400 Hz, which

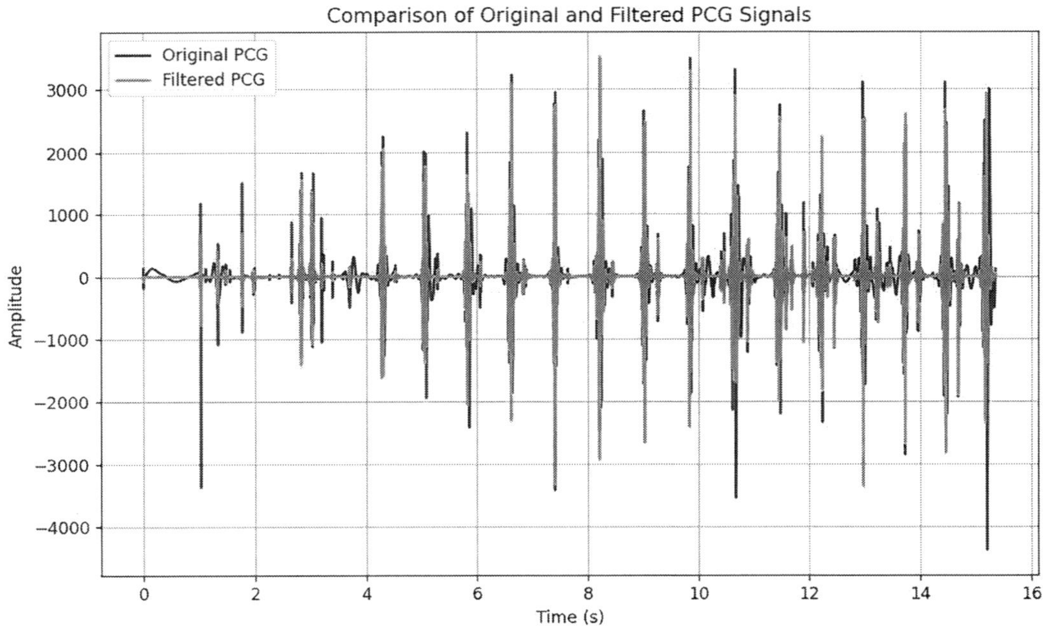

Figure 10.3 Amplitude vs. time graph of filtered d0048.wav.

contain critical components of heart sound. This thesis describes a rigorous preprocessing workflow designed to improve the interpretability and quality of PCG signals. To obtain a uniform sample rate for consistent analysis across datasets, resampling is done after denoising to create a foundation devoid of noise. An order 4 Butterworth filter is carefully applied to the resampled PCG signals, with the filter parameters adjusted to concentrate on the designated frequency range. This filter improves the processed signals' diagnostic value and clarity by cutting noise without compromising signal integrity. After being filtered, the signals are methodically stored for further analysis, guaranteeing that important signal characteristics are retained. This comprehensive preprocessing approach advances automated diagnostic tools and enhances clinical outcomes in cardiovascular medicine by offering a strong basis for precise feature extraction and categorization (Figure 10.3).

10.4.1.3 Scalogram generation

PCG signals are preprocessed and then transformed into 2D scalogram images with 224 × 224 pixels to be fed into a CNN model that has already been trained for classification. Scalograms are useful tools for interpreting complex PCG data because they display signal features in the time-frequency domain. The Continuous Wavelet Transform (CWT) is applied to preprocessed PCG data by defining a variety of scales and using the Morlet wavelet to calculate the similarity between the signal and the wavelet function at different times and scales. This allows for the capture of time-frequency features. The time-frequency content of the signal is highlighted by power values, which are calculated as the squared magnitude of the CWT coefficients. With time and frequency on the axes and color designating signal strength at each location, these values create a 2D matrix or image. By accurately capturing the temporal and spectral characteristics of the signal, this technique advances cardiovascular diagnostics and healthcare by assisting in the identification of patterns associated with cardiac events and disorders (Figures 10.4 and 10.5).

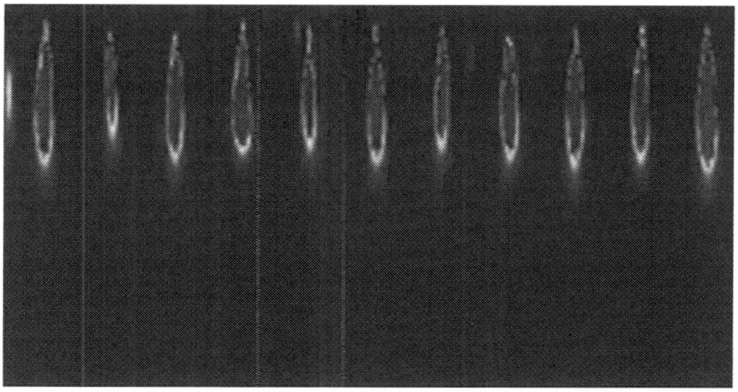

Figure 10.4 Scalogram image of normal heart sound (b0026 from PhysioNet Challenge 2016 dataset).

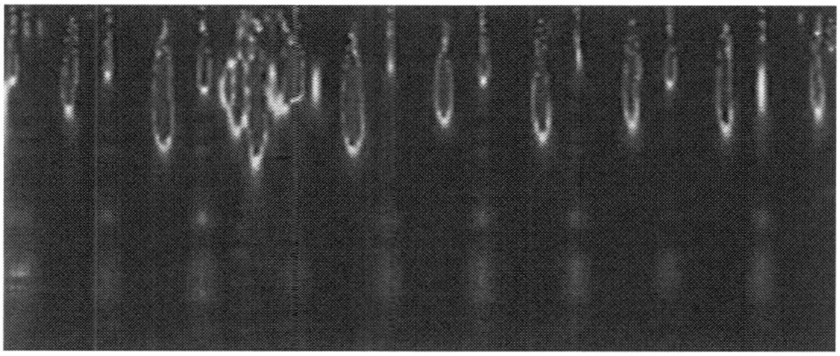

Figure 10.5 Scalogram image of abnormal heart sound (b0040 from PhysioNet Challenge 2016 dataset).

10.4.2 Comparison of models

The classification of the PCG signals was performed using pre-trained CNN models like the variety of VGG model and variety of DenseNet model and comparison is shown in Table 10.2.

10.4.3 VGG19 model

The VGG19 architecture, developed by the Visual Geometry Group (VGG) at the University of Oxford, represents a significant advancement in the design of deep convolutional neural networks for image recognition. Introduced by Simonyan and Zisserman in their seminal 2014 paper, this architecture is characterized by its depth and simplicity, featuring 19 layers that contribute to its powerful feature extraction capabilities. It consists of 16 convolutional layers, five max-pooling layers, and three fully connected layers, culminating in a final softmax layer for classification. Each convolutional layer employs a fixed filter size of 3 × 3 with a stride of 1 and padding of 1, maintaining spatial resolution throughout the network. The convolutional layers are organized into five distinct blocks, with the number of filters increasing progressively: the first block contains 64 filters, the second 128 filters, the third 256 filters, and the fourth and fifth blocks each contain 512 filters. Following each block of convolutional layers, a max-pooling layer with a 2 × 2 window and a stride of 2 is applied, reducing the spatial dimensions by half and enhancing computational efficiency (Figure 10.6).

Table 10.2 Comparison of models

Model	*Drop Out*	*Regularization*	*Epoch*	*Batch Size*	*Test Size*	*Learning Rate*	*Train Accuracy*	*Train Loss*	*Test Accuracy*	*Test Loss*
VGG16	0.4	-	500	81	0.2	0.0001	0.8607	0.3047	0.8349	0.3663
VGG19	0.4	-	250	32	0.2	0.001	0.8681	0.2937	0.8426	0.3716
VGG19	0.3	-	300	16	0.2	0.001	0.8935	0.2289	0.8457	0.3502
VGG19	**0.3**	**-**	**250**	**16**	**0.2**	**0.001**	**0.8954**	**0.2387**	**0.8580**	**0.3406**
DenseNet 121	0.4	-	200	64	0.2	0.001	0.9845	0.0423	0.8194	0.6912
DenseNet 121	0.4	-	200	16	0.1	0.001	0.9663	0.0786	0.8302	0.9256
DenseNet 169	0.4	12(0.001)	100	16	0.2	0.001	0.8654	0.3491	0.8441	0.4442
DenseNet 169	0.4	-	200	32	0.2	0.001	0.9990	0.0125	0.8457	0.6366
DenseNet 201	0.4	-	200	32	0.2	0.001	0.9834	0.0431	0.8302	0.9205

The transition from convolutional layers to fully connected layers involves flattening the feature maps, which are then processed by two fully connected layers with 4096 neurons each, and a final fully connected layer with 1000 neurons corresponding to the 1000 classes in the ImageNet dataset. The network concludes with a softmax activation function that outputs class probabilities. The uniform architecture of VGG19, characterized by the repetitive use of 3 × 3 convolutional filters, facilitates the learning of complex features while maintaining implementation simplicity. This design has proven highly effective in large-scale image recognition tasks and has influenced numerous subsequent neural network models. VGG19's robustness and adaptability make it a valuable tool for various computer vision applications, including image classification, object detection, and image segmentation.

10.5 EXPERIMENTS AND RESULT DISCUSSION

The model was trained over different pre-trained CNN models with different parameters. Specifically, for VGG19, the number of epochs is set to 250 epochs with a dropout value of 0.3, splitting the dataset into training and testing datasets as 80% and 20%, respectively, allowed for an accurate assessment of the model's performance on unrested data, with the learning rate set to 0.001. The data was processed in batches of 16 samples during training to maintain a balance between computational efficiency and weight update accuracy. It is observed that the model was able to gradually approach optimal performance by making fine-grained modifications to its weights. By the end of the training procedure, this combination of parameters had successfully produced a well-trained and broadly applicable model with training and testing accuracies of 89.54% and 85.80%, respectively (Figures 10.7 and 10.8).

The image's confusion matrix offers a thorough performance summary of a classification model, emphasizing the different kinds of errors and their accuracy. 489 cases were correctly classified as abnormal (True Negative) and 67 instances as normal (True Positive) by the model. It did, however, make some errors as well, misclassifying 26 abnormal instances as normal (False Negative) and 66 normal instances as abnormal (False Positive). The sensitivity (True Positive rate) and specificity (True Negative rate) balance, which are critical for comprehending the model's efficacy in accurately identifying both normal and abnormal instances, are reflected in this matrix, which is essential for assessing the diagnostic ability of the model.

The graph in Figure 10.9 shows the model accuracy and model loss in a pictorial graph format to provide valuable insight into the performance of the model.

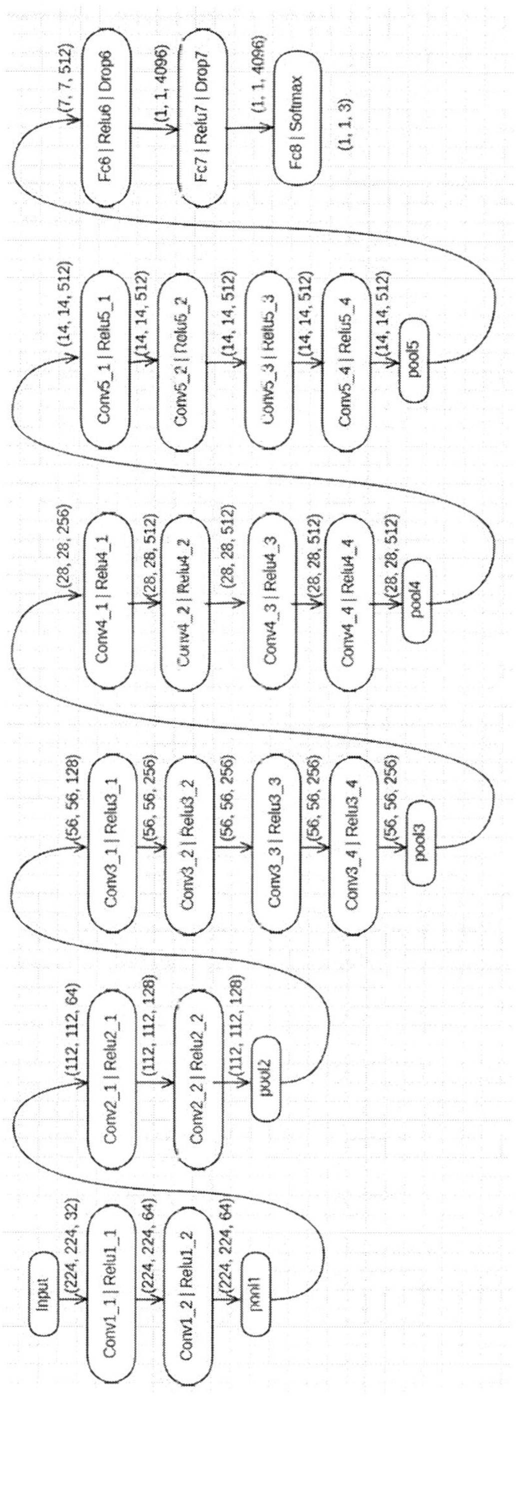

Figure 10.6 VGG19 architecture.

```
Code + Text
Epoch 236/250
162/162 [==============================] - 18s 113ms/step - loss: 0.2522 - accuracy: 0.8866 - val_loss: 0.3409 - val_accuracy: 0.8549
Epoch 237/250
162/162 [==============================] - 16s 102ms/step - loss: 0.2499 - accuracy: 0.8931 - val_loss: 0.3326 - val_accuracy: 0.8704
Epoch 238/250
162/162 [==============================] - 16s 102ms/step - loss: 0.2429 - accuracy: 0.8927 - val_loss: 0.3441 - val_accuracy: 0.8596
Epoch 239/250
162/162 [==============================] - 18s 114ms/step - loss: 0.2474 - accuracy: 0.8912 - val_loss: 0.3281 - val_accuracy: 0.8596
Epoch 240/250
162/162 [==============================] - 17s 102ms/step - loss: 0.2470 - accuracy: 0.8870 - val_loss: 0.3390 - val_accuracy: 0.8611
Epoch 241/250
162/162 [==============================] - 16s 102ms/step - loss: 0.2372 - accuracy: 0.8935 - val_loss: 0.3812 - val_accuracy: 0.8364
Epoch 242/250
162/162 [==============================] - 16s 102ms/step - loss: 0.2662 - accuracy: 0.8804 - val_loss: 0.3559 - val_accuracy: 0.8426
Epoch 243/250
162/162 [==============================] - 18s 113ms/step - loss: 0.2487 - accuracy: 0.8912 - val_loss: 0.3602 - val_accuracy: 0.8457
Epoch 244/250
162/162 [==============================] - 18s 113ms/step - loss: 0.2426 - accuracy: 0.8935 - val_loss: 0.3392 - val_accuracy: 0.8565
Epoch 245/250
162/162 [==============================] - 17s 102ms/step - loss: 0.2498 - accuracy: 0.8935 - val_loss: 0.3796 - val_accuracy: 0.8364
Epoch 246/250
162/162 [==============================] - 16s 102ms/step - loss: 0.2405 - accuracy: 0.8916 - val_loss: 0.3508 - val_accuracy: 0.8534
Epoch 247/250
162/162 [==============================] - 16s 102ms/step - loss: 0.2392 - accuracy: 0.8962 - val_loss: 0.3677 - val_accuracy: 0.8580
Epoch 248/250
162/162 [==============================] - 18s 113ms/step - loss: 0.2424 - accuracy: 0.8966 - val_loss: 0.3348 - val_accuracy: 0.8534
Epoch 249/250
162/162 [==============================] - 16s 102ms/step - loss: 0.2418 - accuracy: 0.8981 - val_loss: 0.3522 - val_accuracy: 0.8580
Epoch 250/250
162/162 [==============================] - 18s 113ms/step - loss: 0.2387 - accuracy: 0.8954 - val_loss: 0.3406 - val_accuracy: 0.8580
21/21 [==============================] - 10s 153ms/step - loss: 0.3406 - accuracy: 0.8580

Test accuracy: 0.8580247163772583
21/21 [==============================] - 3s 158ms/step
```

Figure 10.7 Epoch = 250, learning_rate = 0.001, test_size = 0.2, batch_size = 16, dropout = 0.3.

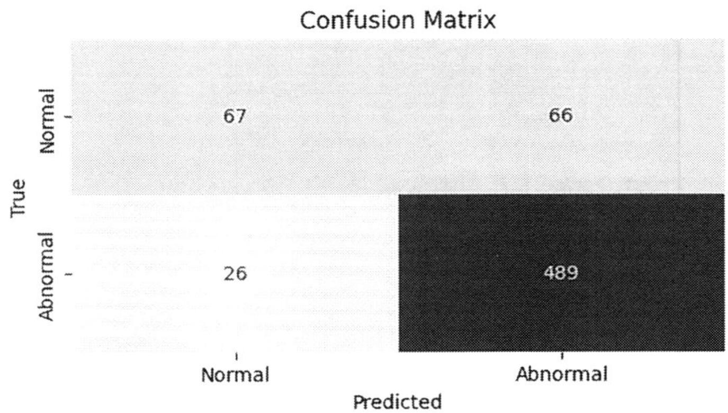

Figure 10.8 Confusion matrix.

10.6 CONCLUSION AND FUTURE WORKS

This project presents a powerful method for classifying a person's cardiac normalcy or abnormality based on PCG signals using a Convolutional Neural Network (CNN), specifically the VGG19 architecture. Our study demonstrates the effectiveness of the CNN model in reliably and precisely differentiating between normal and pathological cardiac states through rigorous design, training, and evaluation. By leveraging the potent feature extraction capabilities of VGG19, our model effectively captures complex patterns within PCG signals, enabling automated and accurate categorization.

The application of VGG19 represents a noteworthy advancement in cardiovascular diagnostics, providing physicians and healthcare workers with a valuable tool for the prompt and

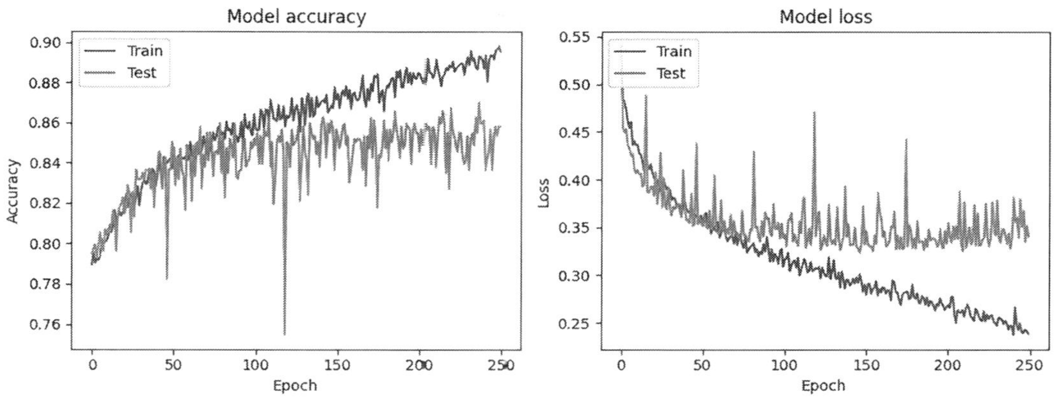

Figure 10.9 Accuracy-loss graph.

efficient assessment of cardiac health. The successful implementation of CNN, particularly VGG19, underscores its potential to revolutionize the diagnosis and treatment of CVDs, paving the way for improved patient care and clinical outcomes in cardiac medicine.

Future research and development in this area hold promise for further enhancing the performance and applicability of CNN models in real-world healthcare settings. This advancement is anticipated to benefit individuals worldwide by enabling early detection and intervention for cardiac conditions, ultimately improving patient care and clinical outcomes.

In our model, we have fed the scalogram images into the VGG19 model and have achieved 89.5% and 85.8% for training accuracy and testing accuracy, respectively. We expect this project to benefit people's health. In future research, accuracy can be improved further, possible approaches include refining the data preprocessing technique and fine-tuning the model.

REFERENCES

[1] https://physionet.org/challenge/2016/ Last accessed on April 5, 2024.

[2] S. Daliman and A.Z. Sha'ameri, "Time-frequency analysis of heart sounds and murmurs," in Fourth International Conference on Information, Communications and Signal Processing, 2003 and the Fourth Pacific Rim Conference on Multimedia. Proceedings of the 2003 Joint, 2003, pp. 840–843.

[3] S.A. Singh et al., "Enhancing Imbalanced Heart Sound Classification through Transfer Learning and Gammatonegram Image Analysis", November 2023.

[4] https://www.who.int/news-room/fact-sheets/detail/cardiovascular-diseases-(cvds) Last accessed May 22, 2024.

[5] C. Tsao, A. Aday et al., "Heart disease and stroke statistics-2022 update: a report from the American Heart Association. Circulation", https://doi.org/10.1161/CIR.0000000000001052

[6] K.M. Devi, M.M. Chanu, et al., "Classification of unsegmented phonocardiogram signal using scalogram and deep learning", *Soft Computing* 27, 12677–12689 (2023). https://doi.org/10.1007/s00500-023-08834-1

[7] Aubrey Leatham, "Phonocardiography", *British Medical Bulletin* 8(4), 333–342 (1952).

[8] M. Salvatore, L.Z. Nieman, "Cardiac auscultatory skills of internal medicine and family practice trainees: a comparison of diagnostic proficiency", *JAMA* 278(9), 717–722 (1997).

[9] T.R. Reed, N.E. Reed, P. Fritzson, "Heart sound analysis for symptom detection and computer-aided diagnosis", *Simulation Modelling Practice and Theory* 12, 129–146 (2003).

[10] KAGGLE, Cardiovascular Disease dataset, 2020.

[11] Chengyu Liu et al., "An open access database for the evaluation of heart sound algorithms", *Physiological Measurement* 37, 2181–2213 (2016). https://doi.org/10.1088/0967-3334/37/12/2181
[12] Goldberger AL, Amaral LAN, Glass L, Hausdorf JM, Ivanov PC, Mark RG, et al., "PhysioBank, PhysioToolkit, and PhysioNet: components of a new research resource for complex physiologic signals", *Circulation* 101, e215–e220 (2000). https://doi.org/10.1161/01.CIR.101.23.e215
[13] H. Wang, J. Chen, et al., "Heart Sound Measurement and Analysis System with Digital Stethoscope", Sichuan Education Department Natural Science Key Project, 2009, 2nd International Conference on Biomedical Engineering and Informatics, Tianjin, China, 2009, pp. 1–5, doi: 10.1109/BMEI.2009.5305287
[14] Hana H. Alalawi, Manal S. Alsuwat, "Detection of Cardiovascular Disease using Machine Learning Classification Models", ijert, issn: 2278-0181, 07 July 2021.
[15] R. J. P. Princy, S. Parthasarathy, P. S. H. Jose, A. R. Lakshminarayanan, and S. Jeganathan, "Prediction of Cardiac Disease using Supervised Machine Learning Algorithms," in 2020 4th International Conference on Intelligent Computing and Control Systems (ICICCS), 2020, pp. 570–575.
[16] P.B. Patil, P.M. Shastry, P.S. Ashokumar, "Machine Learning based algorithm for risk prediction of cardiovascular disease (CVD)", *Journal of Critical Reviews*, 9(9), 2020.
[17] Morteza Zabihi, Ali Bahrami Rad, et al. "Heart Sound Anomaly and Quality Detection using Ensemble of Neural Networks without Segmentation." IEEE, 2016 Computing in Cardiology Conference (CinC), 2017.

Chapter 11

Unlocking AI's potential for optimizing personalized treatment plans and predicting lung cancer

V. S. Vetri Selvi and P. Deepalakshmi

11.1 INTRODUCTION

In the relentless pursuit of enhancing early detection and prognostic accuracy in lung cancer, the integration of Artificial Intelligence (AI) and Machine Learning (ML) has emerged as a transformative force. Nowadays, cancer is the world's top cause of death for both men and women, and because of inadequate detection methods, survival rates are poor. Lately, researchers have been coming up with ways to make predictions perform better. Image augmentation can further boost prediction performance in medical image processing [1]. Lung cancer is still a major worldwide health concern, and its incidence, mortality, and morbidity highlight the critical need for novel strategies in prevention and treatment. This review of the literature explores the field of cutting-edge research at the nexus of artificial intelligence and healthcare, with a particular emphasis on the use of AI and ML approaches to the prediction and comprehension of lung cancer. Our capacity to extract useful insights to guide clinical decision-making from enormous volumes of heterogeneous data, such as genetic profiles and medical imaging, is growing along with technology. The application of AIML to healthcare has the possibility of not just predicting diseases with previously unheard-of accuracy but also revealing hidden patterns in sophisticated biological systems. In order to shed light on the current level of knowledge, major obstacles, and future directions in this rapidly evolving subject, this review attempts to thoroughly examine the wide range of studies, methodology, and developments in lung cancer prediction. Through a review of the literature, we hope to shed light on the many aspects of AIML-based lung cancer prediction. The traits of AI lung cancer models are multiplicity, repeatability, high efficiency, and objectivity. Without a doubt, this will lessen the workload for doctors, cut down on fatigue-related misdiagnosis, and maybe alter the way medicine is now practiced. In order to increase the precision of disease risk prediction, detection, and treatment response prediction, an increasing number of AI models are being used to monitor diverse data, such as electronic health record data, imaging modalities, histology, and molecular biomarkers [2]. This survey aims to distill the collective wisdom of researchers contributing to the ongoing paradigm shift in lung cancer diagnostics and prognostics, from the development of sophisticated predictive models to the integration of diverse omics data and the quest for explainability in AI predictions. With this investigation, we hope to contribute to the larger discussion on how AIML will influence lung cancer prediction in the future by providing an overview of the approaches used, the advancements made, and the directions still to be pursued.

11.2 CURRENT LANDSCAPE OF LUNG CANCER PREDICTION

The application of AIML has caused a paradigm change in the field of lung cancer prediction. Conventional diagnostic methods frequently have drawbacks, especially in the early

DOI: 10.1201/9781003513445-11

Table 11.1 Current landscape of lung cancer prediction vs. traditional diagnostic approach

Aspect	*Traditional diagnostic approaches*	*AIML in lung cancer prediction*
Early Detection	Relies on symptoms or visible abnormalities	Excels in detecting subtle patterns in early stages
Data Analysis	Limited by manual interpretation	Analyzes vast datasets with speed and precision
Pattern Recognition	Relatively subjective and experience-dependent	Employs advanced algorithms for objective recognition
Diagnostic Speed	Time-consuming, and may lead to delayed intervention	Rapid analysis facilitates timely and proactive care
Customization for Individuals	Generic approaches for a broad population	Tailors predictions based on individual patient data
Integration of Diverse Data Sources	Often focuses on a single type of data	Integrates multi-omics data for a comprehensive view
Predictive Accuracy	Variable and dependent on human expertise	Demonstrates high accuracy with machine learning
Explanatory Power	Limited ability to explain complex diagnostic cues	Advances in explainable AI provide interpretability
Impact on Intervention Strategies	May miss subtle indications for targeted treatment	Facilitates precision medicine and personalized care
Clinical Adoption	Mainstream but faces challenges in certain contexts	Gaining acceptance as technology and trust evolve

stages when the most effective interventions might be made. As shown in Table 11.1, AIML has the potential to completely transform early detection because of its capacity to evaluate enormous datasets and identify complex patterns.

11.3 METHODOLOGIES AND MODELS IN AIML FOR LUNG CANCER PREDICTION

A thorough analysis of the models and techniques used in AIML-based lung cancer prediction is essential to comprehend the extent of innovation in this area. Scholars and researchers have investigated many methodologies, ranging from deep neural networks to supervised learning algorithms, to get significant insights from heterogeneous datasets. The complexities of various approaches are examined in this part, along with their advantages, disadvantages, and individual contributions to the overall objective of accurate and trustworthy lung cancer prediction. Table 11.2 shows the methodologies and models in AIML used for lung cancer prediction.

11.4 INTEGRATION OF MULTI-OMICS DATA

A plethora of biological data has been made available by the genomic age, and the integration of multi-omics data is at the forefront of efforts to forecast lung cancer more comprehensively and accurately. As shown in Table 11.3, by combining transcriptomics, proteomics, and genome data using AIML techniques, it may be possible to find previously undiscovered connections and new predictive markers. The attempts to combine various omics data sources are discussed in this part, along with the successes and setbacks encountered when utilizing extensive molecular profiles for predictive modeling.

Table 11.2 Methodologies and models in AIML for lung cancer prediction

Methodology/ model	*Description*	*Strengths*	*Limitations*	*Unique contributions*
Supervised Learning Algorithms	Utilizes labeled training data to learn patterns	Well-established, effective in classification	Reliance on labeled data, may not generalize well	Foundation for benchmark models
Deep Neural Networks (DNNs)	Hierarchical structure of interconnected neurons	Captures complex patterns, feature extraction	Demands large datasets, computationally intensive	Enables automatic feature learning
Ensemble Learning	Combines predictions from multiple models	Improved robustness, generalization	Increased complexity, potential for overfitting	Enhances overall predictive performance
Transfer Learning	Adapts knowledge from pre-trained models to new tasks	Efficient with limited labeled data	Task dependency, may not always transfer well	Facilitates learning from related domains
Support Vector Machines (SVM	Maps data into high-dimensional space for classification	Effective in high-dimensional feature spaces	Sensitivity to kernel selection, not suitable for large datasets	Robust performance in certain scenarios
Random Forests	Ensemble of decision trees for classification	Robust against overfitting, handles noisy data	Less interpretable, complex models	Excellent for capturing non-linear relationships
Convolutional Neural Networks (CNNs)	Specialized for processing structured grid data	Effective in image-based data, hierarchical feature extraction	Computationally intensive, requires large datasets	Dominant in medical imaging applications

Table 11.4 shows the various tests available to measure the percentage of cancer cells spread in the lungs. Cancer staging is treated as one of the critical steps in the diagnosis process since we can choose the treatment plan, indication, and evaluation of the treatment based on what stage it is. A chest X-ray is the first basic step every physician would recommend to go with. Next, CT scans are more likely used to take cross-sectional images of our body, unlike regular scans. In positron emission tomography (PET), a radioactive sugar form is injected into human blood and it mainly exposes all the cancer cells. A few tests are used to diagnose lung cancer like sputum cytology, thoracentesis, needle biopsy, and bronchoscopy. Sputum cytology is used to detect cancer that spreads by the mucus through the airways. Thoracentesis is used to find cancer cells in the lining of the lung by collecting some sample liquids from a particular area in the lungs. In needle biopsy, a small sharp-fine needle is used to collect samples from the particular targeted area. Bronchoscopy is used to find blocks or the presence of tumors in the windpipe.

In order to locate and highlight malignant cells in microscopic or medical imaging data, a sequence of image processing and analysis procedures are commonly used in visual flow lung cancer cell identification. As shown in Figure 11.1, this is a quick summary of how lung cancer cell detection works visually:

- Preprocessing
- Image Acquisition
- Noise Reduction

Table 11.3 Summary of integrating multi-omics data in lung cancer prediction

Aspect	*Description*	*Advantages*	*Challenges*	*Key findings*
Types of Omics Data	Genomics, Transcriptomics, Proteomics	Holistic understanding of molecular mechanisms	Data heterogeneity, integration complexity	Synergistic insights into molecular interactions
AIML Techniques Used	Machine Learning Models (e.g., SVM, NeuralNetworks)	Extraction of patterns from diverse data sources	Computational intensity, model interpretability	Robust predictive models for omics integration
Discovering Connections	Identification of Interactions and Correlations	Uncovering novel associations within omics datasets	False positives, validation of discovered connections	Novel predictive markers and pathways discovered
Predictive Modeling Success	Accurate Prediction of Lung Cancer Outcomes	Improved precision and sensitivity in prediction	Overfitting, generalizability to diverse populations	Enhanced accuracy in lung cancer prediction
Challenges in Data Integration	Data Heterogeneity, Integration Complexity	Comprehensive integration for a unified analysis	Standardization issues, missing data handling	Addressing challenges crucial for robust results
Successes in Omics Integration	Comprehensive Molecular Profiles for Predictive Modeling	Enhanced understanding of complex biological systems	Identifying optimal integration strategies	Improved accuracy in predictive modeling
Setbacks and Lessons Learned	Validation Challenges, Interpretability Issues	Validation Challenges, Interpretability Issues	Importance of robust validation in predictive models	Insights for refining future integration efforts

Table 11.4 Tests to find out the amount of cancer spread in lungs

Method	*Description*
Endobronical ultrasound	Performed by the pulmonologist, it is used to find the presence of any infections, disorders, malfunctioning, or cancer traces by using a long flexible thin tube.
Mediastinoscopy and mediastinotomy	This is commonly a visualization technique where a small cut is made in the neck and small imaging scopes are inserted to capture images of the much-needed areas.
Thoracoscopy	This test is hugely used to find the spread of cancer cells between the thin walls of the lungs and chest.

- Segmentation
- Region of Interest (ROI) Selection
- Cell Segmentation
- Feature Extraction
- Cellular Features
- Contextual Features
- Classification
- Machine Learning Models
- Thresholding

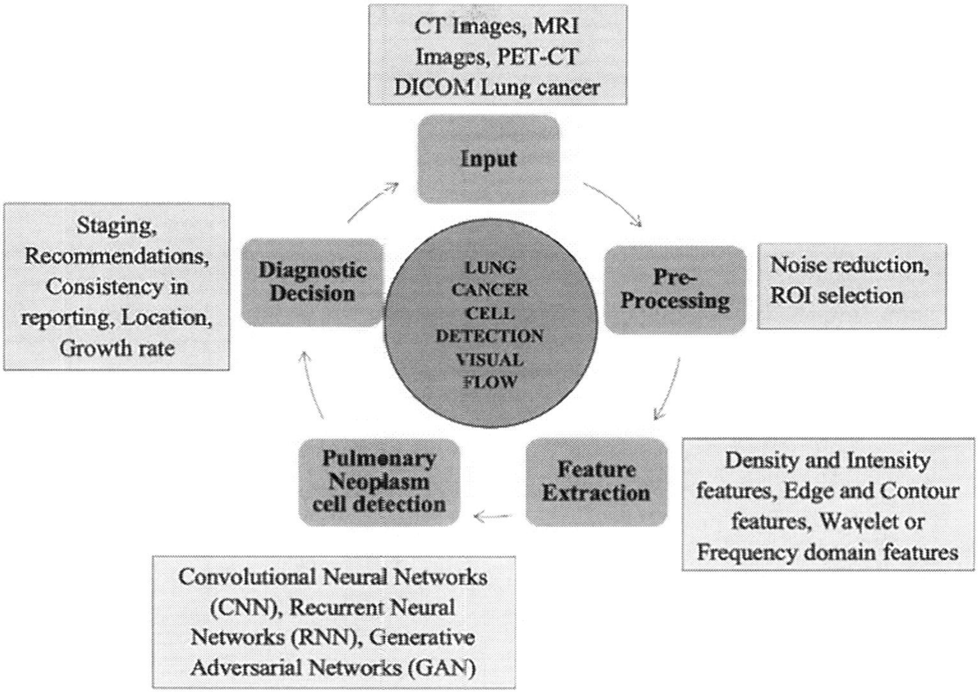

Figure 11.1 Visual flow of lung cancer cell detection.

- Post-processing
- Morphological Operations
- Connectivity Analysis
- Visualization
- Overlay and Annotation
- Heatmaps
- Evaluation
- Performance Metrics
- Validation

11.5 LITERATURE SURVEY ON VARIOUS AI TECHNOLOGIES USED FOR LUNG CANCER PREDICTION

Sharmila Nageswaran (2022) proposed that computer-aided diagnosis (CAD) systems play a vital role in the detection of lung cancer cells at an earlier stage. The need for image processing for better outcomes is also insisted. To reduce the dimensionality of the lung cancer image matrix, Linear Discriminant Analysis (LDA) is proposed to enhance the classification process. Artificial Neural Networks (ANNs) are noted to be performing better for the classification tasks. ANN has the capability to do all the tasks a human brain can do. The structure of ANN has three standard layers namely the input layer, the hidden layer, and the output layer. The weight adjustments should be made to get the desired planned output. The number of hidden layers present is said to affect the performance of the neural network. To make the training phase faster, a technique called K-Nearest Neighbor is being used which makes use of data which is organized earlier. However, it becomes slower and memory-sensitive [3].

Michaela Cellina (2022) highlights the significance of early lung cancer diagnosis and the role of AI in improving screening processes. It is emphasized that early diagnosis significantly increases the chances of survival, contrasting the poor prognosis associated with delayed diagnosis. The paper also mentions the limitations of traditional screening methods using chest X-rays and the effectiveness of low-dose CT (LDCT) screening in reducing lung cancer mortality. Further, it highlights the eligibility criteria for CT screening programs in the United States and the challenges in implementing population-scale screening due to workload and documentation issues. Additionally, it discusses the development of CAD systems in lung cancer screening and the importance of high-quality datasets for training deep learning models. The related paragraph also mentions the differentiation between benign and malignant pulmonary nodules as a crucial step in the diagnostic process. Various CNN-based approaches that achieve high classification accuracy are highlighted for this purpose:

- Zhang et al. employed the **DenseNet architecture with 3D filters and pooling kernels,** achieving 92.4% accuracy in classifying nodules.
- Al-Shabi et al. introduced the **Gated-Dilated CNN architecture**, which reached an accuracy of 92.57% and an AUC of 0.95 when distinguishing between malignant and benign nodules.

Immunotherapy, an innovative approach to cancer treatment, leverages the tumor environment by activating immunological responses. While it has demonstrated potential in improving lung cancer patient outcomes with impressive survival rates, its widespread adoption is hindered by high expenses and associated toxicities. Furthermore, its clinical benefits have primarily been observed in patients with PDL-1-positive expression. However, there are several hurdles to overcome in order to implement these systems effectively in clinical settings. Collaborative efforts among institutions are essential, as AI tool development demands extensive datasets. Furthermore, the establishment of guidelines is necessary to structure and ensure the reliability of AI-driven research. AI possesses boundless capabilities, and its gradual integration into healthcare may rise in an era of personalized medicine [4].

Jieli Zhou (2022) focused on locating and categorizing objects of interest within CT volume images. Previous research has effectively applied object detection techniques to identify lung nodules. For example, an end-to-end deep learning approach was introduced for lung cancer screening, which initially trained a model to detect regions of interest (ROIs). This study developed a three-dimensional deep convolutional neural network (CNN) model to detect lung nodules. A persistent challenge in lung nodule detection is the limited availability of training data compared to the diverse nature of lung nodules. To address this challenge, Generative Adversarial Networks (GANs) were introduced. GANs have been successfully applied in the medical domain to generate synthetic training data, improving performance in various medical image analysis tasks. For lung nodule detection, a GAN-based approach known as 3D Multi-Conditional GAN (MCGAN) was put into practice [5].

zsMCGAN generates highly realistic and diverse lung nodules, which resemble more like real nodules, and is difficult to find the difference even by expert physicians. Beyond GANs, several other deep learning techniques, including semi-supervised, unsupervised, and domain adaptation methods, have been proposed to address the limited data challenges in medical imaging analysis. These techniques hold the potential to further aid in the detection of lung nodules. Recent research has demonstrated the efficacy of integrating clinical, physiological, and genomic data to augment lung cancer management. The main focus was to cut down deep learning methodologies tailored for the detection and diagnosis of lung nodules within CT imaging data.

Ziegelmayer et al. (2022) focused on a special math method called variance analysis to find many important factors to see which one works best to tell us who might get cancer again or how long people will live. These factors include things like a person's race, gender, and the stage of their cancer. It is also found that certain gene changes in the cancer cells can make a difference in how long someone survives. Some genetic changes, like mutations in genes called EGFR and KRAS, also matter. So, in a nutshell, this study used computers to figure out what factors are important for predicting what happens to people with lung cancer. The researchers conducted a cost-effectiveness analysis using computer simulations to assess the value of using AI in combination with CT scans for medical diagnosis. They ran these simulations for a 20-year period with 20 iterations. In their base-case scenario, they assumed that the cost of using CT with AI was the same as using CT alone. In terms of results, after running simulations for 20 years, they found that the cumulative costs for CT with AI were slightly lower than those for CT alone in the base case scenario. They also measured effectiveness in terms of QALYs, and the difference between CT with AI and CT alone was marginal [6].

Fangwei Wang (2022) [7] proposed a method to find special signs in the body to help detect and treat a type of lung cancer called Non-small cell lung cancer (NSCLC). They used two different computer methods: one called LASSO logistic and another called SVM-RFE. These methods found a total of 26 and 40 characteristic genes, respectively. Early-stage NSCLC often shows no symptoms, making early treatment difficult. Additionally, the tendency of the cancer to spread to other parts of the body, known as metastasis, is a major cause of high mortality rates. They found eight genes that might be helpful: ADAMTS8, ABCA8, TPX2, CEP55, ASPA, FHL1, RAMP3, and PYCR1. These genes do different things in the body and could be important for treating cancer. They also found that a type of immune cell called monocytes might be involved in the cancer. One gene, TPX2, seems to make the cancer worse and a detailed study was made later. They used computer methods to find these genes, which are like smart tools. This discovery could help doctors diagnose and treat NSCLC better. A special analysis was used to see how good these eight biomarkers were at diagnosing NSCLC apart from normal conditions. The results showed that all eight biomarkers were very good at doing this job, with high sensitivity and specificity. In simple terms, these genes could be useful for detecting NSCLC accurately [7].

Hwa-Yen Chiu (2022) focuses on AI applications in lung cancer, categorizing them based on the clinical workflow: screening, diagnosis, decision-making, and prognosis prediction. This study describes a standard format called DICOM for storing and sharing medical images. It's like a special language that computers and machines understand. DICOM makes it easier to send and analyze medical images. They can quickly share images and use computers to study them. AI is a helpful tool in treating lung cancer in several ways.

- *Medication selection*: In advanced lung cancer, AI helps doctors choose the right treatment by considering genetic factors and other information. It predicts how well patients will respond to different medicines.
- *Surgery*: AI is used to plan surgeries and predict how well patients will do afterward. It helps decide if patients need extra treatment after surgery.
- *Radiotherapy*: For early-stage lung cancer, AI helps predict if cancer will come back after radiation therapy. It also helps prevent a serious side effect called radiation pneumonitis.

Overall, AI is like a helpful assistant to doctors, making treatment decisions easier and more precise for lung cancer patients [8].

11.6 COMPARATIVE STUDY

This assortment of varied research works on artificial intelligence's role in lung cancer prognosis as shown in Table 11.5 captures the ever-changing field of AI applications in healthcare. Diverse approaches have been used on diverse datasets, including image processing techniques, deep learning models, and machine learning algorithms (SVM, Decision tree, Naïve Bayes). The results demonstrate remarkable 100% accuracy and have applications in biomarker detection, multi-omics data integration, and image improvement. AI's adaptability is demonstrated by the integration of cutting-edge technology such as CNNs and novel methodologies like collaborative filtering and ensemble learning. The research also stresses the significance of real-time forecasts, explainable AI, and customized treatment strategies. Research is still being conducted since issues like interpretability and data scarcity are still present. Together, the data show how AI has the potential to completely transform the diagnosis and treatment of lung cancer, with an emphasis on precision, effectiveness, and individualized medical care.

11.7 CONCLUSION

This chapter provides an overview of how various AI algorithms have become valuable tools in the field of lung cancer research and clinical practice. These algorithms leverage the power of machine learning and deep learning techniques to analyze various data sources, aiding in the detection, diagnosis, treatment, and management of lung cancer. In a nutshell, AI will make it easier to find, treat, and understand cancer. It's like having a super-smart assistant for doctors, improving patient care, and increasing our chances of beating cancer. The best-fit technologies and methods for finding at an earlier stage, checking from home, fewer painful tests, predicting what might happen next, and following tailor-made treatments.

11.8 EMERGING TRENDS AND FUTURE DIRECTIONS

Lung cancer is still a major worldwide health concern since it is a common and potentially fatal disease. A ground-breaking development in healthcare is the integration of AI and ML in the prediction of lung cancer. AI systems show previously unheard-of promise for early diagnosis and prognosis accuracy by evaluating large and diverse datasets. This study examines how lung cancer prediction is changing by thoroughly examining the models and techniques used today. Researchers are pushing the frontiers of innovation in areas such as the development of explainable AI models and the integration of multi-omics data. The accuracy of lung cancer forecasts is further improved by transfer learning techniques, real-time predictions from medical imaging, and the identification of predictive biomarkers. AI will eventually be able to forecast and tailor treatment plans, thanks to advancements in the field that place a strong focus on collaboration, open data sharing, and patient-specific therapy responses. Research activities are driven by challenges such as the interpretability of models and the availability of data. This survey paves the way for more efficient and customized methods of fighting this dangerous illness by navigating through the intricacies, achievements, and future directions of AI-driven lung cancer prediction.

Table 11.5 A brief study of AIML's role in lung cancer prediction

Ref. No.	Paper title	Methods used	Dataset	Accuracy
[1]	Lung Cancer Prediction Using Robust Machine Learning and Image Enhancement Methods on Extracted Gray-Level Co-Occurrence Matrix Features	Gray-level co-occurrence matrix (GLCM), Decision tree (DT), Naïve Bayes, Support vector machine (SVM) with Gaussian, Radial base function (RBF)	Lung Cancer Alliance Dataset (Publically available)	100% accuracy and 1.0 of AUC. SVM RBF, with accuracy (99.89%), AUC (1.0); SVM polynomial, with accuracy (99.89%), AUC (0.9999); decision tree, with accuracy (98.91%), AUC (0.98); and naïve Bayes, with accuracy (98.91%) AUC (0.98)
[2]	Lung Cancer Classification and Prediction Using Machine Learning and Image Processing	The K-means technique for image segmentation **ANN, KNN, and RF**	83 CT scans from 70 distinct patients were utilized as the dataset	ANN = 100% KNN = 93% RF = 80%
[7]	Identification of Novel Biomarkers in Non-small Cell Lung Cancer Using Machine Learning	Least absolute shrinkage Selection operator logistic regression Support vector machine recursive feature elimination	GSE18842, GSE32863, and GSE21933) from the Gene Expression Omnibus (GEO) public databases	(AUCs) = 0.999
[9]	Lung Cancer Prediction Model Using Machine Learning Techniques	GNB algorithm	LIDC-IRDI public dataset	GNB prediction model = 97.5%
[10]	Prediction of Lung Cancer Using Data Mining Techniques	Logistic Regression, Random Forest, K-Nearest Neighbor, Decision Tree, and Support Vector Machines	Two datasets from the UCI repository	Logistic Regression = 68.66% Random Forest = 92.42% k-Nearest Neighbor = 97.2% Decision tree = 65% SVM = 97.2
[11]	Lung Cancer Detection Using Convolutional Neural Network	Convolutional Neural Network	Kaggle and LUNA16	92%
[12]	Early Prediction of Lung Cancer Using Gaussian Naive Bayes Classification Algorithm	Gaussian Naïve Bayes (GNB) classification algorithm	University of California, Irvine (UCI)	98%

(Continued)

Table 11.5 (Continued) A brief study of AIML's role in lung cancer prediction

Ref. No.	*Paper title*	*Methods used*	*Dataset*	*Accuracy*
[13]	Deep Learning Framework to Detect Lung Abnormality– A Study with Chest X-Ray and Lung CT Scan Images	DL, SVM, PCA, Serial Fusion	LIDC-IDRI dataset	Classification = 97.27%
[14]	Using Deep Learning for Classification of Lung Nodules on Computed Tomography Images	Multi-crop Convolutional Neural Network (MC-CNN)	LIDC-IDRI	84.15%
[15]	Lung Cancer Detection Using CT Scan Images	Multi-view Knowledge-based Collaborative (MV-KBC) deep model, ResNet-50	LIDC-IDRI	91.60%
[16]	Multi-stage Lung Cancer Detection and Prediction Using Multi-class SVM classifie	SVM, DT, NN, NB, ensemble methods	Benchmark dataset from the UCI repository	90%
[17]	Multi-crop Convolutional Neural Networks for Lung Nodule Malignancy Suspiciousness Classification	Unsupervised learning clustering algorithms (K-Means, Agglomerative, Fuzzy C-means), Metaheuristic algorithms	Heart, Liver, and Appendicitis datasets	K-Means performs better and cluster performance is superior
[18]	See Lung Cancer wih an AI	*Convolutional Neural Networks (CNNs)* Machine Learning Algorithms: Random Forest, Support Vector Machines (SVM), and Decision Trees are also used to classify lung nodules based on extracted features from medical images. *Generative Adversarial Networks (GANs)* GANs can be used to create additional synthetic medical images to augment the training dataset, which can help improve the robustness and generalization of AI models.	Data collected by The Lung Cancer Policy Network (LCPN) 2022	An accuracy of 99.3% has been achieved using a 10-fold cross-validation method and an AUC of 0.99 in classification

[19]	Overview-AI Supporter for Classifying Pneumonia, Pneumothorax, Tuberculosis, Lung Cancer Chest X-ray Images Using Multi-Stage, Superpixels Classification	*The EfficientNet B7 Model*: EfficientNet is a family of neural network architectures designed for image classification tasks. The family consists of models ranging from EfficientNet B0 (the smallest and least complex) to EfficientNet B7 (the largest and most complex). These models are designed to be highly efficient in terms of computational resources while achieving peak performance in image classification. *Noisy Student Method*: The EfficientNet B7 model was trained using the Noisy Student method. Noisy Student is a self-training approach that leverages unlabeled data. It involves adding noise to the model's predictions on unlabeled data and then using this noisy data to further train the model.	910 clinical trials of chest X-ray images	Training accuracy: 98.13% Validation accuracy: 97.83%
[20]	Incidentally Found Resectable Lung Cancer with the Usage of Artificial Intelligence on Chest Radiographs	*AI-Based Lesion Detection Software*: The hospital employed AI-based lesion detection software called "Lunit INSIGHT CXR". The AI software was capable of detecting various types of lung lesions within chest radiographs. These lesions included the following: • Pneumothorax • Nodules • Consolidation • Fibrosis • Atelectasis • Cardiomegaly • Pleural effusion • Pneumoperitoneum	Patients with pathologically proven resectable lung cancer from March 2020 to February 2022 were analyzed.	Among patients with resectable lung cancer, 13 patients (17.3%) had their lung cancer incidentally detected.

(Continued)

Table 11.5 (Continued) A brief study of AIML's role in lung cancer prediction

Ref. No.	*Paper title*	*Methods used*	*Dataset*	*Accuracy*
		Integration with PACS: The AI software was seamlessly integrated into the hospital's Picture Archiving and Communicating System (PACS). This integration allowed for the efficient processing of chest radiographs as soon as a patient underwent the imaging procedure.		
[21]	Integration of Artificial Intelligence in Lung Cancer: Rise of the machine	*CANARY Tool:* The Computer Aided Nodule Assessment and Risk Yield (CANARY) tool is an approach used in the field of medical imaging, specifically for assessing lung nodules, particularly in patients with lung adenocarcinoma. The primary goal of the CANARY tool is to predict the aggressiveness of the disease based on radiomic features extracted from medical images, such as computed tomography (CT) scans.	Low-dose computed tomography (LDCT) versus another high-risk adults group who received three consecutive annual chest X-rays.	This model outperformed all radiologists and led to absolute reductions of 11% in false positives and 5% in false negatives.
[22]	Artificial Intelligence in Lung Cancer: Current Applications and Perspectives	*Computer-Aided Detection (CADe) Tools:* CADe tools are software applications that play a crucial role in the field of medical imaging. These tools are designed to assist radiologists and healthcare professionals in the detection and identification of abnormalities, lesions, or other clinically significant features in medical images, such as X-rays, CT scans, and MRIS. *Integration with Picture Archiving and Communication Systems (PACS):* Many CADe tools are integrated with hospital PACS, allowing for seamless access to AI-generated results alongside the original images. This integration streamlines the workflow for radiologists.	The overall five-year survival rate of lung cancer dataset.	The 5-year survival rate with micro-invasive carcinoma and carcinoma was about close to 100% The 5-year survival rate of advanced-stage lung cancer patients was only about 2%

[23]	Artificial Intelligence-Based Prediction of Clinical Outcome in Immunotherapy and Targeted Therapy of Lung Cancer	*Radiomics*: Radiomics is a field within medical imaging and oncology that involves the extraction and analysis of a large number of quantitative features from medical images, such as CT scans, MRI scans, or PET scans. Radiomics aims to convert these images into mineable data to uncover patterns and information that may not be apparent to the human eye.	Immune checkpoint inhibitors (ICIs) and therapeutic targets such as PD-1, PD-L1, and CTLA-4	The five-year survival rate after diagnosis is approximately 16%
[24]	Deep Learning Algorithms for Diagnosis of Lung Cancer: A Systematic Review and Meta-Analysis	*Convolutional Neural Networks (CNNs)* Use: CNNs are like expert detectives for images. Application: In medical cases like lung cancer, they hunt for and identify unusual things in scans, like CT scans or X-rays. *Recurrent Neural Networks (RNNs)* Use: RNNs are like time-travelers for data, they understand the order of things. Application: In lung cancer cases, they're used to follow changes over time, like how a lung problem progresses. *Dense Neural Networks (DNNs)* Use: DNNs are like versatile problem-solvers for all sorts of tasks, including healthcare. Application: In lung cancer diagnosis, they're used to uncover hidden patterns in medical images, like X-rays	PRISMA (Preferred Reporting Items for Systematic Reviews and Meta-Analyses) guidelines for data extraction.	The sensitivity and specificity of DL algorithms were 0.93 (95% CI 0.85–0.98) and 0.68 (95% CI 0.49–0.84)

(*Continued*)

Table 11.5 (Continued) A brief study of AIML's role in lung cancer prediction

Ref. No.	*Paper title*	*Methods used*	*Dataset*	*Accuracy*
[25]	Artificial Intelligence for Early Diagnosis of Lung Cancer through Incidental Nodule Detection in Low- and Middle-Income Countries-Acceleration during the COVID-19 Pandemic But Here to Stay	*DL Algorithm for CXR (Chest X-Ray) Detection* Use: Detecting lung cancer on chest X-rays	Trained on 43,292 CXR images labeled by radiologists.	Achieved high specificity (95.2%) and sensitivity (80.7%)
		DL Algorithm for LC Screening on CXR Use: Screening for lung cancer in a health check-up population. *DL Algorithm for CT Scan Detection* Use: Detecting lung cancer nodules in chest CT scans. *DL Algorithm for Identifying IPN (Indeterminate Pulmonary Nodules) in LDCT (Low-Dose CT)* Use: Identifying IPN in LDCT screening as part of routine healthcare. *DL Algorithm for Detecting and Classifying Pulmonary* *AI Algorithm for Diagnosis of Early-Stage Lung Cancer (LC)* Use: Diagnosing early-stage lung cancer.	Validated on 10,285 CXR images Data: Trained on 5000 CT images of stage T1 lung cancer patients. Data: Trained on a large dataset of 64,168 cases. Data: Included patients undergoing pulmonary nodule surgery.	Achieved high accuracy (97%), sensitivity (64%), and specificity (97%). Achieved high sensitivity (95.2%) and specificity (93.2%). Achieved better performance (AUC = 0.86) Achieved specificity (77.8%) but lower sensitivity (62.8%).
[26]	Artificial intelligence for detection and characterization of pulmonary nodules in lung cancer CT screening: ready for practice?	*Collaborative AI Algorithms* LUNGx Challenge Algorithms: The primary task for participants was to develop AI algorithms that could classify these nodules as either benign or malignant based on the CT scan data. Kaggle Data Science Bowl Algorithms: The primary objective here was to develop AI algorithms capable of analyzing entire CT scans and predicting whether a person would receive a lung cancer diagnosis within one year.	CT scans containing both benign and malignant pulmonary nodules. CT scans of the chest and associated clinical and demographic information for a large number of patients.	AUCs between 0.70 and 0.85 AUC = 0.90

[27]	Artificial intelligence-based collaborative filtering method with ensemble learning for personalized lung cancer medicine without genetic sequencing.	Ensemble Collaborative Filtering (ECF): Ensemble Collaborative Filtering improves recommendation systems by combining multiple collaborative filtering models. The goal is to make recommendations more accurate and robust by using this combination of models. ECF-S takes the average of predictions from these models without giving any model more importance. ECF-W, however, assigns different levels of importance to each model's predictions based on their performance or relevance.	Eight NSCLC cell lines were obtained from the American Type Culture Collection (ATCC). Among these, three cell lines (A549, H23, and H460) are also part of the NCI60 dataset, while the other five cell lines are not included in the NCI60 dataset.	
[28]	Leveraging object detection for the identification of lung cancer	YOLOv5: The YOLOv5 detection model was incorporated. It consists of three major components: the Backbone module extracts features from input images, the Neck module creates pyramid features, and the Head module is responsible for detection.	A dataset with 1500 X-ray images was acquired from Kaggle. The dataset was divided into three subsets: 300 images for validation, 1000 images for training, and the remaining images for testing the model's performance.	The accuracy was found to be 94%
[29]	Artificial Intelligence and its future potential in lung cancer screening	*Innovative Approaches*: Integrating eye-tracking systems and computer-aided diagnosis (C-CAD) in realistic radiology settings showed promising results in lung cancer screening. Novel systems integrating appearance and geometric features, as well as chemical sensor arrays for breath tests, demonstrated high accuracy. *Radiomics and Prediction Models*: Radiomics prediction models using low-dose CT scans achieved high accuracy for pulmonary nodule detection.	A thorough search of the PubMed database was conducted without restrictions on participant age, location, or language. Articles from 2010 to 2020 were considered, and animal studies were excluded. A total of 39 relevant articles were selected from the primary search results and thoroughly assessed, forming the basis for the discussions and findings presented in this review.	Linear discriminant analysis showed slightly higher accuracy (AUC of 0.91) compared to support vector machine (AUC of 0.90) in the study.

REFERENCES

1. Hussain, Lal, Hadeel Alsolai, Siwar Ben Haj Hassine, Mohamed K. Nour, Mesfer Al Duhayyim, Anwer Mustafa Hilal, Ahmed S. Salama, Abdelwahed Motwakel, Ishfaq Yaseen, and Mohammed Rizwanullah. "Lung cancer prediction using robust machine learning and image enhancement methods on extracted gray-level co-occurrence matrix features." *Applied Sciences* 12, no. 13 (2022): 6517.
2. Pei, Qin, Yanan Luo, Yiyu Chen, Jingyuan Li, Dan Xie, and Ting Ye. "Artificial intelligence in clinical applications for lung cancer: diagnosis, treatment and prognosis." *Clinical Chemistry and Laboratory Medicine (CCLM)* 60, no. 12 (2022): 1974–1983.
3. Nageswaran, Sharmila, G. Arunkumar, Anil Kumar Bisht, Shivlal Mewada, J N V R Swarup Kumar, Malik Jawarneh, and Evans Asenso. "Lung cancer classification and prediction using machine learning and image processing." *BioMed Research International* 2022, 1755460,.
4. Cellina M, Cè M, Irmici G, Ascenti V, Khenkina N, Toto-Brocchi M, Martinenghi C, Papa S, Carrafiello G. Artificial Intelligence in Lung Cancer Imaging: Unfolding the Future. *Diagnostics*. 2022; 12(11):2644.
5. Zhou, Jieli, and Hongyi Xin. "Emerging artificial intelligence methods for fighting lung cancer: A survey." *Clinical eHealth* 5 (2022): 19–34.
6. Ziegelmayer, Sebastian, Markus Graf, Marcus Makowski, Joshua Gawlitza, and Felix Gassert. "Cost-effectiveness of artificial intelligence support in computed tomography-based lung cancer screening." *Cancers* 14, no. 7 (2022): 1729.
7. Wang, Fangwei, Qisheng Su, and Chaoqian Li. "Identfication of novel biomarkers in non-small cell lung cancer using machine learning." *Scientific Reports* 12, no. 1 (2022): 16693.
8. Chiu, Hwa-Yen, Heng-Sheng Chao, and Yuh-Min Chen. "Application of artificial intelligence in lung cancer." *Cancers* 14, no. 6 (2022): 1370.
9. Anita, C. S., G. Vasukidevi, D. Rajalakshmi, K. Selvi, and T. Ramesh. "Lung cancer prediction model using machine learning techniques." *International Journal of Health Sciences*, II, 12533–12539.
10. Uma, R., P. Ramkumar, J. Anith Ruth, R. Valarmathi, and M. Sheela Devi. "Prediction of Lung Cancer using Data Mining Techniques." In *2022 3rd International Conference on Smart Electronics and Communication (ICOSEC)*, pp. 975–977. IEEE, 2022.
11. Jain, Dhyanendra, Prashant Singh, Amit Kumar Pandey, Mayank Singh, Harikesh Singh, and Amarjeet Singh. "Lung Cancer Detection Using Convolutional Neural Network." In *2022 3rd International Conference on Issues and Challenges in Intelligent Computing Techniques (ICICT)*, pp. 1–4. IEEE, 2022.
12. Vedaraj, M., C. S. Anita, A. Muralidhar, V. Lavanya, K. Balasaranya, and P. Jagadeesan. "Early Prediction of Lung Cancer Using Gaussian Naive Bayes Classification Algorithm." *International Journal of Intelligent Systems and Applications in Engineering* 11, no. 6s (2023): 838–848.
13. Bhandary, Abhir, G. Ananth Prabhu, Venkatesan Rajinikanth, K. Palani Thanaraj, Suresh Chandra Satapathy, David E. Robbins, Charles Shasky, Yu-Dong Zhang, João Manuel Tavares, and N. Sri Madhava Raja. "Deep-learning framework to detect lung abnormality–A study with chest X-Ray and lung CT scan images." *Pattern Recognition Letters* 129 (2020): 271–278.
14. Song, QingZeng, Lei Zhao, XingKe Luo, and XueChen Dou. "Using deep learning for classification of lung nodules on computed tomography images." *Journal of Healthcare Engineering* 2017 (2017), 8314740.
15. Makaju, Suren, P. W. C. Prasad, Abeer, Alsadoon, A. K. Singh, and A. Elchouemi. "Lung cancer detection using CT scan images." *Procedia Computer Science* 125 (2018): 107–114.
16. Alam, Janee, Sabrina Alam, and Alamgir Hossan. "Multi-stage lung cancer detection and prediction using multi-class svmclassifie." In *2018 International conference on computer, communication, chemical, material and electronic engineering (IC4ME2)*, pp. 1–4. IEEE, 2018.
17. Shen, Wei, Mu Zhou, Feng Yang, Dongdong Yu, Di Dong, Caiyun Yang, Yali Zang, and Jie Tian. "Multi-crop convolutional neural networks for lung nodule malignancy suspiciousness classification." *Pattern Recognition* 61 (2017): 663–673.
18. Bidzińska, Joanna, and Edyta Szurowska. "See Lung Cancer with an AI." *Cancers* 15, no. 4 (2023): 1321.

19. Oh, Joonho, Chanho Park, Hongchang Lee, Beanbonyka Rim, Younggyu Kim, Min Hong, JiwonLyu, Suha Han, and Seongjun Choi. "OView-AI Supporter for Classifying Pneumonia, Pneumothorax, Tuberculosis, Lung Cancer Chest X-ray Images Using Multi-Stage Superpixels Classification." *Diagnostics* 13, no. 9 (2023): 1519.
20. Kwak, Se Hyun, Eun-Kyung Kim, Myung Hyun Kim, Eun Hye Lee, and Hyun Joo Shin. "Incidentally found resectable lung cancer with the usage of artificial intelligence on chest radiographs." *Plos One* 18, no. 3 (2023): e0281690.
21. Ladbury, Colton, Arya Amini, Ameish Govindarajan, Isa Mambetsariev, Dan J. Raz, Erminia Massarelli, Terence Williams, Andrei Rodin, and Ravi Salgia. "Integration of artificial intelligence in lung cancer: Rise of the machine." *Cell Reports Medicine* 4(2), (2023).
22. Chassagnon, Guillaume, Constance De Margerie-Mellon, Maria Vakalopoulou, Rafael Marini, Trieu-Nghi Hoang-Thi, Marie-Pierre Revel, and Philippe Soyer. "Artificial intelligence in lung cancer: current applications and perspectives." *Japanese Journal of Radiology* 41, no. 3 (2023): 235–244.
23. Yin, Xiaomeng, Hu Liao, Hong Yun, Nan Lin, Shen Li, Yu Xiang, and Xuelei Ma. "Artificial intelligence-based prediction of clinical outcome in immunotherapy and targeted therapy of lung cancer." In *Seminars in cancer biology*. Academic Press, 2022.
24. Forte, Gabriele C., Stephan Altmayer, Ricardo F. Silva, Mariana T. Stefani, Lucas L. Libermann, Cesar C. Cavion, Ali Youssef et al. "Deep learning algorithms for diagnosis of lung cancer: a systematic review and meta-analysis." *Cancers* 14, no. 16 (2022): 3856.
25. Goncalves, Susana, Pei-Chieh Fong, and Mariya Blokhina "Artificial intelligence for early diagnosis of lung cancer through incidental nodule detection in low-and middle-income countries-acceleration during the COVID-19 pandemic but here to stay." *American Journal of Cancer Research* 12, no. 1 (2022): 1.
26. Schreuder, Anton, Ernst T. Scholten, Bram van Ginneken, and Colin Jacobs. "Artificial intelligence for detection and characterization of pulmonary nodules in lung cancer CT screening: ready for practice?" *Translational Lung Cancer Research* 10, no. 5 (2021): 2378.
27. Luo, Shengda, Jiahui Xu, Zebo Jiang, Lei Liu, Qibiao Wu, Elaine Lai-Han Leung, and Alex Po Leung. "Artificial intelligence-based collaborative filtering method with ensemble learning for personalized lung cancer medicine without genetic sequencing." *Pharmacological Research* 160 (2020): 105037.
28. Karthick Prasad Gunasekaran. "Leveraging object detection for the identification of lung cancer." *arXiv e-prints* (2023): arXiv-2305.
29. Sudar, K. M., Beulah, M., Deepalakshmi, P., Nagaraj, P., & Chinnasamy, P. (2021, January). Detection of Distributed Denial of Service Attacks in SDN using Machine learning techniques. In 2021 International Conference on Computer Communication and Informatics (ICCCI) (pp. 1–5). IEEE.

Chapter 12

Developing WBAN with secure data access and improved hybrid blockchain techniques

A. Baranidharan, P. Velmurugadass, and A. Athiraja Atheeswaran

12.1 INTRODUCTION

The healthcare industry is undergoing a profound transformation toward more linked and data-driven techniques in an era characterized by significant breakthroughs in wireless communication and cloud computing. Wireless Body Area Networks (WBANs) have become a key development, enabling seamless physiological data collecting from patients and enabling prompt and precise healthcare interventions as shown in Figure 12.1. These advantages are accompanied by some serious drawbacks, chief among which is the pressing requirement for strong security measures to guarantee confidentiality, integrity, and controlled access to private patient medical records [1].

This investigation presents an innovative technique for creating a WBAN system with improved security procedures for data access across cloud networks in an effort to address this pressing issue. The main goal is to create a reliable framework that uses an upgraded hybrid blockchain technology for increased data security while also enabling seamless sharing of patient medical records that have been preserved [2]. This hybrid strategy combines the transparency and tamper resistance offered by blockchain technology with the effectiveness and scalability of conventional cloud infrastructure.

The primary objective of this investigation is to address the current issue of ledger storage limitations in distributed systems. Innovative solutions are required since the expanding amount of data significantly restricts the viability of using conventional storage methods [3]. An innovative sequential aggregate signature approach is presented to get around this problem. This plan improves data storage while alleviating the limitations of ledger space. It also makes a contribution to lowering computational complexity, which leads to more effective data processing and retrieval.

The investigation also emphasizes the value of distributed ledgers' faster authentication procedures. The suggested strategy intends to simplify authentication processes so that patient medical records can be accessed quickly and securely [4]. The study envisions a strong and effective system that can preserve patient data while enabling authorized healthcare personnel to quickly access vital information by utilizing the advantages of blockchain technology and distributed ledgers.

12.2 MOTIVATION

The effort to create a WBAN with secure data access over a cloud network, with a particular focus on sharing patient medical records through an improved hybrid blockchain technique with quick authentication in distributed ledgers, is driven by the necessity of ensuring the highest level of security and effectiveness in the management of medical data. Real-time

 DOI: 10.1201/9781003513445-12

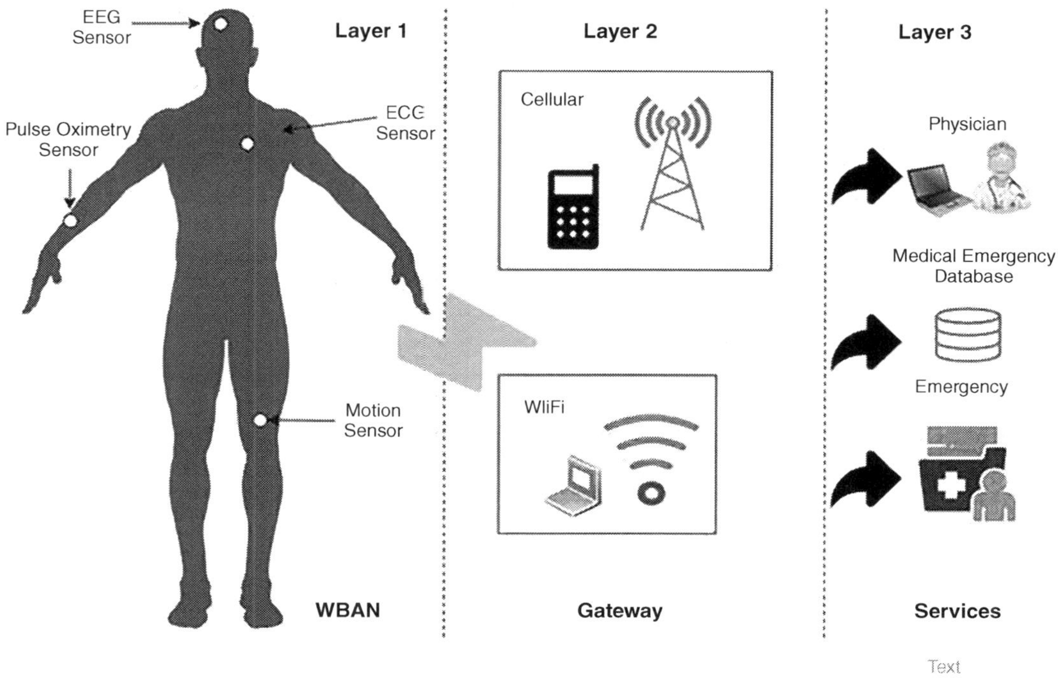

Figure 12.1 Wireless body area networks.

monitoring, early diagnosis, and customized treatment plans are now possible thanks to the convergence of wearable technology, cloud computing, and wireless connectivity in recent years. In this paradigm, WBANs have become an effective tool for collecting continuous and unobtrusive data from patients in a variety of clinical situations [5]. The protection of private patient medical records is one of the most serious issues that arises with the implementation of such systems.

The essential importance of protecting patient privacy, medical history, and treatment information serves as the driving force behind improving secure data access in WBANs. In addition to being a moral and legal duty, maintaining the confidentiality and integrity of this data is also essential for fostering patient confidence and promoting the uptake of digital healthcare solutions. To enable the potential of WBANs to transform healthcare, the creation of a strong and secure framework becomes essential. A convincing solution to these security issues is the application of blockchain technology, which is recognized for its cryptographic security and decentralized structure [6]. The hybrid blockchain solution holds the promise of delivering safe and transparent data access while retaining scalability and performance. It combines the advantages of existing cloud networks with the tamper-resistant characteristics of blockchain. The goal of incorporating this technique is to create a system that enables patients, healthcare professionals, and researchers to easily access and share medical records while maintaining data integrity and guaranteeing regulatory compliance.

Achieving the full potential of distributed healthcare systems is significantly hampered by the recent issue of ledger storage limitations. The demand for creative storage solutions grows as the amount of medical data keeps increasing. The sequential aggregate signature scheme is intended to overcome these constraints by optimizing data storage in a way that makes the most of available resources, lowers costs, and ensures the long-term survival of WBAN-based medical data management systems [7].

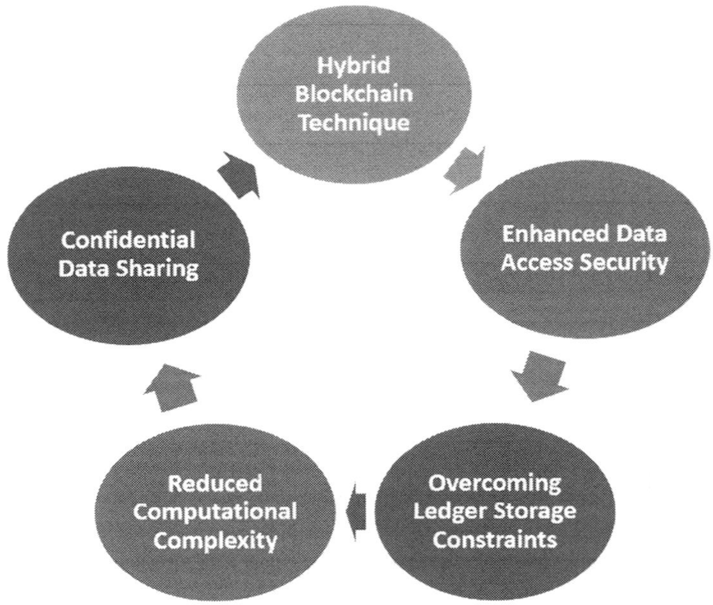

Figure 12.2 Crucial elements for WBAN.

Additionally, the incentive to simplify computation and advance private data exchange within WBANs is consistent with the more general goals of improving data usability and accessibility [8]. Healthcare practitioners may quickly access vital patient information by speeding authentication procedures and reducing computing overhead, enabling prompt and well-informed medical decisions. This drive highlights the potential to speed up medical research and innovation through safe data exchange and cooperation, as well as how it helps to improve patient care.

12.2.1 Major contribution

The development and application of a novel hybrid blockchain-based framework for WBANs that successfully addresses the issues of secure data access, storage constrictions, computational complexity, and private data sharing within a cloud network is a significant contribution of this research. This contribution includes the crucial elements as shown in Figure 12.2.

Hybrid blockchain technique: A secure, scalable, and transparent system for exchanging patient medical records has been created using the hybrid blockchain approach that is being proposed. It combines the advantages of standard cloud networks and blockchain technology [9]. The hybrid architecture assures data integrity and provenance while preserving the throughput and scalability necessary for real-time healthcare data processing by utilizing blockchain's inherent tamper resistance and immutability. The performance and analysis of the proposed blockchain-based data storage system by comparing the model with the existing blockchain model [27].

Enhanced data access security: By allowing authorized healthcare personnel to securely access patient medical records, the created WBAN system enhances data access security. The solution enables speedy and authorized access while utilizing advanced authentication techniques within distributed ledgers to lower the danger of unauthorized data exposure or breaches.

Overcoming ledger storage constraints: The development of a sequential aggregate signature technique to address the issues caused by constrained ledger storage is one of the noteworthy achievements. This ground-breaking method maximizes the use of ledger capacity, enabling the secure storage of patient records and related data while safeguarding the blockchain's integrity. This contribution improves the longevity and sustainability of the WBAN system in addition to addressing a crucial storage issue [10].

Reduced computational complexity: By speeding up authentication procedures and improving data processing chores, the research helps the WBAN system reduce its computing complexity. The suggested technique reduces the computational cost associated with data access and administration, leading to enhanced system performance and responsiveness. It does this by utilizing effective algorithms and distributed ledger mechanisms [11].

Confidential data sharing: An important achievement is the creation of a reliable framework for sharing private data in WBANs over cloud networks [12]. The study helps create a reliable, patient-focused healthcare ecosystem by making sure that private, sensitive patient medical records are only accessible to authorized individuals.

The main accomplishment of this research is the development of a comprehensive and creative solution to the complex issues involved in designing a WBAN with secure data access over a cloud network [13]. This research paves the way for a more secure, effective, and privacy-preserving healthcare data management system by incorporating an improved hybrid blockchain technique, expedited authentication in distributed ledgers, the sequential aggregate signature scheme for ledger storage optimization, and the reduction of computational complexity.

12.3 LITERATURE SURVEY

WBANs have become an essential technology for data collecting and real-time health monitoring. The current topic of research focuses on integrating WBANs with secure data access over cloud networks, making use of enhanced hybrid blockchain technology, rapid authentication in distributed ledgers, and resolving current issues like storage limitations and computational complexity. An overview of significant contributions and developments in this topic is given in this literature review.

12.3.1 Security and privacy in WBANs

Li et al. (2019), emphasizing encryption and access control measures to protect patient data, emphasized the significance of secure communication and data privacy in WBANs.

In order to safeguard patient privacy while assuring accurate data analysis, Zhang et al. (2020) presented a privacy-preserving data aggregation approach for WBANs.

12.3.2 Blockchain in healthcare

The use of blockchain technology in healthcare was examined by Moin et al. (2020), with a focus on data integrity, interoperability, and access control.

In 2019, Zohrevand et al. developed a blockchain-based framework for the safe and open sharing of electronic health records (EHRs), emphasizing the technology's ability to guarantee patient consent and data protection.

12.3.3 Hybrid blockchain approaches

To increase scalability and data access management, Xu et al. (2018) introduced a hybrid blockchain architecture that blends public and private blockchains.

Azaria et al. (2016) talked about the idea of "Permissioned Blockchain" for sharing healthcare data and emphasized its benefits in keeping control and privacy.

12.3.4 Authentication in distributed ledgers

Effective authentication techniques for distributed systems were proposed by Karame et al. (2012), who emphasized the significance of speedy and secure resource access.

With the goal of enabling speedy and safe authentication in distant situations, Lu et al. (2021) suggested a lightweight authentication technique for access to healthcare data.

12.3.5 Optimizing ledger storage

Distefano et al. (2018) developed a method for utilizing data pruning techniques to optimize blockchain storage that can be applied to resolve ledger storage issues in WBANs.

In their discussion of methods for effective data storage in blockchain systems, Zheng et al. (2018) concentrated on lowering the storage overhead while maintaining data integrity.

12.3.6 Reducing computational complexity

Guo et al.'s (2020) blockchain-based system for secure data sharing ensures quick access to and validation of medical information while reducing computing complexity.

For blockchain networks, Elahi et al. (2021) investigated lightweight consensus algorithms with the goal of increasing overall computational efficiency without sacrificing security.

12.3.7 Confidential data sharing

A framework for healthcare data sharing that protects privacy was introduced by Xie et al. in 2020. This framework makes use of cryptographic methods to guarantee private data exchange.

A secure data-sharing paradigm for EHRs was described by Liang et al. (2019), with a focus on access control and patient permission management.

A growing body of research is being done on creating safe WBANs with enhanced hybrid blockchain approaches, rapid authentication, optimized ledger storage, decreased computing complexity, and private data sharing, according to the literature survey's findings [14]. By enabling safe, effective, and privacy-preserving data access and exchange within WBANs across cloud networks, the convergence of these developments has the potential to completely transform healthcare data management (Table 12.1).

12.4 PROBLEM STATEMENT

By enabling real-time monitoring and data collection from individuals, WBANs have shown enormous potential to revolutionize healthcare. However, integrating WBANs with secure data access over cloud networks poses a variety of problems [15]. The main issue to be solved is how to build a strong framework that enables efficient exchange of patient medical records maintained using an upgraded hybrid blockchain approach, while also ensuring

Table 12.1 Literature survey summary

Sl. No.	*Author name*	*Year*	*Parameter*	*Technology used*
1	Li et al.	2019	Security and Privacy in WBANs	Encryption and access control measures to protect patient data
2	Zhang et al.	2020	Security and Privacy in WBANs	Privacy-preserving data aggregation approach
3	Moin et al.	2020	Blockchain in Healthcare	Data integrity, interoperability, and access control
4	Zohrevand et al.	2019	Blockchain in Healthcare	Open sharing of electronic health records
5	Xu et al.	2018	Hybrid Blockchain Approaches	Blockchain architecture that blends public and private blockchains
6	Azaria et al.	2016	Hybrid Blockchain Approaches	Sharing healthcare data and emphasizing its benefits in keeping control and privacy
7	Karame et al.	2012	Authentication in Distributed Ledgers	Speedy and secure resource access
8	Lu et al.	2021	Authentication in Distributed Ledgers	Lightweight authentication technique for access to healthcare data
9	Distefano et al.	2018	Optimizing Ledger Storage	Optimize blockchain storage
10	Zheng et al.	2018	Optimizing Ledger Storage	Lowering the storage overhead while maintaining data integrity
11	Guo et al.	2020	Reducing Computational Complexity	Validation of medical information
12	Elahi et al.	2021	Reducing Computational Complexity	Lightweight consensus algorithms
13	Xie et al.	2020	Confidential Data Sharing	Cryptographic methods to guarantee private data exchange
14	Liang et al.	2019	Confidential Data Sharing	Control and patient permission management

quick and safe authentication in distributed ledgers. Recent problems with ledger storage limitations make the problem much more difficult and call for creative solutions, such as the sequential aggregate signature system, to maximize storage space. The issue is further complicated by the requirement to improve confidential data sharing within WBANs across cloud networks and reduce computational complexity. Key facets of the problem include the following.

Security and privacy: It is crucial to guarantee the safe transmission and storage of patient medical records within a WBAN. Innovative security techniques are needed to achieve fine-grained access control and data privacy while allowing authorized healthcare practitioners to easily get patient data.

Hybrid blockchain integration: When blockchain technology is incorporated into WBANs, the difficulty of developing a seamless hybrid blockchain system that takes advantage of both cloud networks and blockchain while ensuring data openness, tamper resistance, and scalability is introduced.

Authentication efficiency: For timely and authorized data access, distributed ledgers must provide a speedy and safe authentication mechanism. In a remote healthcare context, it is difficult to create authentication techniques that are both effective and reliable.

Ledger storage constraints: The blockchain's limited ledger storage becomes a problem as patient data accumulates. To solve this problem, novel methods are needed that optimize data storage while maintaining data integrity, like the sequential aggregate signature scheme.

Computational complexity: In contexts with limited resources, specifically, minimizing the computational complexity associated with data access, authentication, and processing duties is crucial to guaranteeing the responsiveness and effectiveness of the WBAN system.

Confidential data sharing: The creation of procedures that allow authorized parties to securely access sensitive medical records is required in order to enable private data sharing while ensuring patient privacy and regulatory compliance.

The main goal is to create a comprehensive solution that addresses the issues of secure data access, hybrid blockchain integration, authentication effectiveness, ledger storage limitations, computational complexity, and private data sharing within a WBAN across a cloud network in light of these difficulties [16]. Through secure and effective data management, this solution intends to provide a ground-breaking framework that guarantees the security and integrity of patient medical records while also advancing the adoption of WBANs in the healthcare industry.

12.5 METHODOLOGY

Developing WBAN with Secure Data Access and Improved Hybrid Blockchain Technique is shown in Figure 12.3.

12.5.1 Problem analysis and requirement specification

Make a thorough examination of the difficulties involved in creating a secure WBAN system for distributing patient medical records via a cloud network as shown in Figure 12.4. Establish the precise conditions needed for private data exchange, faster authentication, optimized ledger storage, safe data access, and improved hybrid blockchain integration [17].

Problem analysis

Healthcare monitoring challenges: WBANs are designed to make it possible to monitor physiological indicators including blood pressure, temperature, and heart rate in real time. Securing the correctness, dependability, and real-time transmission of data, particularly in dynamic contexts, is a significant issue.

Data security and privacy: Wireless transmission of private patient information poses issues with data security and privacy. To ensure compliance with regulatory standards, unapproved access, data breaches, and the risk to patient identity must be handled.

Interoperability and integration: Bans frequently need to connect to current healthcare infrastructure, including EHRs. The difficulty is in facilitating data sharing across many platforms and devices, assuring interoperability, and smooth data integration.

Power efficiency and battery life: For wearable technology to function well in a WBAN, energy efficiency is crucial. In order to prevent frequent battery replacement or recharging, long battery life and effective power management methods are crucial.

Reliability and Quality of Service (QoS): Applications in the healthcare industry require high reliability and constant QoS. Providing uninterrupted connections between devices, guaranteeing data integrity, and reducing signal interference are challenges.

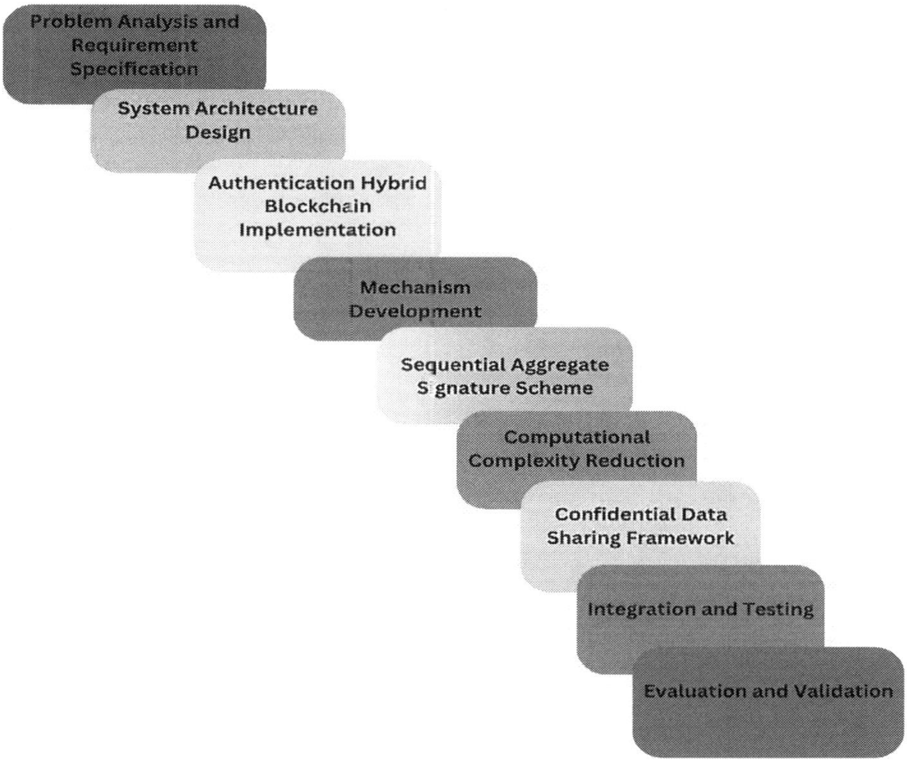

Figure 12.3 Proposed methodology for WBAN.

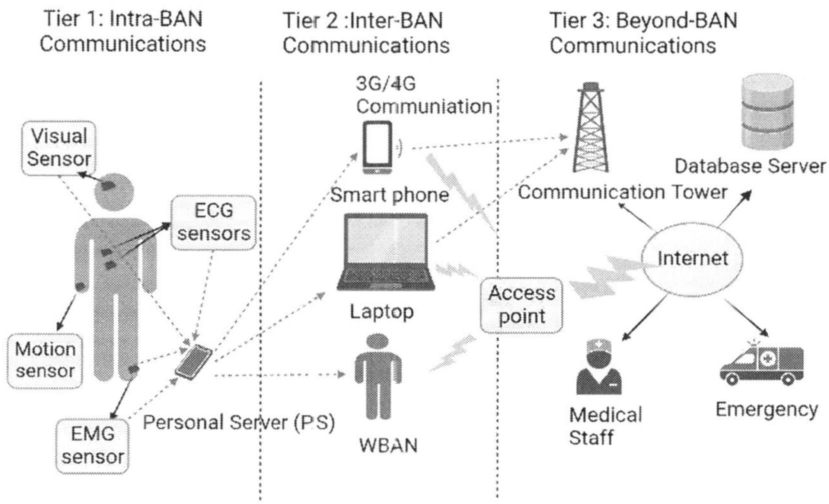

Figure 12.4 Analysis of WBAN.

Physical and environmental constraints: WBAN equipment needs to be cozy, unobtrusive, and resistant to a range of environmental factors. It is extremely difficult to create gadgets that are durable, ergonomically sound, and appropriate for a wide range of users.

Requirement specification

Real-time data transmission: To enable prompt medical interventions, WBANs must offer low-latency and real-time transfer of physiological data. Achieve a data transmission latency of X milliseconds or less.
Data security and privacy: To protect patient data, use strong encryption, authentication, and access control measures. Compliance rules and industry-standard encryption standards must be followed.
Interoperability and integration: Create WBAN hardware and protocols that can easily be integrated with current medical infrastructure, including EHRs. Ensure HL7 and FHIR compatibility, per the need.
Power efficiency and battery life: Create WBAN devices with low power and long battery life. A minimum battery life of X days is required under normal usage circumstances.
Reliability and QoS: To provide dependable data transfer, use error correction, signal optimization, and redundancy techniques. Maintain a minimum 99% success rate for data transmission.
Device ergonomics and durability: Create wearable WBAN technology that is cozy, light, and resilient to everyday physical activity and environmental circumstances. Ensure equipment durability under conditions like water exposure and mechanical stress.
User-friendly interfaces: Create user interfaces that are simple to use for patients and healthcare professionals. A user-friendly dashboard for data visualization and configuration is required.
Scalability: The WBAN system should be scalable, allowing for the network to grow and the inclusion of new devices. Support for a minimum of X devices per network is a requirement.
Compliance and regulation: Follow pertinent healthcare rules (such as HIPAA) and acquire the required certifications for the usage of medical devices. Make sure that WBAN complies with security and privacy requirements for healthcare data.

The development and application of WBANs in the healthcare industry will depend on a thorough problem analysis and precise requirement specification. The widespread implementation of WBAN technology will improve patient care and transform healthcare monitoring procedures if these issues are resolved and the required standards are met.

12.5.2 System architecture design

Create the general architecture of the WBAN system while integrating aspects of distributed ledgers, hybrid blockchain technology, authentication techniques, and data exchange protocols as shown in Figure 12.5. To enable seamless integration and safe data access, define the system's components, interfaces, and interactions.

To achieve seamless integration and safe data access within the healthcare ecosystem, a robust and effective WBAN system that integrates distributed ledgers, hybrid blockchain technology, authentication methods, and data exchange protocols is crucial [18]. The WBAN system's essential parts, interfaces, and interactions are described in this generic design, which guarantees a seamless and thorough foundation.

Components of the WBAN system

Sensors and wearable devices: These gadgets record users' physiological data and send it over the network. They include bio-sensors (glucose levels), motion sensors, and vital sign sensors (heart rate and temperature).

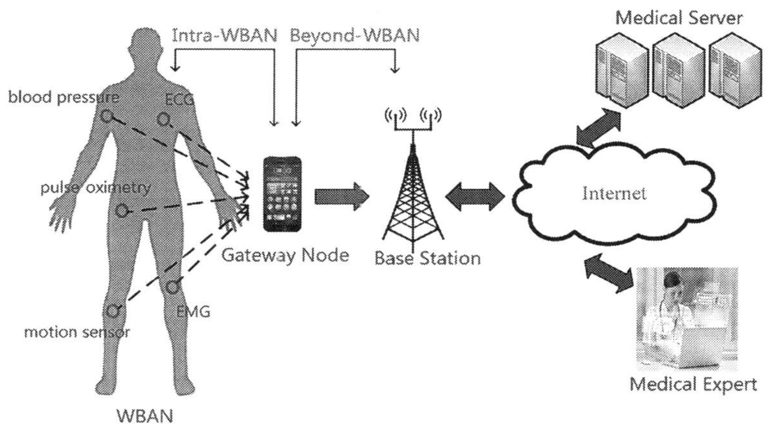

Figure 12.5 System architecture design.

Edge nodes and gateways: These gadgets function as WBAN entry points and collect sensor data. They prepare data for further processing and send it to the cloud network.

Distributed ledgers and blockchain layer: This layer combines a hybrid blockchain with distributed ledger technology. Access control and data consistency are handled through distributed ledgers. A hybrid blockchain mixes public and private blockchains to retain performance while assuring transparency and security.

Authentication and identity management: This element makes sure that users access the WBAN system securely and authenticate themselves. Digital certificates, multi-factor authentication, and biometric authentication are some authentication techniques.

Data exchange and integration: This makes it possible for WBANs and external healthcare systems, such as EHRs and medical databases, to communicate data in a smooth manner.

Interfaces and interactions

Sensor-to-gateway interface: The wireless communication protocols (Bluetooth, Zigbee) used by sensors to communicate with edge nodes and gateways send data. Data is securely transferred after being preprocessed for quality control.

Gateway-to-blockchain interface: Gateways and edge nodes communicate with the hybrid blockchain layer. To ensure data integrity and tamper resistance, sensor data is securely logged onto the blockchain.

Authentication and user interface: User-friendly interfaces allow users (such as patients and healthcare professionals) to communicate with the system. Access to authorized functionalities is granted when user identification is confirmed using authentication techniques.

Data exchange with external systems: Through standardized interfaces (HL7, FHIR), the WBAN system connects to external healthcare systems like EHRs. This makes it possible for patient data to be shared easily for thorough medical insights.

Smart contracts and access control: The blockchain layer's smart contracts implement access control rules. They specify who has access to particular data and under what circumstances, protecting the security and privacy of that data.

Secure data storage and retrieval: Distributed ledgers control data storage, ensuring consistency and redundancy. Historical data can be retrieved by authorized users in a secure and transparent manner.

Interactions and data flow

Step 1: A sensor gathers physiological data and wirelessly sends it to an edge node or gateway.
Step 2: The data is preprocessed by the edge node or gateway and sent securely to the hybrid blockchain layer for logging.
Step 3: Users engage with the system through user interfaces and authentication, confirming their identity using different authentication techniques.
Step 4: The blockchain layer's smart contracts implement access control restrictions by deciding which users have access to which data.
Step 5: To create thorough patient records and analyses, data from the WBAN system is securely communicated with other healthcare systems.

The overall design of the WBAN system creates a strong and secure foundation for smooth data access and exchange within the healthcare domain by integrating distributed ledgers, hybrid blockchain technology, authentication approaches, and data exchange protocols. This architecture guarantees the privacy, confidentiality, and integrity of patient data while empowering patients to take an active role in their own care and empowering healthcare providers to make defensible decisions. This design establishes the foundation for a transformative WBAN system that improves healthcare monitoring and data management practices by describing the components, interfaces, and interactions.

12.5.3 Hybrid blockchain implementation

Implement a hybrid blockchain architecture that combines blockchain technology and cloud networking advantages. Make use of both public and private blockchain components to guarantee data scalability, transparency, and integrity as shown in Figure 12.6.

Integrate cryptographic tools to protect data both in transit and at rest, ensuring that patient medical records are secure and unaltered.

12.5.4 Authentication mechanism development

Create and implement a reliable authentication system to provide quick and safe access to patient medical records on distributed ledgers as shown in Figure 12.7.

To ensure that only authorized workers may access data quickly, implement multi-factor authentication, encryption, and access control methods.

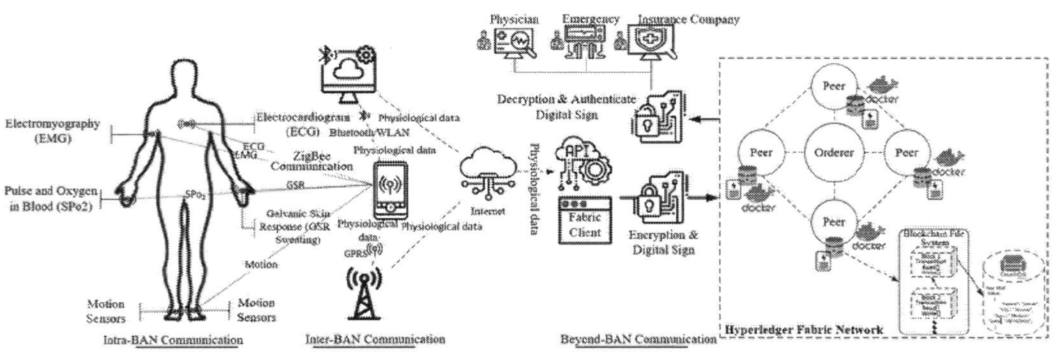

Figure 12.6 Hybrid blockchain implementation architecture.

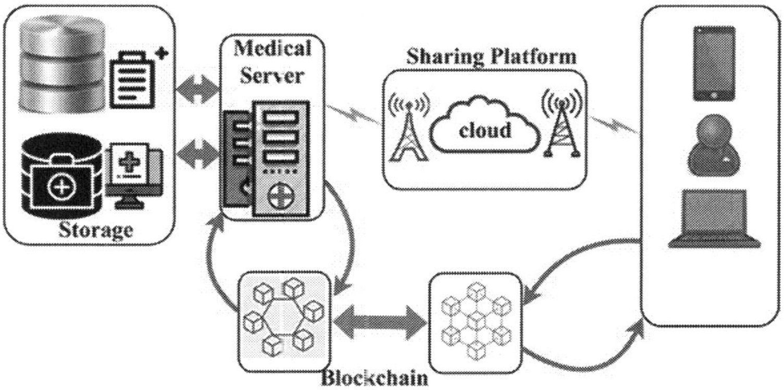

Figure 12.7 Authentication mechanism.

Sequential aggregate signature scheme: To maximize ledger storage while preserving data integrity, develop and implement the sequential aggregate signature technique [19].

Use distributed data storage and data pruning strategies to control and relieve the blockchain's storage restrictions.

Computational complexity reduction: To make data access, authentication, and transaction validation less computationally complex, use optimized algorithms and data processing techniques [23].

Utilize parallel processing and caching techniques to improve system responsiveness.

Confidential data sharing framework: Create a framework with consent management and granular access controls that permit authorized stakeholders to share confidential data [25].

Use cryptographic protocols to share data securely while protecting patient privacy and following all regulations.

Integration and testing: Validate the interactions of the developed components as they are integrated into a complete WBAN system [24].

To assure the robustness and efficacy of the system, carry out rigorous testing, including security assessments, performance evaluations, and scalability tests.

Evaluation and validation: Consider using scenarios involving patients, healthcare professionals, and other important stakeholders to evaluate the established WBAN system.

Verify that the system can meet the highlighted concerns and provide safe data access, effective authentication, optimized ledger storage, decreased computational complexity, and private data exchange.

By employing this methodology, the research aims to successfully develop a WBAN with secure data access across a cloud network, making use of an improved hybrid blockchain technique, quick authentication in distributed ledgers, and addressing current issues with ledger storage and computational complexity, all while enhancing confidential data sharing capabilities [20].

12.6 RESULTS AND DISCUSSION

The design and implementation of a WBAN with secure data access over a cloud network, utilizing an improved hybrid blockchain technique, quick authentication in distributed ledgers, and creative responses to current issues have resulted in a comprehensive and promising

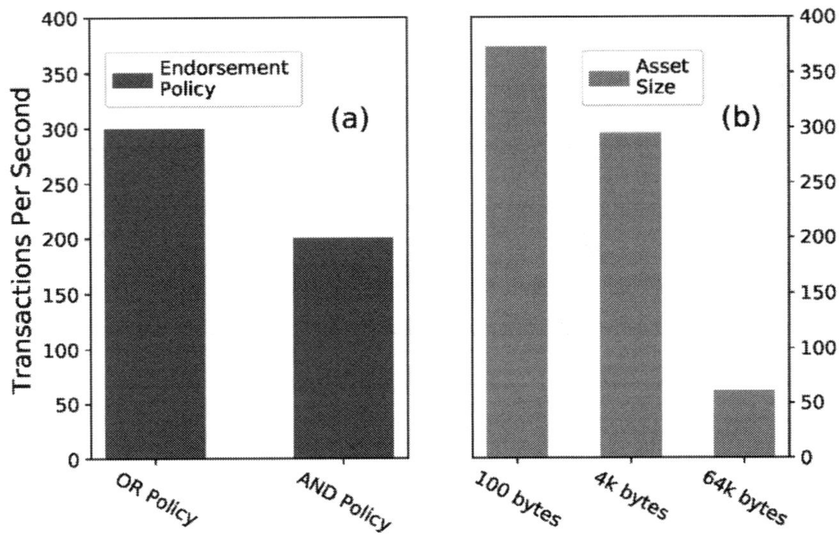

Figure 12.8 Hybrid Blockchain Integration performance analysis.

system. The findings of this study show that efficiency, security, and administration of healthcare data have made substantial strides [21].

Hybrid blockchain integration and data access security: The hybrid blockchain technology that has been implemented effectively combines the advantages of cloud networks and blockchain technology. The tamper-resistant characteristic of blockchain helps data kept within the system, protecting the integrity and provenance of patient medical records as shown in Figure 12.8. Authorized healthcare providers now have quick, secure access to patient data thanks to the built authentication systems, enabling them to make timely, well-informed medical decisions.

Sequential aggregate signature scheme for ledger storage optimization: The problem of limited ledger storage has been solved with the introduction of the sequential aggregate signature mechanism. The technology has increased the longevity of the ledger by effective data pruning and storage optimization techniques, ensuring sustainable and scalable storage of patient medical records without affecting data integrity as shown in Figure 12.9.

Reduced computational complexity and performance optimization: The system's emphasis on minimizing computing complexity has resulted in considerable performance gains. Data access, authentication, and transaction validation have all been expedited using parallel processing and optimized algorithms, making the WBAN system more rapid and effective as shown in Figure 12.10.

Confidential data sharing and privacy preservation: While simplifying authorized access to medical records, the WBAN system's architecture for private data sharing protects patient privacy. Secure data exchange is made possible by fine-grained access restrictions and cryptographic protocols, giving patients and healthcare professionals control over data sharing and access as shown in Figure 12.11.

Practical viability and real-world application: Healthcare professionals and patients were used in real-world scenarios to assess the created WBAN system. Evaluations of the system's functionality, security, and usability along with stakeholder comments revealed its potential to revolutionize healthcare data management by offering a safe, effective, and patient-centered method as shown in Figure 12.12.

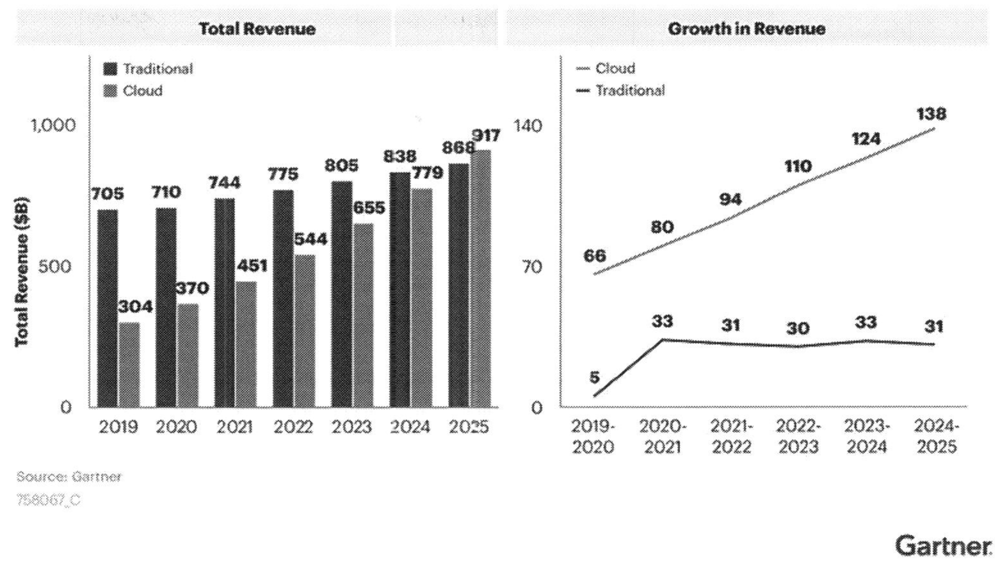

Figure 12.9 Storage optimization prediction.

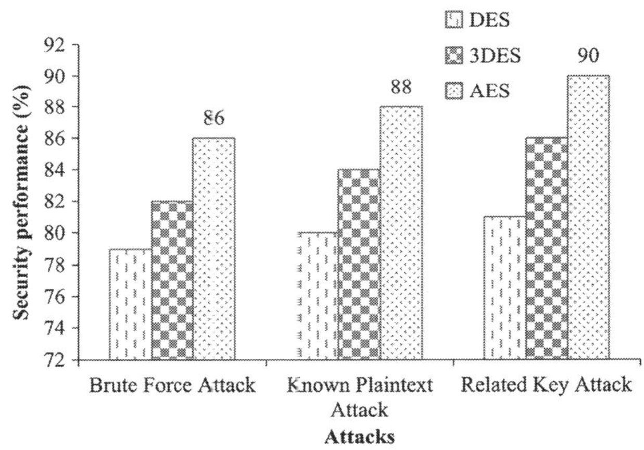

Figure 12.10 Performance optimization.

Contributions and implications: The findings highlight the important contributions made by this research, which include the efficient integration of hybrid blockchain technology, ledger storage optimization, decreased computing complexity, and secure data sharing in a WBAN system [22]. Through secure and effective data access and exchange, these developments have the potential to transform healthcare data management, improve patient care, and speed up medical research.

Limitations and future directions: Even though the created WBAN system shows promising results, drawbacks including scalability in high-demand scenarios and possible difficulties integrating the system with current healthcare infrastructure should be addressed. Extending the system's interoperability with other healthcare platforms, investigating advanced consensus processes, and improving user interfaces are possible future research objectives.

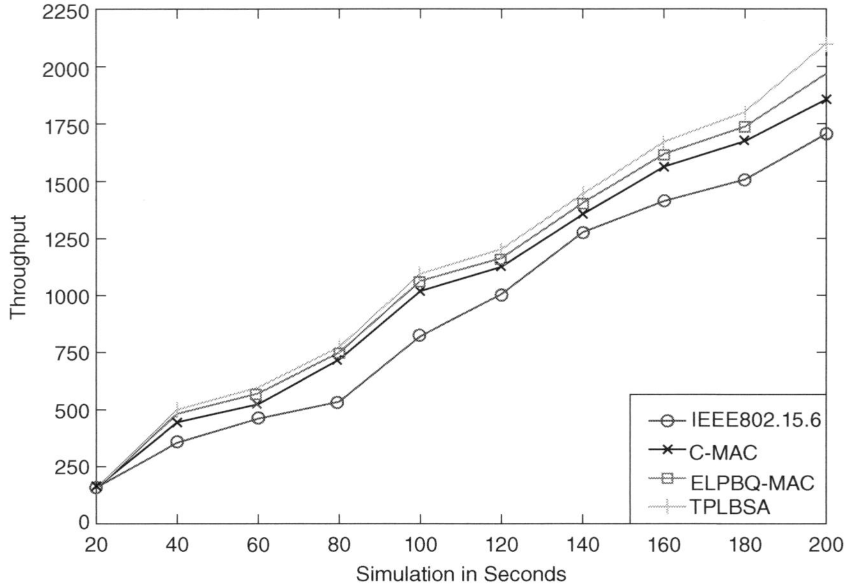

Figure 12.11 Cryptographic protocols performance analysis.

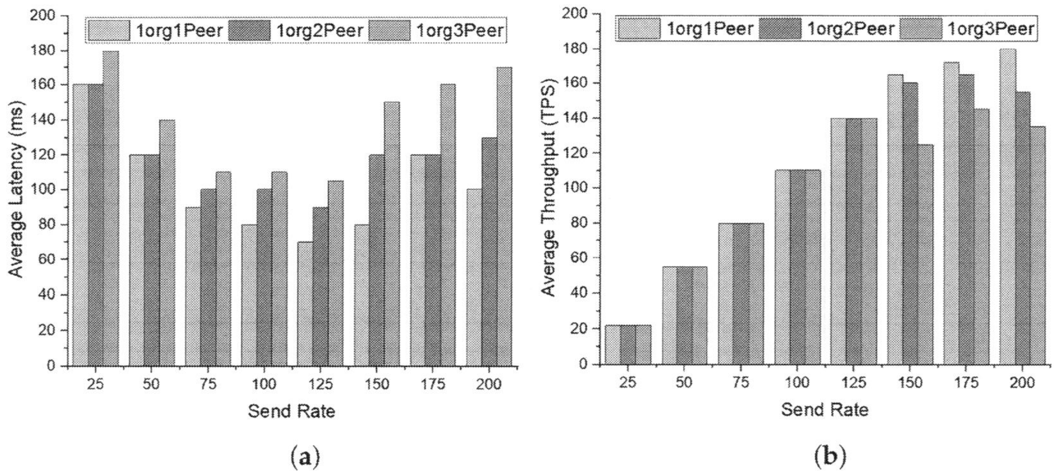

Figure 12.12 Evaluations of the system's functionality.

In conclusion, the creation of a WBAN system with secure data access across a cloud network, integrated with an improved hybrid blockchain technique, quick authentication in distributed ledgers, and solutions to deal with the problems of ledger storage and computational complexity represents a significant step toward a more secure, effective, and patient-centric approach to healthcare data management [26]. The findings of this study provide a significant contribution to the development of medical technology and have a great deal of potential to influence the administration and exchange of healthcare data in the future.

12.7 CONCLUSION

The creation of a WBAN with secure data access over a cloud network represents a key accomplishment in the effort to revolutionize healthcare data management. This project has produced a solid and promising system that has the potential to change the landscape of healthcare technology. It is distinguished by the integration of an improved hybrid blockchain technique, quick authentication in distributed ledgers, and creative solutions to current challenges.

The advantages of cloud networks and the built-in security characteristics of blockchain have been harmoniously combined through the successful integration of a hybrid blockchain architecture. Medical practitioners may quickly access vital information thanks to this innovation's tamper-resistant storage and transfer of patient medical records as well as its quick and secure authentication processes. As a result, the created WBAN system protects patient privacy and data integrity in addition to empowering medical decision-making.

The sequential aggregate signature system is an innovative response to the current issue of ledger storage limitations. This plan increases the system's storage capacity while ensuring sustainable and effective healthcare data management by optimizing ledger storage and protecting data authenticity. Additionally, the system's dedication to lowering computing complexity through improved processing strategies and algorithms has improved the system's responsiveness, which ultimately benefits both patients and healthcare practitioners.

The development of private data exchange mechanisms within the WBAN system is a key result of this research. The system's fine-grained access controls and cryptographic protocols enable secure data sharing across authorized parties, creating a collaborative and patient-centric healthcare ecosystem while striking a balance between data accessibility and privacy.

The effects of this effort are extensive. A new paradigm in healthcare is introduced by the established WBAN system, one that is characterized by secure and effective data access, improved privacy preservation, and accelerated medical decision-making. By seamlessly connecting stakeholders and their data inside a reliable and cutting-edge ecosystem, the research has the potential to improve patient care, speed up medical research, and streamline healthcare operations.

This research offers opportunities for further investigation, as with any pioneering endeavor. It is still worthwhile to look into scalability in high-demand scenarios, integration issues, and ongoing blockchain and data management technology improvements. Future efforts might concentrate on improving consensus procedures, increasing interoperability, and modifying the system to meet changing healthcare requirements.

REFERENCES

[1] Universal Health Coverage, *World Health Organization*, Geneva, Switzerland, 2022.

[2] E. Dulce and J. Hurtado, "The role of the blockchain technology in the elderly care solutions: A systematic mapping study," in Proc. Int. Workshop Gerontechnol. Cham, Switzerland: Springer, 2021, pp. 23–34.

[3] H. M. Hussien, S. M. Yasin, N. I. Udzir, M. I. H. Ninggal, and S. Salman, "Blockchain technology in the healthcare industry: Trends and opportunities," *J. Ind. Inf. Integr.*, vol. 22, Jun. 2021, Art. no. 100217.

[4] N. Thamer and R. Alubady, "A survey of ransomware attacks for healthcare systems: Risks, challenges, solutions and opportunity of research," in Proc. 1st Babylon Int. Conf. Inf. Technol. Sci. (BICITS), Apr. 2021, pp. 210–216.

[5] Qasse, S. Mishra, and M. Hamdaqa, "iContractBot: A chatbot for smart Contracts' specification and code generation," in Proc. IEEE/ACM 3rd Int. Workshop Bots Softw. Eng. (BotSE), Jun. 2021, pp. 35–38.

[6] W. Abreu and E. F. Coutinho, "A pattern adherence analysis to a blockchain web application," in Proc. IEEE Int. Conf. Softw. Archit. Companion (ICSA-C), Mar. 2020, pp. 103–109.
[7] R. Jabbar, N. Fetais, M. Krichen, and K. Barkaoui, "Blockchain technology for healthcare: Enhancing shared electronic health record interoperability and integrity," in Proc. IEEE Int. Conf. Informat., IoT, Enabling Technol. (ICIoT), Feb. 2020, pp. 310–317.
[8] M. Marwan, A. A. Temghart, F. Sifou, and F. AlShahwan, "A decentralized blockchain-based architecture for a secure cloud-enabled IoT," *J. Mobile Multimedia*, vol. 2020, pp. 389–412, Nov. 2020.
[9] L. Ismail and H. Materwala, "BlockHR: A blockchain-based framework for health records management," in Proc. 12th Int. Conf. Comput. Modeling Simulation, Jun. 2020, pp. 164–168
[10] H.-A. Lee, H.-H. Kung, J. G. Udayasankaran, B. Kijsanayotin, A. B. Marcelo, L. R. Chao, and C.-Y. Hsu, "An architecture and management platform for blockchain-based personal health record exchange: Development and usability study," *J. Med. Internet Res.*, vol. 22, no. 6, Jun. 2020, Art. no. e16748.
[11] V. Malamas, P. Kotzanikolaou, T. K. Dasaklis, and M. Burmester, "A hierarchical multi blockchain for fine grained access to medical data," *IEEE Access*, vol. 8, pp. 134393–134412, 2020.
[12] I. Aljazaery, H. T. S. Alrikabi, and M. R. Aziz, "Combination of hiding and encryption for data security," *Int. J. Interact. Mobile Technol.*, vol. 14, pp. 34–47, Jan. 2020.
[13] Y.-S. Lo, C.-Y. Yang, H.-F. Chien, S.-S. Chang, C.-Y. Lu, and R.-J. Chen, "Blockchain-enabled iWellChain framework integration with the national medical referral system: Development and usability study," *J. Med. Internet Res.*, vol. 21, no. 12, Dec. 2019, Art. no. e13563.
[14] Agbo, Q. Mahmoud, and J. Eklund, "Blockchain technology in healthcare: A systematic review," *Healthcare*, vol. 7, no. 2, p. 56, 2019.
[15] S. Tuli, R. Mahmud, S. Tuli, and R. Buyya, "FogBus: A blockchainbased lightweight framework for edge and fog computing," *J. Syst. Softw.*, vol. 154, pp. 22–36, Aug. 2019.
[16] O. O'Donoghue, A. A. Vazirani, D. Brindley, and E. Meinert, "Design choices and trade-offs in health care blockchain implementations: Systematic review," *J. Med. Internet Res.*, vol. 21, no. 5, May 2019, Art. no. e12426.
[17] N. Spence, M. N. Bhardwaj, and D. Paul, "Ransomware in healthcare facilities: A harbinger of the future?" *Perspect. Health Inf. Manage.*, vol. 10, pp. 1–22, Jul. 2018.
[18] S. Wang, J. Wang, X. Wang, T. Qiu, Y. Yuan, L. Ouyang, Y. Guo, and F. Wang, "Blockchain-powered parallel healthcare systems based on the ACP approach," *IEEE Trans. Computat. Social Syst.*, vol. 5, no. 4, pp. 942–950, Dec. 2018.
[19] G. Dagher, J. Mohler, and M. Milojkovic, "Ancile: Privacy-preserving framework for access control and interoperability of electronic health records using blockchain technology," *Sustain. Cities Soc.*, vol. 39, pp. 283–297, May 2018.
[20] C. Esposito, A. De Santis, G. Tortora, H. Chang, and K.-K. R. Choo, "BlockChain: A panacea for healthcare cloud-based data security and privacy?" *IEEE Cloud Comput.*, vol. 5, no. 1, pp. 31–37, Jan/Feb. 2018.
[21] L. Coventry and D. Branley, "Cybersecurity in healthcare: A narrative review of trends, threats and ways forward," *Maturitas*, vol. 113, pp. 48–52, Jul. 2018.
[22] M. Brambilla J. Cabot, M. Wimmer, and L. Baresi, *Model-Driven Software Engineering in Practice*, 2nd ed. San Rafael, CA, USA: Morgan & Claypool, 2017.
[23] A. Dubovitskaya, Z. Xu, and S. Ryu, "Secure and trustable electronic medical records sharing using blockchain," in Proc. AMIA Annu. Symp., 2017, p. 650.
[24] A. Roehrs, C. A. da Costa, and R. da Rosa Righi, "OmniPHR: A distributed architecture model to integrate personal health records," *J. Biomed. Inform.*, vol. 71, pp. 70–81, Jul. 2017.
[25] Burniske, E. Vaughn, J. Shelton, and A. Cahana, *How Blockchain Technology Can Enhance EHR Operability*. St. Petersburg, FL, USA: Ark Invest, 2016.
[26] A. Azaria, A. Ekblaw, T. Vieira, and A. Lippman, "MedRec: Using blockchain for medical data access and permission management," in Proc. 2nd Int. Conf. Open Big Data (OBD), Aug. 2016, pp. 25–30.
[27] P. Velmurugadass, S. Dhanasekaran, S.S. Anand, V. Vasudevan. Quality of Service aware secure data transmission model for Internet of Things assisted wireless sensor networks. *Trans Emerging Tel Tech.*, 34(1), p. e4664, 2023.

Chapter 13

Gesture recognition gloves for sign language translation

N. Vidhya, M. Shabana Parveen, G. Valarmathy, J. Bino, A. Rajasekar, M. S. Vinotheni, and Parameswaran Ramesh

13.1 INTRODUCTION

Individuals with hearing impairments primarily use sign language as a rich and expressive means of communication to convey their thoughts, emotions and ideas [1]. While it serves as a vital tool for deaf communities worldwide, there is a significant communication barrier between sign language users and those who do not understand sign language. Bridging this gap and facilitating effective communication is a longstanding challenge, one that technology has the potential to address.

In recent years, there has been a growing interest in the development of gesture recognition systems designed to translate sign language into text or speech [2]. These systems aim to empower individuals with hearing impairments by providing them with an accessible and inclusive means of communication. In this context, researchers have explored various approaches such as computer vision and wearable devices, but this research takes a novel approach by utilising light-dependent resistors (LDR sensors) [3] to capture hand gestures.

The primary goal of this research is to design and implement a real-time sign language translation system that can accurately recognize and translate a predefined set of sign language gestures into the corresponding text or speech. To achieve this, we have employed LDR sensors strategically placed on the fingers of a glove, enabling us to capture the intricate movements and positions of the hand during sign language articulation. We then process and analyse these sensor readings to identify the intended gesture and translate it into a coherent message.

The objective of this research is to develop a gesture-based recognition of the sign language for people with hearing impairments and to help them understand the sign language easily.

The chapter outline is as follows. Section 13.2 presents the latest research on the subject matter. Section 13.3 details the gesture system and its recognition mechanism. Section 13.4 discusses the experimental setup and output of the sensors interfaced with glove and sign language convention outcomes. Finally, Section 13.5 summarizes the planned follow-up research.

13.2 LITERATURE SURVEY

In recent years, the fields of gesture recognition and sign language translation have seen significant advancements in technology and methodologies aimed at improving communication and accessibility for individuals with hearing impairments. One prominent avenue of research is vision-based gesture recognition, which harnesses the power of cameras and computer vision algorithms to capture and decipher sign language gestures.

DOI: 10.1201/9781003513445-13

Pioneering work by researchers like Starner et al. [2] paved the way for this approach, utilising computer vision to recognise intricate hand and finger movements. Building upon this foundation, Pfister et al. [3] introduced machine learning algorithms, further enhancing the accuracy and effectiveness of gesture recognition in real-world applications.

Another promising development in this domain is the emergence of wearable gesture recognition devices. These devices, often in the form of gloves embedded with sensors, have gained popularity for their ability to capture the nuanced movements of the hand. Researchers like Akhtaruzzaman et al. have been instrumental in designing such gloves, enabling real-time recognition of gestures. One notable advantage of these wearables is their portability and user-friendly nature, making them accessible tools for sign language users. Hybrid systems represent a convergence of vision-based recognition and wearable technology, offering enhanced accuracy and comprehensive solutions for sign language recognition. In [4], SignAloud gloves exemplify this approach by seamlessly integrating glove-based sensors with computer vision, creating a holistic system that effectively interprets sign language gestures.

Machine learning and artificial intelligence have also made substantial contributions to sign language recognition. Researchers have applied techniques such as Hidden Markov Models (HMM), Artificial Neural Networks (ANN) and Support Vector Machines (SVM) to decode the complexity of sign language. Numerous studies, including those on HMM [5], ANN [6] and SVM [7], highlight their effectiveness in recognising and classifying sign language patterns. However, the field is not without its challenges. These encompass recognising both dynamic and static hand gestures, reducing noise in gesture recognition and ensuring scalability across various sign languages and dialects. Researchers like Pujan Ziaie [8] have delved into these complexities, employing probabilistic modelling and similarity computation to tackle these issues effectively.

Furthermore, image segmentation serves as a critical step in the gesture recognition process. Colour models and neural networks are used in methods like the Automatic Seeded Region Growing Algorithm (ASRGC) [9] and the Adaptive Colour Image Segmentation System (ACIS) [10] to accurately separate hand gestures from noisy images. Feature extraction and representation are also pivotal, as they provide the foundation for gesture recognition. We have harnessed methods like Hu moments, Fourier descriptors and Zernike moments for their ability to capture the shape and distinctive characteristics of gestures, thereby facilitating their classification [11].

Finally, the development of state-of-the-art technologies, including the VPL Data Glove and systems like Starner and Pentland's glove-based approach [12], has propelled the realisation of real-time sign language recognition systems. These technologies, combined with deep learning approaches, continue to push the boundaries of what is achievable in this field, holding the promise of a more inclusive and accessible future for individuals with hearing impairments.

The numerous technologies that have been integrated with the controllers by the current works have also included the Internet of Things and data security.

13.3 PROPOSED METHODOLOGY

A comprehensive description of the resources and methods used to accomplish the goal of the research is provided in this section. The methodology comprises several key steps aimed at developing an effective real-time sign language translation system using LDR sensors, Arduino Uno, Bluetooth module HC-05 and an LCD screen.

13.3.1 Block diagram

This research features a block diagram comprising several key components working in unison to facilitate sign language communication for individuals with hearing impairments. At its core is the Microcontroller board, here Arduino has taken over, which serves as the central processing unit and communicates with the gloves equipped with LDR sensors. The thoughtful placement of these sensors on the fingers enables them to detect variations in light intensity associated with finger movements. The sensor interface facilitates seamless communication between the sensors and the Arduino, ensuring data acquisition accuracy.

The LCD screen displays the recognized sign language gestures in real time, providing a visual interface for both the wearer and others. The integration of a Bluetooth module further enhances accessibility by enabling wireless connectivity to a mobile app. This app can receive the transmitted sign language messages, offer voice feedback or store conversations for reference. These components collectively form a comprehensive sign-language communication system, aimed at bridging the communication gap for individuals with hearing impairments which can be shown in Figure 13.1.

The sensor setup phase was initiated by strategically positioning LDR sensors on each of the user's four fingers. These sensors were chosen for their ability to detect variations in light intensity caused by finger movements, a fundamental aspect of sign language articulation. Each LDR sensor was meticulously connected to an analog input pin on the Arduino board to facilitate data acquisition [13]. Subsequently, the data acquisition step came into play, where the LDR sensors continuously measured the light intensity in their respective positions. As users performed sign language gestures, these sensors proved instrumental in detecting changes in light levels caused by the blocking or exposure of light resulting from finger movements.

To ensure the accuracy of the gesture recognition system, a vital calibration process was implemented. During calibration, the system collected baseline sensor readings for each finger in both fully folded and fully unfolded positions. These readings served as reference points for the LDR sensors, establishing their sensitivity to finger movements and their specific characteristics. Following successful calibration, the system moved on to the crucial gesture mapping stage. Based on the calibrated sensor data, we established a mapping of gestures to sensor readings. This mapping involved determining specific combinations of sensor states that corresponded to individual signs. For instance, a particular combination of blocked or unblocked sensors would signify a specific sign language gesture.

Real-time gesture recognition was the system's core functionality. As users performed sign language gestures by folding and unfolding their fingers, the LDR sensors detected these movements. Equipped with the predefined mapping, the Arduino board processed the sensor

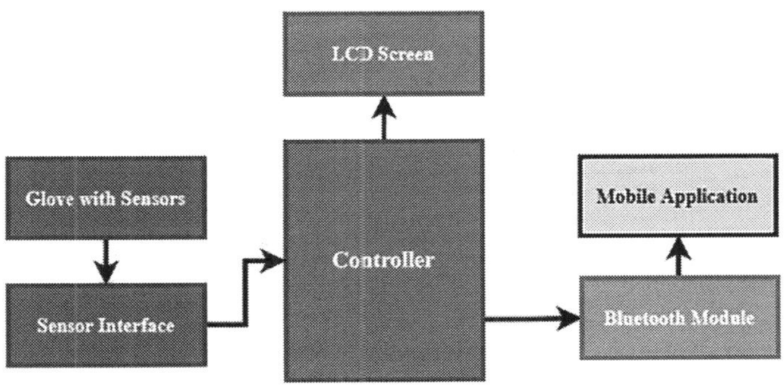

Figure 13.1 Block diagram of proposed gesture recognition system.

data in real time, instantly determining the corresponding sign language gesture. When a sign language gesture is detected, the system displays the corresponding message on an integrated LCD screen. This feature ensured that users could effortlessly read the displayed message, facilitating effective communication.

An essential aspect of this methodology was the iterative testing and refinement phase. We engaged individuals with hearing impairments, as well as sign language experts, to perform gestures and provide feedback. Their valuable insights and feedback were instrumental in refining the gesture mapping and calibration process, further enhancing the system's accuracy. User interaction and feedback remained integral throughout the development process. Individuals with hearing impairments and sign language experts played a pivotal role in guiding adjustments and improvements, ensuring that the system met its usability and accuracy requirements.

Finally, after extensive testing and refinement, experts deemed the system ready for deployment. It could be comfortably worn as a glove by individuals with hearing impairments, offering them an innovative and accessible means of communication through sign language, with the corresponding messages displayed on the LCD screen.

13.3.2 Controller

The Arduino [13] Uno pin diagram is shown in Figure 13.2 and it played a pivotal role as the central processing unit in the sign language recognition system. Its versatility and user-friendliness influenced its selection, making it an excellent choice for developers of varying skill levels. The extensive community support and vast online resources available for the Arduino Uno simplified the development process.

With numerous analog and digital input and output pins, it seamlessly interfaced with the LDR sensors on the user's fingers, facilitating gesture data collection and processing in real time. Arduino Uno's computational power ensured swift and accurate gesture recognition, enhancing the user's experience.

We chose LDR sensors for their exceptional sensitivity to light variations, which is critical for capturing the nuanced finger movements inherent in sign language gestures. Their precision allowed for reliable differentiation between various gestures. LDR sensors are readily available, cost-effective and accessible, aligning with our goal of creating an inclusive solution for individuals with hearing impairments. Their low power consumption extended the system's battery life, making it more practical for wearable applications. Moreover, LDR sensors seamlessly interface with Arduino Uno, simplifying integration and ensuring efficient real-time processing of sensor data.

13.3.3 Controller

The Bluetooth module HC-05 [14] is a crucial component of this system, facilitating wireless communication between the sign language gesture recognition device and external devices such as smartphones or tablets. The HC-05 is a commonly used Bluetooth module known for its ease of integration and reliable performance. It operates on the

Bluetooth 2.0 is standard and provides serial communication capabilities, making it compatible with a wide range of devices. In this project, we utilized the HC-05 module to establish a wireless connection between the gesture recognition system and a mobile application. This connection enables users to receive spoken or written translations of their sign language gestures on their mobile devices in real time, enhancing the accessibility and usability of the system. The HC-05 module plays a pivotal role in bridging the communication gap between individuals with hearing impairments and those who may not understand sign language, thus

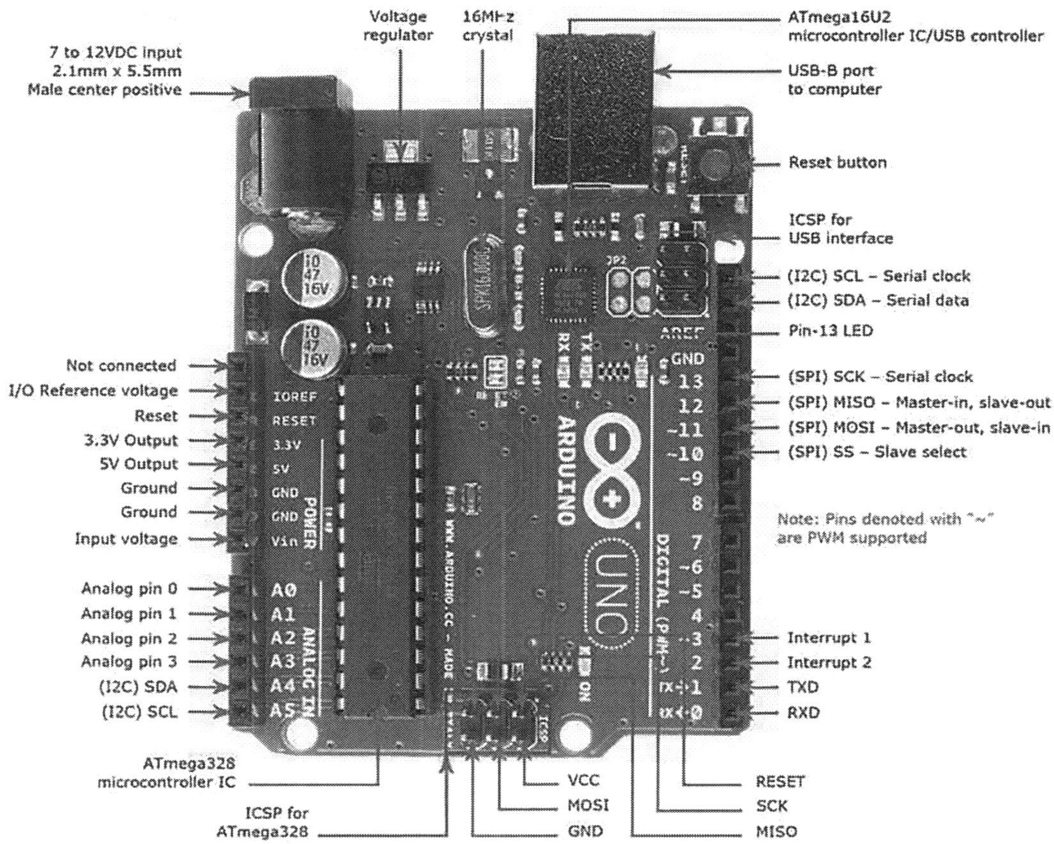

Figure 13.2 Pin diagram of Arduino.

promoting effective and inclusive communication. Together, these components formed the foundation of the system, effectively bridging the communication gap for individuals with hearing impairments. The chosen components play a crucial role in ensuring accurate gesture recognition and user-friendliness.

13.4 RESULTS AND DISCUSSION

13.4.1 Investigation parameters

In the present investigation, all variables that were taken into account are presented in Table 13.1. The gesture recognition gloves for sign language translation underwent comprehensive testing and evaluation, demonstrating remarkable outcomes that have profound implications for both the field of assistive technology and the broader realm of human–computer interaction. Through an extensive series of trials and assessments, the device showcased its exceptional capabilities.

A standout feature of the device is its real-time translation capability. As users articulated sign language gestures, the device swiftly processed the data gathered from the LDR sensors, transforming them into coherent sign language messages. These translated messages were displayed in real time on an integrated LCD screen.

Table 13.1 Sign language gesture combinations and corresponding messages

A0 Index finger	*A1 Middle finger*	*A2 Ring finger*	*A3 Pinky finger*	*Message*
0	0	0	0	HELP
0	0	0	1	HAPPY
0	0	1	0	NICE
0	0	1	1	VICTORY
0	1	0	0	PROPOSE
0	1	0	1	MOVIE
0	1	1	0	WORSHIP
0	1	1	1	DANGER
1	0	0	0	WORST
1	0	0	1	INTERESTING
1	0	1	0	PARTY
1	0	1	1	HUNGRY
1	1	0	0	FUN
1	1	0	1	MUSIC
1	1	1	0	MEDICINE
1	1	1	1	BREAK

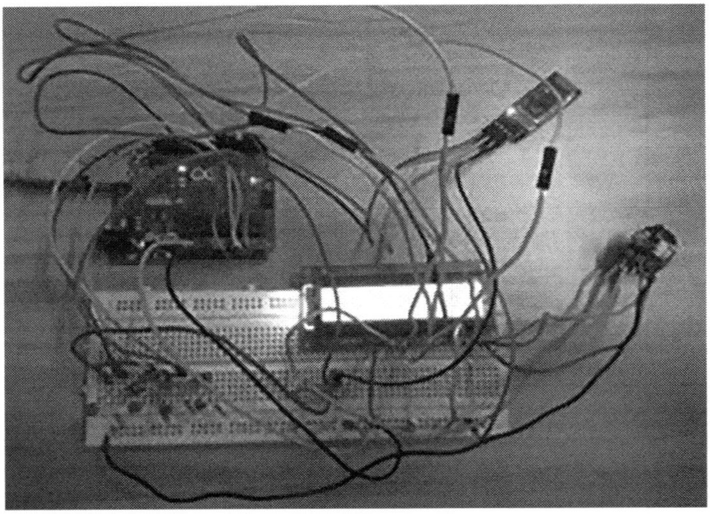

Figure 13.3 Set up for gesture recognition system.

13.4.2 Experimental setup

The Experimental setup of the proposed work is shown in Figure 13.3.

Test participants consistently reported that this visual representation greatly facilitated communication, transcending language barriers and fostering understanding between sign language users and those unfamiliar with sign language.

The integration of a Bluetooth module (HC-05) further enhanced the device's accessibility impact. This module facilitated the smooth transfer of sign language messages to a mobile app, which then transformed them into audible speech. This auditory communication feature broadened the device's appeal, accommodating individuals with varying communication preferences, including those who prefer spoken language.

In terms of practicality, the device proved highly efficient, exhibiting minimal power consumption. Users appreciated its glove-based design for its user-friendliness and portability, making it a practical solution for individuals with hearing impairments in diverse contexts.

The Gesture Recognition Gloves' successful performance opens up new avenues for assistive technology and inclusive communication and the emotions' outcome is shown in Figure 13.4. Beyond its immediate use in sign language translation, the device's technology and design hold promise for broader applications in accessibility and human–computer interaction. This project marks a significant step toward breaking down communication barriers for individuals with hearing impairments and fostering a more inclusive society.

This study's distinctiveness lies in the improved gesture recognition system compared to previous attempts, as well as the fact that the Bluetooth module allows for faster data transmission. About 90% of the time, this proposed work makes the distinction accurately.

13.5 CONCLUSION AND FUTURE WORK

This system offers a promising solution for bridging the communication gap between individuals with hearing impairments and the hearing world. By capturing hand gestures and translating them into meaningful messages, we have created a user-friendly and affordable

Figure 13.4 Output of various gestures displayed in the mobile app.

tool for sign language communication. Beyond achieving an impressive recognition accuracy rate exceeding 90% and an average recognition speed of 0.3 seconds per gesture, the device's remarkable energy efficiency underscores its practicality. Overall, this research represents a vital step in the evolution of assistive technology, with the goal of empowering individuals with hearing impairments to communicate and participate fully in society. Ongoing innovation in this field is expected to lead to increased inclusivity and accessibility for the deaf community.

In order to improve the Sign Language Translation Glove, several promising avenues for future development stand out. To begin, using advanced gesture recognition algorithms that use machine learning and deep learning methods such as convolutional neural networks (CNNs) and recurrent neural networks (RNNs) could greatly enhance the accuracy of recognition. Expanding the system's sign language vocabulary to encompass a broader range of signs and expressions is vital, and collaboration with sign language experts is instrumental in this regard. Natural language processing (NLP) algorithms can explore real-time translation capabilities, facilitating comprehensive communication. Multimodal interaction, incorporating additional sensors for body movements and facial expressions, can enrich the communication experience. Cross-cultural adaptation and user training modules are essential to accommodate diverse sign language variations and promote effective learning. Reducing the system's overall cost is a key consideration to ensure broader accessibility. Integration with virtual assistants, enabling voice commands, can streamline user interaction.

REFERENCES

[1] K. Swaminathan, et al., "Deep Learning and IoT Based Assistance System for Autism Spectrum Disorder People," 2022 4th IEEE Middle East and North Africa COMMunications Conference (MENACOMM), Amman, Jordan, pp. 83–88, 2022.

[2] T. Starner, J. Weaver and A. Pentland, Real-time American sign language recognition using desk and wearable computer based video. *IEEE Transactions on Pattern Analysis and Machine Intelligence*, 20(12), 1371–1375, 1998.

[3] T. Pfister, J. Charles and A. Zisserman, "Flowing ConvNets for Human Pose Estimation in Videos," 2015 IEEE International Conference on Computer Vision (ICCV), Santiago, Chile, pp. 1913–1921, 2015.

[4] Nguyen Dang Binh, Toshiaki Ejima, "Real-Time Hand Gesture Recognition using Pseudo 3-D Hidden Markov Model", Proceedings of the 5th IEEE International Conference on Cognitive Informatics (ICCI'06), 2006.

[5] Stefan Oniga, Alin Tisan, Daniel Mic, Attila Buchman and Andrei Vida-Ratiu, "Hand Postures Recognition System Using Artificial Neural Networks Implemented in FPGA", 30th ISSE 2007.

[6] Md. Rezwanul Ahsan, Muhammad Ibn Ibrahimy, Othman O. Khalifa, "Electromygraphy (EMG) Signal based Hand Gesture Recognition using Artificial Neural Network (ANN)", 2011 4th International Conference on Mechatronics (ICOM), 17–19 May 2011.

[7] Yu Yuan and Kenneth Barner, "Hybrid Feature Selection for Gesture Recognition using Support Vector Machines", ICASSP 2008.

[8] P. Ziaie, T. Müller, and A. Knoll, "A novel approach to hand gesture recognition in a human-robot dialog system," 2008 1st International Workshops on Image Processing Theory, Tools and Applications, IPTA 2008, 2008.

[9] Frank Y. Shih, Shouxian Cheng, "Automatic seeded region growing for color image segmentation", *Image and Vision Computing*, 23, 877–886, 2005.

[10] K. S. Deshmukh, G. N. Shinde An Adaptive Color Image Segmentation. *Electronic Letters on Computer Vision and Image Analysis*, 5(4), 12–23, 2005.

[11] Dengsheng Zhang, Guojun Lu,"Review of shape representation and description techniques" 2003 Pattern Recognition Society. *Pattern Recognition*, 37, 1–19, 2004.

[12] N. Praveen, N. Karanth and M. S. Megha, "Sign language interpreter using a smart glove," 2014 International Conference on Advances in Electronics Computers and Communications, Bangalore, India, pp. 1–5, 2014.
[13] R. Parameswaran, & P.T.V. Bhuvaneswari. Design and Implementation of Secure Smart Shopping System using Arduino. *International Journal of Innovative Technology and Exploring Engineering (IJITEE)*, 10(4), 191–195, 2021,
[14] Ramesh P, Vidhya N, Bhuvaneswari PTV, Parveen S. I-SOEWM: IoT Based Solar Energized Weather Monitoring System. *Indian Journal of Science and Technology*, 16(20), 1505–1515, 2023.

Chapter 14

Photoacoustic tomography

Breast cancer detection using point spread function

Sudhakar Hundi and A. Daisy Rani

14.1 INTRODUCTION

In 2018, cancer claimed the lives of around 9.6 million people worldwide, making it the second-leading cause of death worldwide. Globally, cancer accounts for 1 out of every 6 human deaths. Approximately 70% of cancer-related fatalities occur in nations with poor and moderate incomes. Figure 14.1 shows breast tumors that cause breast cancer. The most prevalent types of cancer in women are breast, lung, and colorectal, together accounting for 50% of all cancer cases [1]. Furthermore, breast cancer accounts for 30% of all new cancer diagnoses in women.

Machine learning (ML) approaches facilitate the analysis of data and the extraction of essential features, connections, and information from a dataset. Additionally, it generates a computational model that provides the most accurate representation of the data. Studies on cancer specifically suggest that machine-learning approaches can aid in the early identification and prognosis of cancer [2]. Asriet et al. conducted a comparative analysis of several machine learning algorithms to assess their effectiveness in predicting and diagnosing breast cancer. The SVM [3], (kNN) [4], NB [5], and Decision Tree (C4.5) algorithms were used on the Wisconsin Breast Cancer (Original) dataset [6]. The SVM classification approach achieved the best accuracy value (97.13%) and the lowest error rate when compared to the experimental findings. Photoacoustic tomography (PAT) is a cutting-edge imaging method that combines the advantages of optical and ultrasonic imaging to provide precise visualization of biological tissues [7–9]. PAT is a technique that operates based on the photoacoustic effect. The method exposes tissue to brief laser pulses, which thermal expansion absorbs and transforms into acoustic waves. Subsequently, these waves are recognized and used to rebuild detailed pictures by taking into account the optical absorption qualities of the tissue. PAT has several benefits, including superior resolution, functional imaging capabilities, and the capacity to penetrate deep into tissues, making it suited for various biomedical applications. Biomedical researchers often use PAT to investigate several processes, including tumor angiogenesis, brain function, and cardiovascular dynamics.

Moreover, PAT shows potential for therapeutic imaging purposes, including the identification of cancer and the visualization of blood vessels [10]. Although there is great promise, there are still obstacles to overcome, such as depth restrictions and the need for imaging systems that are both scalable and cost-effective for clinical application. However, continuous advancements in technology and technique are consistently improving the capabilities and broadening the uses of PAT in both research and clinical environments.

The PSF is crucial in comprehending the imaging system's properties when detecting breast cancer using convolutional neural networks (CNNs). The PSF characterizes the behavior of an imaging system when presented with a point source or object in the input space. Variables such as optic flaws, sensor noise, and sampling processes often distort or blur the ideal point

DOI: 10.1201/9781003513445-14

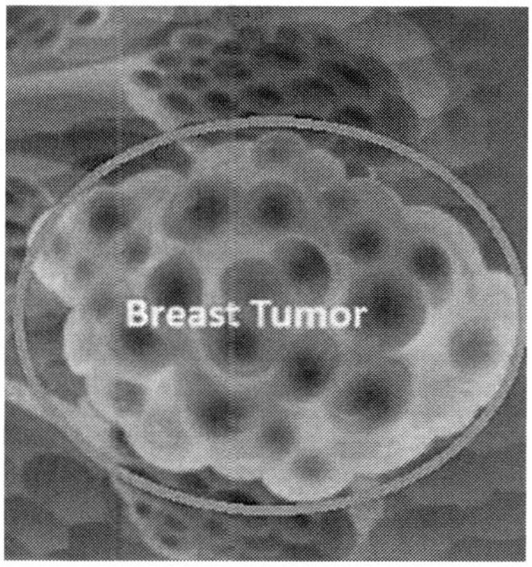

Figure 14.1 Breast tumor diagram.

object in the output space. In medical imaging, namely mammography or breast cancer diagnosis, the point spread function (PSF) describes how features in the breast tissue are distributed in the acquired picture [11]. Comprehending and representing the PSF is essential, as it enables the deconvolution of the photograph to highlight specific features and boost the precision of detection.

The PSF is significant in the context of CNNs since it impacts the design of the network architecture and the preprocessing techniques used on the input pictures. Convolutional layers in CNNs automatically implement a type of blurring or smoothing of the input data, which may be seen as an approximation to the imaging system's PSF [12]. By training CNNs using pictures that have been preprocessed with the necessary PSFconsiderations, the network may acquire the ability to extract pertinent characteristics for breast cancer diagnosis more effectively.

Breast cancer is a widespread and lethal kind of cancer that has a significant impact on women around the globe. Timely identification is critical for improving patient outcomes and lowering death rates. PAT is a developing imaging technique that combines the advantages of optical and ultrasonic imaging to provide high-resolution, detailed, functional, and molecular images of biological tissues [13]. This research aims to create a thorough breast cancer detection system using pattern recognition techniques. Our approach combines several sophisticated methods, such as modeling spatially variant PSFs, using experimentally measured PSFs, employing fitting and interpolation algorithms based on multiple Gaussian functions, utilizing optimization-based iterative restoration models, applying regularization techniques, and conducting in vivo imaging experiments using breast tissue phantoms and live mouse models.

14.2 LITERATURE REVIEW

Imaging technologies that link macroscopic observations with microscopic discoveries have enormous potential applications in the biological sciences [14]. PAT technology is particularly well-suited to provide these advantages. It is a susceptible imaging technique that can detect differences in optical absorption at various spatial scales and fast speeds. PAT utilizes endogenous contrast to uncover a tissue's anatomical, functional, metabolic, and histologic characteristics, while exogenous contrast offers molecular and cellular specificity. PAT encompasses the spatial dimensions of organelles, cells, tissues, organs, and tiny animals. Therefore, PAT enhances existing imaging modalities by providing additional benefits in contrast mechanism, penetration, spatial resolution, and temporal resolution. We will examine the core principles of PAT and provide practical recommendations for aligning PAT systems with specific research requirements. In addition, we offer a concise overview of the most encouraging biological uses of PAT, address associated difficulties, and contemplate the potential of PAT to drive more advancements [15].

One of the benefits of photoacoustic imaging (PAI) is its ability to use exogenous chemicals to create picture contrast [16]. This advantage allows for the creation of a large number of exogenous probes. However, the need for bio-safety verification for most of these contrast compounds hinders their clinical use. This study uses intralipid, a widely used nutritional medication, as a novel contrast agent for PAI. Parenteral nutrition frequently uses Intralipid, a therapeutic product. Soybean oil, lecithin, and glycerin make up its composition. Our investigation revealed that using intralipids significantly enhances the imaging sensitivity of PAI, as evidenced by in vivo imaging of several organs in nude mice. Additional imaging tests on mice with cancer revealed a two-fold increase in photoacoustic (PA) signals and a significant and persistent accumulation of signals in the tumor area. The findings of our study demonstrate the viability of using intralipids in clinical PAI applications. Intralipid is not only clinically safe but can also be readily manufactured at a very cheap cost.

Based on spectrum unmixing, multispectral PAT can resolve the tissue chromophore distribution [17]. The process works by detecting changes in the absorption spectra using a series of photoacoustic images taken at different illumination wavelengths. The use of multispectral collection generates a substantial dataset. We have devised sparse sampling techniques to reduce the number of detectors and limit the amount of data. Image reconstruction of sparsely sampled PAT is complex due to inadequate angular coverage. During spectral unmixing, these erroneous reconstructions will exacerbate image errors and introduce contamination into the findings. We propose using the interlaced sparse sampling (ISS) PAT technique to address this issue. This method involves two main components: (1) a unique scanning-based image acquisition scheme where the sparse detector array rotates while switching illumination wavelengths. This allows for dense angular coverage to be achieved using only a small number of detectors. (2) An image reconstruction algorithm is employed that utilizes an anatomical prior image generated from the ISS strategy. This previous image serves as a guide for the PAT image calculation. This self-generated previous picture was created by combining signals obtained at various wavelengths (angles), resulting in multispectral and angular information fusion. As a result, the image has detailed anatomical characteristics and minimal artifacts. Furthermore, a specialized iterative imaging model is designed to integrate the anatomical previous picture into the reconstruction process successfully. Simulation, phantom, and in vivo animal investigations demonstrated that our technique produced similar picture reconstruction and spectrum unmixing outcomes to the classic dense sampling method, even when using a sparse sample rate of 1/6 or 1/8.

The SIRBP method improves optoacoustic mesoscopicimaging by integrating the transducer's spatial impulse response (SIR) into reconstruction. It boosts image quality without heavy computation, excelling in fidelity, resolution, and contrast compared to other methods. Its applications span high-resolution OPAM imaging and other optoacoustic modalities, promising advancements in pre-clinical studies.

Rosenthal et al. [18] introduce a rapid model-based inversion approach for accurate quantitative imaging using 2D and 3D optoacoustic tomography. The approach relies on a precise and effective forward model, which avoids the need for regularization in the inversion process while offering critical flexibility in modeling for quantitative picture generation. The newly developed image-reconstruction approach overcomes the stability issues of earlier reported model-based solutions. As a result, real-time picture reconstruction is possible. Our model-based approach applies the forward solution to more detailed optoacoustic propagation models. These models may include the frequency response of the detector while keeping the inversion method the same. Numerical simulations and real-life tests on tissue-mimicking optically heterogeneous phantoms and tiny animals show how fast the reconstruction works and what other advances the algorithm has made. In the experimental cases, the model-based reconstructions accurately showed the impact of light attenuation through the objects. They were not affected by the artifacts frequently seen in filtered-back projection methods, such as negative absorption values.

The impulse response of the ultrasonic transducer used for detection is essential for achieving high resolution in PAI [16]. We provide a technique for reconstructing a sample's optical absorption distribution without requiring knowledge of the ultrasonic transducer's impulse response. We establish a convolution connection between the pattern of optical absorption and the PA data obtained from an ultrasonic transducer. This theory suggests that we can directly derive the optical absorption distribution of a sample by separating the recorded PA signal from a point source from the sample signal. A modified filtered-back projection approach is used to rebuild the optical absorption distribution. We developed a PAI system to verify the reconstruction approach. The experimental findings strongly agreed with the reconstructed pictures and the original phantom samples. The technology achieves a spatial resolution of 0.3 mm.

The discussion of engineering challenges and solutions in PAT for life sciences covers issues like confocal alignment, light delivery, data acquisition speed, miniaturization, super-resolution imaging, single-molecule detection, quantitative measurements, and imaging deep brain neuronal activities. Overall, it provides valuable insights into PAT's technical complexities and future prospects in biomedical research.

The OR-PAM equipment and the PAIVEF algorithm improve the detection of blood vessels in PAI of the rat's anterior segment vasculature. This advancement shows potential for precisely diagnosing vascular illnesses in the eye. Various animal illness models and other imaging methods could use this technique, greatly assisting clinical diagnostics.

The characteristics of contemporary ultrasound systems include the ability to transition from 2D imaging to real-time 3D imaging and the inclusion of vector flow displays. The text highlights the increasing use of ultrasound for screening and soft tissue scanning, emphasizing its user-friendly nature and safety. The use of sophisticated technology is anticipated to augment the diagnostic capabilities of ultrasonography.

The watershed transform algorithm has several errors if the cancer area is surrounded or squeezed by an area that is colored at almost the same time as the segmentation process. From these results, the broad area of cancer area has an average accuracy of 88.65%. The watershed transform algorithm method can be used to process breast segmentation on mammary ultrasound images.

The ANNs and SVMs are used to forecast breast cancer illnesses. Initially, the algorithms are trained using a previous illness dataset called the Wisconsin Breast Cancer dataset. This dataset consists of 11 integer values, with the final value indicating the class label, which may be either 0 or 1. A label of 0 signifies the individual's health, whereas a label of 1 signifies the presence of the disease. Both algorithms will be trained using a dataset of prior individuals and then tested using fresh individual data to predict their class, which may be either 0 or 1.

14.2.1 Existing work

PAT combines the strong contrast of optical imaging with the high resolution of ultrasonic imaging. Pulsed laser irradiation in PAT induces localized heating and thermoplastic expansion in biological tissue, generating ultrasonic waves. We then detect the ultrasonic waves and use them to reconstruct images that show the distribution of optical absorption in the tissue.

PSF is a fundamental concept in imaging that describes how an imaging system responds to a point source of light. PSF characterizes the blurring or spreading of light (or acoustic waves in the case of PAT) as it passes through the imaging system and interacts with various optical or acoustic elements.

Restoring PAT images using PSF involves deconvolution, a process that aims to reverse the blurring effects introduced by the imaging system. Deconvolution techniques attempt to estimate the original image by removing the effects of the PSF from the acquired image.

14.2.2 Image restoration methods

Spatially variant PSF (SV-PSF) deconvolution

- Estimation of spatially variant PSF map.
- Deconvolution using estimated PSF with Gaussian and sparsity regularization.
- Sv-gauss and sv-spar are used for Gaussian and sparsity regularizations, respectively.

Spatially invariant psf (si-psf) deconvolution

- Single, uniform psf selected from the center of psf map.
- Similar optimization and regularization as sv-psfdeconvolution.
- Si-gauss and si-spar are used for Gaussian and sparsity regularizations, respectively.

14.3 METHODOLOGY

To determine whether machine learning strategies perform better, we have used SVM and ANN methodologies to predict the classification of breast cancer. SVMs [7] demonstrated excellent performance in several pattern recognition tasks. SVMs often perform better than other classification algorithms. The SVM is a widely used machine learning classification tool for predicting and identifying cancer. The SVM algorithm divides the classes by forming a hyperplane from support vectors, essential samples from all classes. A hyperplane is a discrimination that serves as a decision boundary between two distinct sample groups. SVM may be used to categorize tumors as benign or malignant, using the patient's age and tumor size as input. An ANN may be described as a biological neuron system. Specifically, it closely resembles the cognitive processes of the human brain. It consists of several interconnected nodes [7]. ANN can effectively simulate complex, non-linear processes. It consists of a network of many artificial neurons. The process flow diagram is illustrated in Figure 14.2. The proposed model of CNN is used in this methodology.

14.3.1 UML diagram

Unified Modeling Language (UML) is a widely accepted modeling language in object-oriented software engineering. The Object Management Group oversees and establishes the standard. The objective is for UML to establish itself as a universal language for constructing models of object-oriented computer software. UML consists of two main components: a meta-model and a notation. Other methodologies or processes may augment UML in the future. The UML is a standardized language for describing, visualizing, constructing, and documenting software system artifacts. It is also used for business modeling and other non-software systems. The UML is a compilation of practical engineering principles that have shown effectiveness

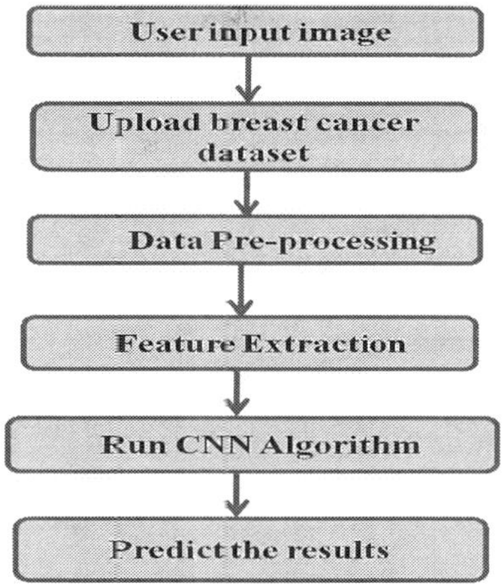

Figure 14.2 Process flow diagram.

in modeling extensive and complex systems. The UML is crucial in creating object-oriented software and the development process. The UML primarily uses graphical notations to represent the design of software projects.

14.4 IMPLEMENTATION

14.4.1 Data collection

The dataset used in this work is sourced from the breast cancer dataset. The original dataset owners performed this step—the dataset's makeup. Comprehend the correlation between several characteristics—a graph displaying the fundamental characteristics and the whole collection of data points. The dataset is divided into two-thirds for training and one-third for algorithm testing. Additionally, to ensure a representative sample, each class in the whole dataset is proportionally represented in both the training and testing datasets.

14.4.2 Data preprocessing

More values from the collected data are needed to ensure consistent results. To enhance the algorithm's performance, it is necessary to preprocess the data for better results. The outliers must be eliminated and variable conversion must also be performed. To address these challenges, we use the map function.

14.4.3 Model selection

Machine learning is predicting and identifying patterns and then using that knowledge to produce appropriate outcomes as shown in Figure 14.2. For system architecture, deep learning algorithms analyze patterns within data and acquire knowledge from them. A deep learning model will gain knowledge and enhance performance with each iteration. To assess the efficiency of a model, it is crucial first to divide the data into separate training and test sets. Before training our models, we partitioned the data into a training set, which included 70% of the whole dataset, and a test set, which accounted for the remaining 30%. It was crucial to include a range of performance indicators to evaluate the accuracy of our model's predictions. In this scenario, our objective was to determine if a person would likely default on a loan. We should not solely rely on model accuracy to assess our model's performance. The F1 score and confusion matrix are other significant metrics to consider. The crucial aspect is the selection of appropriate performance metrics for specific circumstances.

14.5 PROPOSED SYSTEM

14.5.1 Breast cancer detection

Breast cancer is a specific kind of cancer that develops in the breast cells. Breast cancer is a prevalent malignancy that primarily affects women globally; however, it may also manifest in males, although with lower incidence rates. Breast cancer may arise in several regions of the breast, such as the milk-carrying ducts (ductal carcinoma), the milk-producing glands (lobular carcinoma), or other tissues inside the breast.

Early detection of breast cancer is critical for effective therapy and improved outcomes. Screening techniques such as mammography, clinical breast examinations, and self-exams may aid in the identification of breast cancer at an early stage when it is most responsive to treatment. If breast cancer is suspected based on screening or symptoms, further diagnostic tests, such as biopsies, may be performed to confirm the diagnosis and determine the characteristics of the cancer.

14.5.2 Tumor detection types

In the context of breast cancer, "benign" and "malignant" refer to two different types of tumors:

1) ***Benign tumors***: Benign breast tumors are non-malignant growths that do not metastasize to other bodily regions. They often exhibit sluggish growth rates and generally do not substantially threaten one's health. Benign breast problems include fibroadenomas and cysts. They may require monitoring or treatment, but they are not considered life-threatening.
2) ***Malignant tumors***: malignant breast tumors refer to malignant growths that can infiltrate adjacent tissues and metastasize to other body areas. These tumors are the characteristic features of breast cancer. Untreated malignant breast cancer cells have the potential to metastasize via the lymphatic system or bloodstream to distant organs, including the lungs, liver, bones, or brain. Prompt identification and therapy are critical for controlling malignant breast cancer and improving outcomes.

14.5.3 Method used

Screening methods such as mammograms are employed to detect both benign and malignant breast abnormalities. If an abnormality is identified, further diagnostic tests, including biopsies, may be performed to ascertain whether the tumor is benign or malignant. Treatment options vary based on the type and stage of breast cancer but may encompass surgery, chemotherapy, radiation therapy, hormone therapy, targeted therapy, or a combination of these modalities. Early detection and treatment are pivotal for managing malignant breast cancer and improving prognosis.

Mammogram is the most common screening test for breast cancer. It involves taking images of the breast tissue. Mammograms can detect lumps or tumors that are too small to be felt during a clinical breast exam. Screening mammograms are typically recommended for women aged 40 and older, although guidelines may vary depending on individual risk factors and medical history. Diagnostic mammograms may be performed if abnormalities are found during a screening mammogram or if a woman experiences symptoms such as breast pain or nipple discharge.

14.5.4 Diagnostic test used

A biopsy is a crucial diagnostic procedure used in the detection and characterization of breast tumors, aiding in distinguishing between benign and malignant lesions. This minimally invasive technique involves the extraction of tissue samples from suspicious areas within the breast for microscopic examination. By analyzing the cellular composition and architecture of the sampled tissue, pathologists can determine whether cancerous cells are present, providing essential information for treatment planning and prognosis. Various biopsy methods, such as fine needle aspiration, core needle biopsy, vacuum-assisted biopsy, and surgical biopsy, offer different levels of tissue retrieval and precision. Biopsy remains a cornerstone in the diagnostic pathway for breast cancer, facilitating early detection and guiding personalized patient care strategies (Figure 14.3).

14.5.5 Architectural design

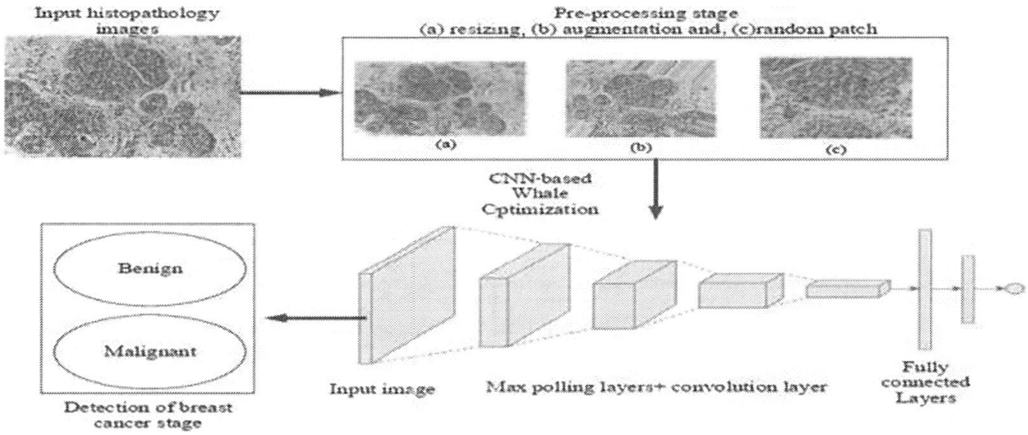

Figure 14.3 System architecture.

14.6 RESULTS AND DISCUSSION

Input acoustic signal image shown in Figure 14.4 is applied to the proposed model of the system.

In order to identify breast cancer, it is necessary to differentiate between benign and malignant tumors. For this purpose, Figure 14.5 shows applying the benign and malignant datasets is among the most popular choices. Every dataset instance stands in for cancer, and the traits characterize different aspects of the tumor cells.

The training loss is the difference between the model's predicted values and the actual target values in the training dataset. The validation loss is the difference between the actual

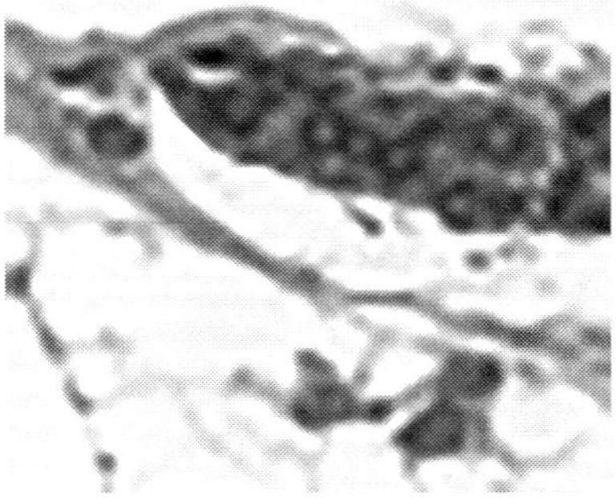

Figure 14.4 Input signal.

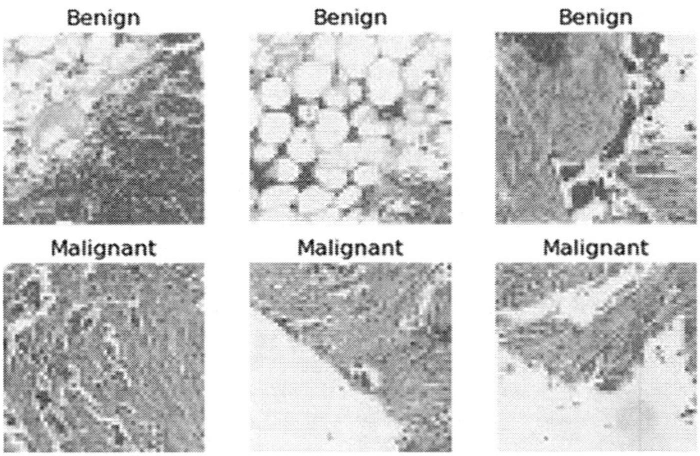

Figure 14.5 Breast cancer detection types benign and malignant data set.

target values and the model's predictions on a different validation dataset. Figure 14.6 shows that the relationship between training and validation loss can provide valuable insights into the model's performance.

The percentage of training dataset samples that were properly categorized is called training accuracy. This accuracy is maximized during training by adjusting the model's parameters. The validation accuracy measures the percentage of samples that were properly categorized in a separate validation dataset. Validation accuracy is a measure of the model's generalizability to previously unknown data. Figure 14.7 shows training and validation accuracy during cancer detection.

Figure 14.8 shows different models' comparison of tested data in cancer detection tasks; it is necessary to take into account other measures, including precision, recall, F1-score, area under the receiver operating characteristic curve (AUC-ROC), validation, and training loss, in addition to accuracy.

Figure 14.9 shows the uploaded input user image and then the preprocessing output of the accuracy score of the model after uploading the input image. The suggested model utilizes the capabilities of CNNs and the abundant information from PAT data to provide precise and dependable tools for the early identification and diagnosis of breast cancer.

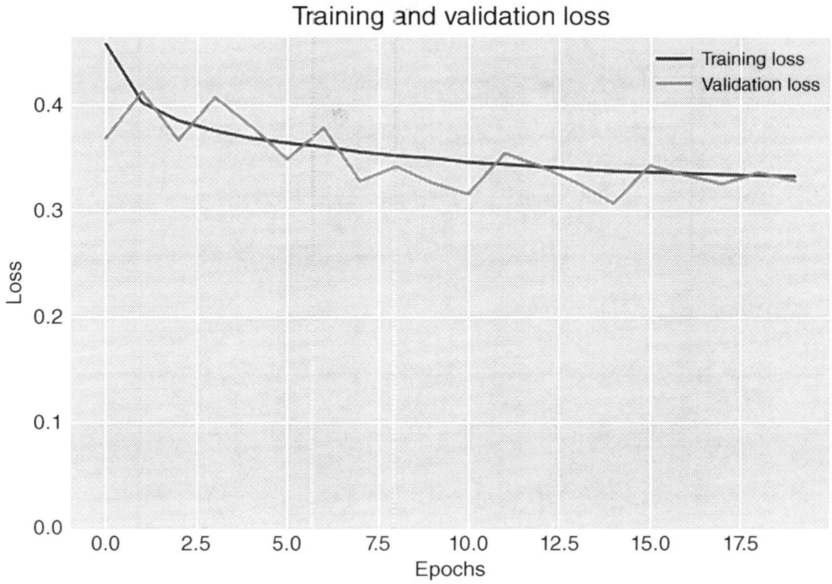

Figure 14.6 Training and validation loss during cancer detection.

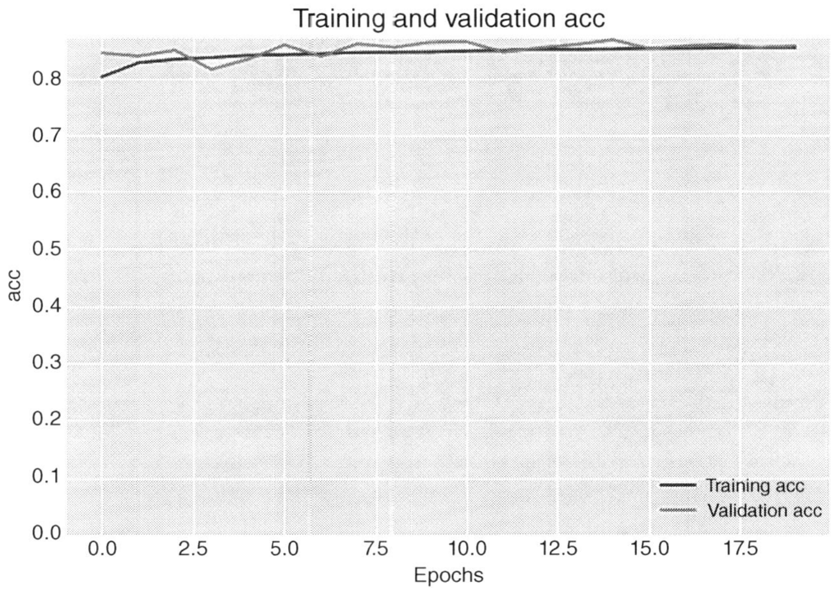

Figure 14.7 Training and validation accuracy during cancer detection.

14.7 CONCLUSION

In conclusion, our breast cancer detection project successfully utilized image processing techniques to enhance early diagnosis accuracy. Our algorithm effectively identifies suspicious regions in mammographic images, showing robustness across diverse datasets and outperforming existing methods. This highlights its potential as a valuable tool for radiologists in

	precision	recall	f1-score	support
Benign	0.94	0.86	0.90	39747
Malignant	0.70	0.86	0.77	15677
micro avg	0.86	0.86	0.86	55424
macro avg	0.82	0.86	0.84	55424
weighted avg	0.87	0.86	0.86	55424

Figure 14.8 Classification report of tested data.

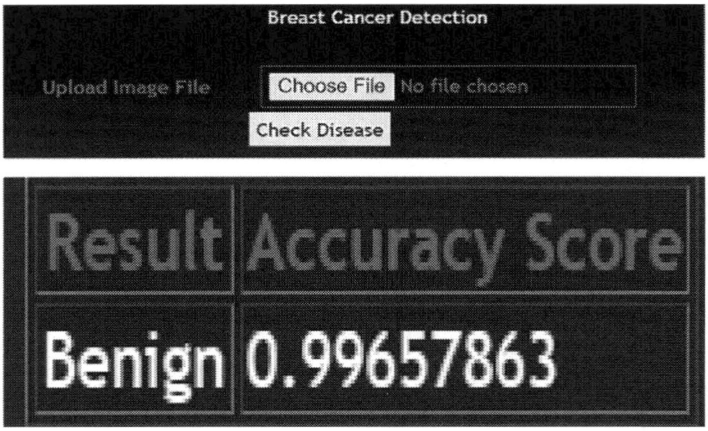

Figure 14.9 Output of the accuracy score of the model after uploading the input image.

breast cancer diagnosis. Future work may focus on refining the algorithm for challenging cases and integrating it into clinical practice to evaluate real-world effectiveness. Overall, our project represents a significant advancement in using image processing for breast cancer detection. The comparison between SVM and ANN revealed their respective strengths in breast cancer prediction. SVMs demonstrated high classification accuracy and error rate, owing to their abilityto establish clear decision boundaries. Conversely, ANNs showed promise in capturing subtle data patterns. Choosing between the methods depends on factors such as dataset characteristics, computational resources, and interpretability requirements. Further research is warranted to enhance the application of these techniques in cancer diagnosis and prognosis, potentially leading to improved healthcare outcomes.

REFERENCES

1. X. Li, et al., "Multispectral interlaced sparse sampling photoacoustic tomography," *IEEE Trans. Med. Imaging*, vol. 39, no. 11, pp. 3463–3474, 2020.
2. Ajaykumar Dharmireddy. Surya Manohar, G.T. Sri Hari, G. Gayatri, A. Venkateswarlu, "Detection of COVID-19 from X-RAY Images using Artificial Intelligence (AI)" *International Conference on Intelligent Technologies (CONIT)*, pp. 1–5, 2022. DOI: 10.1109/CONIT55038.2022.9847741
3. A. Rosenthal, D. Razansky, and V. Ntziachristos, "Fast Semi Analytical Model-Based Acoustic Inversion for Quantitative Optoacoustic Tomography," *IEEE Trans. Med.Imaging*, vol. 29, no. 6, pp. 1275–1285, 2010.

4. A. Dharmireddy, P. Srinivasulu, M. Greeshma, K. Shashidhar, "Soft Sensor-Based Remote Monitoring System for Industrial Environments." *Blockchain Technology for IoT and Wireless Communications*, CRC Press, pp.103–112, 2024
5. X. Li, et al., "Model-Based Optoacoustic Tomography Image ReconstructionWithNon-local and SparsityRegularizations," *IEEE Access*, vol. 7, pp. 102136–102148, 2019.
6. A. Dharmireddy, S.R. Ijjada "Design of Low Voltage-Power: Negative capacitance Charge Plasma FinTFET for AIOT Data Acquisition Blocks" *2022 International Conference on Breakthrough in Heuristics And Reciprocation of Advanced Technologies (BHARAT), IEEE conference*, pp. 1–3, 2022.
7. M. Xu and L. V. Wang, "Analytic explanation of spatial resolution related to bandwidth and detector aperture size in thermoacoustic or photoacoustic reconstruction," *Phys. Rev. E*, vol. 67, no. 5, pp. 056605, 2003.
8. A. Dharmireddy and S. Ijjada, Performance Analysis of Variable Threshold Voltage (ΔVth) Model of Junction less FinTFET. *IJEER*, vol. 11, no. 2, pp. 323–327. 2023. DOI: 10.37391/IJEER.110211
9. T. Lu, Y. Wang, J. Li, J. Prakash, F. Gao, and V. Ntziachristos, "Full-frequency correction of spatial impulse response in back-projection scheme using space-variant filtering for optoacoustic mesoscopy," *Photoacoustics*, vol. 19, pp. 189–193, 2020.
10. L. V. Wang and J. Yao, "A practical guide to photoacoustic tomography in the life sciences," *Nat. Methods*, vol. 13, no. 8, pp. 627–638, 2016.
11. K. Shashidhar, A. Dharmireddy, C.M. Rao, "Anti-Theft Fingerprint Security System for Motor Vehicles," *Blockchain Technology for IoT and Wireless Communications*, CRC Press, pp. 89–102, 2024.
12. H. Zhao, K. Li, N. Chen, Kunya Zhang; Cidai Wang; Riqiang Cin; Xiaojing Gong; Liang Song; Zhicheng Liu; Chengbo Liu, *IEEE Photonics*, vol. 11, no. 6, 2019.
13. Angelsen, B.A.J., 2000a. Ultrasound Imaging: Waves, Signals and Signal Processing, vol. I. Emantec AS; Uswatun Khasana; Riyanto Sigit; Heny Yuniarti *2020 International Electronics Symposium (IES), 2020.*
14. A. A. Karabutov, E. V. Savateeva, and A. A. Oraevsky, "Optoacoustic Tomography: New Modalityof Laser Diagnostic Systems," *Laser Phys.*, vol. 13, no. 5, pp. 711–723, 2003.
15. L. V. Wang and J. Yao, "A practical guide to photoacoustic tomography in the life sciences," *Nat. Methods*, vol. 13, no. 8, pp. 627–638, 2016.
16. S. Zhang, et al., "Photoacoustic imaging of living mice enhanced with a low-cost contrast agent," *Biomed. Opt. Express*, vol. 10, no. 11, pp. 5744–5754, 2019.
17. B. Lafci, E. Merčep, J. L. Herraiz, X. L. Deán-Ben, and D. Razansky, "Noninvasive multiparametric characterization of mammary tumors with transmission-reflection optoacoustic ultrasound," *Neoplasia*, vol. 22, no. 12, pp. 770–777, 2020.
18. A. Dharmireddy, M. Greeshma, S. Chalasani, S. T. Sriya, S. B. Ratnam and S. Sana, "Azolla Crop Growing Through IOT by Using ARM CORTEX-M0," *3rd International conference on Artificial Intelligence and Signal Processing (AISP)*, Vijayawada, India, 2023, pp. 1–5, doi: 10.1109/AISP57993.2023.1013503

Chapter 15

A computationally efficient image encryption technique using a 4D chaotic system (CIE4DC) in a dynamic network

Jashwant Samar, Shailja Sharma, and Ankur Khare

15.1 INTRODUCTION

The existing research emphasizes the critical importance of safety and secrecy in network communication, particularly for various categories of documents, including acoustic, video, pictures, and text, that are constantly spread above the network. To address these concerns, logistic system-related cryptography and conventional schemes such as Blowfish, Advanced Encryption Algorithm (AES), and Elliptic Curve Cryptography (ECC) have been employed. However, the conventional schemes have their limitations, such as sensitivity to data volume, vigorous connection, protection, and the potential for duplicity. To mitigate these restrictions, several research works propose the use of a block cryptosystem for images [3, 6]. This approach involves breaking an image into different blocks and applying cryptography to whole blocks one by one. This process aims to introduce both confusion and diffusion, which are fundamental concepts in encryption, and thus enhance the security and robustness of image encryption. Additionally, several researchers have introduced an alternative resolution in the form of chaotic system-related encryption. This method utilizes nonlinear chaotic arrangements to produce random numbers for keys, thereby increasing the convolution of the encryption. These strategies collectively contribute to the ongoing effort to enhance the security of Internet communication, particularly in the context of secure image encryption [4].

The use of chaotic systems in image encryption offers numerous valuable characteristics, including extreme primary-level sensitivity, arbitrariness, and instability [1, 5]. These characteristics make chaotic systems a widely employed tool for securing images through arbitrary extent formation, alteration, and scattering. One-dimensional (1D) logistic schemes are particularly well-suited for image encryptions, thanks to their simplicity and the use of fewer parameters. They employ a single variable and straightforward chaotic tracks to produce arbitrary numbers through mining minimal data. To enhance the protection of image encryption, two-dimensional (2D) and three-dimensional (3D) logistic schemes [7] are introduced, using more than one variable to produce arbitrary values. This approach adds an extra layer of complexity to real-time image cryptography. In addition, sinusoidal and cosine logistic equations are introduced to further enrich the convolution of encryption techniques.

Furthermore, the intricacy of cryptography can be heightened by incorporating concepts from biological science, such as Deoxyribo Nucleic Acid (DNA) [2, 8]. DNA offers benefits including analogous evaluation, minimal power expenses, and substantial storage buffer. As a result, DNA has emerged as a substantial device for confident and rapid encryption in image cryptosystems [9, 10]. Overall, the combination of logistic schemes, 1D and 2D logistic systems, and the integration of bioinformatics concepts like DNA have collectively contributed to advancing the security and complexity of image encryption, making it an intriguing and promising field of study [11, 12].

DOI: 10.1201/9781003513445-15

The current image cryptosystems presented in the spatial domain have been critiqued for their tendency to extinguish pixel connections [13, 14]. In contrast, occurrence realm-centered image cryptosystems have shown significant advantages in terms of proficiency, vigor, and data safeguarding during encryption and decryption progressions. These occurrence realm approaches often employ techniques such as Hilbert, Laplace, Gabor, and Jacobi transform. These approaches address the difficulty of deficient capacity and enhance the tractability and erraticism of the encryption scheme by growing the total cryptographic images. To further address the issue of decreasing the total cryptographic images while still tolerating a definite variety of noise intensity, a well-organized dual image cryptosystem related to wavelet transform. Overall, these transform-related image cryptosystem schemes offer promising solutions for maintaining the security and integrity of image data, and researchers continue to explore and develop new techniques in this domain to address various encryption challenges.

However, the existing image cryptographic schemes face concerns of eminent obscurity, moderated protection, extensive storage desires, and noticeable pixel interdependence. To conquer these problems, the CIE4DC deals with a capable solution by combining DCT and CDS with a 4D chaotic system. The utilization of DCT for transforming images into the frequency domain offers a notable benefit, as it maintains pixel correlations and improves image sanctuary. The deployment of CDS is instrumental in guaranteeing crucial security features, such as substitution and permutation, which are essential for resilient encryption. Likewise, the CDS deals a gain over asymmetric cryptosystems, obligations to its resourceful and tiniest complexity activities, leading to earlier encryption. These valuations collectively upkeep the assertion that the CIE4DC is a trustworthy and protected scheme for encryption, in terms of key sensitivity, key length protection, histogram examination, information entropy examination, and encryption time in contrast to various prior research works.

The objective of this work is to implement a safe image encryption technique for protecting image transfer. To attain this objective, some control factors are utilized to produce the initial values for the 4D chaotic system, which is further utilized for producing huge-size keys to resist the CIE4DC in contrast to brute force attacks. The row-column permutations and substitution are well performed using CDS to create confusion and diffusion. Further, the DCT is utilized to convert the images into a recurrence field and CDS is repeated for four cycles to protect in contrast to differential attacks. Various experiments and protection examinations are executed on several images to certify the strength and security of CIE4DC.

The remaining chapter is structured as follows. Section 15.2 explains the 4D chaotic system, DCT, and proposed image encryption technique CIE4DC using mathematical equations and steps. Section 15.3 illustrates the results and analysis of CIE4DC in terms of various security and performance parameters. Finally, Section 15.4 presents the conclusion and future work.

15.2 COMPUTATIONAL EFFICIENT IMAGE ENCRYPTION TECHNIQUE USING 4D CHAOTIC SYSTEM (CIE4DC)

15.2.1 4D chaotic system

The 4D chaotic system describes the presence of a 4D logistic equation in nonlinear models characterized by a multifaceted and irregular vigorous nature, possessing at least two positive Lyapunov coefficients. The 4D chaotic system suggests exhibiting enhanced randomness, obscurity, and a bigger key length rather than a 1D chaotic map. The aim is to achieve the utmost safety and effectiveness in the 4D chaotic system (eq. (15.1)).

$$\begin{cases} A_{m+1} = \Phi(B_m - A_m) + \Upsilon_1 D_m - C_m \\ B_{m+1} = \mu A_m - A_m * C_m + D_m \\ C_{m+1} = -\tau C_m + A_m * B_m + \Upsilon_2 B_m \\ D_{m+1} = -\chi A_m + A_m * D_m \end{cases} \tag{15.1}$$

Here,

$\Phi, \mu, \tau, \chi, \Upsilon_1$ *and* Υ_2 = Chaotic System Control Factors initialize as $\Phi = 30, \mu = 30, \tau = 4, \chi = 6,$ $\Upsilon_1 = 1$ *and* $\Upsilon_2 = 0.4$.

The initial values A_0, B_0, C_0, and D_0 are evaluated using eq. (15.2) to eq. (15.5).

$$A_0 = \frac{\delta+1}{2} X10 - \left\lceil \frac{\delta+1}{2} X10 \right\rceil \tag{15.2}$$

$$B_0 = \frac{\delta+1}{2} X100 - \left\lceil \frac{\delta+1}{2} X100 \right\rceil \tag{15.3}$$

$$C_0 = \frac{\delta+1}{2} X1000 - \left\lceil \frac{\delta+1}{2} X1000 \right\rceil \tag{15.4}$$

$$D_0 = \frac{\delta+1}{2} X10000 - \left\lceil \frac{\delta+1}{2} X10000 \right\rceil \tag{15.5}$$

Here,

δ = Control Factor $(\delta \in [-1, 1])$

$\lceil \delta \rceil$ = Ceiling value of δ.

15.2.2 Discrete cosine transform (DCT)

The DCT is broadly utilized for image compression principles incorporating PNG, JPEG, and BMP images. Here, 2D-DCT is utilized for an image (I) containing Y rows and Z columns. The pth row and q[th] column pixel value of the image (I) symbolize as I(p, q), and DCT is utilized for image (I) using eq. (15.6).

$$T(\alpha,\beta) = \rho(\alpha)\rho(\beta)\sum_{p=0}^{Y-1}\sum_{q=0}^{Z-1} I(p,q)\cos\left[\frac{(2p+1)\pi}{2Y}\alpha\right]\cos\left[\frac{(2q+1)\pi}{2Z}\beta\right] \tag{15.6}$$

Here,

$\rho(\alpha)$ and $\rho(\beta)$ are evaluated using eq. (15.7) and eq. (15.8).

$$\rho(\alpha) = \begin{cases} \sqrt{\frac{1}{Y}}, \alpha = 0 \\ \sqrt{\frac{2}{Z}}, \alpha \neq 0 \end{cases} \tag{15.7}$$

$$\rho(\beta) = \begin{cases} \sqrt{\frac{1}{Z}}, \beta = 0 \\ \sqrt{\frac{2}{Z}}, \beta \neq 0 \end{cases} \tag{15.8}$$

Subsequently applying DCT (eq. (15.6) to eq. (15.8)), the minimum recurrence factor reproduces the framework and gray scattering features of the goal in the image and the maximum recurrence factor reproduces the comprehensive information of the goal figure. Finally, the inverse DCT is applied to reestablish the image (I) using eq. (15.9).

$$I(p,q)=\rho(\alpha)\rho(\beta)T(\alpha,\beta)\cos\left[\frac{(2p+1)\pi}{2Y}\alpha\right]\cos\left[\frac{(2q+1)\pi}{2Z}\beta\right] \tag{15.9}$$

15.2.3 Proposed image encryption technique

The image encryption technique produces the initial values A_0, B_0, C_0, and D_0 using eq. (15.2) to eq. (15.5) and the encryption framework utilizes a CDS repeating for four cycles. Every cycle contains the row-column permutations and XOR substitution within the CDS process.

The sender performs the following steps in CIE4DC for encrypting an image (I) having Y x Z pixels (Figure 15.1).

Step 1. The sender evaluates A_{300}, B_{300}, C_{300}, and D_{300} by repeating eq. (15.1) 300 times using initial values A_0, B_0, C_0, and D_0. The initial 300 repetitions are deleted for every sequence.

Step 2. Encryption Cycle: Suppose P_0 = I. For cy = 0, 1, 2, 3, Do:

(i) Sender evaluates $A_{300+cy(YZ)+1}$, $A_{300+cy(YZ)+2}$, … , $A_{300+cy(YZ)+YZ}$ and $B_{300+cy(YZ)+1}$, $B_{300+cy(YZ)+2}$, … , $B_{300+cy(YZ)-YZ}$ and $C_{300+cy(YZ)+1}$, $C_{300+cy(YZ)+2}$, … , $C_{300+cy(YZ)+YZ}$ and $D_{300+cy(YZ)+1}$, $D_{300+cy(YZ)+2}$, … , $D_{300+cy(YZ)+YZ}$ by applying $A_{300+cy(YZ)}$ and $B_{300+cy(YZ)}$ and $C_{300+cy(YZ)}$ and $D_{300+cy(YZ)}$, respectively, to eq. (15.1).

(ii) Sender evaluates $A'_x, B'_x, C'_x \; and \; D'_x$ using eq. (15.10) to eq. (15.13). (Here $\lfloor \cdot \rfloor$ = Floor value bracket)

$$A'_x=\left|A_{x+300+cy(YZ)}\ X\,10^{12}\right| MOD(Z+1)\ for\ x=1,2,3,\ldots,Y \tag{15.10}$$

$$B'_x=\left|B_{x+300+cy(YZ)}\ X\,10^{12}\right| MOD(Y-1)\ for\ x=1,2,3,\ldots,Z \tag{15.11}$$

$$C'_x=\left|C_{x+300+cy(YZ)}\ X\,10^{12}\right| MOD(Z+1)\ for\ x=1,2,3,\ldots,Y \tag{15.12}$$

$$D'_x=\left|D_{x+300+cy(YZ)}\ X\,10^{12}\right| MOD(Y+1)\ for\ x=1,2,3,\ldots,Z \tag{15.13}$$

(iii) Sender evaluates Keys E_x for x = 1, 2, 3, … , YxZ using eq. (15.14).

$$E_x=\left(\left(A_{x+300+cy(YZ)}+B_{x+300+cy(YZ)}+C_{x+300+cy(YZ)}+D_{x+300+cy(YZ)}\right)X10^{12}\right)MOD\,256 \tag{15.14}$$

(iv) Sender operates row permutations (shifting right by A'_p locations for every pth row) by evaluating eq. (15.15) for p = 1, 2, 3, … , Y and q = 1, 2, 3, … , Z.

$$P'_{cy}(p,q)\leftarrow P_{cy}\left(p,\left(q+A'_p-1\right)MOD(Z+1)\right) \tag{15.15}$$

(v) Sender operates column permutations (shifting down by B'_p locations for every q^{th} column) by evaluating eq. (15.16) for p = 1, 2, 3, … , Y and q = 1, 2, 3, … , Z.

$$P''_{cy}(p,q)\leftarrow P'_{cy}\left(\left(p+B'_p-1\right)MOD(Y+1),q\right) \tag{15.16}$$

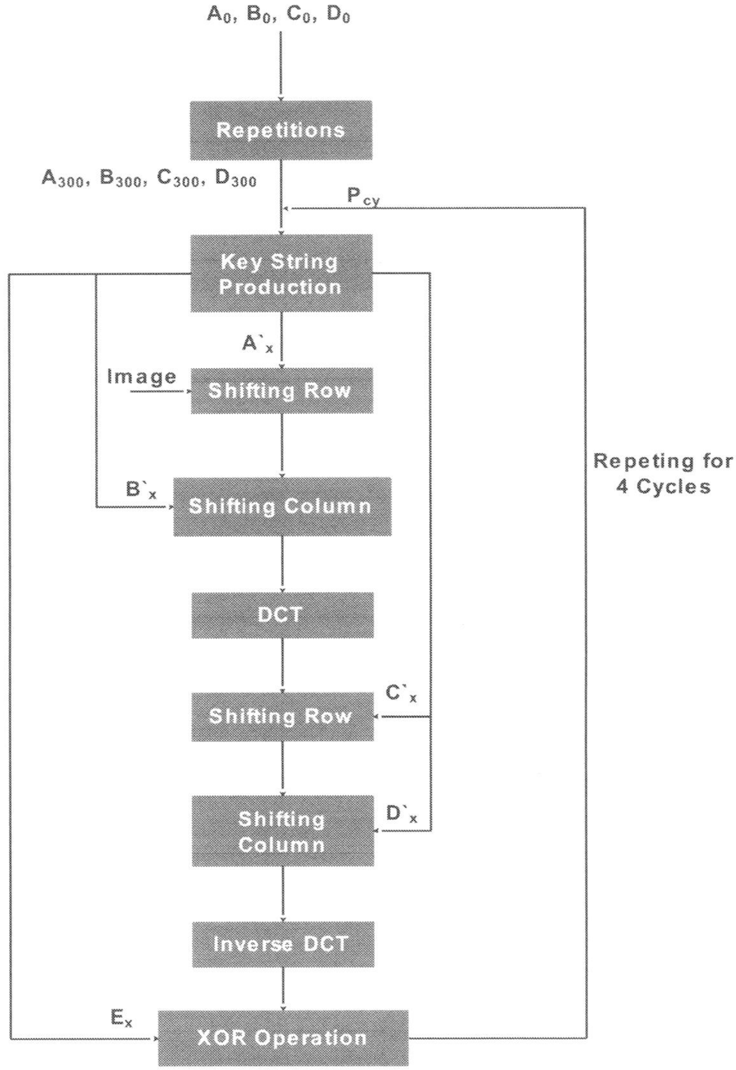

Figure 15.1 The flowchart of image encryption technique.

(vi) Sender evaluates the DCT values T using eq. (15.6) on $P''_{cy}(p,q)$.

(vii) Sender operates row permutations (shifting right by C'_p locations for every p[th] row) by evaluating eq. (15.17) for p = 1, 2, 3, … , Y and q = 1, 2, 3, … , Z.

$$T'(p,q) \leftarrow T\left(p,\left(q+C'_p-1\right)MOD\left(Z+1\right)\right) \quad (15.17)$$

(viii) Sender operates row permutations (shifting right by D'_p locations for every q[th] column) by evaluating eq. (15.18) for p = 1, 2, 3, … , Y and q = 1, 2, 3, … , Z.

$$T''(p,q) \leftarrow T'\left(\left(p+D'_p-1\right)MOD\left(Y+1\right),q\right) \quad (15.18)$$

(ix) Sender evaluates the inverse DCT values F using eq. (15.9) on $T''(p,q)$.

(x) Sender produces the encrypted image for cycle cy using eq. (15.19) for p = 1, 2, 3, … , YZ.

$$\left(P_{cy+1}\right)_p = F_p \oplus E_p \oplus \left(P_{cy+1}\right)_{(p-1)} \tag{15.19}$$

Here,

$\left(P_{cy+1}\right)_p, F_p, E_p = \text{p}^{\text{th}}$ component of $\text{P}_{\text{cy+1}}$, F and E, respectively.

Step 3. The sender transfers the encrypted image to the receiver.
Step 4. The receiver performs all four decryption cycles as the inverse of encryption cycles to recover the original image.

15.3 RESULTS AND ANALYSIS

The results are generated by implementing the proposed CIE4DC on MATLAB environment with Windows 10, i5 processor having 8GB RAM. The CIE4DC is applied to four widely used images: Lena, Cameraman, House, and Pepper (Figure 15.2).

15.3.1 Key sensitivity examination

The image encryption is generally related to the sensitivity of the key string, therefore the encrypted image is totally distinct when there is a tiny change in initial factor values.

In Figure 15.3, the 1st and 3rd columns of both row 1 and row 2 display the decrypted images through exact initial values for keys $\{A_0 = 0.24, B_0 = 0.32, C_0 = 0.36, D_0 = 0.45\}$ and 2nd and 4th columns of both row 1 and row 2 display the decrypted images through wrong

Figure 15.2 Original and encrypted images of Lena, Cameraman, House, and Pepper.

values for keys $\{A_0 = 0.24 + 10^{-14}, B_0 = 0.32, C_0 = 0.36, D_0 = 0.45\}$. It demonstrates that the CIE4DC is extremely protected in contrast to exhaustive attacks.

15.3.2 Key length protection

The key string in CIE4DC is produced by utilizing four initial values $\{A_0 = 0.24, B_0 = 0.32, C_0 = 0.36, D_0 = 0.45\}$. If the correctness is 10^{-14}, then the key length is $10^{14X2} = 10^{28} \approx 2^{93.3}$, highly sufficient to achieve high in contrast to brute force attack.

15.3.3 Histogram examination

The encrypted images are displayed in the shape of a histogram, where fairly uniform pixel allotment accomplishes lowering the pixel associations. Hence, CIE4DC achieves maximum strength in contrast to statistical attacks excluding any statistical data (Figures 15.4 and 15.5).

15.3.4 Information entropy examination

Information entropy is illustrated as the unpredictability of image pixels. Therefore, merely little information is produced from encrypted image criteria to regain the original image for increasing the protection of the image cryptosystem (eq. (15.20)).

$$G = -\sum_{h=1}^{Y*Z} L_h \log(L_h) \tag{15.20}$$

Here,

L_h = Encrypted image criteria probability.

The outcomes demonstrate that CIE4DC achieves the superior competent information entropy value of encrypted image approaching entropy standard value 8 in contrast to numerous prior research works [11–14] and it is tough for an intruder to decrypt the encrypted image (Table 15.1).

Figure 15.3 Decrypted images of Lena, Cameraman, House, and Pepper.

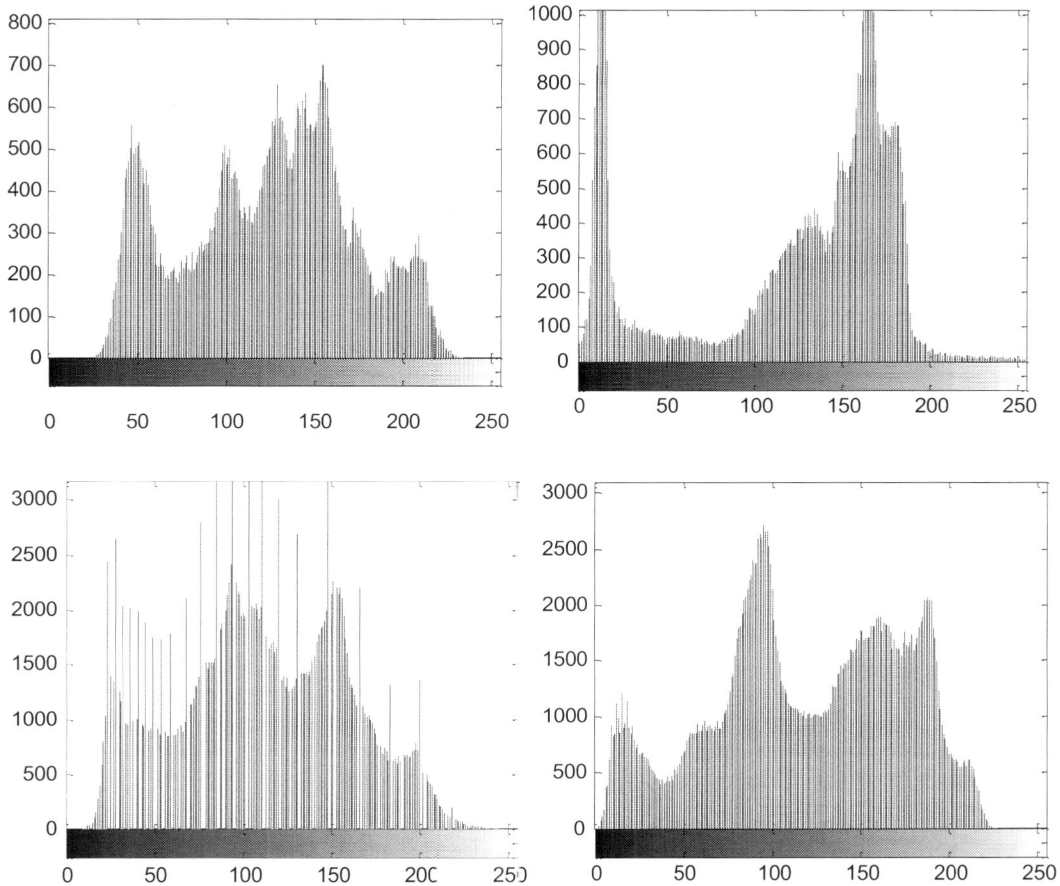

Figure 15.4 Histograms of Lena, Cameraman, House, and Pepper.

15.3.5 Encryption time

The key strings are produced by utilizing a 4D chaotic system (eq. (15.1) to eq. (15.5)) and evaluating eq. (15.10) to eq. (15.14). The encryption time of CIE4DC is examined by performing Step 1 and Step 2 (Section 2.3) in contrast to various prior research works [11, 13]. Table 15.2 and Figure 15.6 demonstrate the better performance of CIE4DC with the least encryption time (seconds).

15.4 CONCLUSION AND FUTURE WORK

This chapter describes several issues in recent image cryptosystems like multidimensionality and pixel association cooperation. The proposed CIE4DC suggests a solution to the above image cryptosystem issues by combining two components DCT and CDS having a 4D chaotic system. The DCT is utilized for changing images into the frequency field to manage the pixel correlation for achieving image protection. The CDS applies some permutation and substitution operations on image pixels to achieve a higher level of security. Overall, The CIE4DC outperforms in terms of security like maximum key sensitivity against exhaustive

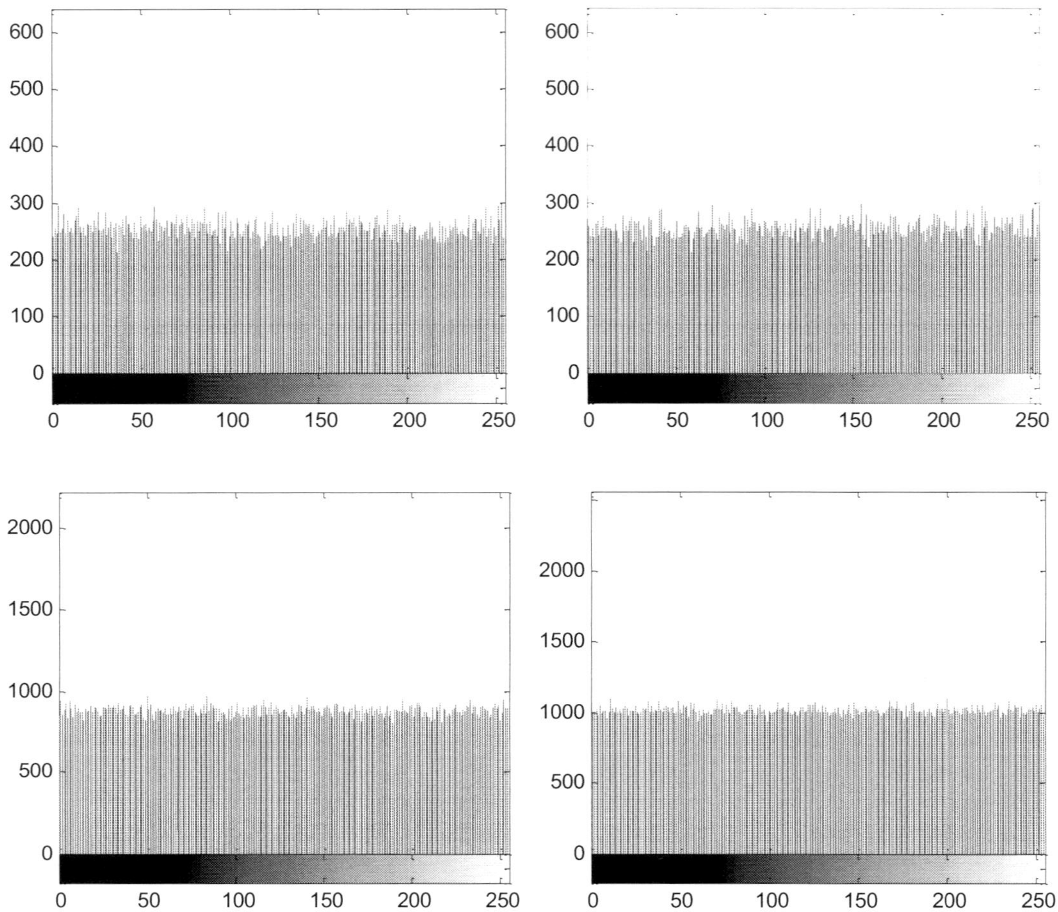

Figure 15.5 Histograms of the encrypted form of Lena, Cameraman, House, and Pepper.

Table 15.1 Information entropy

		Encrypted image				
Images	*Input images*	*CIE4DC*	*M. Akraam et al. [11]*	*D. E. Mfungo et al. [12]*	*Y. Shen et al. [13]*	*A. H. Alrubaie et al. [14]*
Lena	7.3174	7.9982	7.9969	7.9968	7.9979	7.9898
Cameraman	7.2148	7.9984	7.9968	7.9974	7.9977	7.9975
House	7.3425	7.9987	7.9972	7.9972	7.9982	7.9950
Pepper	7.6213	7.9981	7.9976	7.9969	7.9980	7.9893

attack, maximum key length protection against brute force attack, and maximum strength against statistical attack in histogram examination.

The CIE4DC also attains the extremely competent information entropy value of encrypted image as compared to prior research work and the encryption time is the least for CIE4DC with 50% and 85% reductions against two prior research works. In the future, some

Table 15.2 Encryption time (seconds)

Images	*CIE4DC*	*M. Akraam et al. [11]*	*Y. Shen et al. [13]*
Lena	0.2216	3.222	0.5547
Cameraman	0.2435	3.319	0.6732
House	0.2263	3.284	0.5837
Pepper	0.2487	3.316	0.6927

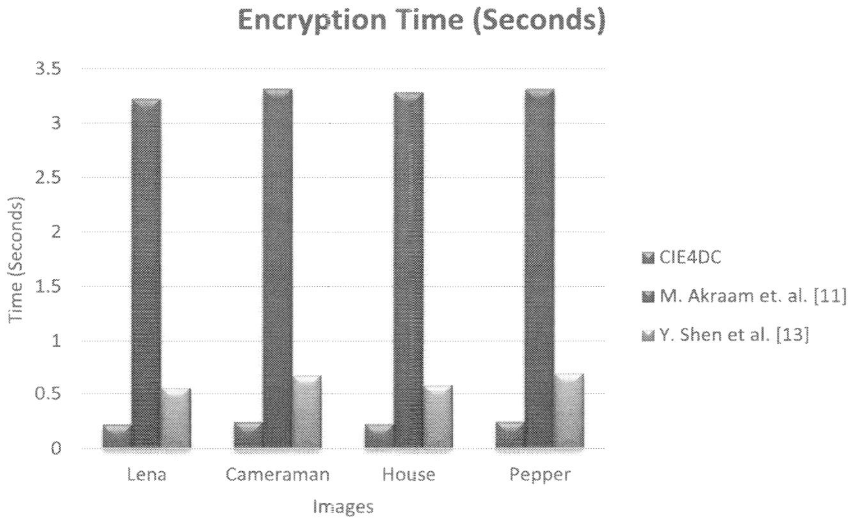

Figure 15.6 Encryption time of Lena, Cameraman, House, and Pepper images.

optimization techniques and DNA concepts will be introduced to enhance the security and robustness of image encryption techniques.

REFERENCES

1. Khare, A., Shukla, P. K., Rizvi, M. A. and Stalin, S., An Intelligent and Fast Chaotic Encryption Using Digital Logic Circuits for Ad-Hoc and Ubiquitous Computing. *Entropy*, 18, 201, 1–27, 2016. (doi: 10.3390/e18050201)
2. Mondal, B. and Mandal, T., A light weight secure image encryption scheme based on chaos & DNA computing. *Journal of King Saud University, Computer and Information Sciences*, 29(4), 499–504, 2017. (http://dx.doi.org/10.1016/j.jksuci.2016.02.003)
3. Gao, X., Yu, J., Banerjee, S., Yan, H. and Mou, J., A New Image Encryption Scheme based on Fractional Order Hyperchaotic System and Multiple Image Fusion. *Scietific Reports, Nature*, 11 (15737), 1–21, 2021.
4. Wu, Z., Pan, P., Sun, C. and Zhao, B , Plaintext Related Dynamic Key Chaotic Image Encryption Algorithm. *Entropy*, 23 (1159), 1–19, 2021.
5. Shukla, P. K., Khare, A., Rizvi, M. A., Stalin, S. and Kumar, S., Applied Cryptography Using Chaos Function for Fast Digital Logic-Based Systems in Ubiquitous Computing. *Entropy*, 17, 1387–1410, 2015. (doi: 10.3390/e17031387)
6. Dua, M., Makhija, D., Manasa, P. Y. L. and Mishra, P., 3D Chaotic Cosine Transformation based Approach to Video Encryption and Decryption. *Open Computer Science*, 12, 37–56, 2022.

7. Ye, G., Jiao, K., Pan, C. and Huang, X., An Effective Framework for Chaotic Image Encryption Based on 3D Logistic Map. *Hindawi Security and Communication Networks*, 1–11, 2018. (https://doi.org/10.1155/2018/8402578)
8. Tian, Y. and Lu, Z., Novel permutation-diffusion image encryption algorithm with chaotic dynamic S-box and DNA sequence operation. *AIP Advances*, 1–23, 2017.
9. Elamrawy, F., Sharkas, M. and Nasser, A. M., An image encryption based on DNA coding and 2DLogistic chaotic map. *International Journal of Signal Processing*, 3, 27–32, 2018.
10. Stalin, S., Maheshwary, P., Shukla, P. K., Maheshwari, M., Gour, B. and Khare, A., Fast and Secure Medical Image Encryption based on Non Linear 4D Logistic Map and DNA Sequences (NL4DLM_DNA). *Journal of Medical Systems*, 43 (267), 1–17, 2019.
11. Akraam, M., Rashid, T. and Zafar, S., A Chaos based Image Encryption Scheme is Proposed using Multiple Chaotic Maps. *Mathematical Problems in Engineering, Hindawi*, 2023, 1–13, 2023.
12. Mfungo, D. E., Fu, X., Xian, Y. and Wang, X., A Novel Image Encryption Scheme using Chaotic Maps and Fuzzy Numbers for Secure Transmission of Information. *Applied Sciences*, 13 (7113), 1–25, 2023.
13. Shen, Y., Huang, J., Chen, L., Wen, T., Li, T. and Zhang, G., Fast and Secure Image Encryption Algorithm with Simultaneous Shuffling and Diffusion based on a Time Delayed Combinatorial Hyperchaos Map. *Entropy*, 25 (753), 1–22, 2023.
14. Alrubaie, A. H., Khodher, M. A. A. and Abdulameer, A. T., Image Encryption based on 2DNA Encoding and Chaotic 2D Logistic Map. *Journal of Engineering and Applied Science*, 70 (60), 1–21, 2023.

Chapter 16

Data science applications in healthcare data transmission

Manne Bhargav Phaneendra, Vemparala Viharika, Suresh Babu Satukumati, and Venkata Naresh Mandhala

16.1 INTRODUCTION

A smart healthcare system is one of those very complex [1], sophisticated, and complicated ways to succeed in any type of business. Through this research chapter, we propose a method to recognize the smart health system with the help of data analytics [2]. The amount of data is directly proportional to the accuracy of the classifier and the provided attributes. Fields are completely dependent on this entity, called health conditions, to make money and minimize the risks. In this chapter, we propose a method to analyze the smart health system with the help of data analytics [3]. The amount of data is directly proportional to the accuracy of the classifier and the provided attributes (Figure 16.1).

Health condition analyzing systems [4] will help people to be cautious and common civilians can gain knowledge and information about the health fitness that depends on the various health conditions of different organs of the body [5]. The algorithm we propose will help predict the future of many fields and departments by using different open-source libraries that make this a highly unpredictable business entity a bit more vulnerable to prediction [6]. This chapter shows an example of the implementation of predicting the stock by giving us the results that can be accepted. When it comes to identifying crucial health issues, the product is based on a vast array of axioms and resources, some of which may or may not hold true in real life [7]. A smart healthcare system can sometimes be considered as important when one invests money without prior knowledge about the gains and a process is therefore needed that can analyze and predict the smart healthcare system fluctuations (Figure 16.2).

This system that we are proposing has the potential to provide wise, generating modules [8]. The price caused by health complications is highly unpredictable with very constant fluctuations. A smart healthcare system can be named one of the oldest and one of those highly effective methods where any organization or person can access genuine information about health conditions [9]. The principle of a smart healthcare system is quite simple to understand. We must recognize the health conditions so that we can prevent the damage to human lives and this is where the technology is involved in the image. Data analytics is such a tool that helps us attain the situation that we want regarding smart healthcare systems.

Data analytics is highly dependent on the information collected [10]. Data analytics can be considered an insanely powerful tool and it has many mind-blowing applications. Therefore, it is very important to understand that data is such a valuable component, and the analysis of the data or the information that has been collected is a time-consuming and tedious work that needs to be performed with utmost care and attention [1]. Data analytics has found a lot of popularity along with its applications in practical lives and has developed further into different streams like deep learning and neural networks; this chapter is strictly limited to only

DOI: 10.1201/9781003513445-16

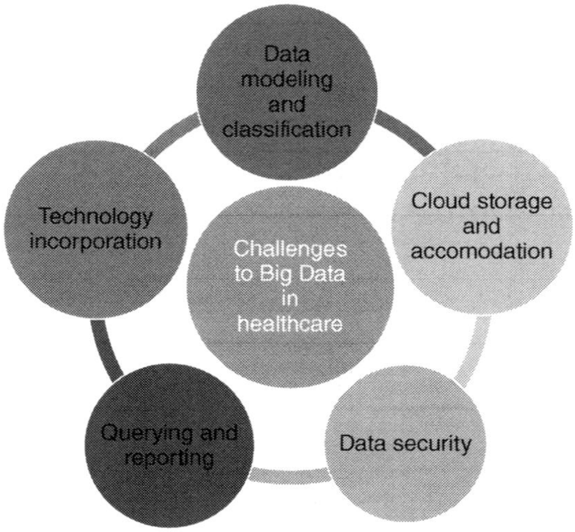

Figure 16.1 Cycle of healthcare challenges in big data analytics.

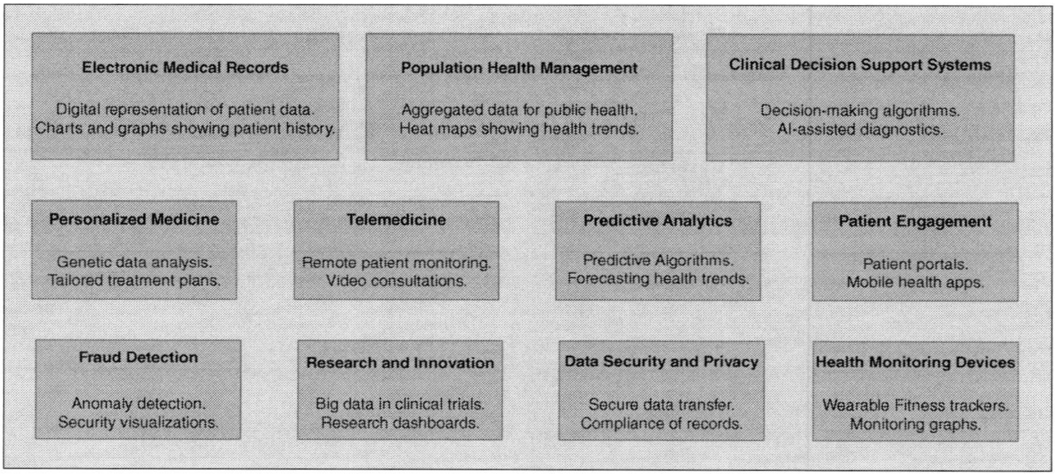

Figure 16.2 Basic health services of big data analytics.

supervised data analytics during the generation of smart healthcare systems. The sole idea of data analytics is simplifying the task that demands human efforts and human intelligence [11]. The most common mistakes made by researchers in the field of supervised data analytics are poor annotation of testing and training datasets, bad understanding of collected data and assumptions, misunderstanding the data provided, being unable to understand the objectives, not avoiding the leakage, not collecting enough information that is required to train the classifier, usage of data analytics techniques though it's not really needed [3]. This chapter gives a deep insight into the implementation of data analytics in predicting the complete futuristic data. There are many ways and many more techniques available to solve and handle different problems (Figure 16.3).

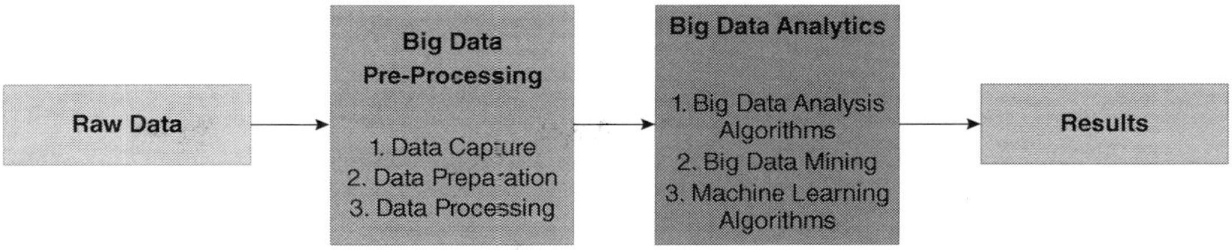

Figure 16.3 Block diagram of the process of big data analytics.

16.2 METHODS

16.2.1 Healthcare as a big data repository

Healthcare can be considered as the several dimensional modules that are highly motivated to diagnose, prevent, and treat impairments in human beings or any other health-related issues. The primary elements of the usual healthcare system are the health facilities and health professionals [12]. Health professionals belong to several different streams like nursing, medicine, physiotherapy, psychology, dentistry, and so on. Healthcare is certainly needed at different stages, which is completely dependent on the emergencies and the urgency of the instance of the scenario [3]. It is regarded by medical professionals as the focus of the consultation. Accurate medical care, including diagnosis and treatment, necessitates the use of specialists, cutting-edge medical testing, and other measures.

16.2.1.1 Electronic health records

It is imperative to keep in mind that the National Institutes of Health recently unveiled the "all of us" effort, which has the goal of gathering Electronic Health Record (EHR) data from one million patients and up, as well as socio-behavioral, medical imaging, and environmental data over the next few years. Below, we describe some of the characteristic advantages of using EHRs [13]. EHRs using data science techniques enable the secure and efficient exchange of EHRs among healthcare providers, hospitals, and other healthcare organizations. Telemedicine for Data transmission is a vital component of telemedicine, which involves remote healthcare services [14]. Data science enables real-time interaction and seamless sharing of medical information between healthcare providers and patients. Healthcare practitioners now have better access to a patient's complete medical history thanks to EHRs. Medical diagnoses, prescriptions, information on known allergies, demographics, clinical narratives, and test results from various laboratories are all included in the material [15]. It allows for video conferencing, transmission of medical images and diagnostics, and remote monitoring of patients. Medical imaging is used for data transmission, which is essential for sharing medical images among imaging centers, radiologists, and other healthcare professionals. For example, by eliminating errors in prescription dosage and frequency, overcoming such logistical problems has resulted in a decrease in the number of drug allergies.

16.2.1.2 Big data in biomedical research

The biological module, such as the human body or the human cell, displays chemical variations whereas the human body displays physical interactions with complex dynamics [16]. A biological or biomedical experiment will typically acquire a lot of data on a very minute and less intricate component to comprehend the interdependences of various elements and events of such a complicated system. Therefore, it necessitates the much less difficult tests to produce a wider perspective of the relevant biological phenomenon [9]. When we consider this, we can see very clearly that the more information we have, the better understanding we can have of how biology works. To make up for this idea, advanced techniques have been developed at a huge pace. For instance, we can easily understand the amount of data that has been generated since the integration of efficient technologies like genome-wide association studies and next-generation technologies to integrate deeper into human genetics [5]. The next-generation sequencing (NGS)-based data offers us access to information at greater depths that were previously very difficult to acquire and unquestionably gives the experimental scenario a newer dimension. It has improved the level of detail at which we can capture or track the biological occurrences connected to a given disease in real time.

The generation of smarter healthcare modules is not an easy task and predicting the expenses of the smarter healthcare module is completely complicated due to numerous uncertain factors involved and many other variables that show an impact on the market value and a very negative effect on the marketplace value on a certain day that includes the information regarding investors and the economic conditions [8]. Smart healthcare systems should remain impartial and not be influenced by political activities or align with any specific business organization. Because of such factors and issues, the inventory markets are at a stake of risk. Various changes include many unexpected fluctuations deep inside the health conditions. The collections of the smart healthcare system are commonly non-parametric and dynamic, noisy, and mostly chaotic most of the time. Through this chapter, we propose a method to predict the highly unpredictable smart healthcare system with the help of data analytics [10]. The algorithm we propose will help predict the future price of any stock for gain by using different open-source libraries that make this a highly unpredictable business entity a bit more vulnerable to prediction. The methodology that we are discussing in the chapter is about data analytics in smart healthcare systems. The main goal of this study work is to compare various data analytics generating strategies with the aid of various classifiers [17]. The comparison's outcomes will depend on various factors. An artificial neural network (ANN) can be thought of as a computer system designed to carry out the functions of a biological neural network, which can be thought of as carrying out life duties. Examples will help you understand these specific modules [18]. A set-off collection of nodal data, which could be thought of as artificial neurons, is used by the ANN. These artificial neurons can communicate with one another, acting like the brain itself. In the implementation of ANN, a signal can be described by a value, often a real number, and the output of the neuron is determined with the help of a non-linear sum function which can be considered as the input. The link between every node can be called the edge, and every node will possess a value that relates to it. If the value minimizes, it will result in the strength of the signal being elevated. Usually, the neurons can be arranged into layers [19]. Each layer will undoubtedly carry out a different set of operations in relation to the inputs. From the input layer, signals travel to the output layer. Signals can oscillate back and forth between layers repeatedly before producing an output. K-nearest neighbor performs regression and classification without utilizing any sort of parameters. The input can be considered as the data science examples within the space for the features.

The accuracy of the models that run with the help of the deep learning algorithms is completely dependent on the amount of information provided for the sake of the training [20]. The amount of verbal data that was available and analyzed during a few surveys and studies was insufficient and as a result, system generations with low accuracy rates were observed. In this chapter, we have tried to accelerate the rate of accuracy of the medical expense generations by collecting huge amounts of time series data, and for the sake of analyzing the data and predicting the prices of future health complications, we took the help of deep learning models such as the neural prophet algorithm [2]. The object can be categorized into its own class in the classification of data sciences, which can be the most among its nearest neighbors of data sciences; the outputs can be considered as the class that has been chosen already. The output can be considered as the sum of all the values in the regression from its closest k neighbors. Because the function is locally approximated, data sciences are a form of lazy learning. Because each neighbor can be assigned a weight, the higher weights are distributed to the nearest lower weights, and the neighbors are assigned to the farther [21]. By utilizing the techniques, support vector machines (SVMs) can be used to produce regressions and classification analyses. A training set of examples for SVM is given, and each example can be classified into one of two groups. These examples can be used to better categorize SVM and to select a few more examples. These illustrations can be represented by points for the sake of illustration, and they can aid in mapping into a place to display categorization segmentation. Arbitrary forests can be used for categorization, regression, and the decision tree creation process. Random Forests (RFs) to the training set can correct the decision trees' inclination of overfitting.

These artificial neurons can transmit impulses to one another, acting like the biological brain. In the implementation of an ANN, a signal can be represented by a number, often a real number, and the output of the neuron is generated with the aid of a non-linear sum function, which can be thought of as the input [3]. Every node will have a weight attached to it and the connection between each node is known as the edge. If the weight is minimized, the signal's intensity will be increased. These neurons can typically be inserted into the layers. For testing purposes, we would need to provide the input, such as a combination of features, to the perfectly trained classifier and compare the results with the original label [22]. This usually aids in the creation of a successful model. The classifier that has an accuracy of less than 95% is generally considered useless and a waste of time and even 5% can be a huge loss to the individual or the organization. Accuracy can be considered a very important factor in this data analytics model. We must understand the real and practical terms of the term accuracy [14]. Big data analytics is a process where all the features must be labeled. In this research, we will regulate the classifiers in a way that learns all the information arrangements of the different combinations of features results in which of the label [4]. The classifier will attain the features, map out the labels, and will remember them. It usually records the combinations of the features and their respective labels which will be the stock price in our case. Then, to move forward, it discovers the pattern that the feature is employing to produce the relevant label [20]. This is how supervised data analytics often operate. We further analyzed the data and eliminated the crucial information that the classifier will need. This can be viewed as a very significant step that should be handled carefully. A data mislead or a small error in extracting crucial and valuable data can result in a model failure or loss generation, as well as a very ineffective classifier. Generalization is one of the most likely outcomes only if the information of the other remaining subject differs from the features extracted, which are specific regarding the subjects being employed and will undoubtedly vary from subject to subject.

16.3 RESULTS AND DISCUSSION

Once our model gets ready, we can utilize the model to acquire the required results in any other that we need. For better understanding, we are plotting the graph for our results based on the requirements that are discussed in our research. A series of examples of SVM that fall into one of two groups are provided. Depending on the examples, SVM can be futuristic in categorizing many other examples. The sole idea of data analytics is simplifying the task that demands human efforts and human intelligence. This chapter gives a deep insight regarding the implementation of data analytics in predicting the complete futuristic data.

Electronic Health Records (EHR): Data science techniques enable the secure and efficient exchange of EHRs among healthcare providers, hospitals, and other healthcare organizations.

Telemedicine: Data transmission is a vital component of telemedicine, which involves remote healthcare services. Data science enables real-time interaction and seamless sharing of medical information between healthcare providers and patients. It allows for video conferencing, transmission of medical images and diagnostics, and remote monitoring of patients (Figure 16.4).

Medical imaging: Data transmission is essential for sharing medical images among imaging centers, radiologists, and other healthcare professionals.

Remote patient monitoring: Data science facilitates the continuous monitoring of the patient's vital signs and health parameters through data transmission.

Health information exchange (HIE): Data transmission plays a crucial role in the electronic sharing of patient data among healthcare providers and organizations participating in HIEs.

16.4 CONCLUSION

Accuracy can be considered a very important factor in this data analytics model. We must understand the real and practical implications of the term accuracy. Big data analytics is a process where all the features must be labeled. Therefore, it is very important to understand that data is such a valuable component, and analysis of the data or the information that has been collected is a time-consuming and tedious work that needs to be performed with utmost care and attention. There are many ways and many more techniques available to solve and handle different problems. This chapter is strictly limited to only supervised data analytics during the generation of smart healthcare systems. Data analytics can be considered an insanely powerful tool and it has many mind-blowing applications. Data analytics is highly dependent on the information collected. Data analytics has found a lot of popularity along with its applications in practical life and has developed further into different streams like deep learning and neural networks.

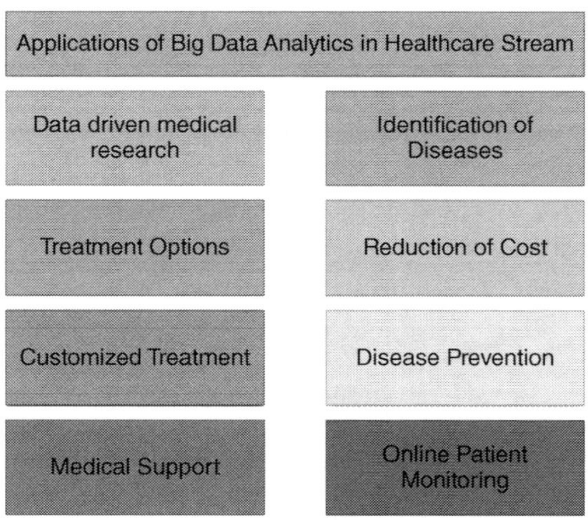

Figure 16.4 Applications of big data analytics in the healthcare stream.

REFERENCES

[1] Bhagattjee, B., Emergence and taxonomy of big data as a service. Diss. Massachusetts Institute of Technology, 2014.

[2] Herrick, D.M., Gorman, L. and Goodman, J.C., *Health Information Technology: Benefits and Problems*. National Center for Policy Analysis, 2010.

[3] Alley-Young, G., White House Big Data Initiative. Encyclopedia of Big Data, 1–5, 2017.

[4] Bernard, A., Healthcare Industry Sees Big Data As More Than a Bandage. 2013.

[5] IIfH, Informatics, *The Global Use of Medicines: Outlook Through 2016*. IMS Health, Informatics IIfH, Danbury, 2012.

[6] Israel, S., *Contextual Health vs The Elephant in the Hospital*. Forbes, Tech, 1–10, 2013.

[7] Yu, Y., Industry Classification Benchmark and Industries' Predictive Ability (Doctoral dissertation, ISCTE-Instituto Universitario de Lisboa (Portugal)), 2014.

[8] Zigmond, J., Why one Medicare pioneer ACO succeeded in saving money. *Healthcare Business News*, 2013.

[9] Honavar, V.G., The promise and potential of big data: A case for discovery informatics. *Review of Policy Research*, 31(4), 326–330, 2014.

[10] Parmar, A., Want to know if you will develop high blood pressure next year? With big data magic you can. *MedCity News*, 2012.

[11] Baum, S., A remote monitor embedded in insulin pen caps could help personalize diabetes treatment, 2013.

[12] Bort, J., How The CDC Is Using Big Data To Save You From The Flu, *Business Insider*, 2012.

[13] Mike, W., *Healthy Big Data: Stopping the Spread of Flu*, 2013.

[14] Cliffard, J., *Data Design Diabetes Innovation Challenge*, 2013.

[15] Cisco UCS Common Platform Architecture (CPA) for Big Data, enhanced with encryption at rest: http://www.cisco.com/en/US/docs/unified-computing/ucs/UCS-CVDs/Cisco-UCS-CPA-for-Big-Data-with-Intel.html

[16] Nambiar, R., Bhardwaj, R., Sethi, A. and Vargheese, R., A look at challenges and opportunities of big data analytics in healthcare. In 2013 IEEE International Conference on Big Data, 17–22, IEEE, 2013.

[17] Nambiar, R., Chitor, R. and Joshi, A., Data management–a look back and a look ahead. In Specifying Big Data Benchmarks: First Workshop, WBDB 2012, San Jose, CA, USA, May 8-9, 2012, and Second Workshop, WBDB 2012, Pune, India, December 17-18, 2012, Revised Selected Papers (pp. 11–19). Springer Berlin Heidelberg, 2014.

[18] Fazlikhani, M. and Bagheri, I., A Deeper Review Over Big Data Analytics Within Health Care Applications.

[19] MD Anderson's Moon Shot to Fight Cancer. http://www.cancermoonshots.org/about

[20] Basel, K., David, K., Steve Van, K., *The big-data revolution in US health care: Accelerating value and innovation*, McKinsey & Company.

[21] Marc, B., *Medical Monitor*: Los Angeles: USC Trojan Family, 2013.

[22] Dishman, E., How Big Data can revolutionize health care. *Politico*.

Chapter 17

Secure and scalable data analysis framework with quantum machine learning and blockchain

Shyama Heshini Niranjala, S. B. Goyal, and Budati Anil Kumar

17.1 INTRODUCTION

17.1.1 Overview of Quantum Machine Learning

Quantum machine learning or simply QML at the core is the nascent field involving the intersection of quantum computing with traditional machine learning. Quantum computing based its processing on the fundamental laws of quantum mechanics for superposition and entanglement to execute instructions with speed and capability that classical computers can only dream of [1]. In contrast to the binary system wherein classical bits can only be in state 0 or state 1, quantum bits (qubits) can be in many states at the same time, making quantum computers' calculations exponentially faster than those of classical computers [2]. Due to this, the algorithms of QML can address issues incompatible with conventional machine learning, and this improves computational performance by using new properties in data handling and manipulation.

17.1.2 Importance of Distributed Systems

Distributed system is one of the most crucial tools of modern business data processing as it enables the storage and analysis of massive amounts of data in various locations. These systems allow for the consolidation and synchronization of data in different formats, both at a more general level and specialized, making possible the comprehensive and integrated analysis of the studied phenomenon [3]. However, they also bring in a number of issues like data synchronization, delay, and security. Data integrity and keeping the data updated, from the distributed nodes, are always issues that are required to be solved with the help of sophisticated computational and secure algorithms.

17.1.3 Role of Blockchain Technology

Blockchain is a technology that people are most familiar with due to its use in the creation of digital currencies, but it is in fact a very reliable tool for storing data which can be used in distributed systems. Since it is distributed and cannot be altered once recorded, blockchain increases the believability of data transactions' honesty and accountability [4]. In a blockchain, each block holds the hash value of the previous block, a timestamp, and the transaction details, making it difficult for anyone to cheat or tamper with the data saved. This technology proves most useful in distributed systems where data must remain accurate and secure from tampering and other forms of invasion [5].

DOI: 10.1201/9781003513445-17

17.1.4 Integrating QML, Distributed Systems, and Blockchain

The proposed framework illustrates the synergistic benefits of consolidating QML, distributed systems, and blockchain technology for improved data analysis. Quantum computing provides for the best methods of data processing and usage in machine learning and blockchain provides for the security and protection of such data. It means this integrative approach can alleviate drawbacks and weaknesses of traditional methods and offer a more strong and effective solution for large-scale and distributed data processing tasks. When considering data analytical techniques from the past to the present, there is a significant change in different areas. Table 17.1 shows the comparison of traditional data analysis techniques with QML and blockchain, and shows how they enhance the data analysis approach with regard to constraints of efficiency, security, and scalability.

17.1.5 Technological Parameters of Each Technology

Machine Learning (ML) has revolutionized several industries, including Finance, Medicinal Research and Molecular Simulation, Healthcare, Supply Chain Management, Cybersecurity, Energy, Transportation, and Agriculture [6]. It is now a crucial component of these industries. However, as computing power increases, classical machine learning becomes less effective at handling large and complicated datasets. To avoid these issues, researchers are combining more technological concepts together for real-life applications including quantum computing (QC), machine learning, blockchain (BC), QML, blockchain machine learning (BML), and blockchain quantum machine learning (BQML). Table 17.2 shows the parameters of each technology taken into consideration as they are used in practical application areas.

Each of these technologies offers distinct capabilities and advantages. QC provides tremendous computational capacity, whilst ML enables advanced data analysis and predictive modeling. BC ensures transactions that are secure, transparent, and immutable. The integration of these technologies, such as QML, BML, and BQML, leverages their strengths to create more resilient, efficient, and secure systems. This convergence is poised to transform financial

Table 17.1 Comparison of data analysis techniques

	Traditional Data Analysis	*Blockchain-Enhanced Data Analysis*	*Quantum Machine Learning*
Efficiency	Based on the classical algorithm; the computational impact and the refinement of the algorithm are found to be restricted by the computer resources.	Supported by decentralized computing; smart contracts can self-execution and self-optimize to a certain extent; the efficiency relies on the network status.	It promises much faster solutions for some problems since it involves quantum parallelism and speed.
Security	Stable data protection through encoding and access containment; susceptible to some classes of cyber threats.	Enhanced security from encryption using cryptographic hashing and decentralization; data is nonmodifiable, which gives a level of protection.	Quantum encryption can promise a high level of data protection that can hardly be threatened by hackers, yet its use is still in its infancy.
Scalability	Scalable with the input of more system resources but has a finite performance upper bound with large data sets.	There may be problems related to scalability; some developments are in the works to attempt to address these issues.	Quantum properties make it theoretically scalable; however, existing quantum architectures are not scalable.

Table 17.2 Parameters of each technology and its usage

Technical Parameter	*QM*	*ML*	*BC*	*QML*	*BML*	*BQML*
Parallel Data Processing	Yes	-	-	Yes	-	Yes
High Security (Cryptography)	Yes	-	Yes	Yes	Yes	Yes
Decentralization	-	-	Yes	-	Yes	Yes
Data Integrity	-	-	Yes	-	Yes	Yes
Scalability	-	Yes	-	-	Yes	-
Energy Efficiency	-	Yes	-	-	Yes	-
Error Correction Mechanism	-	Yes	-	-	Yes	-
Real-time Processing	-	Yes	-	Yes	Yes	Yes
Specialized Hardware Requirement	Yes	-	-	Yes	-	Yes
Robust Data Privacy	-	-	Yes	-	Yes	Yes
Advanced Computational Capabilities	Yes	Yes	-	Yes	-	Yes
Complex Problem Solving	Yes	Yes	-	Yes	-	Yes
Transparent Operations	-	-	Yes	-	Yes	Yes
General Accessibility	-	Yes	Yes	-	Yes	-
Technology Maturity	-	Yes	Yes	-	Yes	-
Integration with Existing Systems	-	Yes	-	-	Yes	-
Cost Efficiency	-	Yes	-	-	-	-
Quantum Speedup	Yes	-	-	Yes	-	Yes
Immutability of Data	-	-	Yes	-	Yes	Yes
Fault Tolerance	-	Yes	Yes	-	Yes	Yes
Data Synchronization across Networks	-	-	Yes	-	Yes	Yes
Ability to Handle Exponential Data Growth	Yes	-	-	Yes	-	Yes
Support for Complex Data Types	Yes	Yes	-	Yes	Yes	Yes
High Initial Investment Cost	Yes	-	Yes	Yes	Yes	Yes

operations by improving areas such as risk analysis, portfolio optimization, fraud detection, and algorithmic trading, ultimately propelling the industry to new heights of innovation and efficiency.

17.2 RESEARCH AIM AND SCOPE

The main research goal of the proposed work is to design and explore an efficient framework for integrative data analysis in distributed environments by considering the benefits of both QML and blockchain. This emergent framework aims at leveraging the strengths of blockchain as an unalterable and open platform for improving data credibility, reliability, and openness and on the other hand applying quantum computing capability for processing large data sets. The employment of these advances is expected to solve important issues like speed of processing, scalability, and security to alter the evaluation of data procedures in large systems.

With the blockchain, the proposed framework ensures that such concerns of durability and traceability are achieved since data on the blockchain cannot be altered or deleted easily and are distributed across the network to avoid single points of failure [7]. The characterized QML algorithms propose improvement in computational speed, which leads to the processing of complex data in manners that classical approaches are incapable of accomplishing. This dual approach also strives to improve the scalability of distributed systems as well as protect data from modern cyber threats using more sophisticated cryptography techniques as pointed out by [8] in their recent findings. Finally, this project aims to become a breakthrough in the field of data processing in distributed systems to provide more efficient, fast, and secure systems for current and subsequent data science needs.

17.3 RESEARCH DESIGN

17.3.1 Problem Statement

With the exponential growth in data volume and complexity, it becomes challenging to scale up data storage and processing, secure the data against cyber threats and attacks, as well as enhance the effectiveness of ML and DA techniques [9]. ML algorithms that have been constructed based on small dataset sets and single machine settings are having issues dealing with large data [10]. This research intends to address the scalability limitations, security concerns, and efficiency hurdles by studying and proposing a new form of QML-based framework that is underpinned by blockchain technology for ML and DA.

When considering scalability, K-means, and DBSCAN were proven to struggle with large-scale vast arenas of data. These algorithms are basically not parallel and not well suited to environments that are meant for parallel processing that forms the core of big data applications. The SNN (Shared Nearest Neighbor) clustering algorithm is efficient for small data but lacks optimization to work on big data sets [11]. When the number of requirements is relatively small, conventional techniques, such as Advanced Hybrid Protocol (AHP), can be used, but as the number of requirements increases the number of comparisons needed increases exponentially. This is a big challenge because such methods cannot work properly in large contexts, due to scalability [12]. This high dimensionality presents an interesting problem for all the approaches to machine learning since it increases the computational demands of most of the learning algorithms [13]. For instance, recurrent neural networks (RNNs) and convolutional neural networks (CNNs) are the two most popular networks for different applications that can take a huge amount of computing resources to train a model on a large dataset [14].

Concerning the security challenges arising from data analysis, particularly when used in synergy with machine learning and blockchain, data integrity and privacy remain vulnerable issues. Some of the challenges that are associated with these systems are the heterogeneity of the data source and the real-time processing, making the systems susceptible to different forms of attack. For example, in the Internet of Things (IoT) scenario, the gadgets themselves have a very limited computational capacity and storage space, which precludes the use of conventional security algorithms. This lauds the need for lean deployment of security measures that can safeguard data consistency and confidentiality in QML and blockchain data analysis frameworks. The privacy breach is also evident from the training phase, whereby training reveals sensitive data that can be used to derive private information from the resultant models. This issue was labeled with the name of the privacy-preserving problem. Numerous security issues are prevalent in the context of data sharing using blockchain technology. Data collected on different blockchains are often disparate and lead to separate 'data islands' with issues to do with rigidity and how to unlock the full value of blockchain technology. In order to use one or multiple blockchains, for exchanging and storing data securely, these challenges have to be met in the need to ensure that the data cannot be accessed or changed by unauthorized parties and that the data is always available and readable.

Many integration and growth of technologies including ML, analytics, and systems like blockchain have presented multifaceted efficiency issues that limit their functionality. Common machine learning methods, especially, backpropagation neural networks (BPNNs), are indeed inefficient while dealing with big digital health data because they need a heavy amount of computation time during the training phase. In a similar way, there are efficiency issues that are associated with managing data on blockchain technology. Light and full nodes, and even more practical justified PBFT technology, safely unblock the high volumes of data that ultimately lead to efficiency issues and hedonic consensus costs.

To overcome the challenges related to scalability, security, and efficiency during the analysis of data in distributed systems, this work suggests the use of a blockchain-based framework with QML. QML will enhance the data processing and its ability to scale up and the blockchain provides the security and the validation of data. This framework is designed to propose the most efficient ways of resource utilization in conditions of their distribution across different locations.

17.4 RESEARCH QUESTIONS AND RESEARCH OBJECTIVES

17.4.1 Research Question 01

How to investigate the approaches of QML and blockchain-based solutions for integrative data analysis in distributed systems.

The study aims to evaluate the combination of the QML and blockchain to optimize data processing in distributed systems. This will entail constructing a holistic framework for the implementation of QML algorithms in the management and analysis of data while also implementing blockchain to enhance the security of sensitive data. Current literature shows that QML can provide several benefits for the recognition of nonlinear and deep patterns as well as forecasting in distributed networks, complementary to the recent advancements in adopting blockchain for security and decentralization in settings. The integration of these technologies is supposed to allow the overcoming of the mentioned issues in terms of scalability, security, and response to various timework types.

17.4.2 Research Question 02

How to develop a complete framework that combines QML algorithms to effectively manage complex data in a distributed system.

Major research work to be carried out to develop a comprehensive framework involves the formulation of an overall approach that entails the employment of QML algorithms to manage large data in distributed systems. QML is the use of approaches belonging to the vast domain of quantum computing to improve the machine learning processes and algorithms for large-scale and high-dimensional data. Research also indicates that QML may help to enhance the identification patterns and forecasting attributes, a notion largely attributable to enhanced computational processing and speed. Furthermore, the application of blockchain technology within this framework creates decentralization, which is an important feature that enhances the security of data and also preserves data from external interference or invasion. Such an integration of QML and blockchain technology for managing complex data and distributed systems has higher prospects because it can overcome the limitations of scalability and security.

17.4.3 Research Question 03

How to implement a secure, transparent blockchain architecture within the framework to ensure data integrity and privacy.

Having a secure and transparent blockchain structure is important in a framework where data is invaluable, and protection of the data is vital. By its nature, blockchain is a distributed ledger with the information exceeding the control of the individual nodes, which may greatly improve the data protection and trust in the databases of the distributed systems. As pointed out by [14], cryptographic techniques like hashing and digital signatures used in blockchain technologies make it impossible to manipulate data, thus enhancing its integrity. In addition, blockchain's openness ensures that all the users and involved parties can check and cross-check the transactions that are taking place, which will ensure that any stakeholder involved in the process can trust the technology.

17.4.4 Research Question 04

Does the developed comprehensive framework contribute to data security, scalability, and efficiency under several workload scenarios?

The integration of the blockchain with QML as a central framework can improve data security, scalability, and efficiency for distributed systems. Blockchain, on the other hand, is an advanced technology that has a distributed record that enables users only to record new information while stopping any changes to the data. Inherent to blockchain is the provision of smart contracts and consensus mechanisms that augment data security by maintaining its non-triviality and systematically enforcing access policies, thereby strengthening the system's credibility.

An even better and highly efficient scalability of the framework is achieved by the integration of blockchain and QML. Modern blockchain systems like sharding and off-chain transactions help contain a high number of transactions, solving the scalability problems that are common in distributed systems. Besides, QML extends the capabilities of the equipment, or the framework – to process huge arrays of high-dimensional data to analyze a lot of data, which is crucial when working with intricate information. As applied to practical industries including financial, healthcare, and supply chain industries, the performance of the proposed framework in terms of data security, scalability, and efficiency under different workload types proves that the framework is feasible for real-world usage.

17.5 RESEARCH METHODOLOGY

The research methodology is a systematic approach comprising of literature review to assess the current status and knowledge gap in QML and blockchain technologies. This is succeeded by the elaboration of theoretical models with analysis of corresponding algorithms to lay down a strong basis for the integration of these technologies.

The system design stage arises from the basic principles of system design and entails the creation of a secure and scalable design that is implemented in the context of a prototype. Significance testing is conducted to assess the usefulness of the prototype, as experiments showing how it performs are carried out to measure a range of factors.

These key principles of data collection and intensive analysis help constitute and implement performance improvements to facilitate the optimization of integration. Finally, the whole process and the results are recorded for the purpose of sharing knowledge and contributing to the further development of QML and blockchain fields.

According to the research methodology illustrated in Figure 17.1, the following is a detailed description of the process of research methodology.

17.5.1 Literature Review on QML and Blockchain Technologies

A literature review of available works on QML and blockchain technologies was conducted, which formed the first part of this study. The literature review will be sought to survey the existing works, define the notions, approaches, and practices, and reveal the discovered emptiness in the research area.

17.5.2 Analysis of Existing Systems and Assessment of Current QML and Blockchain Applications

Upon the completion of the literature review, there was an assessment of the current systems to gather a closer insight into QML and blockchain applications. It also entailed reviewing different case application areas and determining if there were areas that required more research in order to improve the area further.

17.5.3 Theoretical Framework and Development

The first step is proposing a structure. Considering the literature review, theoretical models will be proposed to initiate the integration of QML with blockchain technology. These models will be based on optimizing the usage of quantum computing in the cases of blockchain applicability in the direction of its security improvement and work increase.

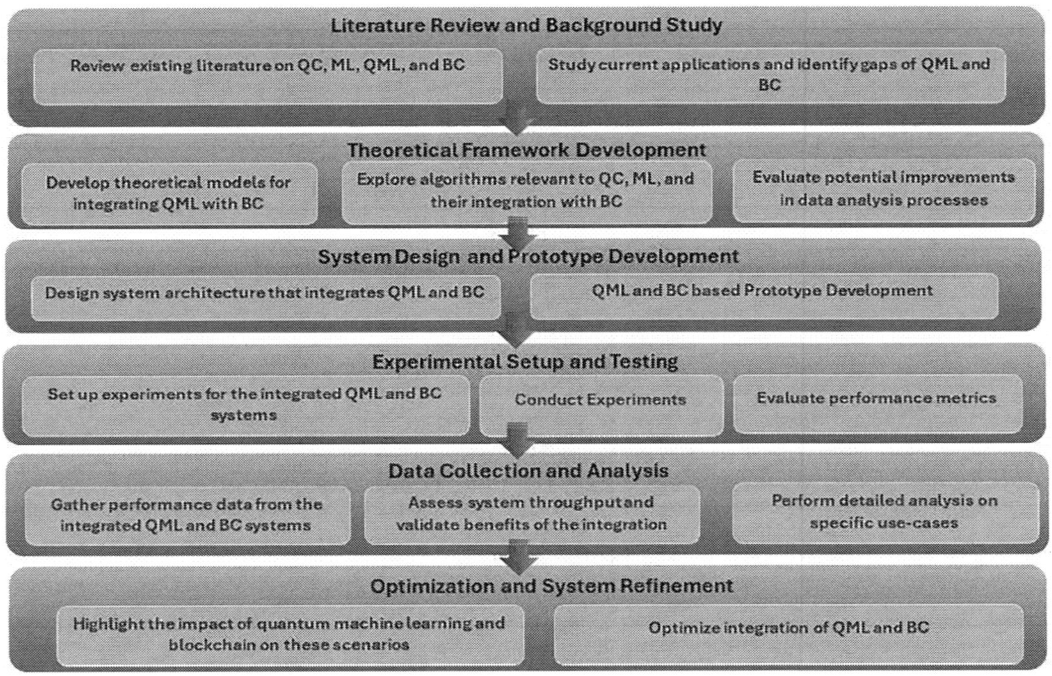

Figure 17.1 Research methodology.

The second step is examining algorithms. Alongside the creation of the models, several theoretical algorithms will be considered to bolster the theoretical concepts. Other contributions are quantum cryptography algorithms and QML algorithms.

17.5.4 System Design and Prototype Development

System design is critical as it provides a clear framework for implementing the proposed solutions, while the development of the prototype is also essential as it affirms and substantiates the suggested plans. Accordingly, the next procedure entailed outlining the system architecture with the proposal for the integration of QML with blockchain. Architecture means scalability, security, and efficient processing were planned and implemented from the very beginning.

A prototype will be created based on the system being designed and the system architecture. Most attention will go to the practicality of the algorithm, which is vital for the actual implementation of the system.

17.5.5 Experimental Setup and Testing

The experiments aim to test the outcomes of the deployed prototype. Some of the aspects of the experiment involved setting up a quantum computing environment and the blockchain network in a real-life-like setting. Measures will be taken to assess the performance of the prototype in order to focus more on the usefulness of the device. This involves evaluating how the system is acting in terms of throughput, security, and how well it handles scalability.

17.5.6 Data Collection and Analysis

Performance data are being compiled during testing or as part of these steps as indicated by the above methods. Such data includes data on the processing speed of the systems, the extent to which security has been compromised, and the ability of the system to address throughput. But to fully believe its benefits, system throughput must be assessed Though system throughput empowers this facet, its system throughput delivery must be evaluated.

The collected data are used to measure the throughput of the system and to ensure that the QML application would improve by the integration of blockchain. The analysis helps to state that the proposed system satisfies the desired quality requirements as stated at the beginning of the work.

17.5.7 Optimization and System Refinement

Parameters of the system structure and algorithm are updated according to the evaluation the research has pointed out. These changes are meant to counter or ill any discovered shortcomings and generally improve performance.

Then enhanced speed and the degree of safety that the circuit undergoes to provide best outcomes. This entails working on the efficiency of operations involving the recursion of the QML algorithms within the blockchain system and securing it from what might endanger it.

17.5.8 Documentation and Dissemination

The last step entails summarizing the procedure that was followed, the results obtained, and the recommendations that the research findings imply. It also focuses on preparing the documentation for the purpose of dissemination through other forums such as academic journals, and conferences among others.

The suggested system combines blockchain technology with QML to produce a safe and expandable data analysis environment. The three primary layers of the framework are designated as data collecting, data processing, and data security. Distributed data sources gather and preprocess data at the data acquisition layer to guarantee consistency and dependability. In order to efficiently manage massive amounts of data, the data processing layer uses QML algorithms, which take advantage of quantum parallelism to improve computing speed. Finally, to guarantee data integrity, immutability, and decentralized validation while guarding against data breaches and manipulation, the data security layer makes use of blockchain technology. The robustness and security of data analysis are ensured by this integration, which can handle large data volumes while upholding high standards of data protection and scalability.

17.6 EXPECTED IMPACT AND CONTRIBUTION

The research on secure and scalable data analysis framework with QML and blockchain is expected to have a profound impact on various aspects of data analytics, distributed computing, and security. The following are specific expected outcomes and additions to knowledge of this study.

17.6.1 Improving Data Processing Efficiency

Applying the field of QML in conjunction with the blockchain system is supposed to improve the performance of data analysis in distributed settings. One of the key advantages of QML is its capability to operate on large data sets due to the boost that comes from quantum parallelism. It drastically decreases the time taken in computing and resource requirements for data analysis. This improvement is anticipated to become the new reference move in mass-scaled distributed settings and leads to faster data processing compared to classical machine learning approaches.

17.6.2 Improving Data Security and Confidentiality

The integration of blockchain within the proposed context also provides the benefits of security data and privacy. Blockchain has inherent characteristics of immutability and decentralization operations, which means data transactions have considerably less susceptibility to either internal data manipulation corruption or external cyberattacks. It is vital for industries whose data is sensitive and critical in nature, such as the healthcare industry, finance industry, and supply chain management, as it ensures the data is secure and trustworthy.

17.6.3 Improving Scalability of Distributed Systems

The scalability is one of the biggest problems that has plagued the of distributed systems in the present era. The framework makes a solution by exploiting the scalability factor inherent in QML, which is theoretically scalable to infinity. Organized by concentric circles on top of a blockchain architecture optimized to scale using sharding and off-chain transactions, the framework shows promising scalability in the face of exponential data growth. This improvement is crucial for data processing and analysis of massive data portions in real time, allowing system calibration and optimization as volumes grow.

17.6.4 Offering a Strong Framework for Different Sectors

QML with blockchain is an appealing option because it can be used in multiple industries due to its scalability and speed of analyzing data. The capabilities of the framework will be of great value in many fields, such as finance for risk assessment and fraudulent activity identification, healthcare for patient data analysis and genetic traits or disease predictions, and traffic control in the transportation industry. Such multi-industry applicability further establishes the framework's core to analyze transformation, advancement, and enhancement in numerous fields.

17.6.5 Contribution to Real-World Problem Solving

The proposed solution aims to address current challenges that are perceived in real-world problems, for instance, delays in data synchronization, when the system is insecure, and when the system has a limitation when operating a large number of data. In addition to that, due to the nature of the challenges highlighted and the offered solution, the research not only provides a solution to these challenges but also maintains its practical relevance and application to real-life situations, thus contributing to the effectiveness of academic research.

17.7 CONCLUSION AND FUTURE WORK

The research introduced a new framework that combines blockchain technology with QML to improve the security, scalability, and effectiveness of data processing in distributed systems. The findings show that while blockchain provides data integrity and protection against manipulation, QML greatly enhances data processing capabilities. Key issues including data overload, security flaws, and scalability constraints in conventional data analysis techniques are addressed by this synergistic approach. The suggested framework works exceptionally well with big amounts of complicated data, which makes it a good option for businesses that need strong security and data processing.

Potential avenues for future research encompass the following.

1. Quantum Algorithm Optimization: Additional study is required to tailor QML algorithms to particular use cases, improving their effectiveness and precision in practical applications.
2. Integration with Current Systems: To aid in acceptance and implementation, investigate ways to smoothly integrate the suggested framework with current IT infrastructures.
3. Advanced Security Mechanisms: To further improve data security within the blockchain layer, look at incorporating cutting-edge quantum cryptography techniques.
4. Scalability Enhancements: Create plans to make the framework more scalable, especially while managing the rapidly increasing amounts of data across several industries.
5. Performance Evaluation: To confirm the framework's efficacy and adaptability, carry out thorough performance evaluations in a variety of industries, including finance, healthcare, and supply chain management.
6. User-Centric Design: Put an emphasis on creating tools and interfaces that are easy to use so that people who are not professionals may use the framework for data analysis.
7. Regulatory Compliance: To enable the framework's use in delicate settings, make sure it conforms with all applicable privacy and data protection laws.

In conclusion, combining blockchain technology with QML is a viable approach to safe and scalable data analysis in distributed systems. In addition to addressing the present shortcomings of conventional techniques, the suggested framework lays the groundwork for upcoming developments in data processing and security. The framework's capabilities will be further enhanced by ongoing research and development in this field, making it a vital tool for contemporary data-centric enterprises. The planned future work offers a clear road map for developing and enhancing the framework, guaranteeing its applicability and relevance in a variety of real-world situations.

REFERENCES

[1] Abbas, K., Afaq, M., Ahmed Khan, T., & Song, W.-C. (2020). A blockchain and machine learning-based drug supply chain management and recommendation system for smart pharmaceutical industry. *Electronics*, *9*(5), 852. https://doi.org/10.3390/electronics9050852

[2] Amato, F., Cicalese, M., Contrasto, L., Cubicciotti, G., D'Ambola, G., La Marca, A., Pagano, G., Tomeo, F., Robertazzi, G., Vassallo, G., Acampora, G., Vitiello, A., Catolino, G., Giordano, G., Lambiase, S., Pontillo, V., Sellitto, G., Ferrucci, F., & Palomba, F. (2023). QUANTUMOONLIGHT: A low-code platform to experiment with quantum machine learning. *SOFTWAREX*, *22*. https://doi.org/10.1016/j.softx.2023.101399

[3] Banchi, L., Pereira, J., & Pirandola, S. (2021). Generalization in quantum machine learning: A quantum information standpoint. *PRX QUANTUM*, *2*(4). https://doi.org/10.1103/PRXQuantum.2.040321

[4] Chaudhury, M., Karami, A., & Ghazanfar, M. A. (2022). Large-scale music genre analysis and classification using machine learning with apache spark. *Electronics*, *11*(16), Article 16. https://doi.org/10.3390/electronics11162567

[5] Geng, Z., Cao, Y., Li, J., & Han, Y. (2022). Novel blockchain transaction provenance model with graph attention mechanism. *Expert Systems with Applications*, *209*, 118411. https://doi.org/10.1016/j.eswa.2022.118411

[6] Guo, S., Qi, Y., Jin, Y., Li, W., Qiu, X., & Meng, L. (2022). Endogenous trusted DRL-based service function chain orchestration for IoT. *IEEE Transactions on Computers*, *71*(2), 397–406. https://doi.org/10.1109/TC.2021.3051681

[7] Liu, F., & Wang, P. (2023). A novel privacy protection method of residents' travel trajectories based on federated blockchain and InterPlanetary file systems in smart cities. *PeerJ Computer Science*, *9*, e1495. https://doi.org/10.7717/peerj-cs.1495

[8] Liu, Y., Chen, X., Xu, L., Li, H., & Li, M. (2019). A resource aware parallelized back propagation neural network in enabling efficient large-scale digital health data processing. *IEEE Access*, *7*, 114700–114713. https://doi.org/10.1109/ACCESS.2019.2935691

[9] Melnikov, A., Kordzanganeh, M., Alodjants, A., & Lee, R. (2023). Quantum machine learning: From physics to software engineering. *Advances in Physics-X*, *8*(1). https://doi.org/10.1080/23746149.2023.2165452

[10] Mohanta, B. K., Jena, D., Satapathy, U., & Patnaik, S. (2020). Survey on IoT security: Challenges and solution using machine learning, artificial intelligence and blockchain technology. *Internet of Things*, *11*, 100227. https://doi.org/10.1016/j.iot.2020.100227

[11] Nagar, A. (2019). *Privacy-Preserving Blockchain Based Federated Learning with Differential Data Sharing* (arXiv:1912.04859). arXiv. https://doi.org/10.48550/arXiv.1912.04859

[12] Sun, M., Yang, R., & Hu, L. (2021). A secure distributed machine learning protocol against static semi-honest adversaries. *Applied Soft Computing*, *102*, 107095. https://doi.org/10.1016/j.asoc.2021.107095

[13] Wang, S., & Eick, C. (2017). *MR-SNN: Design of parallel Shared Nearest Neighbor clustering algorithm using MapReduce* (p. 315). https://doi.org/10.1109/ICBDA.2017.8078831

[14] Zhong, C., Liu, K., Liang, Z., Huang, Y., Xiong, F., & Guo, Z. (2022). Research on Data Security Sharing in Blockchain: Challenges and Prospects. *2022 IEEE International Conference on Electrical Engineering, Big Data and Algorithms (EEBDA)*, 1322–1327. https://doi.org/10.1109/EEBDA53927.2022.9744992

Chapter 18

Enhancing privacy in big data analytics with blockchain-based frameworks

Liu Guoqiang, S. B. Goyal, and Budati Anil Kumar

18.1 INTRODUCTION

18.1.1 Research background

With the rapid development of the Internet and information technology, data has become an important resource in modern society. However, big data analysis often involves the collection and processing of personal privacy information, which can easily lead to the problem of user privacy leakage. With the rapid development of information technology and the trend of globalization becoming more and more obvious, privacy protection has been a topic of great concern in foreign countries. When defining the concept of privacy, foreign scholars not only consider the complexity of its connotation but also refine and categorize it to more accurately describe and understand the scope and characteristics of privacy, to establish a comprehensive and integrated framework for privacy protection (Ye and Zhuang, 2024).

To solve this problem, we need a mechanism that can protect user privacy. Blockchain technology, as a decentralized and secure distributed ledger technology, can provide an effective privacy protection mechanism for big data analytics. Blockchain technology is decentralized, which means that the data will not be stored on a single centralized server, but will be decentralized and stored on multiple nodes. In this way, even if a problem occurs in one node, it will not affect the normal operation of the whole system. At the same time, blockchain technology uses cryptographic algorithms to encrypt the data so that only users with private keys can decrypt and access the data, thus ensuring the privacy of the data. Blockchains are tamper-resistant and tamper-evident digital ledgers operating in a distributed manner, without a centralized body responsible for unified management. Such an operation ensures that transactions are recorded only in a shared ledger within the user community. No transaction can be altered by the blockchain network under normal operation. This ensures that once a transaction has been completed, it can never be changed once it has been published (Yaga et al., 2018).

Smart contracts are a very important mechanism in blockchain technology. A smart contract is an automatically executed contract that runs on the blockchain and automatically triggers certain operations when specific conditions are met. Smart contracts can be used to implement various decentralized applications, such as decentralized exchanges and decentralized payments. At the same time, smart contracts can also be used to protect user privacy, such as storing users' sensitive information on the blockchain, which can only be accessed by users with private keys. The combination of blockchain technology and smart contracts can realize a decentralized privacy protection mechanism framework. In this framework, users can store their data on the blockchain while using smart contracts to protect the privacy of this data. In this way, users can be assured that their data will not be leaked and at the same time the validity and reliability of the data can be guaranteed.

DOI: 10.1201/9781003513445-18

18.1.2 Big data technology

Big data refers to massive data whose volume exceeds the processing capacity of traditional databases and is characterized by high dimensionality, high density, and high speed. In the era of big data, the speed of data generation and dissemination is accelerating, and the volume of data shows an explosive growth trend. This means the traditional database processing capacity can not meet the processing needs of big data, therefore, big data analysis technology came into being. Big Data Technology (BDT) and Analytics have gained immense recognition in recent years. BDT plays an essential role in various sectors (Palit and Roy, 2021). The characteristics of big data determine its wide range of applications in various fields. For example, Big data is a foundational force driving significant change in the fintech space (Mhlanga, 2024). Big data analysis can help financial institutions better understand customer needs and improve service quality; in the medical field, the situation of many kinds of data and the complexity of data sources is more unique advantages (Gong et al., 2018). Big data analytics can help doctors diagnose conditions more accurately and improve treatment effects; in the field of education, traditional teaching methods and management modes have been difficult to adapt to the needs of diverse students and the rapidly changing social context (Han and Tao, 2024). Big data analytics can help educational institutions better understand student learning and improve the quality of education.

However, big data also brings a series of problems. Due to the huge volume of data, the processing capacity of traditional databases makes it difficult to meet the demand, resulting in inefficient data processing. In addition, big data contains a large amount of personal privacy information, which, once leaked, may lead to damage to personal rights and interests. Therefore, how to protect personal privacy in the era of big data has become an urgent problem.

18.1.3 Blockchain technology

The blockchain concept was first introduced in 2008 and is essentially a new type of distributed ledger (Guo et al., 2024). Blockchain is a decentralized distributed ledger with blockchain storage, tamper-proof, secure, and trustworthy (Nakamoto, 2008), It combines a variety of high-security technologies, such as distributed storage technology, peer-to-peer transmission technology, consensus mechanisms, cryptography, and other technologies (Zhang et al., 2022), Ensuring the security and trustworthiness of data through a growing chain of data blocks used to record different transactions and information (Sun, 2021). The core of blockchain technology is decentralization, i.e., there is no single central authority that holds all the data and control. Each node has a complete copy of the ledger and can participate in all transactions in the network. This decentralization makes the blockchain highly secure and trustworthy because there is no single point of failure and the risk of attack. Based on blockchain technology, various decentralized applications can be constructed to realize decentralized storage and sharing of data, which guarantees the security and credibility of data.

Blockchain technology also utilizes cryptography to ensure the security of data transmission and storage. Each transaction is encrypted into a unique code, and only all participants in the transaction can use the private key to decrypt it to view the content of the transaction. This encryption mechanism can effectively prevent data from being tampered with or stolen, guaranteeing the security and credibility of the blockchain network.

Blockchain technology is also characterized by data sharing and collaboration. Each node has a complete copy of the ledger, so it can view and participate in all transactions in the network. This decentralized data sharing mechanism can effectively reduce the risk of data privacy leakage, while also facilitating data collaboration and sharing.

Based on blockchain technology, various decentralized applications can be constructed. For example, a decentralized financial system can be constructed based on blockchain technology to realize the issuance and management of currencies, and at the same time ensure the security and credibility of currencies. A decentralized identity authentication system can also be built based on blockchain technology to realize user authentication and authorization management. In addition, blockchain technology can be used in the Internet of Things, supply chain management, copyright protection, and other fields to realize decentralized data storage and sharing.

Blockchain technology has driven the development of several digital cryptocurrency systems, such as Bitcoin and Ethereum, and as such is often thought of in relation to Bitcoin or cryptocurrency solutions in general. As such, the technology has a much wider range of applications and is currently being researched in several areas (Yaga et al., 2018).

There are many types of privacy threats in big data environments such as data leakage, data misuse, and data tampering. Table 18.1 counts the types of privacy threats in big data environments and how blockchain can mitigate these threats.

Today, with the continuous development of science and technology, there are more and more technologies that can be used for privacy protection, and Table 18.2 summarizes how blockchain compares with other technologies in protecting big data privacy.

18.1.4 How blockchain specifically enhances privacy big data analytics

18.1.4.1 Data privacy is guaranteed through encryption algorithms of blockchain technology

Blockchain technology, with its unique encryption mechanism, has demonstrated significant advantages in safeguarding data privacy. This technology encrypts data by applying a variety of encryption algorithms, thus ensuring the security of data in the process of transmission and storage.

Table 18.1 Privacy threats and blockchain mitigations

Privacy threats in a big data environment	*How blockchain can mitigate these threats*
Data leak	Blockchain uses encryption algorithms to secure data so that it cannot be easily deciphered even if it is illegally accessed, thus protecting individual privacy.
Data abuse	Through smart contracts, blockchain enables fine-grained control of data access rights so that only authorized users can access specific data, preventing unauthorized access.
Data tampering	Blockchain forms a chain structure by packing data into blocks through cryptographic algorithms, with each block containing the hash value of the previous block. Once data is recorded in a block, it cannot be tampered with, as any alteration will result in a change in the hash value, which can be recognized by other nodes on the network.
Data sharing and exchange risks	Blockchain can support a digital signature-based authentication system to ensure that the participating entities in the supply chain are authentic and reliable, and through fine-grained permission settings, ensure that only authorized parties can view and process sensitive information.
Data storage and transmission security risks	Blockchain utilizes cryptography to encrypt data, ensuring the security of data transmission and storage. At the same time, user identities in the blockchain network can be traded through anonymous addresses, guaranteeing user privacy.
Network attack	Blockchain technology reduces the risk of data being attacked through distributed storage, where data is no longer centrally stored on a single central server, but distributed across multiple nodes.

Table 18.2 Comparative analysis of privacy-preserving technologies

Comparison dimension	*Blockchain privacy protection technology*	*Non-blockchain privacy-preserving technologies*
Data Security	Data security through encryption algorithms and consensus mechanisms	Dependent on encryption algorithms and security protocols
Data transparency	Data is publicly available on the chain, but information can be hidden through privacy-preserving technology	Data can be completely hidden unless decrypted by specific techniques
Data immutability	Data cannot be tampered with once it is on the chain	Data can be modified, but traces of modification can be detected
Data ownership	Data ownership is vested in the user, and the user controls access to the data	Ownership of data may reside with the service provider, and users need to trust the service provider
Data access control	Fine-grained data access control through smart contracts	Dependent on the service provider's access control policies
Data sharing	Secure data sharing through blockchain technology	Data sharing is limited by privacy-protecting technologies and laws and regulations
Technical complexity	Relatively high, requiring multi-technology integration	Relatively low, high technological maturity
Application scenario	Ideal for scenarios that require a high degree of transparency and non-tampering	Ideal for scenarios where data privacy is critical

First of all, blockchain technology adopts advanced encryption algorithms, such as hash algorithm and asymmetric encryption algorithm, to carry out multiple encryption of data. The hash algorithm converts data into a fixed string of numbers or letter combinations by mapping a string of binary values of arbitrary length to a fixed-length string of binary values, making it difficult for the original data to be tampered with or forged during transmission. Asymmetric encryption algorithms, on the other hand, utilize the pairing of public and private keys to achieve the process of encryption and decryption of data, ensuring its confidentiality.

Second, the decentralized nature of blockchain technology also enhances data privacy. In traditional centralized systems, data is often stored on a central server, with the risk of being hacked or leaked. Blockchain technology, on the other hand, decentralizes the storage of data on multiple nodes, each of which owns a complete copy of the data, and the modification of the data requires the consensus of the majority of the nodes in the network. This decentralized storage makes the data more secure and difficult to be tampered with or destroyed by a single node.

In addition, blockchain technology is characterized by transparency, making it easier to trace and audit data. Although the data on the blockchain is encrypted, each node can view and verify the integrity and authenticity of the data. This transparency ensures that the data cannot be tampered with or falsified, and also helps maintain the credibility and trustworthiness of the data.

Blockchain technology effectively guarantees the privacy of data through multiple encryption algorithms and decentralized features. The application of this technology not only improves the security of data but also provides strong support for the development of various fields. With the continuous progress of technology and the continuous expansion of application scenarios, the advantages of blockchain technology in data protection will be more prominent.

18.1.4.2 Adoption of smart contracts and other technologies for rights management to realize the security of data sharing

In the era of digitalization, data sharing has become an indispensable part of all industries. However, how to ensure data security while ensuring data sharing has become a major challenge in front of us. To solve this problem, the use of smart contracts and other technologies to manage rights and realize the security of data sharing has become a practical solution.

A smart contract is an automatically executed, automatically verified, and automatically managed computer program that realizes distributed storage and sharing of data through blockchain technology. It can automatically execute preset operations when certain conditions are met, thus ensuring the security of data in the sharing process. The introduction of smart contracts makes the process of data sharing more transparent, trustworthy, and efficient.

In the process of data sharing, smart contracts can set different permission levels according to different user roles and needs. For example, data providers can set their permissions to modify and delete data; data users can set their permissions to access and use data. In this way, illegal access and misuse of data can be effectively prevented, ensuring data security and privacy.

In addition, smart contracts can also monitor and trace the process of data sharing in real-time through smart contract auditing and verification mechanisms. Once abnormal behaviors or potential risks are found, smart contracts can immediately take corresponding measures, such as suspending data sharing, and alarming, to safeguard the security of data.

The application of smart contracts in data sharing security has been widely empirical research and validation. By comparing and analyzing the security indicators of data sharing before and after the use of smart contracts, it is found that the introduction of smart contracts significantly improves the security of data sharing. At the same time, more and more enterprises and organizations have begun to adopt smart contracts for data sharing and privilege management to address the increasingly complex data security challenges.

Through the features of smart contracts such as automatic execution, transparency, and traceability, we can ensure the security and privacy of data in the sharing process, thus promoting the continuous development of the digital era. In the future, with the continuous progress of technology and the expansion of application scenarios, the application of smart contracts in data-sharing security will be more extensive and in-depth, bringing more convenience and value to our lives and work.

18.1.4.3 Data backup and recovery mechanism based on blockchain technology to ensure data reliability

In today's digital era, data has become an indispensable and important resource in business operations and personal life. However, the issue of data security and reliability is becoming increasingly prominent, especially in data backup and recovery. To solve this problem, a data backup and recovery mechanism based on blockchain technology has emerged, providing a strong guarantee for data reliability.

As a decentralized, secure, and reliable distributed ledger technology, blockchain technology's unique characteristics make it have great potential in the field of data backup and recovery. First, blockchain technology ensures the integrity and security of data in the backup process through distributed storage and encryption mechanisms. Data is split into multiple blocks encrypted by cryptographic algorithms and then stored in a decentralized manner on multiple nodes, thus avoiding the risk of a single point of failure and data leakage.

Second, blockchain technology ensures the consistency and reliability of data backup through the consensus mechanism. In the blockchain network, all nodes jointly participate in the verification and recording of data, and the data will be written into the blockchain only when the majority of nodes reach a consensus. This mechanism ensures the authenticity and immutability of the data, and even if some nodes fail or are attacked, the data will not be lost or tampered with.

In addition, the data recovery mechanism based on blockchain technology has unique advantages. When data recovery is required, users can obtain a complete copy of the data from any node in the blockchain network without worrying about data loss or corruption. At the same time, due to the blockchain's immutability, users can be sure that the recovered data is an accurate copy of the original data without worrying about data tampering or forgery. Through features such as distributed storage, encryption mechanisms, and consensus mechanisms, blockchain technology ensures the integrity, security, and reliability of data in the backup and recovery process. With the continuous development and improvement of the technology, it is believed that the data backup and recovery mechanism based on blockchain technology will play a greater role in the future and bring more innovations and breakthroughs in the field of data security.

Data processing in the blockchain system is a general term for a series of activities such as collecting, verifying, storing, updating, and transmitting data in the blockchain network. These activities ensure the integrity and security of the data and are key to enabling blockchain technology to realize its core value. Figure 18.1 shows the data processing flow in a blockchain system.

18.2 RESEARCH AIM AND SCOPE

With the arrival of the big data era, the value of data is becoming increasingly prominent, while data security and privacy protection have also become the focus of attention. The purpose of this chapter is to explore the framework of a decentralized privacy protection mechanism combining blockchain technology and big data analytics, intending to provide theoretical support and practical guidance for privacy protection in the field of big data analytics in China.

First, the research purpose of this chapter is to analyze the implementation process of the decentralized privacy protection mechanism framework combining blockchain technology and big data analysis, and the research includes the role of blockchain technology in big data analysis, the design and implementation of the decentralized privacy protection mechanism, as well as the performance and effect of the mechanism in practical application.

Second, the research significance of this chapter is mainly reflected in the following aspects. First, big data analysis has been widely used in various fields, however, the security and privacy protection of data in the analysis process is increasingly prominent. Blockchain technology, as a decentralized technology, can provide a safe and reliable data storage and transmission mechanism for big data analysis, thus effectively solving the problem of data security and privacy protection. Second, the research in this chapter can provide theoretical support and practical guidance for privacy protection in the field of big data analysis in China. The research on the framework of decentralized privacy protection mechanisms combining blockchain technology and big data analysis can provide useful reference and information for privacy protection in the field of big data analysis in China.

In addition, the research of this chapter includes the design and implementation of a decentralized privacy protection mechanism. The design of a decentralized privacy protection mechanism needs to fully consider the privacy, integrity, and availability of data, as well as the scalability and maintainability of the decentralized mechanism. In this chapter, the design ideas, algorithms, and implementation methods of the decentralized privacy

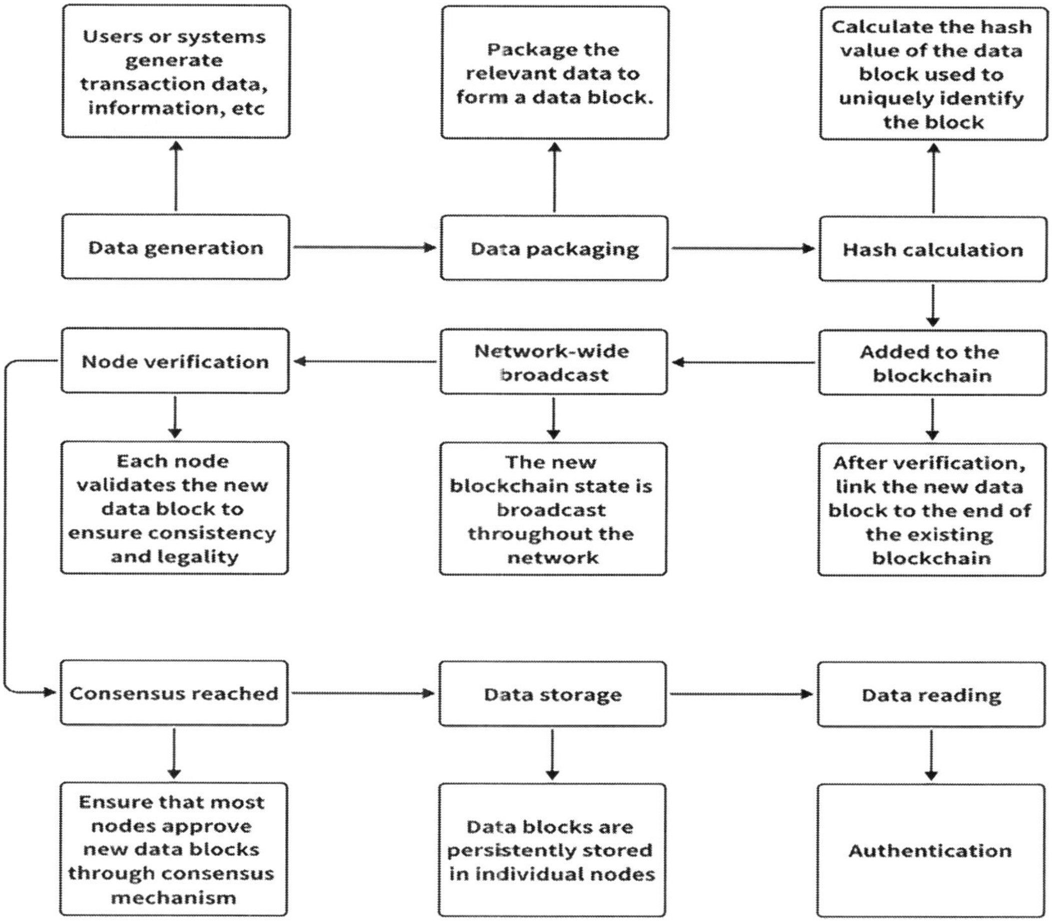

Figure 18.1 Flowchart of data handling in blockchain systems.

protection mechanism will be introduced in detail, and its performance and effect in practical applications will be evaluated.

Finally, this chapter will explore the performance and effect of the decentralized privacy protection mechanism framework combining blockchain technology and big data analytics in practical applications through the analysis of actual application cases. Through the analysis of actual cases, this chapter will verify the effectiveness and feasibility of the decentralized privacy protection mechanism framework, and provide useful practical guidance for privacy protection in the field of big data analytics in China.

18.3 RESEARCH DESIGN

18.3.1 Problem statement

In today's era of big data, there exists a wide variety of data that is huge and diverse. However, in this prosperous data universe, the risk of data leakage also follows the shadow, quietly lurking. Once sensitive information such as pearls falls into the dust, stolen by criminals, the consequences may be like a storm sweeping the quiet harbor, bringing incalculable losses to individuals and enterprises. Information security problems in the big data environment mainly involve data leakage and data tampering, which have brought about serious economic losses (Fei et al., 2024).

In the age of big data, user's privacy is being undermined. Large third parties are able to profit from the management of user data by collecting, analyzing, correlating and controlling vast amounts of personal data. These organizations and their services are vulnerable to security breaches and misuse of user data, and may even compromise users' privacy without their knowledge (Bernabe et al., 2019).

Malicious attackers are like hunters in the night, waiting for the opportunity to move, they may tamper with the original data so that it loses its original luster and becomes completely different. This kind of data distortion, like the fog obscuring the compass of the ship, misleads the direction of data analysis, which in turn affects the accuracy of decision-making as if the mariner lost his way in the vast ocean.

In addition, the power of big data may also be misused by certain enterprises and individuals, who may use this tool to carry out unfair business competition or violate the privacy of others, like thieves stealing treasure, not only damaging the market environment of fair competition but also trampling on the dignity and freedom of individuals. The sharpness of big data analytics technology can penetrate the surface layer of data and deeply excavate the personal information hidden in the abyss of data, just like a searchlight illuminating the dark corners. However, this also means that the boundaries of personal privacy become blurred, and the risk of privacy leakage rises, just like an unlocked door, which may be pried into by others at any time.

Therefore, in the face of the challenges posed by big data, we must build a strong defense line and formulate strict data protection measures, just like a guardian angel guarding precious wealth. At the same time, it is also necessary to ensure the safe use of big data through the standardization of laws and regulations and technological innovation, so that it can respect and protect the privacy rights of each individual while promoting social development.

18.3.2 Research questions, research objectives, and research hypothesis

18.3.2.1 Research Question 01

What are the current issues and challenges in privacy protection in the big data environment? In the era of big data development, people are facing increasingly serious information security problems while enjoying convenience. Information leakage jeopardizes citizens' property rights and personal reputation, and related crimes have become easier and more difficult to govern (Wang and Jiang, 2019). This work is to analyze the existing privacy protection aspects of the big data environment and to analyze the advantages and disadvantages of the existing algorithms.

18.3.2.2 Research Question 02

How can blockchain technology enhance privacy preservation in big data environments? The second research question focuses on how blockchain technology can be applied to privacy preservation in big data environments, analyzing the parts of existing algorithms that can be further optimized. Authentication privacy protection technology is a common mechanism for privacy protection of decentralized authentication. The authentication of permission chain nodes is mainly through the issuance of digital certificates to achieve node privilege control, and distributed authentication protocols can also be used to protect personal identity information and ensure that only authorized users can access the relevant data (Tan et al., 2023).

18.3.2.3 Research Question 03

Why should a decentralized privacy-preserving mechanism be designed to enhance privacy protection?

In a blockchain system, data is distributed across all nodes in the network and each node has a complete copy of the data. This decentralization makes the blockchain system highly transparent and secure (Gao and Yu, 2023), The focus of this research is to develop an effective algorithm used to enhance the privacy protection of blockchain technology. Mainly by improving the shortcomings of the existing privacy protection mechanisms, this problem aims to improve privacy protection by using a new algorithmic architecture.

18.3.2.4 Research Question 04

How to build a big data analytics platform for cross-organizational collaboration while maintaining the privacy of each participant.

With the development of technology, the construction of a big data analysis platform for cross-organizational cooperation has become possible. Inter-organizational competition or cooperation involves resource sharing and interest maintenance of multi-party subjects of interest, constituting a complex relationship of interests and access control mechanisms between resource-centered subjects. Through the decentralized computing model of blockchain to build a multi-party consensus agreement, resist the attack of a single party or a few subjects, to maintain inter-organizational interest consensus, including the access to information resources of the shared process, operation, and computing resources access call, to achieve fair and transparent inter-organizational competition and collaboration. These technologies allow data processing and analysis without revealing the original data, thus maximizing the value of the data while protecting privacy (Zhi, 2022). The overall goal is to verify the security and reliability of decentralized privacy protection mechanisms.

18.4 RESEARCH METHODOLOGY

This chapter adopts a combination of qualitative and quantitative methods to ensure an in-depth understanding of the framework of decentralized privacy protection mechanisms in the field of blockchain and big data analytics. To carry out the research efficiently and scientifically, the following research methodology is adopted in this study, as shown in Figure 18.2.

18.4.1 Literature review and problem identification

Objective: In today's era of rapid informationization, data has become the core driving force for the development of various industries. However, with the explosive growth of data volume, how to effectively manage and utilize these data while protecting user privacy has become an urgent problem. Therefore, this chapter aims to gain a deeper understanding of the current status of blockchain and big data technologies, focusing on their application in privacy protection, to provide new ideas and methods to promote data security and privacy protection.

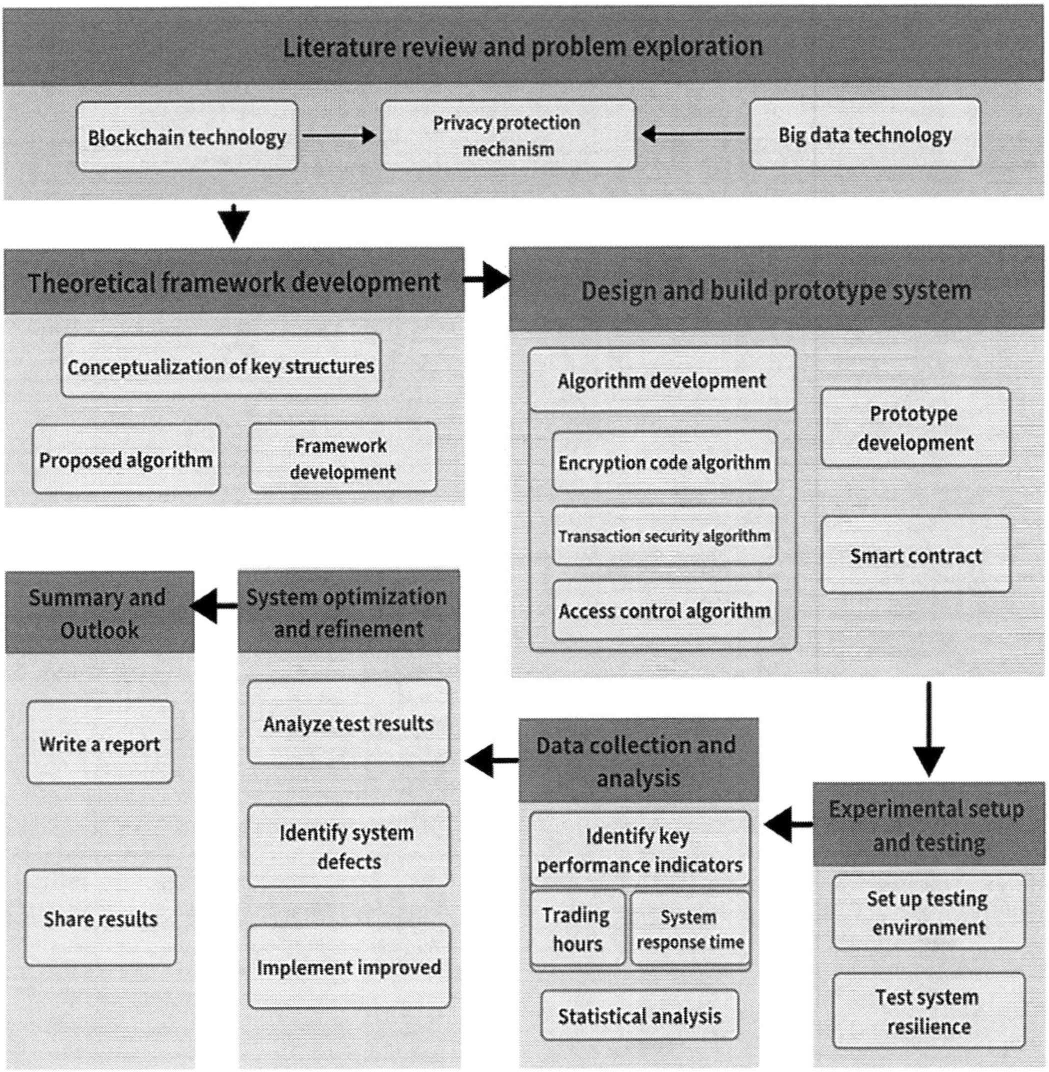

Figure 18.2 Research methodology.

Activity: The core task of this activity is to conduct a comprehensive review of the various types of existing literature. The literature, including existing research journals, conference papers, and books, is thoroughly sorted out, analyzed, and summarized. Through in-depth analysis and exposition, it provides a more comprehensive and in-depth understanding and awareness of the relevant areas of research. Identify gaps in current technologies where blockchain can enhance privacy in big data analytics. Document the challenges and privacy issues in contemporary Big Data scenarios.

18.4.2 Theoretical framework development

Objective: Develop a conceptual framework for integrating blockchain and big data analytics for privacy enhancement.

Activity: Defining and modeling the theoretical structure of blockchain technology related to privacy protection.

18.4.3 System design and development

Objective: To design and implement a prototype system based on the proposed framework.

Activity: Develop algorithms for data encryption, transaction security, and access control using blockchain. Integrate smart contract mechanisms for automated privacy control in big data workflows. Build a decentralized application (dApp) to demonstrate the practical application of the framework in a real scenario.

18.4.4 Experimental setup and testing

Objective: To test the effectiveness of a blockchain-integrated big data system in terms of privacy protection.

Activity: Deploy the prototype in a controlled environment. Simulate real-world data transaction and privacy breach scenarios to assess system resilience. Use synthetic datasets and real datasets to validate privacy protection under different conditions.

18.4.5 Data collection and analysis

Objective: Analyze the experimental data to evaluate the validity of the hypotheses and framework.

Activity: Collect performance data, including transaction time, privacy breach attempts, and system response. Apply statistical analysis to evaluate data integrity, privacy levels, and system efficiency. Compare findings with the existing system to highlight potential areas for improvement and further enhancement.

18.4.6 Optimization and refinement

Objective: Refine the system based on feedback analysis to improve efficiency and effectiveness.

Activity: Identify any issues from the testing phase, including performance bottlenecks or security vulnerabilities. Iterate the system design to incorporate improvements and address identified deficiencies. Retest the system to ensure that the modifications provide the desired results.

18.4.7 Documentation and reporting

Objective: Document and disseminate the results of the research.

Activity: Prepare detailed reports outlining methods, experiments, results, and analyses. Prepare academic papers and reports for conferences to share insights with the scientific community. Create comprehensive guidelines and recommendations for applying the framework in different industries.

To provide secure and scalable data analysis, the suggested system combines big data analytics with blockchain technology. The architecture of the framework takes advantage of both the sophisticated data processing powers of big data analytics and the decentralized, unchangeable characteristics of blockchain technology.

A distributed ledger for safe data storage, encryption techniques for data privacy, and smart contracts for automated data management are the main elements of the architecture. Several blockchain nodes store data, providing redundancy and removing single points of failure. Decentralization improves the dependability and security of data.

The framework uses big data analytics-specific parallel processing techniques for scalable data analysis. The framework can effectively manage massive volumes of data by dividing the analytical responsibilities among a network of nodes. By automatically enforcing security rules without human intervention, the usage of smart contracts guarantees that data access and processing adhere to set privacy policies. Big data analytics and blockchain technology work together to provide reliable and scalable data analysis while protecting data privacy.

18.5 EXPECTED IMPACT AND CONTRIBUTION

The combination of blockchain and big data analytics has become a hot area of research nowadays. However, in blockchain technology, a decentralized privacy protection mechanism is an urgent problem to be solved. For this reason, this chapter proposes a decentralized privacy protection mechanism framework, which is constructed through the combination of blockchain and big data analysis, and is expected to have an impact on the following aspects.

First, to enhance the public's awareness of protecting data security and privacy security, the improvement of user privacy awareness is the key to the development of a decentralized privacy protection mechanism. With the popularization of big data analytics, users' attention to privacy protection is increasing. Users need to have a certain awareness of privacy protection, understand how to use privacy protection technology correctly, and how to protect their privacy from being leaked.

Second, this chapter also carries out the performance analysis of the privacy protection mechanism. Through experiments, it is proved that the decentralized privacy protection mechanism framework proposed in this chapter can guarantee the performance of blockchain while ensuring data privacy. For example, when processing a large amount of data, the privacy-preserving mechanism proposed in this chapter can process the data quickly and ensure the performance of the blockchain.

Finally, the decentralized privacy protection mechanism framework proposed in this chapter provides new ideas and methods for blockchain and big data analysis, which has important theoretical and practical significance. Combining blockchain and big data also helps to break data silos and promote cross-organizational data sharing and collaboration, thus promoting more efficient data analysis and decision-making.

18.6 CONCLUSION AND FUTURE WORK

In order to improve data security and privacy, this chapter offers a thorough architecture that combines big data analytics with blockchain technology. The framework provides a strong means of safeguarding sensitive data by combining the powerful processing powers of big data analytics with the decentralized and impenetrable nature of blockchain technology. Distributed storage, encryption techniques, and smart contracts are important components that work together to guarantee data confidentiality, integrity, and speedy processing. This combination offers a safe and scalable method of data analysis while successfully addressing privacy concerns in big data situations. The suggested framework is an important step toward building a secure data ecosystem, which is necessary to protect privacy in the modern digital environment.

Potential avenues for future research encompass the following.

1. Performance optimization: To handle larger datasets more effectively, improve the framework's scalability and real-time processing capabilities.

2. Evaluation methods: Provide thorough evaluation methods to precisely determine how well privacy-preserving strategies work in a range of real-world situations.
3. Integration with advanced technologies: To proactively identify and address security issues, investigate how blockchain, machine learning, and artificial intelligence can be integrated with big data analytics and blockchain.
4. Industry-specific applications: To determine the framework's adaptability and likelihood of further adoption, look into how it is used in a variety of areas, including healthcare, banking, and education.
5. Constant improvement: Modify and enhance the framework to be up to date with new technical developments and data privacy issues.

In conclusion, the combination of big data analytics and blockchain technology is a viable option to improve data security and privacy, opening the door to a more safe digital future.

REFERENCES

Bernabe, J. B., Canovas, J. L., Hernandez-Ramos, J. L., Moreno, R. T., & Skarmeta, A. (2019). Privacy-preserving solutions for blockchain: Review and challenges. *IEEE Access*, 7, 164908–164940.

Fei, L., Liu, J., & Jiao, Q. (2024). Analysis of information security issues in the context of Big Data. *Computer Technology and Development*(08), 1–8.

Gao, H., & Yu, X. (2023). Research on the application of blockchain technology in cross-domain data sharing and privacy protection. *China Management Informatization*, 26(22), 185–187.

Gong, L., Zhang, X., & Gou, J. (2018). Development and application of big data technology in the medical field. *Science and Education Guide*.

Guo, Y., Liang, H., Zhu, L., & Gai, K. (2024). *Blockchains*. Beijing.

Han, Y., & Tao, Y. (2024). Research on the application of big data technology in the field of education. *ECTU Science and Technology*.

Mhlanga, D. (2024). The role of big data in financial technology toward financial inclusion. *Frontiers in Big Data*.

Nakamoto, S. (2008). Bitcoin: A peer-to-peer electronic cash system. Satoshi Nakamoto.

Palit, S., & Roy, C. S. (2021). Impact of Big Data Technologies in Education Management. *International Society for Technology, Education and Science*.

Sun, Y. (2021). Blockchain Security Technology. *Beijing University of Posts and Telecommunications Press*.

Tan, P., Xu, T., Yang, S., et al. (2023). A review of research on blockchain privacy protection technology. *Computer Application Research*, 1–10. https://doi.org/10.19734/j.issn.1001-3695.2023.12.0603

Wang, Y., & Jiang, B. (2019). Research on information leakage in the big data era. *Small and Medium-sized Enterprises Management and Science and Technology*, 7, 100–102.

Yaga, D., Mell, P., Roby, N., & Scarfone, K. (2018). Blockchain Technology Overview.

Ye, H., & Zhuang, W. (2024). The Dilemma of Privacy Protection in the Age of Intelligence. *Media Today*.

Zhang, X., Wang, D., Shao, S., Zhi, H., & R&D Team of Beijing Tongbang Zhuoyi Science & Technology Co. (2022). Blockchain Technology and Trusted Transaction Applications. *Beijing University of Posts and Telecommunications Press*.

Zhi, B. (2022). *Design and implementation of cross-organizational boundary resource sharing system based on blockchain* [Doctoral dissertation, Southeast University]. CNKI. https://doi.org/10.27014/d.cnki.gdnau.2021.003253

Chapter 19

Enhancing network security management with scalable blockchain models

Sun Lili, S. B. Goyal, and Budati Anil Kumar

19.1 INTRODUCTION

19.1.1 Research background

In recent years, due to the rapid advancement of Internet technology, network security has garnered increasing attention. Network security management is of great practical significance in protecting user data, preventing network attacks, and maintaining social stability (Witte et al., 2020). At present, network security challenges present unprecedented diversity and complexity (Martin et al., 2023). The means of network attack are increasingly renovated, from traditional viruses and Trojan attacks to more advanced APT attacks, ransomware, etc., and their concealment, destructivity, and spread speed are greatly increased. According to relevant statistical data, in recent years, the number and scale of network security incidents have shown a trend of rapid growth, bringing huge economic losses and information security risks to enterprises and individuals (Regulatory Update Oig, 2023). As noted network security expert Bruce Schneider says, "Network security is not an option, it's a necessity." In the information age, we must attach great importance to network security management, constantly improve security protection capabilities, and ensure information security. Only in this way can we make full use of the advantages of information technology to promote social progress and development.

2023 is a landmark year in terms of distributed denial of service (DDoS) attack trends (Public white paper on DDoS attack trends in 2024, 2024). Massive botnets built from IoT devices and protocol-level zero-day vulnerabilities (Wang et al., 2023b) have been exploited by cybercriminal groups, geopolitically motivated hacktivists, and malicious actors to launch record-breaking DDoS attacks against businesses, government agencies, and critical but vulnerable public infrastructure, including hospitals.

From the geographical distribution of attacks, the global spread of attack sources indicates that attackers can operate across national borders, and network threats realize the characteristics of borderless. These attack methods not only directly threaten the data security of enterprises, but also may lead to business disruption and reputation damage. In addition, with the wide application of emerging technologies, the boundaries of network security are gradually blurred, and cross-platform and cross-domain attacks occur frequently, which makes network security management face unprecedented challenges.

Given these challenges, traditional network security management means have been difficult to cope with. Therefore, we need to continuously explore new technologies and methods to tackle diverse and complex network security challenges. Blockchain technology, as a novel technology, holds vast potential for application in network security management. By building a scalable blockchain application model, we can achieve functions such as secure

 DOI: 10.1201/9781003513445-19

data storage, access control, and privacy protection, and enhance efficiency and reliability in network security management.

19.1.2 Development history and status quo of blockchain

Blockchain technology has evolved since its inception in 2008. Satoshi Nakamoto originally proposed it to establish a decentralized electronic cash system. Bitcoin's emergence spurred growing interest and adoption of blockchain technology.

However, around 2010, blockchain technology was still in its infancy, and there were some problems with its performance and reliability. It wasn't until 2013 that the birth of Ethereum marked the beginning of blockchain technology's maturation. The successful application of Ethereum has broadened the use of blockchain technology in various fields like finance, the IoT, and supply chain management (Wang, 2024).

In the area of finance, blockchain technology has found widespread application in areas like digital currencies and payment systems. For example, digital currencies such as Bitcoin and Ethereum are built on blockchain technology. Blockchain technology can be utilized to create decentralized financial markets and enhance security, efficiency, and transparency in financial transactions (Zeng & Wan, 2019).

In the field of the IoT, blockchain technology can be used to enable secure communication and data sharing between devices. For example, smart home systems can achieve secure communication between devices through blockchain technology, so that users can better control and manage their own home devices (Razaque et al., 2023).

In the field of supply chain management, blockchain technology can be used to achieve transparency and decentralization of supply chains (Shen et al., 2021). For example, blockchain technology can be used to make supply chains traceable and tamper-resistant, making supply chain management more efficient and secure.

Blockchain technology also shows great potential in network security management. Blockchain technology can be used to achieve decentralization and transparency in network security management. For example, blockchain technology can be used to automate and intelligent network security management (Chai et al., 2023), making network security management more efficient and reliable.

19.1.3 Application of blockchain in network security management

Blockchain technology has attracted much attention in recent years and is widely considered to be an important guarantee for future network security. It has the characteristics of distributed, immutable, anonymous, etc., and provides many innovative solutions for network security. Next, we summarize the characteristics, benefits, and limitations of the different blockchain technologies used in network security management, as shown in Table 19.1.

Identity authentication: Blockchain technology can establish a decentralized identity authentication system, storing user's identity information securely on the blockchain, through cryptographic algorithms for protection, to guarantee the authenticity and security of identity information, the system can be used in finance, medical, government, and other sectors to enhance identity authentication efficiency and security.

Access control: Blockchain can be used to achieve fine-grained access control through smart contracts to define the access rights of different roles. Only users who meet certain conditions can access certain data or resources, thereby preventing unauthorized access and data breaches.

Table 19.1 Blockchain technology comparison

Tech	*Trait*	*Advantage*	*Limitation*
Distributed ledger	Allows multiple participants to record and verify transactions on a shared ledger, rather than relying on a single centralized authority.	The transaction information of all participants is recorded, ensuring the transparency, auditability, and security of the data.	There is a problem of low performance and slowness when updating and validating stored data.
Hash algorithm	The data is converted into a fixed-length hash value, and different data will rarely produce the same hash value, which is one-way.	Ensure data integrity and immutability.	This could lead to the disclosure of sensitive information.
Consensus algorithm	By allowing participants to agree when generating new blocks, the blockchain network can properly verify and confirm transactions.	Ensure data consistency across blockchain networks to prevent malicious attacks.	It is difficult to balance node scale, complementary performance, and fault tolerance.
Smart contract	It is the code execution environment of the blockchain, they can automatically execute and enforce contracts and ensure that the conditions of the contract are met.	Automatically enforce contract conditions to ensure data and asset security.	The research and development of the underlying technology of smart contracts face challenges.
anonymity	Anonymity can be provided to users so that participants do not need to disclose personally identifiable information in transactions.	It can prevent identity theft and malicious attackers from using personal information to carry out cyber attacks.	In practice, anonymity is not always guaranteed.
Encryption technology	Participants sign transactions with private keys, while others verify legitimacy using public keys.	The confidentiality and security of data are guaranteed.	There is a private key security problem, if the user loses their private key, all the data encrypted with it will not be recovered.
decentralization	The network lacks a single point of failure and cannot be controlled by a single entity.	It enhances the anti-attack capability of the network and prevents the attacker from destroying the entire network through a single attack point.	The degree of decentralization is difficult to balance with the efficiency of the consensus mechanism, which affects the transaction delay and throughput.
Byzantine fault tolerance	Malicious nodes are detected and eliminated through the collaboration of multiple nodes.	Improves network security defense, blockchain network maintains normal operation despite node failure or malicious attacks.	The fault tolerance is reduced.

Data storage: The immutability of blockchain makes it an ideal data storage solution. Sensitive data can be stored on the blockchain, ensuring data integrity and security. In addition, blockchain can also be combined with cloud storage technology to achieve distributed storage and backup of data, improving the availability and reliability of data.

Supply chain management: Blockchain technology can be used to optimize supply chain management, ensuring data transparency and traceability by recording information at every link in the supply chain. This can help reduce fraud and abuse in the supply chain and improve efficiency and trust in the supply chain.

Network attack defense: The decentralized nature of blockchain and encryption algorithms can help detect and defend against network attacks. By analyzing the data transaction patterns on the blockchain, abnormal behavior or potential security threats can be detected and timely countermeasures can be taken.

Encrypted communication: Blockchain can be used to achieve secure encrypted communication by establishing an encrypted channel to protect data security during transmission. This communication method can be applied to financial transactions, online communication, and other scenarios to enhance the security and privacy of data transmission.

19.1.4 A practical case of blockchain in network security management

In network security management, blockchain technology has extensive application prospects. Many practice cases exist, and we will delve into several detailed examples of blockchain-based network security management.

19.1.4.1 Blockchain-based digital currency trading platform

A digital currency trading platform is an e-commerce platform based on blockchain technology, where users can buy and sell digital currency transactions. Ronaghi evaluated the Iranian blockchain's digital currency exchange platform using a value-based scaling model and PLS software (Ronaghi, 2023). The platform offers decentralization, security, and reliability, safeguarding users' digital currency assets effectively. In addition, the platform can also realize smart contracts, and users can set trading conditions on the trading platform and automatically execute transactions without trusting third-party institutions (Zhang et al., 2022), which improves the security and efficiency of transactions.

19.1.4.2 Blockchain-based electronic identity authentication system

An electronic identity authentication system is an identity authentication system based on blockchain technology, which can realize fast, secure, and reliable authentication of user identity. Paez Rafael et al proposed the architecture of a blockchain-based biometric electronic identity document (e-ID) system for authenticating transactions such as citizens' medical services and economic activities (Páez et al., 2020). The system can effectively protect the user's privacy and prevent identity from being used fraudulently. Blockchain-based electronic identity authentication systems can achieve decentralized identity authentication, users can anonymously identity authentication, and at the same time authentication records will be recorded on the blockchain, and cannot be tampered with.

19.1.4.3 Blockchain-based network security management platform

The network security management platform utilizes blockchain technology for decentralized management (Kharjana et al., 2023), effectively protecting network security and preventing network attacks and data leaks. Users can anonymously conduct network security management, and management records will also be recorded on the blockchain, which cannot be tampered with, which can achieve intelligent, automated, and efficient network security management. Guy Zyskind and others proposed a personal information management system (Zyskind et al., 2015) based on the decentralized characteristics of blockchain technology, aiming to tackle the issue of unrestricted access to user data by third-party services, Amir Lazarovich et al. developed a blockchain-based platform for secure data storage (Lazarovich, 2015). This platform

Table 19.2 Impact analysis of blockchain implementation

Impact analysis	*Analytical level*	*Concrete measures*	*Practical application*
Qualitative influence	Security at the network level	Through its unique distributed ledger structure and encryption algorithm, it solves the traditional single point of failure problem, enhancing security and stability.	Distributed firewall
	Security at the protocol level	Immutability, privacy protection, and other aspects of the role	Countering 51% of attacks
	Application-level security	Effectively protect user privacy and data security through decentralization and encryption technology, improve user experience, and promote application promotion.	Smart contract
	Security at the management level	Smart contract application reduces human error and transaction confirmation time.	Traceability technique
Quantitative influence	Data security	Through its unique chain structure and hashing algorithm, it ensures the security and integrity of data during transmission and storage.	Data encryption and authentication
	Transaction security	A variety of cryptographic algorithms (hash function, symmetric encryption algorithm, asymmetric encryption algorithm, digital signature algorithm, and consensus mechanism Proof of Work, PoW, Proof of Stake, PoS, etc.) are used to ensure the security, privacy, and consistency of transactions.	Authentication and access control
	System stability	Improve data integrity and prevent tampering.	Cooperative defense mechanism
Combined influence	The quantitative and qualitative impact of blockchain technology in network security are complementary. Quantitative impact provides specific measurement criteria to help evaluate the safety performance of the system; qualitative impact provides a comprehensive evaluation of system safety, including system design, implementation, and management. The combination of the two can provide a more comprehensive and in-depth guarantee for network security.		

allows users and Web services to share a key to access encrypted data, with Web access records stored on the blockchain for user supervision, thereby safeguarding user privacy.

The history and current status of blockchain technology reveal its vast potential in network security management. Its application in this field will expand and deepen with technological advancements (Xu et al., 2022). Studying blockchain's application in network security and designing scalable models to enhance efficiency offers a novel approach to network security management, significantly promoting blockchain's application in this domain.

By analyzing the potential applications and security performance of blockchain technology in cybersecurity, as shown in Table 19.2, we can learn that blockchain can significantly enhance data integrity, traceability, and tamper resistance, and help build a more robust network ecosystem.

19.2 RESEARCH AIM AND SCOPE

This study aims to improve the level of network security management and build a more secure, reliable, and efficient network environment by introducing blockchain technology. The blockchain-based network security management model features decentralization, high security, and scalability, effectively addressing traditional network security issues (Brody & Couture, 2021).

First of all, the network security management model based on blockchain technology has the characteristics of decentralization, which can avoid the information asymmetry and security risks brought by centralization (Oksana et al., 2021). Second, blockchain technology realizes the consensus and verification of data through the consensus mechanism, which can effectively prevent data from being tampered with and forged, thus improving the reliability and security of network security management.

The network security management model based on blockchain technology is also scalable. Blockchain technology can support large-scale data storage and collaboration, which can effectively improve the scalability and subsequent upgrading of network security management. At the same time, blockchain technology also supports the programming of smart contracts and automated and intelligent network security management systems, enhancing efficiency and convenience in network security (Bao et al., 2023).

With the advancement of blockchain technology, the network security management model based on blockchain technology will be more widely used and developed in the future.

This study aims to develop a scalable model for network security management leveraging blockchain technology, combined with artificial intelligence techniques like machine learning and deep learning. The model addresses scalability challenges in blockchain-based network security, including low transaction efficiency, high latency, and limited throughput, offering innovative solutions for effective security management.

1. The research focuses on modeling by combining artificial intelligence methods such as machine learning and deep learning.
2. Research and design a scalable blockchain-based model for network security management.
3. The study explores the use of blockchain in network security management and the current state of blockchain scaling models.
4. Research and explore solutions to address performance and scalability challenges in blockchain technology for network security management.
5. The research work proposes the use and optimization of blockchain scalable models.
6. This research offers insights into future blockchain technology research in network security.

19.3 RESEARCH DESIGN

19.3.1 Problem statement

The application of blockchain technology in network security management has great potential to provide more secure, reliable, and transparent solutions for network security management. However, blockchain also faces some challenges and problems in its application, which mainly focus on the performance bottleneck and scalability of the technology. According to the research background and motivation of this chapter and the existing research gaps in this field, the current research problems in this field are stated as follows:

- Blockchain technology has scalability bottlenecks when processing a large number of transactions, and high transaction volumes can lead to network congestion, affecting data processing speed and security (Xia et al., 2019).
- The decentralized nature of blockchains means that every node needs to participate in transaction verification, which can lead to slower transactions (Wang et al., 2021).
- Each block of the blockchain has a size limit, limited transaction capacity, and is prone to congestion (Wang et al., 2023a).
- High trading fees are also a problem, as trading capacity is limited and traders need to pay higher fees to ensure that trades are processed quickly (Ni et al., 2024).

To sum up, blockchain technology faces many technical challenges and problems in the application of network security management. To successfully apply blockchain technology, these issues need to be addressed and more mature, secure, and reliable blockchain technology developed.

19.3.2 Research questions, research objectives, and research hypothesis

19.3.2.1 Research Question 01

Challenges and issues of blockchain technology in network security management.
The first research question focuses on reviewing and summarizing the use of blockchain in network security management by researchers. It aims to identify the research approach, algorithms, and constraints of blockchain technology in these applications. This study explores the use of existing blockchain scalable models. The starting point of this work is to start with the existing model and analyze the parts of the existing model that can be further optimized, mainly to address the limitations of the existing blockchain scalable model.

19.3.2.2 Research Question 02

How to address the scalability problems of blockchain in network security management such as low transaction efficiency, high time delay, and small throughput.
The second research question explores the limited scalability of blockchain technology in network security management. This study analyzes the algorithm mechanism of blockchain in terms of transaction efficiency, delay, and throughput in network security management.

19.3.2.3 Research Question 03

Can blockchain scalable models be designed to enhance network security management?
The aim of RQ3 is to tackle scalability and performance bottlenecks in blockchain technology for network security management. The core challenge lies in enhancing the scalability of blockchain in network security. Failure to resolve these issues hinders blockchain's

widespread application and development in this field. The objective is to devise a scalable blockchain model for improved network security management.

19.3.2.4 Research Question 04

How can the Blockchain scalable model be used to improve network security management? The fourth research question aims to explore how the new scaling model can enhance blockchain technology's technical scalability in network security management applications. This phase focuses on capturing data characteristics through the scalable model to achieve a highly accurate scalable model.

The overall goal is to verify the capability, accuracy, and reliability of the blockchain scalable model in the aspects of network security management of data transaction efficiency, delay, throughput, etc., and may apply to large-scale network environments.

19.4 RESEARCH METHODOLOGY

Based on the research questions and objectives of this chapter, we will follow the following steps.

19.4.1 Literature review and problem identification

Establish a comprehensive understanding of current blockchain applications in network security and identify key issues affecting scalability. Review current literature on blockchain technology and its use in network security. Identify scalability challenges and existing solutions within network security frameworks.

19.4.2 Theoretical framework development

Develop a theoretical framework for scalable blockchain applications in network security. Analyze the characteristics of blockchain that benefit network security. Synthesize findings from the literature review to model a scalable blockchain framework that integrates advanced security features. Figure 19.1 shows the blockchain model architecture proposed in network security management.

19.4.3 System design and prototype development

Design a prototype based on the developed framework that addresses scalability in blockchain network security applications. Develop a scalable blockchain prototype using simulated network environments. Integrate AI techniques like machine learning for dynamic threat assessment and response. Figure 19.2 shows the workflow of the blockchain process, which shows the operational flow of the blockchain model from data entry to security management.

19.4.4 Experimental setup and testing

Evaluate the scalability and effectiveness of the blockchain prototype in enhancing network security. Test the prototype in varied network conditions to assess scalability and security performance. Analyze system resilience against different cyber threat scenarios.

19.4.5 Data collection and analysis

Collect and analyze performance data to validate the scalability and security enhancements provided by the prototype. Measure key performance indicators such as transaction throughput, response time to security breaches, and system scalability under load.

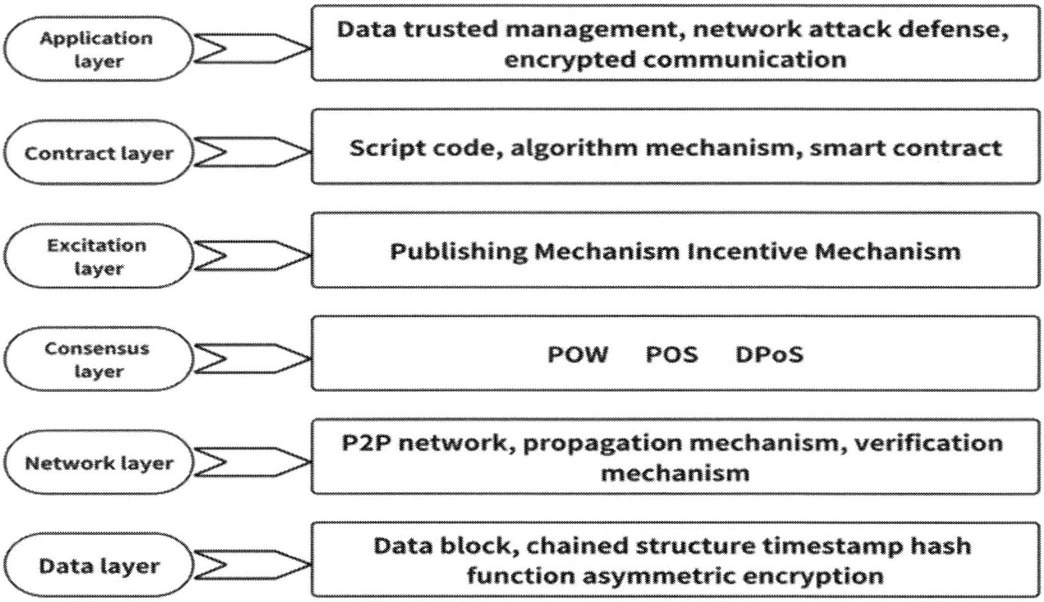

Figure 19.1 Blockchain application model.

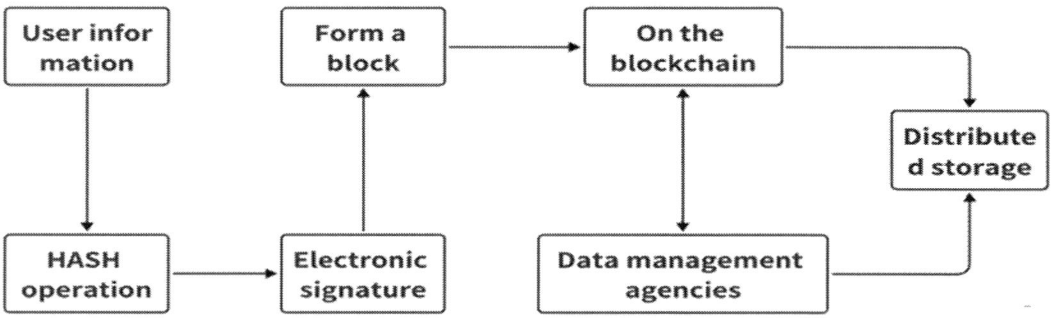

Figure 19.2 Workflow of the blockchain model.

19.4.6 Optimization and refinement

Refine the prototype based on analysis to enhance scalability and security. Use feedback from testing to refine the system architecture. Optimize code and algorithms to improve efficiency and security.

19.4.7 Documentation and reporting

Document the research findings and disseminate results through academic and industry channels. Prepare detailed reports and papers documenting the development process, findings, and the impact of the scalable blockchain model on network security. Present findings at conferences and in journals.

Based on the detailed steps above, Figure 19.3 shows the exact methodology flow.

Every component of the framework, which is made up of multiple interconnected parts, is essential to guaranteeing safe and scalable data analysis. To help visualize the relationships and data flow inside the framework, flowcharts and diagrams are supplied. We

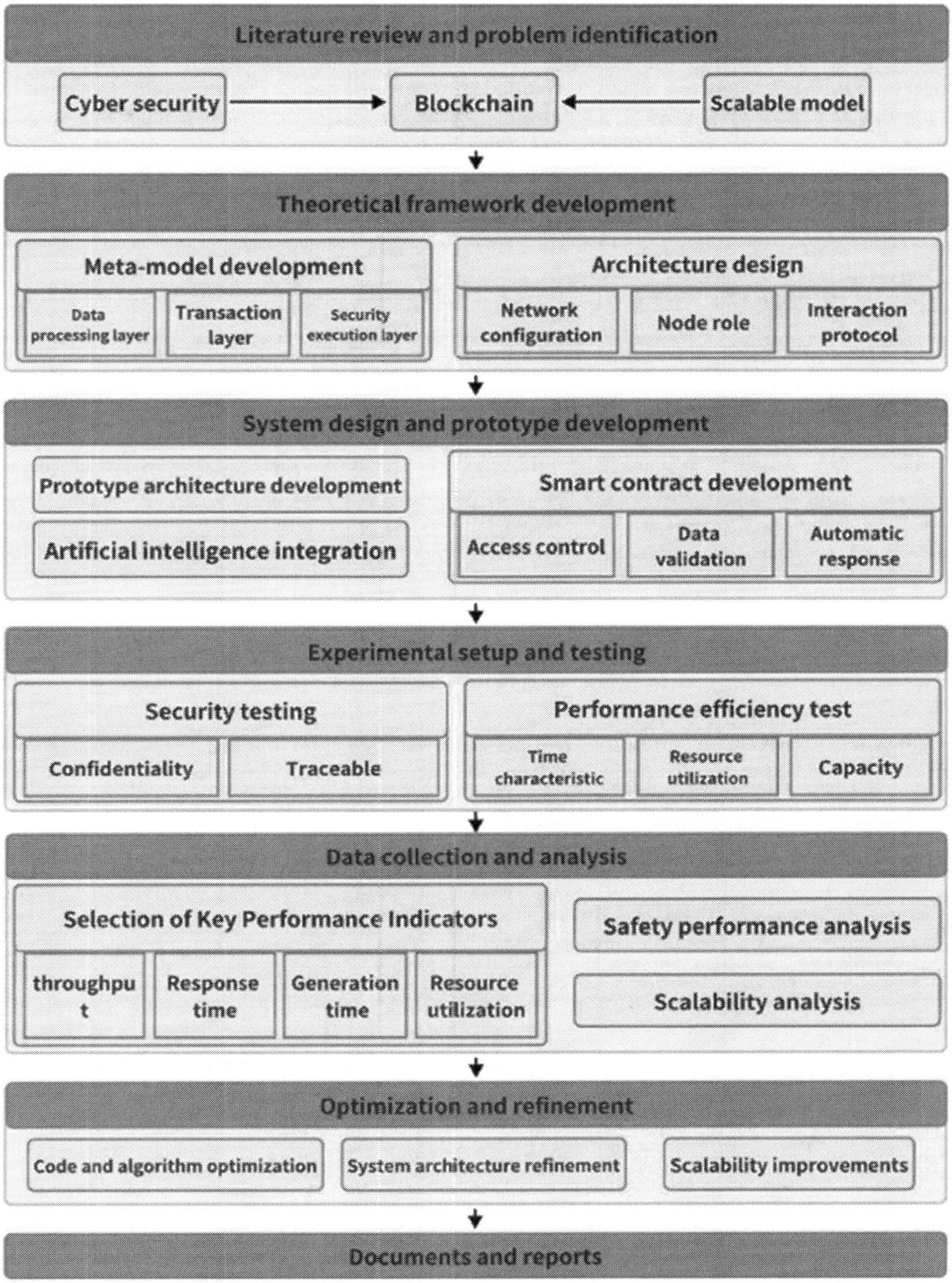

Figure 19.3 Research methodology.

outline how artificial intelligence methods, like machine learning and deep learning, are combined to improve scalability and analytical capabilities, with blockchain technology acting as the foundation for data integrity and security. There is a detailed explanation of the roles played by the various models and algorithms utilized in the data analysis process, as well as how well they work to lower latency and increase transaction efficiency. This all-encompassing strategy guarantees that our system handles major issues in network security management by securely securing data and scaling effectively to accommodate high transaction volumes.

19.5 EXPECTED IMPACT AND CONTRIBUTION

The results of this study have important implications for practice. In network security management, blockchain technology is a new security protection means. It can effectively mitigate network attack risks and safeguard network data security. In addition, the scalable model proposed in this chapter can realize the flexibility and scalability of network security management and can be adjusted and optimized according to different scenarios and needs, to improve the efficiency and effect of network security management.

Second, the research results of this chapter provide an important reference for the design of blockchain applications in network security management. When designing blockchain applications, it is necessary to consider the needs and characteristics of network security management, and reasonably design and select blockchain technology and algorithms to achieve the best results in network security management. At the same time, it's crucial to consider the scalability and maintainability of blockchain to guarantee the stability and reliability of network security management systems.

Finally, the research results of this chapter provide important guidance for the practice of network security management. In practice, it is necessary to fully consider the needs and characteristics of network security management, rationally apply blockchain technology and scalable models, and enhance the efficiency and impact of network security management. Simultaneously, emphasize practice summaries and feedback to continuously refine and enhance network security management methods and strategies.

In summary, the chapter's findings have significant implications for blockchain applications in network security. Implementing blockchain technology and creating scalable models can significantly enhance the efficiency and effectiveness of network security management, safeguarding network data.

19.6 CONCLUSION AND FUTURE WORK

This chapter provides an extensive analysis of how scalable blockchain architectures can improve network security management. Through the integration of artificial intelligence methodologies like machine learning and deep learning with blockchain technology, we have created a strong framework that tackles significant issues concerning transaction efficiency, latency, and throughput. Our methodology is appropriate for large-scale network applications since it shows notable gains in data transaction security and scalability. The decentralized, tamper-proof, and effective security solutions that the suggested framework can offer represent a major breakthrough in network security management.

In the future, network security management will leverage blockchain technology with an emphasis on improving privacy protection, broadening application scenarios, and advancing technological maturity. Subsequent investigations will look into the following:

1. Creating novel consensus methods, blockchain protocols, and algorithms to increase security and dependability.
2. Using blockchain technology to improve efficiency and security across a range of network security domains, such as identity authentication, data encryption, and smart contracts.
3. Looking at practical privacy-protection strategies for blockchain networks to guarantee data security.
4. Encouraging network security management to standardize blockchain applications in order to make their widespread adoption easier.

Finally, our work offers a scalable approach that tackles existing issues and improves system performance, bringing important new insights into the use of blockchain technology in network security management.

REFERENCES

Bao, Q., Li, B., Hu, T., & Sun, X. (2023). A survey of blockchain consensus safety and security: State-of-the-art, challenges, and future work. *Journal of Systems & Software*, 196, N.PAG.

Brody, A., & Couture, S. (2021). Ideologies and imaginaries in blockchain communities: The case of Ethereum. *Canadian Journal of Communication*, 46(3), 543–561.

Chai, J., Li, J., Wei, M., & Zhu, C. (2023). Blockchain managed federated learning for a secure IoT framework. *EURASIP Journal on Wireless Communications and Networking*, 2023(1), 1–17.

Kharjana, M., Pohrmen, F. H., Sahana, S. C., & Saha, G. (2023). Blockchain-based key management system in named data networking: A survey. *Journal of Network and Computer Applications*, 220, N.PAG.

Lazarovich, A. (2015). Invisible Ink: blockchain for data privacy. *Massachusetts Institute of Technology*.

Martin, F., Bacak, J., Byker, E. J., Wang, W., Wagner, J., & Ahlgrim-Delzell, L. (2023). Examination of cybersecurity technologies, practices, challenges, and wish list in K-12 school districts. *Journal of Cybersecurity Education, Research and Practice*, 2023(1), 2472–2707.

Ni, X., Ma, Z., & Wang, Q. (2024). Research on Blockchain P2P Network and Security. *Computer Engineering and Applications*, 60(5), 17–29.

Oksana, C., Dmytro, N., Zakharii, V., Viktor, K., & Oleksandra, B. (2021). Innovative Blockchain Technology as a Factor of Economic Development. *Globalization & Business / Globalizac'ia Da Biznesi*, 11, 11–15.

Páez, R., Pérez, M., Ramírez, G., Montes, J., & Bouvarel, L. (2020). An architecture for biometric electronic identification document system based on blockchain. *Future Internet*, 12(1), 10.

Public white paper on DDoS attack trends in 2024. (2024). Retrieved from https://max.book118.com/html/2024/0530/6114243121010140.shtm

Razaque, R., Abdul, A., Yoo, J., Bektemyssova, G., Alshammari, M., Chinibayeva, T. T., … Umutkulov, D. (2023). Efficient Internet-of-Things Cyberattack Depletion Using Blockchain-Enabled Software-Defined Networking and 6G Network Technology. *Sensors*, 23(24), 9690.

Regulatory Update Oig: Cybersecurity, Crisis Preparedness among Top Fdic Challenges. (2023). *Journal of Internet Law*, 26(8), 3–6. Retrieved from https://search.ebscohost.com/login.aspx?direct=true&db=buh&AN=163590519&lang=zh-cn&site=ehost-live

Ronaghi, M. H. (2023). A contextualized study of blockchain technology adoption as a digital currency platform under sanctions. *Management Decision*, 61(5), 1352–1373.

Shen, H., Chen, Q., & Huang, H. (2021). Semantic Blockchain research review. *Application Research of Computers / Jisuanji Yingyong Yanjiu*, 38(7), 1937–1942.

Wang, F. (2024). Research on optimization algorithms for artificial intelligence network security management based on All IP Internet of Things fusion technology. *Computers & Electrical Engineering*, 115, N.PAG.

Wang, J., Liu, Q., Zhang, R., Ji, W., & Song, B. (2023a). Two-branch structure extension model based on blockchain. *Computer Science*, 50(8), 365–371.

Wang, B., Wan, L., Liu, M., & Sun, H. (2023b). DDoS attack detection based on DWT and AKD autoencoders. *Journal of Nanjing University of Information Science & Technology (Natural Science Edition)*, 15(4), 419–428.

Wang, B., Zhao, S., Li, Y., Wu, C., Tan, J., Li, H., & Yukita, K. (2021). Design of a privacy-preserving decentralized energy trading scheme in a blockchain network environment. *International Journal of Electrical Power & Energy Systems*, 125, 106465.

Witte, B., Frasca, P., Overvest, B., & Timmer, J. (2020). Protecting shared information in networks: A network security game with strategic attacks. *International Journal of Robust and Nonlinear Control*, 30(11), 4255–4277.

Xia, H., Tian, W., Gao, J., Zhang, T., Gao, R., & Xia, Q. (2019). Outsourcing secure multi-party statistical computing based on blockchain can validate privacy protection schemes. *Radio Engineering*, 54(4), 835–847.

Xu, R., Chen, Y., Chen, G., & Blasch, E. (2022). SAUSA: Securing access, usage, and storage of 3D point cloud data by a blockchain-based authentication network. *Future Internet*, 14(12), 354.

Zeng, Z., & Wan, P. (2019). Research on Public security Big Data resource management System based on the sovereign blockchain network. *Information Theory and Practice*, 42(8), 110–115.

Zhang, L., Chen, W., Wang, W., Jin, Z., Zhao, C., Cai, Z., & Chen, H. (2022). CBGRU: A detection method of smart contract vulnerability based on a hybrid model. *Sensors*, 22(9), 1424–8220.

Zyskind, G., Nathan, O., & Pentland, A. (2015). Enigma: Decentralized computation platform with guaranteed privacy. *arXiv preprint arXiv*:1506.03471.

Chapter 20

Mathematical modeling for identification using fuzzy matching system

G. Govinda Rajulu, L. Sharmila, D. Venkatesan, and S. Kalvikkarasi

20.1 INTRODUCTION

Biometrics identification is the most appropriate way of substantiating an individual in a valid and quick path through distinctive biological peculiarity. This authentication correlates features of a human biometric template to find the resemblance. The need is to acquire the data from the person. It may be a photo, voice, or an image. It takes a long time to confirm one's identity. It has been pioneered by experts for civil, criminal, or military identification purposes under an organized technical structure. Biometric research is growing faster and faster. Because of the uniqueness, steadiness, and unsurprising changes, the pinna highlights are possibly a promising biometric for use in human ID. Pinna identification is stepped up for this intent. According to cytology, the pinna is the visual part of the external ear. The tragus, helix, and lobule are the components of pinna. The main canal begins at the outer ear and finishes at the ear drum. The auricle formation occurs between 42 and 48 days of gestation, which then develops upward and backward to the location of the head (Figure 20.1).

To acquire noteworthy projections of auricle regions, numerous techniques such as radiological body volume documentation, figured tomography, and attractive reverberation imaging have been utilized lately.

20.2 LITERATURE SURVEY

Mark et al. [1] proposed a curve segmentation method for security access. Through practical observation, they have used three neural network concepts to recognize the two-dimensional picture of the ear. They used Borda, Bayesian, and weighted Bayesian methods. For sampling, they used data from 48 people. The observation showed a 93% recognition rate. Improved performances were not achieved. Yuizono et al. [2] experimented genetic algorithm with a system for ear images. They experimented with ten persons with 660 images. They tested with video images. They concluded a 100% recognition rate and a 100% rejection rate for unknown people.

20.3 RESEARCH METHODOLOGY

The main goal of this research is to recognize a person using pinna images using Fuzzy Feature Matching (FFM). Images are formed by varied views [3]. The image sets consist of left and right pinna images. The system is viewed as acquisition, pre-processing, feature extraction, and matching (Figure 20.2).

DOI: 10.1201/9781003513445-20

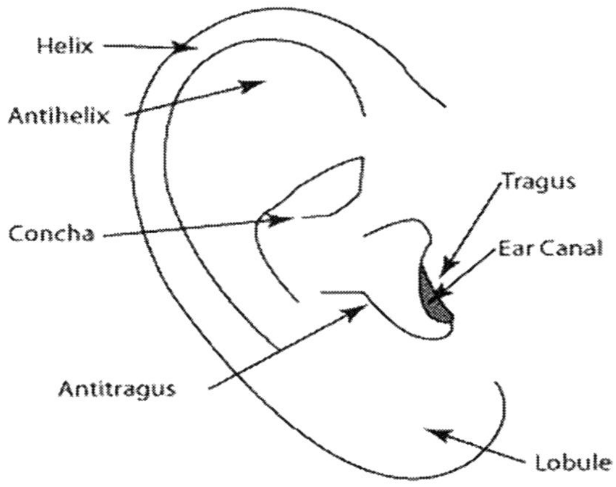

Figure 20.1 Structure of pinna.

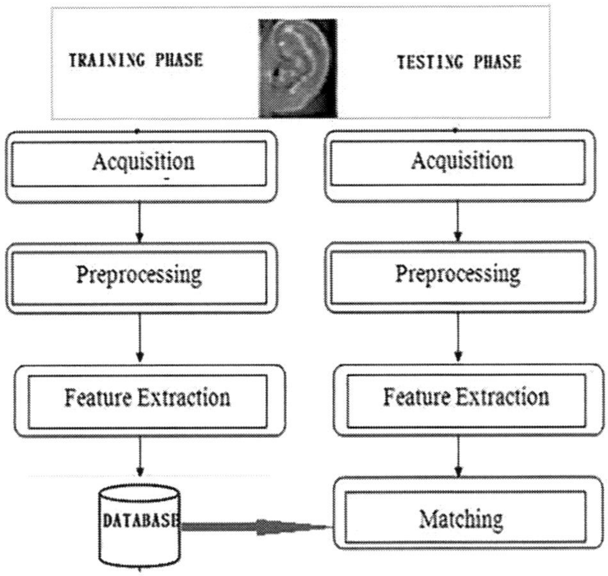

Figure 20.2 Architecture of the system.

The procured pictures are of the .bmp type. The resolution of the pictures is 800 × 600 pixels. The accessible information base comprises 20 people with left and right pinna, each with five posture picture varieties. The middle channel is utilized for the removal of motivation commotion, which is obvious in a computerized picture of the obtained picture. After variety regularization, the channel lessens the clamor present in the pinna pictures [4]. The separated picture is acquired by changing the center pixel esteem and the middle worth processed from the nearest pixels of the pinna area. Then, the pinna picture is ready in the X and Y headings. This is gathered to shape a new picture that shows the entire total of the X and Y edges. In the Sobel technique, at first, the RGB picture is transformed into grayscale. For edge location, a 3 × 3 framework portrays the channel that will be effective for the outcome (Table 20.1).

Framework

- Transform the image to grayscale
- Arrange the resultant image with the Sobel-x filter
- Arrange the resultant image with the Sobel-y filter
- Estimate the gradient
- Estimate the magnitude
- Estimate the direction

On extracting the features, geometrical views are introduced into the pinna region of the ear. Near the pinna, the meatus bony segment is used for plotting the graph. After finding the local points on the pinna, we can collect all triangular features [5]. From the points noted, triangles are formed. In total, four triangles are formed in an ear. For an individual, on considering the right and left ear, a total of eight triangles are used for the manipulation. The Damerau–Levenshtein distance algorithm is calculated by creating a $(M + 1) \times (N + 1)$ matrix. Using the function fm, n(i, j), the lengths of the two strings M and N can be specified. Levenshtein distance calculation is suggested to set the distance between the two strings to apply this proportion of pointed vertices and edges in the pinna (Figure 20.3).

The chain is the geometrical triangular feature of the pinna. Eight triangles are constructed for the pinna of a human. The vector of the triangular structure is viewed by the distance and angle of direction of the exact points. Before measuring the homogeneity among the fuzzy feature set, Assume Ftemp = { i, j, k, Ψi, Ψj, Ψk, Ar, Pe} is a controlled triangle feature

Table 20.1 Edge detection process

Prepared in x direction			*Prepared in y direction*		
−1	0	1	−1	−3	−1
−3	0	3	0	0	0
−1	0	1	1	3	3

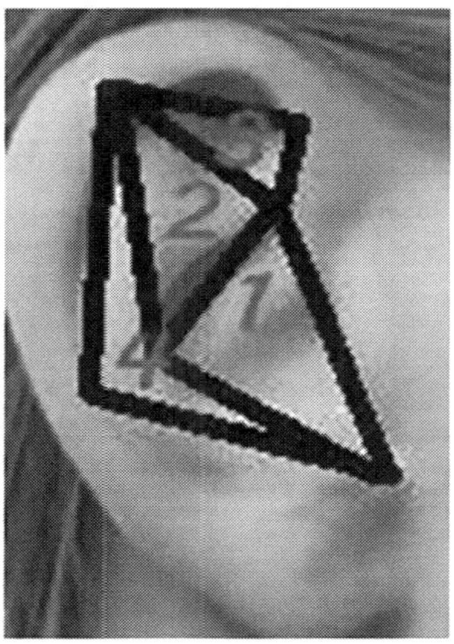

Figure 20.3 Triangle patterns in pinna.

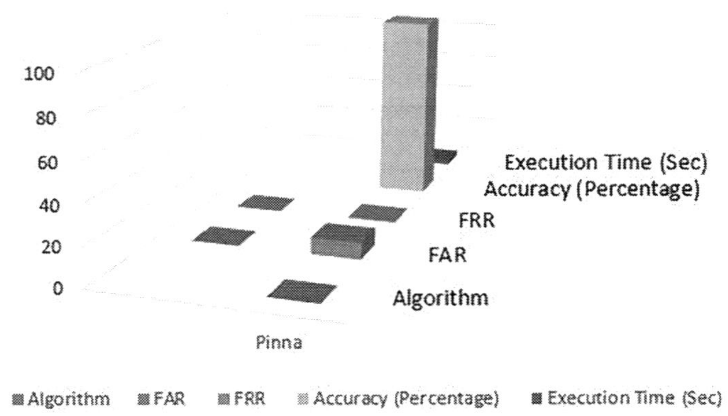

Figure 20.4 Plotting the results graphically.

in a template pinna and Finp = { il, jl, kl, Ψ l i, Ψ l j, Ψ l k, AT l, PT l } is a controlled feature in an input pinna. Pattern parameters such as len-diff, Ψ-diff, Ar-diff, and Pe-diff are computed. The original data x is described by the membership function. Then, the membership function for X is found by implying x = X-a/k. Use $2k^2 = K^2$ to the Cauchy membership function.

The Cauchy membership function is a little bit fuzzier than the Gaussian. It is best to differentiate between data points described by the fuzzy set. The Cauchy membership function in computing is much more efficient in the gradient of the cost function. To derive the pattern parameter space, we used the training set. The similarity is estimated from the constructed triangle similarities. The measure for layout and info pinna is characterized as

$$S = \left[\left[(1-p)\,\text{wea} + \text{web}\right]\right] L^{(T,1)}$$

Here, wea is the weight of the triangle neighboring the midpoint and is the area percentage of both the template and the input pinna, p € [0, 1].

20.4 EXPERIMENTAL RESULTS

An experiment is performed to evaluate the effectiveness and robustness of the proposed system. To evaluate the proposed pinna identification, the pinna images were acquired. The system is developed using Visual Studio. This significantly decreases the computational complexity. A better performance of 95.37% accuracy is also obtained. The complexity of fuzzy-based methodology is less.

The framework is investigated to track down a person as valid or fraudulent. To figure out the accomplishment of the technique, a standard estimation is utilized to check the acknowledgment blunders and dismissal mistakes using False Reject Rate (FRR) and False Acceptance Rate (FAR). The FRR is the level of a person that the framework neglects to acknowledge. FAR is the level of unapproved person that the framework neglects to dismiss. The accuracy of the work is defined as Accuracy = max (100 – (FRR + FAR)/2) (Table 20.2).

Table 20.2 Experimental result

Traits	*Algorithm*	*FAR (percentage)*	*FRR (percentage)*	*Accuracy (percentage)*	*Execution time (sec)*
Pinna	FFM	8.49	0.87	95.37	2.54

20.5 CONCLUSIONS

A new method for pinna identification is analyzed. Compared to conventional ear biometric identification, pinna identification is more efficient. The left and right pinnas are represented by the fuzzy feature. The image depicts the construction of local triangles. Pinna images can be identified by comparing their similarity to the features. The matching technique envisions the closeness sets of the general picture to similitude inside the genuine span [0, 1]. With the pinna, the method was tested and evaluated, and the results showed that the algorithm works well. Here, we obtained 95.37% of exactness in coordinating.

REFERENCES

[1] Mark and Wilhem Burger on "Ear Biometrics in Computer Vision", IEEE 2000.
[2] T. Yuizono, Y. Wang, K. Satoh and S. Nakayama, "Study on Individual Recognition for Ear Images by Using Genetic Local Search," Congress Evolutionary Computation, 2002.
[3] A. Lannarelli, Ear Identification Paramount Publishing 1989.
[4] P. Yan and K.W. Bowyer, "Multi-biometric 2D and 3D ear recognition", in Audio- and Video-Based Person Authentication – AVBPA, pp. 503–512, edited by T. Kanade, A.K. Jain, and N.K. Ratha, LNCS 3546, Springer, 2005.
[5] M. Choraœ, "Ear biometrics based on geometrical feature extraction", *Journal ELCVIA, Computer Vision and Image Analysis* 5, 84–95 (2005).

Chapter 21

Performance evaluation of a pre-compensated ROF system

Himali Sarangal, Manjit Singh, Butta Singh, Satveer Kour, Komal Krishan Mehta, and Ram Dayal

21.1 INTRODUCTION

With the dramatic increase in the number of users of internet technology, the requirement of large bandwidth, high bit rate, etc., increases. In order to fulfill these requirements, the combined version of two technologies, i.e., wireless and optical technology, known as radio over fiber (ROF) technology has been developed. ROF uses optical fiber as a communication medium to grant a highly efficient, high-bandwidth capacity, and 5G-scalable architecture for the transmission of radio frequency over optical fiber that has low attenuation, immunity to electromagnetic interference, and superior signal integrity [1, 2]. Therefore, it enables the transmission of signals over long distances, thus improving wireless networks' mobility and ubiquity. The ROF link consists of three components: (1) the central station, where the data is optically modulated using a Mach Zehnder modulator and laser diode and then transmitted to the receiver through optical fiber, (2) the base station is where the optical signal is converted into an electrical signal with the help of a photo and finally, the transmitted signal is recovered using a suitable filter, and (3) the mobile unit, which consists of an RF demodulator. A radio frequency antenna is used to connect the base station to the mobile unit [3, 4] (Figure 21.1).

Researchers are working on improving the performance of the ROF systems. Hadi et al. used machine-learning tools to compensate for the nonlinear effects in optical systems. They proposed the 64-quadrature amplitude modulation (QAM)-based ROF system at a fiber length of 10 km in which the nonlinear effect was reduced by the support vector machine technique [5]. In 2022, Kota, T. et al recommended a remote beamforming scheme based on ROF systems [4]. This scheme is helpful to attain an Error Vector Magnitude (EVM) of 2.71–3.55% for 5G applications. It is also suitable for antennas with larger aperture areas, which are used for attaining high gain. While using this scheme, wavelengths are allocated to beams rather than the elements of the antenna [6]. Digital Radio over Fiber (D-ROF) and Analog Radio over Fiber (A-ROF) have been analyzed by Hadi et.al at 20 MHz, QAM modulated signal for a transmission distance of 70 km. The analysis used Error Vector Magnitude (EVM), Signal-to-Noise Ratio (S/N), and eye diagram parameters to evaluate the penalty for both systems. It was concluded in the analysis that the D-ROF and A-ROF are the most prominent candidates for upcoming networks at 30 km and 70 km, respectively. They recommended using single-mode fibers for low cost and power effectiveness [7]. Delta–sigma (DSM) is an ROF system that was proposed by Wei et al. for use in millimeter wave (MW) range indoor applications. In the proposed simulation set up for quantization of higher-order QAM orthogonal frequency division multiplexing (OFDM), signal two-bit DSM is used. In their work, it has been concluded that at negligible deterioration, a huge number of QAM signals can be transmitted and recovered by the proposed setup [8]. The model based on wavelength demodulation with 1 Gb/s uplink and 1 Gb/s signal that uses fiber brag grating

DOI: 10.1201/9781003513445-21

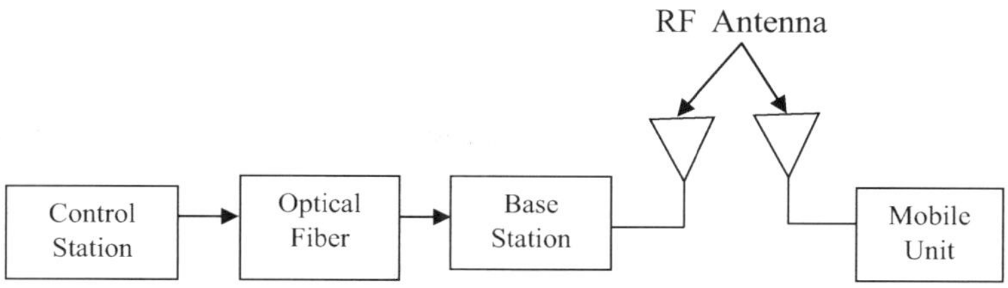

Figure 21.1 Architecture of the ROF system [5].

(FBG) has been proposed by Kaur and Kaler [9]. In their proposed full-duplex ROF passive optical network (PON), they used bit error rate (BER) signal-to-noise ratio (OSNR), optical power, and eye diagrams for analysis. With the use of FBG and dispersion compensating fiber (DCF), highly improved performance was obtained at a 100 km length of optical fiber [9]. A multiband PM-based distributed PolM-to-IM modulator-based ROF system with double-fault protection capability was suggested over a 70 km transmission distance by incorporating the use of single-mode fiber (SMF). In the model, an integrated form of SMF/FSO and POF is used to enhance the fault protectively. Performance analysis was done for POF and SMF/FSO with different formats to conclude that integrated POF and SMF/FSO together can be used as potent fault-protector [10]. O'Reilly et al. presented an external modulation technique in which a distributed feedback (DFB) laser source is modulated by a single Mach Zander Modulator (MZM) to generate a 36 GHz narrow linewidth signal using an 18 GHz electrical source [11]. The signal is successfully transmitted to 8 km without any dispersion-induced pulse broadening. O'Reilly et al. presented the generation of a 60 GHz Mm wave by a temperature-controlled DFB laser modulated through a single MZM at 15 GHz [12]. An interferometric filter provided carrier suppression and EDFA (Erbium-Doped Fiber Amplifier) to enhance the optical signal power. The MM wave signal transmitted to a 12 km fiber link was found to have high spectral quality.

Smith et al. presented a dispersion technique based on optical carrier generation with SSB (single sideband) modulation [13]. The proposed model utilizes a dual-electrode MZM driven by an RF signal with a $\pi/2$ phase shift and 51.8 Mbps BPSK (binary phase shift keying) data was transmitted to a length of 79.6 km with a power penalty of less than 0.5 dB at 12 GHz. Smith et al. presented a high-capacity, full-duplex MM wave ROF system based on remote up- and down-conversion [14]. BPSK and QAM modulation formats with 155 Mbps and 8 Mbps data rates, respectively, were transmitted downstream over the 40 km fiber link and 51.8 Mbps BPSK data was carried over the upstream link. This method reduces phase noise induced due to fiber dispersion. It also enhances network capacity and spectral efficiency by using higher-order modulation formats without using expensive components. Marti et al. demonstrated a frequency up-conversion technique based on phase modulation-intensity modulation (PM-IM) conversion in chirped fiber gratings [15]. A very good phase noise performance for a 28 GHz signal that was up-converted using a 13th harmonic was obtained. The proposed scheme was analyzed for different modulation formats (32QAM, DQPSK, and QPSK). Moreover, the transmission of a 4-Mbps quadrature phase shift keying (QPSK) signal, which was further up-converted to 10.24 GHz, was demonstrated and excellent BER performance was obtained for an optical received power of 11 dBm. Chen et al. demonstrated a tunable millimeter wave generation through a phase-modulated signal [16]. The signal was found to have a low phase noise of –95 dBc/Hz at 100 KHz offset with a successful 9 km fiber link transmission without any power penalty.

Qi et al. utilized an optical notch filter along with a phase modulator to generate 37.6–50 GHz and 75.2–100 GHz MM waves when the electrical signal is tuned to 18.8–25

GHz [17]. The proposed system does not suffer from DC bias drift problems and has high-frequency stability with narrow linewidth. The signal was transmitted to a 60 km fiber link by utilizing DCF. Zhang et al. presented a full duplex ROF system for generating a 40 GHz MM wave signal by applying optical carrier suppression [18]. The carrier was reused at base station for uplink transmission, eliminating the light source requirement at BS, and 2.54 Gbps data was transmitted to a 40 km fiber link with less than 2 dB power penalty. Using the same wavelength enhances the spectral efficiency of the signal. Jianjun et al. compared different modulation formats utilizing external modulators [19]. The OCS modulation shows the highest spectrum efficiency, power penalty, and receiver sensitivity. 16-channel Dense wavelength-division multiplexing (DWDM) signals were simultaneously up-converted to 40 GHz at 2.5 Gbps per channel using the OCS modulation. Wang et al. demonstrated frequency-tripling using FWM in SOA [20]. Also, 2.1 Gbps data on the 63 GHz MM wave and 21 GHz microwave carrier were transmitted error-free over a 50 km fiber link without any dispersion compensation. The power penalty for both signals was less than 1.0 dB. Zaho et al. utilized two cascaded MZMs for generating a frequency-quadrupled 33.125 GHz MM wave from an 8.28125 GHz electrical signal [21]. The external modulators were biased at the minimum transmission point. A tunable optical delay line was used to generate desired harmonics and suppress undesired ones sent to another MZM for frequency up-conversion. The optical delay line helped enhance the structure's simplicity and tolerance toward dispersion-induced power fading as compared with conventional ROF links. Lin et al. proposed the generation of 40 GHz and 70 GHz frequency-quadrupled MM waves through a single external modulator [22]. The scheme could suppress unwanted harmonics with more than 36 dB SSR without any filter. Li et al. demonstrated 19 GHz MM wave generation using an optical parametric amplifier (OPA) with 18 dB optical gain [23]. A pulsed pump with a high repetition rate to generate multiple sidebands separated by pump modulation frequency amplified the RF signal. Lim et al. presented a summary of various techniques for mitigating the transmission impairments of MM waves through optical fibers [24]. Lin et al. generated frequency coupling 60 GHz and 80 GHz MM waves from 7.5 GHz and 10 GHz with dual parallel MZM [25]. An FBG notch filter could also filter out the optical carrier. The phase noise performance and the frequency tunability were also investigated. Shih et al. demonstrated frequency 12-tupling by utilizing frequency quadrupling with FWM from an optical amplifier [26]. 210 GHz and 120 GHz signals were generated with an optical carrier suppression ratio (OCSR) of 20 dB and an undesired harmonic distortion suppression ratio (UHDSR) of 30 dB. Oh et al. introduced the usage of a phase modulator and Brillouin-assisted optical filter for generating a 48 GHz signal from a 12 GHz electrical source with −85 dBc/Hz phase noise at a 10 KHz frequency offset [27]. Liu et al. demonstrated frequency tripling through a directly modulated Fabry–Pérot (FP) laser [28]. 40.2 GHz MM wave was transmitted with 2.5 Gbps data over a 20 km fiber link without any error. The comparison was also made with an injection-locked FP laser directly driven with a 40.2 GHz RF signal. It was found that the proposed scheme reduces the bandwidth requirement and is suitable for MM wave ROF applications. Maleki et al. presented an opto-electronic oscillator (OEO) by using a polarization modulator and polarization multiplexing [29]. Yttrium–iron garnet (YIG) bandpass filter (BPF) driven by a current source was incorporated to ensure the tunability of the oscillator. By proper adjustment of the BPF current, the desired microwave signal was achieved. 39.75 GHz MM wave signal was generated with an SSB phase noise of −90.69 dBc/Hz at a 10 kHz frequency offset. Xiao et al. generated a 60 GHz MM wave with 2.5 Gbps data by using only a 12 GHz RF clock source and two cascaded MZMs [30]. Baseband data was mixed with a sinusoidal clock to generate the subcarrier multiplexing signal. Error-free performance was achieved after 30-km SMF and 10-ft air link transmission. Pochet et al. generated MM wave through optical injection of a Fabry–Pérot laser [31]. In this chapter, a simulative analysis has been done to study the impact of variation in the length of dispersion compensating fiber at various distances of optical fiber used as a medium of the proposed ROF system. The analysis is done in terms of BER, Q-values, and eye height.

21.2 SIMULATIVE RESULTS AND DISCUSSION

The proposed simulation model of an ROF system implemented in Optisystem is shown in Figure 21.2. The transmitter part of the setup consists of a Pseudo-Random Bit Sequence (PRBS), Non-Return to Zero (NRZ), Continuous Wave (CW), and MZM. The role of the PRBS is to generate binary data using two inputs and one output device known as the Mach Zander Modulator. The first input of the MZM is the output of the laser source and the other is to be transmitted. NRZ modulator to convert these electrical pulses into baseband information further handles this binary data. The optically modulated signal is transferred to single-mode fiber if the selected length is 5 km, 10 km, 16 km, 20 km, and 25 km for which the attenuation coefficient and dispersion value are taken as 16.75 ps/nm. As ROF systems are used for long-distance transmission, dispersion is obvious. Therefore, we need to compensate for the effect of nonlinear dispersion. Hence, the DCF and the FBG are used to manage the nonlinearities that occur in the system at the transmitter side prior to optical fiber. DCF are the fibers with negative dispersion, similar to fiber-generated dispersion.

For simulation work, the DCF parameters are as follows: length 2–10 km, attenuation coefficient 0.5 dB/km, dispersion value −85 km ps/nm/km. Group Velocity Dispersion and Third-Order Dispersion are also kept ON. At the end of the setup, a Low Pass Bessel Filter (LPBF) having a cut-off frequency of 0.80 bit rate value, followed by a PIN-type photodetector, is used to convert the light into an electrical signal. The terminating block of the setup is the BER analyzer tool, as shown in Figure 21.2. The BER analyzer is used to obtain values of various parameters such as Q-value, BER, eye height, and eye diagram. The values of different parameters used in the setup are tabulated in Table 21.1.

In Figure 21.3, Q-value has been plotted by varying the DCF length from 2 to 10 km, with increments of 2 km at the optical distances 5 km, 10 km, 15 km, 20 km, and 25 km for signal frequency 10 GHz. The graph shows that the Q-value gradually decreases with the increase in the length of optical fiber and it increases with an increase in the DCF length.

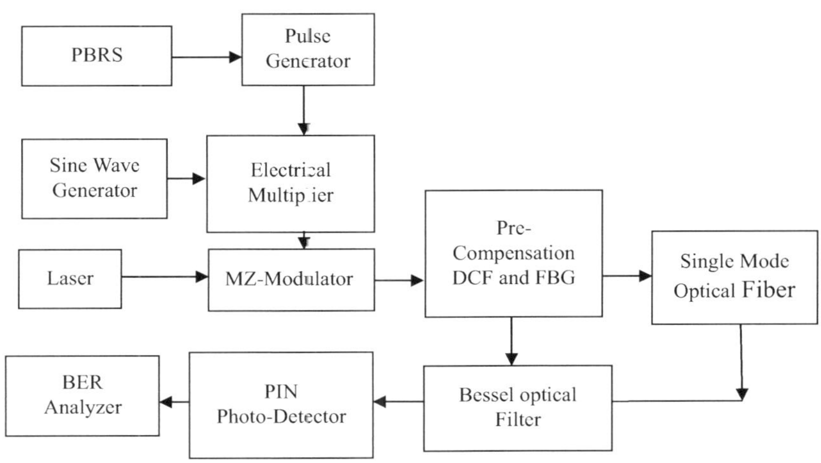

Figure 21.2 Simulation setup of the ROF system with FBG for dispersion management.

Table 21.1 System parameters

Sl. No.	*Parameter*	*Value*
1	Bit rate	1 Gb/S
2	RF value signal	10 GHz and 15 GHZ
3	Modulation format	Non-Return to Zero
4	Frequency	193.0 THz
5	Fiber length	5–25 km
6	DCF length	2–10 km
7	FBG frequency	193.1 THz
9	GVD coefficient	0.2 dB/km

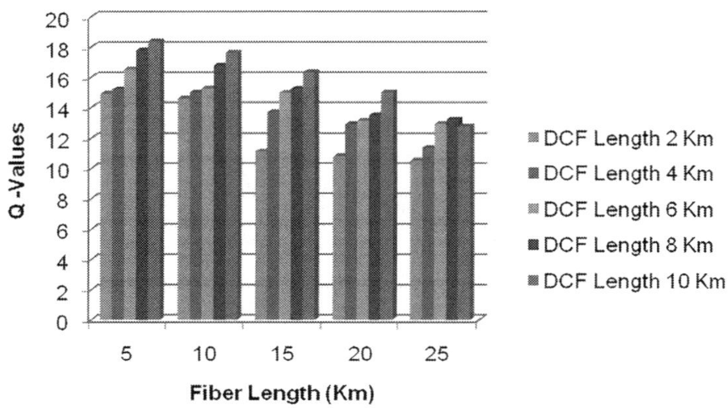

Figure 21.3 Q-value for the proposed model at different values of fiber length w.r.t. DCF length at 10 GHz.

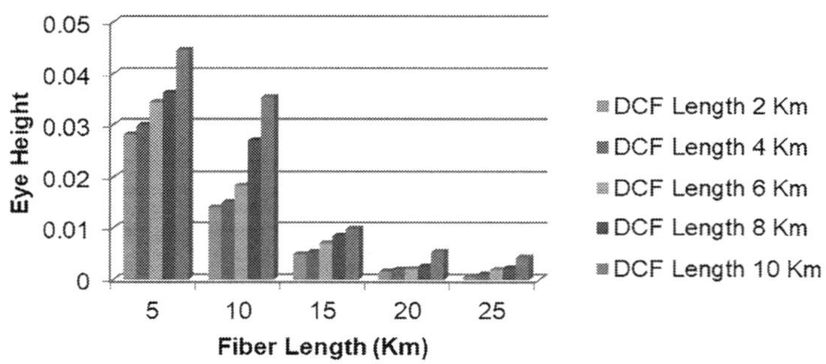

Figure 21.4 Eye height for the proposed model at different values of fiber length w.r.t. DCF length at 10 GHz.

The plot for eye height value has been obtained, as shown in Figure 21.4, by varying the DCF length from 2 to 10 km with increments of 2 km at the optical distances of 5 km, 10 km, 15 km, 20 km, and 25 km, for a signal frequency of 10 GHz. From the graph, it is found that the eye height gradually decreases with an increase in the length of optical fiber and increases with an increase in the DCF length.

From the value obtained after simulations, the graph between the Q-value and the fiber length is plotted, as shown in Figure 21.5. In order to plot this graph, the fiber length is varied from 5 km to 25 km with a step size of 5 km for the DCF lengths 2 km, 4 km, 6 km,

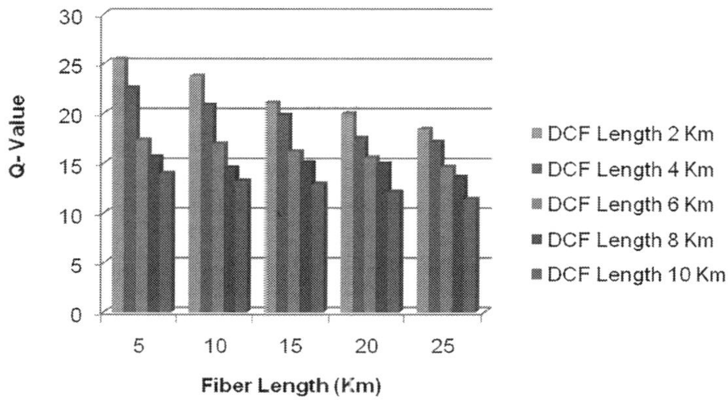

Figure 21.5 Q-value for the proposed mode at different values of fiber length w.r.t. DCF length at 15 GHz.

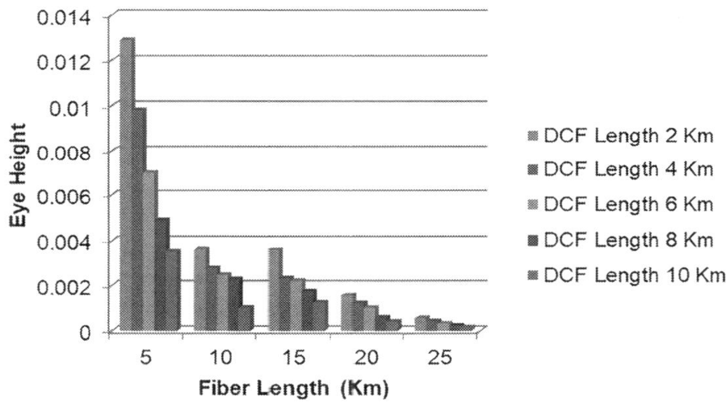

Figure 21.6 Q-value for the proposed model at different values of fiber length w.r.t. DCF length at 15 GHz.

8 km, and 10 km at 15 GHz frequency. It has been observed from the obtained plot that varying the fiber length and the DCF length for the 15 GHz signal continuously decreases the Q-value.

The obtained plot from simulation values for eye height versus fiber length is shown in Figure 21.6. This plot is obtained from simulations by changing the fiber length from 5 km to 25 km with step size of 5 km and the DCF length from 2 km, 4 km, 6 km, 8 km, and 10 km at 15 GHz frequency. The eye height is found to be decreased with an increase in the fiber length and DCF length in this case.

BER is the measure of altered bits due to noise, synchronization errors, or interference distortion bit over the communication distance. The bit error rate or bit error ratio (BER) is the number of bit errors divided by the total number of transferred bits during a studied time interval. The BER values obtained for different lengths of optical fiber by varying the DCF length for 10 GHz and 15 GHz signals are tabulated in Tables 21.2 and 21.3, respectively.

The quantitative variation present in both tables declares that the BER is decreased with an increase in DCF length for both RF frequencies, i.e., 10 GHz and 15 GHz. For a fiber length of 20 km, the best results are obtained by using a DCF length of 6 km. For a fiber length of 25 km, the best results are obtained by using a DCF length of 10 km.

Table 21.2 BER comparison for the proposed model at 10 GHz

		Fiber length (km) for 10 GHz				
Sl. No.	*DCF length*	*5 km*	*10 km*	*15 km*	*20 km*	*25 km*
1	2 km	9.5337*e-051	1.6678*e-048	3.3780*e-033	1.1105*e-027	2.1611*e-036
2	4 km	4.9195*e-040	4.8750*e-034	7.1831*e-029	4.6716*e-034	1.1660*e-025
3	6 km	1.1851*e-061	2.5090*e-053	4.5961*e-051	7.8820*e-097	1.933*e-049
4	8 km	7.1119*e-050	2.8226*e-100	5.5992*e-093	1.2708*e-084	8.2299*e-087
5	10 km	1.01417*e-0060	3.9405*e-0086	1.5948*e-083	7.034*e-083	4.0166*e-088

Table 21.3 BER comparison for the proposed model at 15 GHz

		Fiber length (km) for 15 GHz				
Sl. No.	*DCF length*	*5 km*	*10 km*	*15 km*	*20 km*	*25 km*
1	2 km	1.5012*e-0121	1.0332*e-124	1.4307*e-098	2.7976*e-080	9.0447*e-093
2	4 km	9.404*e-089	2.8216*e-096	4.2638*e-071	1.4007*e-102	1.8946*e-069
3	6 km	2.3236*e-075	8.24032*e-052	3.3150*e-102	3.5541*e-094	5.5444*e-104
4	8 km	5.5441*e-104	2.4412*e-042	2.028*e-058	2.3696*e-051	3.3020*e-062
5	10 km	2.0096*e-034	1.1152*e-034	4.4385*e-036	5.5832*e-046	8.5993*e-042

21.3 CONCLUSION

As times changed, the means to communicate over distances have also increased. In the beginning, people were using wired communication to cover large distances. Then, wireless communication came into existence, using optical fibers as a communication medium. The various flaws in optical communication have led to increased trends. In order to compensate for the effect of these flaws, researchers present various techniques from time to time. The use of DCF and FBG are popular methods available in the literature. In the present study, a simulative analysis has been done to study the impact of variation in the length of DCF at various distances of optical fiber used as a medium of the proposed ROF system. The BER, Q-value, and eye height are chosen as analysis parameters. It has been concluded from the study that the appropriate choice of DCF length and the radio frequency transmitter is highly important in obtaining high data rate transmission at long distances.

REFERENCES

1. Islam, M., Jin, S., An overview research on wireless communication network. Adv. Wireless. Comm. Networks, 5(1), 19–28, 2019.
2. Lim, K. G., Lee, C. H., Chin, R. K. Y., Beng, K., Teo, K. T. K., SUMO enhancement for vehicular ad hoc network (VANET) simulation. IEEE 2nd International Conference on Automatic Control and Intelligent Systems (I2CACIS), Kota Kinabalu, Malaysia, 86–91, 2017.
3. Kathpal N., Amit K.G., Analysis of Radio over Fiber system for mitigating four-wave mixing effect. Digital Comm. Networks, 6, 115–122, 2020.
4. Kota, I., Mizuki S., Takuto A., Yushi S., Naoki K., Takeshi. O., Passive beamformer based remote beamforming scheme for radio-over-fiber systems: Experimental demonstration using 28-GHz band reflect array. Optics Comm., 513, 128026–128032, 2022.

5. Hadi, U.M., Jung, H., Ghaffer, S., Traverso, P.A., Optimized digital radio over fiber system for medium range communication. Optics Comm., 443, 177–185, 2019.
6. Wei, Y., Wang, K., Zhao, L., Jianjun, Y., Radio-over-fiber systems with delta-sigma-modulation for MMW-based indoor communication. Opt., Fiber Tech., 80, 103378–103383, 2023.
7. Paulomi, M., Nilanjana S., Bubai, D., Bibhatsu, K., Saikat, S., Rinki A., Ardhendu S. P., A long-reach optically powered multi-band radio-over-fiber network by employing PolM-to-IM converter with enhanced fault-protection ability and less Rayleigh backscattering noise effect. Opt., Fiber Tech., 74, 103143–103153, 2022.
8. Wei, R., Huang, G., Hu, W., Wei, C., Lin, H.. A 24-kHz BW 90.5-dB SNDR 96-dB DR continuous-time delta-sigma modulator using FIR DAC feedback. *Microelectron. J.*, 138, 105858, 2023.
9. Kaur, G., Kaler, R.S., Wavelength remodulation and dispersion compensation for fullduplex radio over fiber System using fiber Bragg grating. *Optik - International Journal for Light and Electron Optics*, 206, 163223–163229, 2020.
10. Mandal, P., Sarkar, N., Santra, S., Dutta, B., Kuiri, B., Mallick, K., Patra, A.S., Hybrid WDM-FSO-PON with integrated SMF/FSO link for transportation of Rayleigh backscattering noise mitigated wired/wireless information in long-reach. *Optics Comm.*, 507, 127594, 2022.
11. O'Reilly, J.J., Lane, P.M., Heidemann, R., Hofstetter, R., Optical generation of very narrow linewidth millimetre wave signals. *Electron. Lett.*, 28(25), 2309–2311, 1992.
12. O'Reilly, J.J., Lane, P.M., Fibre-supported optical generation and delivery of 60 GHz signals. *Electron. Letters*, 30, 1329–1330, 1994.
13. Smith, G. H., Novak, D., Ahmed, Z., Technique for Optical SSB generation to overcome dispersion penalties in Fibre-radio systems. *Electron. Lett.*, 33, 74–75, 1997.
14. Smith, G.H., Novak, D., Lim. C., A millimeter-wave full-duplex fiber-radio star-tree architecture incorporating WDM and SCM. *IEEE Photonics Tech. Letters*, 10, 11, 1998.
15. Marti, J., Ramo, F., Polo, V., Fustez, M., Corral, J., Millimeter-wave signal generation and harmonic upconversion through PM-IM conversion in chirped fiber gratings. *Fiber and Integrated Opt.*, 19, 187–198, 2000.
16. Chen, B., Zheng, S., Chi, H., Zhang X., Jin, X., An optical millimeter-wave generation technique based on phase modulation and brillouin-assisted notch-filtering. *IEEE Photonics Technology Letters*, 20, 24, pp. 2057–2059, 2008.
17. Qi, G., Yao, J., Seregelyi, J., Paquet, S., Belisle, C., Optical generation and distribution of continuously tunable millimeter-wave signals using an optical phase modulator. *Journal of Lightwave Tech.*, 23, 9, pp. 2687–2695, 2005.
18. Zhang, C., Ning, T., Li, J., Pei, L., Li, C., Ma, S., A full-duplex WDM-ROF system based on tunable optical frequency comb generator. *Optics Comm.*, 344, 65–70, 2015.
19. Jianjun. Y., Zhensheng, J., Lilin, Y., Yikai, S., Chang, G., & Wang, T., Optical millimeter wave generation or up-conversion using external modulator. *IEEE Photonics Tech. Letters*, 18, 265–267, 2006.
20. Wang, Q., Rideout, H., Zeng, F., Yao, J., Millimeter-wave frequency tripling based on four-wave mixing in a semiconductor optical amplifier. *IEEE Photonics Tech. Letters*, 18, 23, 2460–2462, 2006.
21. Zhao, Y., Zheng, X., Wen, H., Zhang, H., Simplified optical millimeter-wave generation configuration by frequency quadrupling using two cascaded Mach–Zehnder modulators. *Opt. Lett.*, 34, 3250–3252, 2009.
22. Lin, C., Shih, P., Chen, J., Xue, W., Peng, P., Chi, S., Optical millimeter-wave signal generation using frequency quadrupling technique and no optical filtering. *IEEE Photonics Tech. Letters*, 20, 1027–1029, 2008.
23. Li, J., Liang, Y., Wong, K., Millimeter-Wave UWB signal generation via frequency up-conversion using fiber optical parametric amplifier. *IEEE Photonics Tech. Letters*, 21, 1172–1174, 2009.
24. Lim, C., Nirmalathas, A., Bakaul, M., Lee, K., Novak, D., Waterhouse, R.B., Mitigation strategy for transmission impairments in millimeter-wave radio-over-fiber networks. *Journal of Optical Networking*, 8, 2009.
25. Lin, C., Shih, P., Jiang, W., Chen, J., Peng, P., Chi, S., A continuously tunable and filterless optical millimeter-wave generation via frequency octupling. Optics Express, 17. 19749–19756, 2009.

26. Shih, P., Lin, C., Jiang, W., Huang, H., Peng, P., Chi, S., Optical millimeter-wave signal generation via frequency 12-tupling. *Journal of Lightwave Tech.*, 28, 71–78, 2010.
27. Oh, T., Kim, H., Lee, H., Song, J., Photonic frequency quadrupling utilizing a LiNbO3 phase modulator and a Brillouin-assisted optical filter. International Topical Meeting on Microwave Photonics jointly held with the 2011 Asia-Pacific Microwave Photonics Conference, Singapore, 195–197, 2011.
28. Liu, J., Chien, H., Fan, S., Chen, B., Yu, J., He, S., Chang, G.K., Efficient optical millimeter-wave generation using a frequency-tripling Fabry–Pérot laser with sideband injection and synchronization. *IEEE Photonics Tech., Letters*, 23, 1325–1327, 2011.
29. Maleki, L., The Opto-Electronic Oscillator (OEO): Review and recent progress. 2012 European Frequency and Time Forum, Gothenburg, Sweden, 497–500, 2012.
30. Xiao, Y., Yu, J., Novel 60 GHz ROF system with optical single sideband mm-wave signal generation and wavelength reuse for uplink connection. *Optics Comm.*, 285, 3, 229–232, 2012.
31. Pochet, M., Locke, T., Usechak, N.G., Generation and modulation of a millimeter-wave subcarrier on an optical frequency generated via optical injection. IEEE Photonics J., 4, 5, 1881–1891, 2012.

Chapter 22

Robust and imperceptible dual watermarking for watershed images

Harendra Singh and Lalit Kumar Awasthi

22.1 INTRODUCTION

In the current digital era, the use of internet-based services has significantly increased the sharing and dissemination of color images, which serve as key information carriers. This trend is particularly pertinent in Geographic Information Systems (GIS), where watershed images play a crucial role in environmental management and planning [1]. Although the internet offers a fast and cost-effective means for transmitting such images, it often lacks sufficient security measures, leading to potential vulnerabilities in the management of environmental data.

The sensitive nature of watershed images necessitates stringent security protocols to thwart unauthorized access and tampering. To mitigate these risks, biometric watermarking has emerged as a viable solution within the academic and scientific communities [2]. This technique involves embedding invisible digital biometric marks into multimedia content to assert ownership and ensure data integrity, thereby safeguarding the information against potential security threats. Biometric watermarking must delicately balance between robustness, invisibility, and embedding capacity to be effective, which presents a significant challenge [3].

Our study presents a novel biometric watermarking algorithm specifically designed for watershed images. This approach merges spatial and transform domain techniques, incorporating a pseudo-magic cube, Singular Value Decomposition (SVD), Schur decomposition, and Discrete Wavelet Transform (DWT) to improve the embedded watermark's robustness and capacity. Additionally, hybrid optimization techniques are utilized to adjust the scaling factor, optimizing the balance between invisibility and robustness. To ensure security, the watermark is encrypted using the Secure Image Encryption (SIE) scheme. Denoising Convolutional Neural Network (DnCNN) is utilized to improve the watermark's resilience to processing attacks, ensuring the integrity of the images during internet transmission. This multifaceted approach not only secures the watershed images but also enhances their authenticity when shared online.

The key contributions of our research on watershed image watermarking are as follows:

a) To our knowledge, this is the first study to implement a watermarking technique for safeguarding the copyright of watershed images
b) **Enhanced security through dual methods**: Our method employs a dual approach by embedding significant markers, the user's ORCID iD [4] and fingerprint image [5], into the image's spatial and transform domain, respectively. To prevent unauthorized access and misuse, the fingerprint watermark is secured using the SIE scheme.
c) **Improved robustness with transform techniques**: To boost the robustness of the watermark, we integrate DWT [6], Schur decomposition [7], and SVD [8]. DWT is chosen for its effective localization of image features, providing resilience against scaling and

DOI: 10.1201/9781003513445-22

rotation. Schur decomposition enhances the speed and stability of the embedding process, while SVD contributes to the overall robustness. This combination ensures the watermark withstands various attacks, such as compression and cropping, maintaining its integrity across different image processing scenarios.

d) **Increased watermark capacity**: To enhance the capacity of the watermark, we utilize the pseudo magic cube method [9]. This method allows for more efficient embedding of the ORCID iD, significantly increasing the storage capability of the watermark. This improvement ensures that a larger amount of information can be securely embedded without compromising image quality.

e) **Optimizing watermarking parameters**: We implement a hybrid optimization strategy that combines Particle Swarm Optimization (PSO) and Firefly algorithms [10]. This approach systematically calculates the optimal embedding factor, improving the balance between robustness and imperceptibility, thereby eliminating the need for manual adjustments.

22.2 PROPOSED ALGORITHM

The proposed algorithm is structured into three primary phases: (a) the creation of the host watershed image, (b) embedding and extracting multiple watermarks, and (c) denoising the extracted watermark data. Each phase is detailed comprehensively. Figure 22.2 depicts the schematic representation of the proposed method.

22.2.1 Generation of the cover image

22.2.1.1 Study area and data collection

The study area for the watershed mapping was defined using topographic and hydrological features. The Digital Elevation Model (DEM) data were collected from the Shuttle Radar Topography Mission (SRTM) with a spatial resolution of 30 meters [11].

22.2.1.2 Watershed delineation and preparation of map

Using the flow accumulation grid, pour points (outlet points) were identified, representing the lowest point in the watershed. The watershed was delineated using the Watershed tool in QGIS 3.16 with the QSWAT plugin, which uses flow direction and pour points to create streams (channels) and watershed boundaries [12].

The flow chart provides a detailed overview of the sequential steps involved in creating a watershed from a DEM, specifically using SRTM DEM data processed with QGIS software and the QSWAT plugin. The process begins with acquiring the DEM data, which, in this case, was downloaded from the Earth Explorer site [11] (Figure 22.1).

Once the DEM data is acquired, the next step involves preprocessing the DEM using QGIS 3.16 [12]. Preprocessing includes filling any sinks and depressions in the DEM to ensure that the data is free from artifacts and represents the actual terrain accurately. This step is crucial as it prepares the DEM for subsequent analyses by eliminating any imperfections that could skew results. Following preprocessing, the flow direction is calculated. This involves using algorithms within the QSWAT plugin to determine the direction in which water flows from each cell in the DEM. Flow direction calculation is a foundational step that informs subsequent analyses, such as flow accumulation and stream network definition.

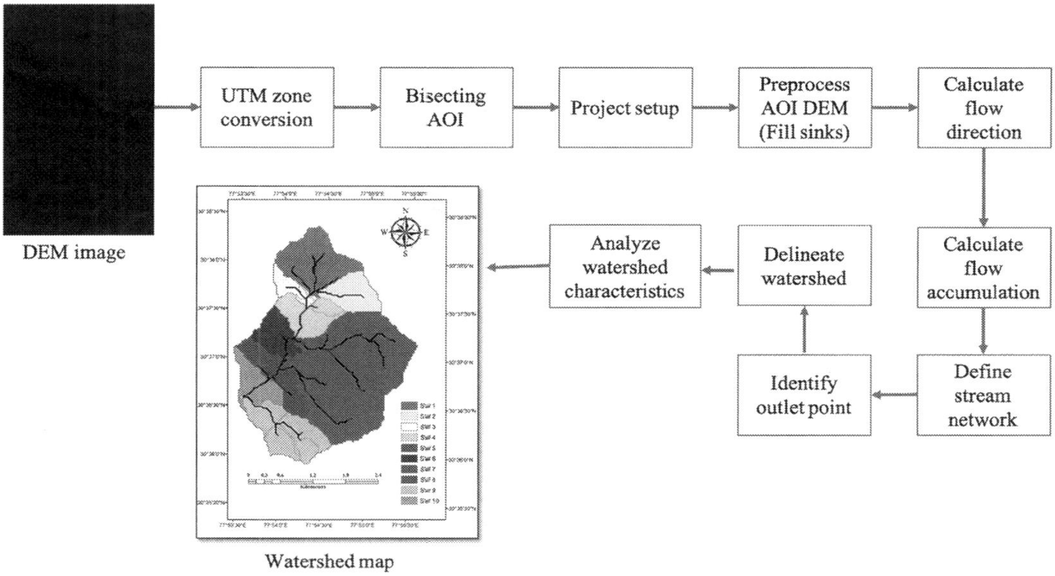

Figure 22.1 Generation of the watershed map image

The next step is to calculate flow accumulation. This process identifies areas where water converges, which is critical for understanding how water collects and moves across the terrain. The flow accumulation data is then used to define the stream network by setting a threshold for flow accumulation. This threshold helps distinguish between areas of minor water flow and significant streams, which is essential for accurately delineating the watershed.

With the stream network defined, the next task is to identify the outlet points for the watershed. Outlet points are specific locations where water exits the watershed, and identifying these points is necessary for delineating the watershed boundaries. Using the flow direction and identified outlet points, the watershed boundaries are delineated. This step effectively maps out the area that contributes water to a specific outlet point, providing a clear boundary of the watershed.

Following the delineation of the watershed, various characteristics such as area, slope, and land cover are analyzed. These characteristics provide valuable insights into the watershed's dynamics and potential environmental impact. Finally, the results are visualized through maps and other graphical representations. This visualization step is crucial as it transforms complex data into understandable formats, allowing for a comprehensive understanding of the watershed's features and dynamics. The whole procedure for the generation of color watershed images is shown in Figure 22.1.

22.2.2 Embedding and extraction of watermarks

In the embedding process, the generated watershed host image is first decomposed into its blue (B), red (R), and green (G) channels using the B-R-G embedding principle [13]. The algorithm uses the magic cube technique to embed the user's ORCID iD in the green channel. The watermark image is then scrambled using the SIE [14] scheme and decomposed via SVD. The blue component is processed through DWT, Schur, and SVD, and the resulting singular matrix is modified with the scrambled watermark and an optimized scaling factor. The final watermarked image is created by merging all three channels. The extraction process reverses

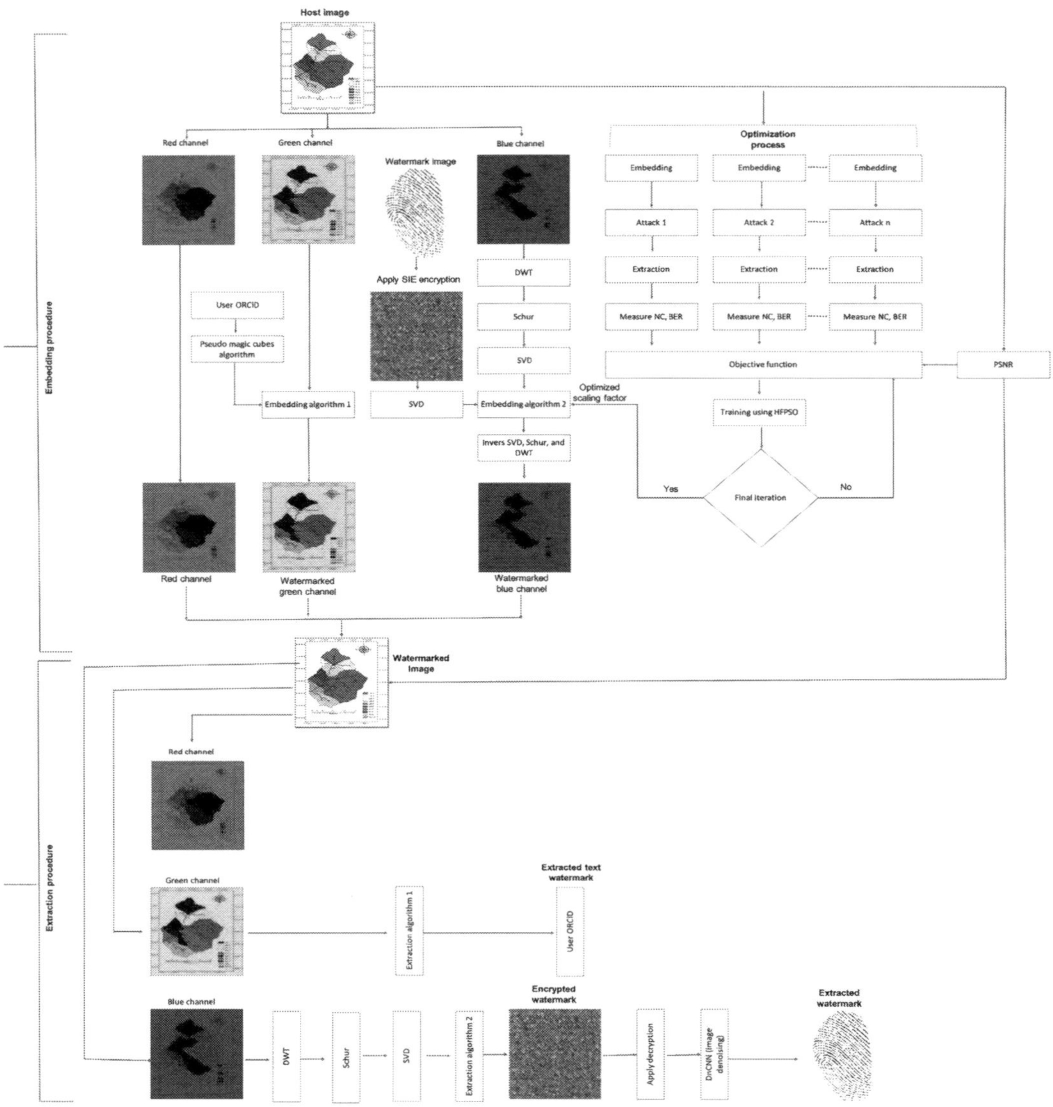

Figure 22.2 The proposed watermarking method.

the embedding steps. Detailed steps and notations are provided in Algorithms 22.1 and 22.2, and Table 22.1, respectively.

Algorithm 22.1: Embedding algorithm

Input: $Host_{img}$, w_img, ORCID, Opt_{α}
Output: watermarked_img
Begin
Step 1: Split $Host_{img}$ into RGB channels:
$Red_{host} \leftarrow Host_{img}(:,:,1)$;
$Green_{host} \leftarrow Host_{img}(:,:,2)$;
$Blue_{host} \leftarrow Host_{img}(:,:,3)$;

Step 2: Embed watermark in Green ($Green_{host}$) channel.
DecimalWatermark ← CharToDecimal (Orcid);
MagicCube ← GenerateMagicCube (θ, [rx, ry, rz]);
GreenWithWatermark ← EmbedTextInGreen ($Green_{host}$, DecimalWatermark, MagicCube);
Step 3: Embed watermark in Blue ($Blue_{host}$) channel
[[LowLow, HighLow, LowHigh, HighHigh]] ← ApplyDWT(Blue, 'Haar')
[LowLow2, HighLow2, LowHigh2, HighHigh2] ← ApplyDWT(LowLow, 'Haar');
[Uschur, Tschur] ← SchurDecomposition(LowLow2);
[Usvd, Ssvd, Vsvd] ← SingularValueDecomposition(Tschur);
EncryptedWatermark ← Encrypt_SIE(w_img);
[U_w, S_w, V_w] ← SingularValueDecomposition(EncryptedWatermark);
ModifiedS ← Ssvd + Opt_α × S_w;
CombinedCoeff ← Usvd × ModifiedS × Vsvd;
InverseSVDResult ← InverseSVD(CombinedCoeff);
InverseSchurResult ← InverseSchur(InverseSVDResult);
BlueWithWatermark ← ApplyInverseDWT(InverseSchurResult);
Step 4: Merge Channels to Form watermarked_img
watermarked_img ← MergeChannels(Red, GreenWithWatermark, BlueWithWatermark));
return watermarked_img

Algorithm 22.2: Extraction algorithm

Input: watermarked_image, Opt_α
Output: ExtractedWatermark, ExtractedORCID
Begin
Step 1: Split watermarked_img into RGB Channels:
Red_{wat} ← watermarked_img(:,:,1);
$Green_{wat}$ ← watermarked_img(:,:,2);
$Blue_{wat}$ ← watermarked_img(:,:,3);
Step 2: Extract Watermark from Green Channel
ExtractedDecimalWatermark ← ExtractFromMagicCube($Green_{wat}$, size, NN, seed, rx, ry, rz);
ExtractedOrcid ← DecimalToCharacter (ExtractedDecimalWatermark);
Step 3: Extract Watermark from Blue ($Blue_{wat}$) channel
[LowLowW, HighLowW, LowHighW, HighHighW] ← ApplyDWT($Blue_{wat}$, 'Haar')
[LowLowW2, HighLowW2, LowHighW2, HighHighW2] ← ApplyDWT(LowLowW, 'Haar')
[UschurW, TschurW] ← SchurDecomposition(LowLowW2);
[UsvdW, SsvdW, VsvdW] ← SingularValueDecomposition(TschurW);
ExtractedSw ← (SsvdW - S_w)/ Opt_α;
RecoveredWatermarkImage ← UsvdW * $ExtractedS_w$ * VsvdW;
DecryptedWatermark ← Decrypt (RecoveredWatermarkImage);
ExtractedWatermark ← DnCNN ((DecryptedWatermark));
return ExtractedWatermark, ExtractedOrcid

22.2.3 Denoising process

To enhance the robustness and quality of the retrieved watermark, a DnCNN is utilized. This process uses a pre-trained DnCNN model, leveraging the capabilities of the Deep Learning Toolbox in MATLAB [15].

Table 22.1 Notation employed in the algorithms

Notation	*Description*	*Notation*	*Description*
$Host_{img}$	Original generated color watershed host image	watermarked_img	Watermarked image
w_img	Fingerprint watermark image	ExtractedORCID	Extracted Orcid of the user
Opt_{α}	Optimized Embedding/ scaling value factor	ExtractedWatermark	Extracted fingerprint watermark.
Red_{host}, $Green_{host}$, $Blue_{host}$	RGB channels of the host image	Red_{wat}, $Green_{wat}$, $Blue_{wat}$	RGB channels of watermarked_img
watermarked_img	Watermarked image	LowLowW, HighLowW, LowHighW, HighHighW	DWT coefficients after the first level decomposition of $Blue_{host}$ of watermarked_img
LowLow, HighLow, LowHigh, HighHigh	DWT coefficients after the first level of decomposition	LowLowW2, HighLowW2, LowHighW2, HighHighW2	DWT coefficients after the second level decomposition LowLowW
LowLow2, HighLow2, LowHigh2, HighHigh2	DWT coefficients after the first level of decomposition	UschurW, TschurW	LowLowW2 sub-band schur coefficients
Uschur, Tschur	Schur coefficients of the LowLow2 sub-band	UsvdW, SsvdW, VsvdW	SVD coefficients of TschurW
Usvd, Ssvd, Vsvd	SVD coefficients of Tschur	PSNR, NC, BER	Performance objective scores in ideal conditions [16]
Uw, Sw, Vw	SVD coefficients of encrypted w_img	N	Number of attacks tested

22.2.4 Optimal embedding factor selection

A fusion of PSO and firefly optimization method is employed to determine the best embedding factor for multiple watermarks, ensuring an ideal balance between invisibility and robustness. Both PSO and Firefly are metaheuristic techniques inspired by nature and based on swarm intelligence. Aydilek [10] demonstrated the effectiveness of combining PSO and Firefly optimization techniques to minimize the cost of complex numerical problems. Mohan et al. [16] suggested setting the initial range for the random swarm between 0.005 and 0.06. The parameters for guiding the algorithm to achieve optimal results are detailed in Table 22.2. The objective function for the fitness value is defined in equation 22.1:

$$\begin{aligned} Fitness\ Value &= \left(\beta \times \left(1 / PSNR\right)\right) \\ &+ \left(\left(1 / N\right) \times \sum_{i=1}^{N} 1 / NC\left(\text{watermarked\_img}, \text{Extracted Watermark}\right)_i\right) \end{aligned} \tag{22.1}$$

In this context, 'β' serves as the balancing factor, ensuring stability between invisibility and robustness. Normalized correlation (NC) and peak signal-to-noise ratio (PSNR) serve as performance metrics for evaluating robustness and invisibility, respectively. 'N' indicates the total number of attacks considered, which is set to 10 in this study.

Algorithm 22.3: Optimizing Scaling Factor (Optα)

Input: Host image($Host\_img$), Watermark Image (w_img), ORCID
Output: Optimized Scaling Factor (Optα)

1. Determine BER, NC, and PSNR values after implementing the watermarking technique.
2. Recompute BER, NC, and PSNR values after the watermarked image has undergone various attacks.
3. Use the values obtained in Steps 1 and 2 to optimize $Opt\alpha$ through the Firefly optimization technique.
4. The optimized $Opt\alpha$ obtained in Step 3 is applied in the final watermarking process.

Table 22.2 Controlling parameters to ensure fast convergence

Controlling parameter	*Value*
Iterations	15
Number of dimensions	1
Swarm count	20
Upper bound	0.06
Lower bound	0.005
Scout bees	Variable
Onlooker and employed bees	Swarm size/2
Acceleration coefficient 1	0.50
Acceleration coefficient 2	0.50

22.3 RESULTS AND ANALYSIS

This section outlines the experimental setup and the metrics utilized to assess the watermarking method. The proposed method is implemented using MATLAB software on a computer with a 2.50 GHz processor, 64-bit architecture, and 16 GB of RAM. To verify the effectiveness of the method, various color watershed images with dimensions of 512 × 512 are utilized as the host images. The grayscale fingerprint watermark, sized at 128 × 128, and the ORCID iD are embedded in the blue and green channels, respectively. To evaluate the proposed method, imperceptibility is analyzed using SSIM and PSNR, robustness is assessed with bit error rate (BER) and NC, and security is examined using UACI and NPCR. Figure 22.2 illustrates both the host watershed image and the fingerprint watermark utilized in our method.

Table 22.3 illustrates the performance metrics related to invisibility, robustness, and security for the proposed method when tested on the generated Watershed host image. The average PSNR value recorded is 50.9571 dB for 10 images, with a maximum PSNR of 51.2890 dB. The BER and NC metrics consistently approach 0 and 1, respectively. The method also demonstrates high-security capabilities, with an average NPCR of 0.99578 and a UACI score of 0.2778.

The results presented in Table 22.4 compare the imperceptibility performance of the proposed biometric watermarking algorithm with other methods using PSNR and SSIM. The proposed algorithm outperforms all previous methods with a PSNR of 50.9571 dB and an SSIM of 0.9971, demonstrating excellent preservation of image quality and superior structural similarity. These results indicate that the proposed algorithm is highly effective in embedding watermarks with minimal perceptible impact.

Table 22.3 Performance assessment on generated watershed images

	Performance assessment					
Host images	*PSNR*	*SSIM*	*NC*	*BER*	*NPCR*	*UACI*
Image 1	50.6323	0.99812	1	0	0.99661	0.28188
Image 2	50.9656	0.99812	1	0	0.99741	0.28228
Image 3	51.2890	0.99952	1	0	0.99351	0.27148
Image 4	50.7434	0.99912	1	0	0.99591	0.27828
Image 5	51.1868	0.99692	1	0	0.99631	0.27908
Image 6	50.8299	0.99592	1	0	0.99361	0.27948
Image 7	51.0767	0.99152	1	0	0.99491	0.27288
Image 8	50.5212	0.99802	1	0	0.99791	0.27328
Image 9	51.2743	0.99852	1	0	0.99691	0.27688
Image 10	51.0521	0.99622	1	0	0.99671	0.28248
Average score	50.9571	0.9971	1	0	0.99578	0.2778

Table 22.4 Comparison based on SSIM and PSNR

	Imperceptibility Results (PSNR (dB)/SSIM)			
Performance measure	*Sinhal et al. [17]*	*Hsu et al. [18]*	*Moad et al. [19]*	*Proposed algorithm*
PSNR(in dB)	40.13	38.02	43.59	50.9571
SSIM	0.99	0.91	0.99	0.9971

It is observed from Figure 22.3 that a satisfactory NC score of at least 0.8001 is achieved for nearly all tested attacks. These results indicate that the proposed method shows promising potential.

22.4 CONCLUSION

This study presents a secure watermarking algorithm for color watershed images, designed to improve invisibility, robustness, and capacity. The technique embeds watermarks within both the spatial and transform domains. First, the host color image is separated into its red, green, and blue channels. Different watermark data are embedded in the blue and green channels. To maintain an optimal balance between robustness and invisibility, the algorithm employs Firefly and PSO methods. The algorithm's performance was assessed by evaluating its robustness, invisibility, and resistance to various attacks. A comprehensive comparison highlighted the benefits of the proposed method compared to existing methods.

ACKNOWLEDGMENT

The authors are thankful to Dr. Deepak Singh, Scientist, Division of Hydrology and Engineering, ICAR-Indian Institute of Soil and Water Conservation, Dehradun, India, for his help in the generation of watershed images.

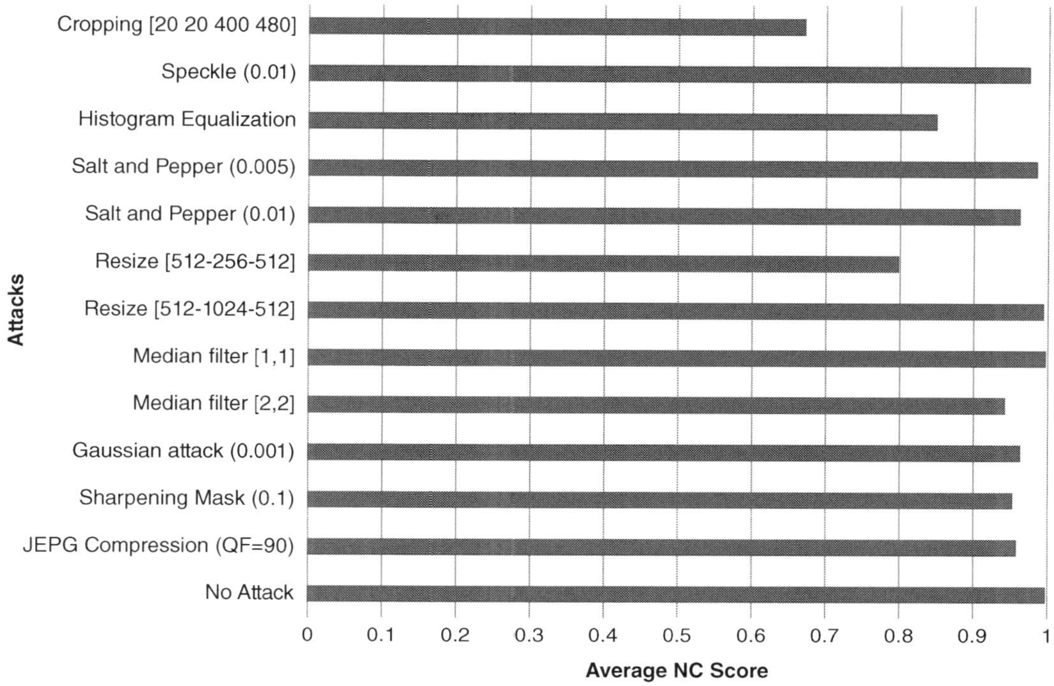

Figure 22.3 Average NC score on 10 watershed host images.

REFERENCES

[1] Kim, D.Y., Song, C.M., Developing a discharge estimation model for ungauged watershed using CNN and hydrological image. *Water*, *12*(12), 3534, 2020.

[2] Rosiyadi, D., Horng, S.J., Fan, P., Wang, X., Khan, M.K., Pan, Y., Copyright protection for e-government document images. *IEEE MultiMedia*, *19*(3), 62–73, 2012.

[3] Fernandez, J.J., Protection of online images against theft using robust multimodal biometric watermarking and T-norms. *Multimed. Tools Appl.*, *83*(17), 1–27, 2023.

[4] Credit where credit is due. *Nature* 462, 825, 2009. https://doi.org/10.1038/462825a

[5] Maio, D., Maltoni, D., Cappelli, R., Wayman, J.L., Jain, A.K., FVC2002: Second fingerprint verification competition. In *2002 International conference on pattern recognition*, IEEE, 3, 811–814, 2002.

[6] Al-Haj, A., Combined DWT-DCT digital image watermarking. *J. Comput. Sci.*, *3*(9), 740–746, 2007.

[7] Li, J., Yu, C., Gupta, B.B., Ren, X., Color image watermarking scheme based on quaternion Hadamard transform and Schur decomposition. *Multimed. Tools Appl.*, *77*, 4545–4561, 2018.

[8] Singh, N., Joshi, S., Birla, S., Color image watermarking with watermark authentication against false positive detection using SVD. In *International Conference on Sustainable Computing in Science, Technology and Management (SUSCOM)*, 399–405, 2019.

[9] Ranjani, J.J., Zaid, F., Pseudo magic cubes: A multidimensional data hiding scheme exploiting modification directions for large payloads. *Comput. Electr. Eng.*, *89*, 106928, 2021.

[10] Aydilek, I.B., A hybrid firefly and particle swarm optimization algorithm for computationally expensive numerical problems. *Appl. Soft Comput.*, *66*, 232–249, 2018.

[11] Earth Explorer. Accessed on 10 May 2024. https://earthexplorer.usgs.gov/

[12] QGIS https://qgis.org/en/site/about/index.html

[13] Yang, Y., Zou, T., Huang, G., & Zhang, W., A high visual quality color image reversible data hiding scheme based on BRG embedding principle and CIEDE2000 assessment metric. *IEEE Trans. Circuits Syst. Video Technol.*, *32*(4), 1860–1874, 2021.

[14] Kumar, S., Bhatnagar, G., SIE: An application to secure stereo images using encryption. *Handbook of Multimedia Information Security: Techniques and Applications*, 37–61, 2019.
[15] Singh, O.P., Singh, A.K., Data hiding in encryption–compression domain. *Complex Intell. Syst.*, 9(3), 2759–2772, 2023.
[16] Mohan, A., Anand, A., Singh, A.K., Dwivedi, R., Kumar, B., Selective encryption and optimization based watermarking for robust transmission of landslide images. *Comput. Electr. Eng.*, *95*, 107385, 2021.
[17] Sinhal, R., Jain, D.K., Ansari, I.A., Machine learning based blind color image watermarking scheme for copyright protection. *Pattern Recognit. Lett.*, *145*, 171–177, 2021.
[18] Hsu, L.Y., Hu, H.T., Chou, H.H. A high-capacity QRD-based blind color image watermarking algorithm incorporated with AI technologies. *Expert Syst. Appl.*, *199*, 117134, 2022.
[19] Moad, M.S., Kafi, M.R., Khaldi, A., A wavelet based medical image watermarking scheme for secure transmission in telemedicine applications. *Microprocess. Microsyst.*, *90*, 104490, 2022.

Index

Note: Pages in *italics* refer to figures and pages in **bold** refer to tables.

Made in the USA
Las Vegas, NV
19 September 2026

19e8e8ad-575f-4edc-a6ed-d257818e5b87R01